THE POET AND
THE ANTIQUARIES

THE POET AND
THE ANTIQUARIES

Chaucerian Scholarship and the
Rise of Literary History, 1532–1635

Megan L. Cook

PENN

UNIVERSITY OF PENNSYLVANIA PRESS

PHILADELPHIA

PUBLISHED IN COOPERATION WITH FOLGER SHAKESPEARE LIBRARY

Published by
University of Pennsylvania Press
Philadelphia, Pennsylvania 19104-4112
www.upenn.edu/pennpress

Printed in the United States of America on acid-free paper
10 9 8 7 6 5 4 3 2 1

Library of Congress Cataloging-in-Publication Data
Names: Cook, Megan L. (Megan Leigh), 1981– author.
Title: The poet and the antiquaries : Chaucerian scholarship
    and the rise of literary history, 1532–1635 / Megan L. Cook.
Description: 1st edition. | Philadelphia : University of
    Pennsylvania Press, [2019] | "Published in cooperation with
    Folger Shakespeare Library". | Includes bibliographical
    references and index.
Identifiers: LCCN 2018051760 | ISBN 9780812250824
    (hardcover)
Subjects: LCSH: Chaucer, Geoffrey, –1400—
    Criticism and interpretation—History. | Chaucer,
    Geoffrey, –1400—Influence. | English literature—
    Early modern, 1500–1700—History and criticism. |
    Antiquarians—England—History—16th century. |
    Antiquarians—England—History—17th century. |
    Medievalism—England—History—16th century. |
    Medievalism—England—History—17th century. |
    Civilization, Medieval, in literature.
Classification: LCC PR1924 .C594 2019 | DDC 821/.1—dc23
LC record available at https://lccn.loc.gov/2018051760

For Linda Cook-Toren and Ruth Ann VanZanten

CONTENTS

A NOTE ON SPELLING AND PUNCTUATION

Throughout, I have silently expanded abbreviations and regularized i/j and u/v spellings. Punctuation from the original sources is maintained.

"Only by Thy Books"

Knowing Chaucer in Early Modern England

In 1598, one "H.B." contributed a curious prefatory poem to a new edition of Chaucer's collected works. Produced under the auspices of the school-teacher Thomas Speght, *The workes of our Antient and Learned English poet, Geffrey Chaucer* distinguished itself from previous collections by the great deal of supplementary material it added to Chaucer's poems. Perhaps most notable is an extensive glossary, the first large-scale lexicon of Middle English in print. The significance of Speght's additions is not lost on H.B., whose poem stages the following dialogue between Chaucer and a latter-day reader. It begins:

> Reader.
> Where hast thou dwelt, good Geffrey, all this while,
> Unknowne to us, save only by thy bookes?
>
> Chaucer.
> In haulks and hernes, God wot, and in Exile,
> Where none vouchsaft to yeeld me words or lookes:
> Till one which saw me there, and knew my Friends,
> Did bring me forth: such grace sometime God sends:
>
> Reader.
> But who is he that hath thy Books repar'd,
> And added more, whereby thou art more graced?

Chaucer.
The self same man who hath no labor spar'd,
To helpe what time and writers had defaced:
And made old words, which were unknown of many,
So plaine, that now they may be known of any.[1]

This exchange encapsulates the way that many early modern readers must have
seen themselves in relation to Chaucer. The Reader is solicitous and polite,
even delighted, but interested less in Chaucer's stories than in the authorial
persona revealed through them. Chaucer's archaic diction—the alliterative
"haulks" (nooks) and "hernes" (crannies) and "God wot" (God knows)—
marks him as temporally distant from the reader, and he seems grateful for
his interlocutor's attentions, which are described as a kind of divine intervention ("such grace").

What differentiates this piece from earlier poems celebrating the affective bond between Chaucer and his readers ("my friends") is the prominence
of the editorial figure who mediates their relationship. This is not really a poem
in praise of Chaucer at all, but a panegyric to Speght. Chaucer is "unknown"
and "in exile" prior to Speght's efforts; editorial intervention and the conse-
quent improvement of the text bring forth Chaucer to his proper place, where
he can express his thanks to the "man who hath no labor spar'd / To helpe
what time and writers had defaced." In this poem, as Stephanie Trigg writes,
"author, editor, and reader are apparently bound together in ties of love and
mutual obligation, of mutually flattering recognition and knowledge," but
without Speght's antiquarian interventions, the connection between the reader
and the author would dissolve.[2]

By foregrounding Speght's involvement, H.B.'s poem emphasizes an aspect of Renaissance encounters with Chaucer—and with Middle English
writing more generally—which often passes unmarked in discussions of early
modern uses of the medieval, and which this book seeks to illuminate. This
is the vital role that early modern scholarly intermediaries played in shaping
later readers' understanding of Chaucer and his contemporaries, whether
through their involvement in printed editions of Middle English texts, their
role in forming collections of medieval books and documents, or in their ge-
nerically varied writings about the English past, which range from handbooks
of rhetoric to discourses on religious history. Through these activities, antiquarians played a key role not only in the construction and dissemination of
broad narratives about the English past, but also in some of the earliest ar-

ticulations of what we might term literary history, especially as it concerns Chaucer. In this, they respond to claims found in Chaucer's own works: Chaucer, in A. C. Spearing's terms, "was the father of English literary history—the first English poet to conceive of his work as an addition, however humble, to the great monuments of the classical past and as continuing to exist in a future over which he would have no control."[3] At the same time, however, they—like many of Chaucer's readers, from the fifteenth-century to the present—respond to the remarkably malleable authorial self-presentation found in Chaucer's writings, a flexibility that makes not only his writings but the authorial figure behind them available for an especially wide array of interpretations and appropriations.[4]

The story of how Chaucer's work came to occupy an exceptional place in English literary history offers revealing insight into the ways texts and authors acquire political, historical, and social meaning far beyond that which might have adhered to them at the moment of composition.[5] Much of this story can be told through the six folio editions of Chaucer's *Works* that were printed between 1532 and 1602.[6] Though large and necessarily costly, the collected works seem to have become the preferred or at least expected vehicle for Chaucer in print, judging by the fact that no shorter or smaller printed volumes of Chaucer appeared in this period. Both in their length (eventually more than four hundred pages) and their impressive folio size, these are the largest collections of poetry printed in England during this period. All were produced with substantial involvement of individuals connected with antiquarian communities, and all bear evidence of the scholarly habits and intellectual investments characteristic of those communities.

Antiquarians, in other words, were largely responsible for the kind of work that enables the reader and Chaucer to reunite in H.B.'s poem. By reading the archive of Chaucer's reception in a way that foregrounds this work, this book seeks a fuller understanding of the ways that Chaucer and his writings were read and transmitted in early modern England. Antiquarian material makes profoundly visible the fact that Chaucer—already widely known to English readers—functioned in a wide range of historical discourses in this period, some concerned with his literary merits but many more simply eager to leverage his preexisting fame.[7] This fame, and Chaucer's ability to signify venerability and Englishness in so many different contexts, made him a prime site at which to link a nascent concept of vernacular literary history with ideas about national and linguistic identity both past and present.

Of Chaucer's early modern readers, perhaps no group had as outsize an impact as those courtiers, chroniclers, heralds, and scholars whose attention to the English past might earn them the label "antiquarian." Antiquarians sought, in William Camden's famous words, "to restore antiquity to Britaine, and Britain to his antiquity" (ut Britanniae antiquitatem et suae antiquitati Britanniam restituerem).[8] While antiquarian scholars constituted a relatively small number of Chaucer's readers in late Tudor England, they were a uniquely influential minority. In the printed folio editions, the antiquarian view of Chaucer announces itself in dedications, explanatory notes, and even in the selection and arrangement of texts, including many that are now recognized as apocryphal.[9] As antiquarians prepared editions of his *Works* and circulated copies of his poems and lists of his titles, they became arbiters of what constituted "Chaucer" and how it should be situated in relation to other literary, linguistic, and historical material. References to Chaucer and other medieval writers are woven through major works of antiquarian scholarship like John Leland's *De Viris Illustribus* (1530s) and Camden's *Britannia* (1586), and a number of antiquarians, like Francis Thynne (1545?–1608) and Elias Ashmole (1617–1692), annotated their own copies of Middle English texts in manuscript or in print. Taken together, these materials show that antiquarian and other scholarly readers constitute a significant and frequently overlooked site for the reception of Middle English literature in early modern England.

More important, in reading and reproducing Chaucer, antiquarians shaped the experiences of a much larger swath of readers. When nonantiquarians read Chaucer, it was typically in the printed folio editions, shaped by the antiquarian interests of the scholars who produced them. From 1532 until the middle of the eighteenth century, the typical reader encountered Chaucer in books whose contents and supplementary materials were determined not by poets or literary critics but by antiquarians for whom interest in Chaucer was just one facet of a much broader engagement in the English past. In this sense, Tudor antiquarians acted as a kind of filter through which nearly all post-1532 readers encountered Chaucer and his texts. Readers who relied upon the editions produced by William Thynne (1532, revised 1542 and 1550), John Stow (1561) and Thomas Speght (1598 and 1602) include George Puttenham, Sir Philip Sidney, William Shakespeare, Edmund Spenser, Samuel Pepys, John Milton, and John Dryden, as well as the authors of lesser-known adaptations of Chaucer's poems like the ribald *Cobler of Canterburie* (1590, likely written by Robert Greene), Francis Kynaston's Latin translation of *Troilus and Criseyde* (pub. 1635), and *Chaucer New Painted* by William Painter (1623). In the decades around the turn of the seventeenth century, Anne Bowyer, mother of the antiquary and collector Elias Ashmole, copied out extracts from Chaucer into her commonplace book (now Bodleian Library MS Ashmole 51) while the noblewoman Elizabeth Danvers (1545/50–1630) was said by John Aubrey to have "Chaucer at her fingers' ends."[10]

Antiquarian Readers?

In this book, I define the idea of the antiquarian capaciously, as someone with a professional or abiding personal interest in the details of the English past. The writings and textual work of the readers I study here draw upon the same rhetorical and literary-historical discourses that made Chaucer an indispensable symbol for cultural and linguistic excellence in the English past, but their authors interweave these discourses with wide-ranging narratives about nationhood, language, and history. With a few notable exceptions, these writers did not consider themselves poets or poetic commentators; instead, they wrote first and foremost as chroniclers, religious polemicists, historians, and specialists in genealogy and heraldry.

Renaissance antiquarianism had its roots in humanism, and, like other forms of humanistic inquiry, it sought the recovery of the past through an improved understanding of ancient records and texts.[11] Humanistic readers, as described by Lisa Jardine and Anthony Grafton in their influential account of the scholar and author Gabriel Harvey, often studied their texts "for action," focusing primarily on those aspects of the past—including philosophy, style, and aesthetics—perceived as informing the present in a positive way. This is a method of reading that, in Jardine and Grafton's words, is "intended to *give rise to something else*."[12] Antiquarian readers, by contrast, often dwelled on the past for its own sake. While they shared a humanistic tendency to valorize Greek and Roman texts, the work of English antiquarians also addressed itself to the more recent, post-Roman past. One particularly notable outcome of this approach was the rise of Anglo-Saxon studies at Cambridge, but an appetite for research into place-names, family trees, and the history of certain institutions—such as that required for the compilation of heraldic treatises, chronicle histories, and legal scholarship—also created a class of readers with the practical skills needed for detailed research using later medieval texts and documents.

Interest in Chaucer enters antiquarian discourse at, or close to, its inception. For many sixteenth- and seventeenth-century scholars, the paradigmatic English antiquarian was John Leland (ca. 1503–1552), who, in addition to producing a significant body of Latin and Greek poetry, undertook an extensive program of research and writing about the English past. Leland is remembered today for his conflict with the Italian historiographer Polydore Vergil, with whom he quarreled over the historical existence of King Arthur, and for his "laborious journey"—actually a series of as many as five journeys—to monastic libraries in the years leading up to the dissolution of the monastic houses under Henry VIII.[13] While Leland was no champion of vernacular literature, his *De Viris Illustribus*, a posthumously circulated collection of bibliographic and biographical notes on learned Englishmen, features an extended entry on Chaucer, as well as one on John Gower. Although his claims about Chaucer's life largely appear to be based on hearsay and tradition rather than archival evidence, as I discuss in my second chapter, Leland's writings on Chaucer's life would form the core of Chaucer's biography until the eighteenth century.

While Leland was closely associated with the court of Henry VIII, over the course of the century, antiquarian studies came to flourish in the universities and in the city of London as well.[14] With this, came new, large-scale projects that sought to interpret the material and textual remains of the medieval past. At Cambridge, Matthew Parker (1504–1575), archbishop of Canterbury and vice-chancellor of the university, assembled a team of Anglo-Saxon scholars whose research into medieval English texts was intended, in part, to provide evidence for the historical independence of the English church.[15] In 1586, William Camden published the first edition of the extraordinarily popular *Britannia*, with a special emphasis on the physical and cultural legacy of the Roman occupation of Britain.[16] While Camden began and ended his career at the University of Oxford, he spent much of his professional life living and working in London, and the social and scholarly networks that he helped to foster were important conduits for medieval studies at the end of the sixteenth century.

The most significant of these networks was the Society of Antiquaries. Around 1586, Camden and his pupil, the lawyer and manuscript collector Sir Robert Cotton, established the group to share and discuss research on topics related to the English past.[17] Attendance was by invitation only, and members were expected to present papers upon two preset topics; the best responses were preserved in the society's records.[18] The papers collected in Thomas

Hearne's *Curious Discourses* (1720, revised and expanded 1771) reveal a kind of intellectual piecework system in which individual members focused on highly specific and technical aspects of the set topic, with the understanding that their work would be complemented or perhaps challenged by the contributions of other members. The Society of Antiquaries met consistently for about twenty years.[19] Members were heralds, lawyers, and schoolteachers; topics discussed at meetings reflected the interests of participants and ranged from the history of coinage in Britain to the origins of units of land measurement to the historical duties of officers of the royal household.

Aside from Camden and Cotton, the best-known member of the Society of Antiquaries was John Stow, who bears a special relationship to the history of Chaucer in print. Stow's crabbed handwriting can be found in a large number of surviving manuscripts and documents, including several fifteenth-century collections containing works by Chaucer.[20] From this primary-source research, Stow produced two highly influential works whose titles evoke the temporal sweep and geographical specificity characteristic of antiquarian scholarship in the later sixteenth century: *The Annales of England, faithfully collected out of the most authenticall Authors, Records, and other Monuments of Antiquitie, from the first inhabitation untill this present yeere 1592* and *A Survay of London: Contayning the Originall, Antiquity, Increase, Moderne estate, and description of that Citie, written in the yeare 1598.* Chaucer is mentioned in these works—as he is other notable works of Tudor scholarship like John Bale's *Illustrium Majoris Britanniae Scriptorum*, John Foxe's *Actes and Monuments*, Raphael Holinshed's *Chronicles*, and William Camden's *Britannia*—but his life and writings are in no way their major focus. These references do not encompass the full scope of Stow's engagement with Chaucer, however: earlier in his career, he had been the motivating force behind the 1561 edition of Chaucer's *Works*, expanding it to include more than a dozen new poems (many apocryphal) largely drawn from two fifteenth-century literary manuscripts now at Trinity College, Cambridge.[21] He also contributed material to a new account of Chaucer's life that was published in the 1598 edition of the *Works* and appears to have taken an abiding interest in Chaucer's contemporary John Lydgate as well.

Viewed on its own, Stow's edition of Chaucer is interesting, but when we approach it in the context of an entire career, it becomes legible as something connected to larger currents of scholarly practice and historiographic thought. When the antiquarian commentary is foregrounded as a significant strand of Chaucerian reception in its own right—a strand that quite often precedes and enables more recognizably literary forms of response—an alternative "secret history" of Chaucerian reading begins to emerge. For many antiquarians, Chaucer was more than an exemplary poet. He was a figure whose outsize prominence in emerging literary histories made him essential to broader accounts of English cultural and political development. As a result, while the early modern period witnessed some of the most celebrated reworkings of Chaucer's verse and stories, it also saw continued efforts to articulate Chaucer's significance in other forms of writing: histories, biographies, and lexicographical works, as well as prefatory materials designed to introduce readers to a poet who seemed, in the decades after the English Reformation and amid a rapidly evolving vernacular tongue, newly distant from the present. These other writings—and the ways that they shaped the publication, preservation, transmission, and reception of works attributed to Chaucer, and the corpus of Middle English writing more broadly—are the principal subject of this book.

Why Chaucer?

Rather than being fixed in a single cultural role as "the father of English poetry," in paraliterary materials Chaucer emerges as a surprisingly mobile figure, whose writings can be appropriated for a variety of historical, religious, and scholarly purposes, and who comes equipped with an increasingly robust biographical narrative.[22] While Chaucer is of undisputed poetic importance, for many readers and writers in the early modern period, he matters as much or more for other reasons, some of which might seem startling from the vantage point of the twenty-first century: Chaucer is celebrated as an alchemist, an intellectual, a courtier, a religious reformer, and above all an Englishman, whose writing serves to endow the English nation with a vernacular suited to its status as an emerging power. At times, commentary invested in these aspects of Chaucer's persona can seem quite divorced from the aesthetic or poetic dimensions of his texts, but I will argue throughout this book that these quasi-historical and biographical readings do much to dictate conventional understandings of specific texts, to shape Chaucer's canon, and to determine the presentation of his works in print.

Chaucer's works were far from the only Middle English texts circulating in Tudor England, however. Printers put forth new editions of works by Lydgate, Gower, and Langland, not to mention anonymous devotional works and popular romance. Prefatory epistles attached to printed editions of Gower's *Confessio Amantis* (1532), Langland's *Piers Plowman* (1555), and Lydgate's *Troy Book* (1555) all praise the lasting virtues of the "olde English" used in these poems. Writings from the past were neither culturally nor intellectually inert: in the hands of printer Robert Crowley, Langland's fourteenth-century alliterative poem *Piers Plowman* found a new audience among readers concerned with religious prophecy, and alchemic adepts took interest in passages from Gower, Lydgate, and Chaucer that seemed to speak to their art.[23] Medieval texts and records, in both print and manuscript, remained an important source for historiographers and chroniclers. When public theater was established in London in the early 1560s, writers for the stage drew both on earlier forms of performance and on earlier written texts for inspiration.[24]

Despite the diversity of these encounters with the medieval past, my focus remains on Chaucer, because early modern readers themselves so very often turned to Chaucer when they self-consciously reflected on the historical trajectory of English literature. For these readers, marking Chaucer's historical distance becomes a way of underscoring the antiquity of the English poetic tradition, while also giving Chaucer an exceptional place in that tradition. At once representative of his historical moment and ahead of his time, Chaucer took on a special, even paradoxical, role in accounts in the development of poetic, linguistic, and national modernity in England (or, rather, the English-speaking community, since such commentary usually ignores the presence of other vernaculars like Welsh and Cornish in the British Isles).

Perhaps unsurprisingly, given that Chaucer has the longest continuous reception history of any author writing in English, responses to Chaucer and his works constitute a larger body of written commentary than that associated with any other English author until the rise of Shakespeare studies in the eighteenth century. The copiousness of the written record related to Chaucer reflects his appeal to an unusually broad range of readers and commentators, from poets and rhetoricians to chroniclers and clerics. These readers sought out and made reference to Chaucer not only because of his reputation as an exemplary poet, but also because of his perceived status as an innovator in the field of Englishness itself, whose linguistic and lexical contributions to national excellence just happened to take the form of literary writings. While Chaucer had always held pride of place among English poets, in early modern England interest in his life and writing substantially outstripped interest in his contemporaries and immediate followers and no other Middle English writer is subject to the same degree of biographical speculation.[25]

The early modern encounter between antiquarians and Chaucer continues to reverberate in medieval studies today. In some cases, most notably
Thomas Usk's *Testament of Love* and the anonymous dream vision *The Floure and
the Leafe* (both of which are printed in Chaucer's *Works*), sixteenth- and early
seventeenth-century editions serve as records of works for which no earlier
manuscript survives.[26] In the case of better-attested works, early editions may
still provide variant readings drawn from otherwise-untraced manuscripts; for
example, William Thynne's 1532 edition provides the only complete text of the
Book of the Duchess. More broadly, the version of Chaucer and his works found
in these antiquarian editions has structured much subsequent literary and scholarly engagement with medieval English literature. In the linguistic realm, these
editions kept not just Chaucer's texts but the language of those texts in the
hands of Tudor and Stuart readers, offering later writers a rich vocabulary for
archaism and allusion and inaugurating a long-standing strain of medievalism
in English writing.[27] Later still, their very real textual faults would help to
motivate the activities of eighteenth- and nineteenth-century editors, who
approached Chaucer armed with both philological methods and a stronger understanding of Middle English.[28]

Reading in an Expanded Archive

By taking up evidence of extraliterary readings of Chaucer in early modern
England and by considering the scholarly and intellectual milieu that informed
those readings, this book seeks to map the mutually constitutive relationship
between a nascent discourse of vernacular English literary history and understandings of the English past more broadly. Within this discourse, Chaucer
served as the native historical foundation for the work of later English poets
in much the same way that Anglo-Saxon Christianity became proof of the
English church's historical independence from Rome, and, in common law,
earlier cases acted as precedent for later legal decisions. In each case, the medieval example could be cited to place early modern practices—poetic, religious, or legal—on historical footing. Because it is deeply invested in questions
of historical change and continuity, any study of Chaucer's status in early modern England is also, in part, a study in periodization. Accordingly, my analysis draws on previous studies of Renaissance attitudes toward the postclassical,
pre-Reformation past, especially those that foreground the ways that postmedieval ideologies shaped the fate of medieval texts and manuscripts. Such work

is a reminder that periodization is never simply a chronological question and that, as Margreta de Grazia writes, the divide between the medieval and the Renaissance "works less as a historical marker than as a massive value judgment, determining what matters and what does not."[29]

Chaucer's early modern reception epitomizes the way that periodization plays with conventional, linear notions of temporality. Beginning in the early sixteenth century, Chaucer emerged as a figure capable of both exemplifying his historical moment *and* transcending it through the enduring literary value of his work, making him at once "proleptically modern" and representative of the past.[30] As a result, Chaucer's works were treated not only as sources of readerly pleasure and poetic exemplarity but also as documentary evidence of England's linguistic, cultural, and political past. Even as Chaucer remained an important reference point for later poets, Renaissance scholars worked to situate his life and writings in an increasingly dense web of knowledge about the past, reading him at once as a historical source and as a literary historical source.

Chaucer's presence in a wide range of extrapoetic discourses means that people in early modern England had available to them a figure who, in aggregate, might have looked very different from the poet that we know today, in terms of both what was believed about his life and writing and the significance that was accorded to it. The ability to occupy a position of national importance in both poetic and historical registers set Chaucer apart both from his co-medievals and from later authors, although Gower, Lydgate, and Langland would each at times play a Chaucer-like role in later commentary. The chapters that follow use Chaucer's early modern bibliography to trace his function in overlapping discourses of nationhood, cultural identity, and literary tradition. I move from the early sixteenth century to the middle of the seventeenth, showing how subsequent generations of commentators built upon one another's worth to refine and elaborate their understanding of Chaucer and his role in English national identity. By attending to the wider frame in which Chaucer's works were read and reproduced, this book as a whole seeks a more comprehensive understanding of the early modern reception of Middle English writing, as well as a clearer view of the links between literary history, linguistic identity, and ideas about a shared, national past. Reading Chaucer's reception in an expanded archive offers a new degree of context to a rich body of previous scholarship that prioritizes poetic and dramatic responses to medieval works and allows me to foreground questions of nationalism and history in new ways.[31]

This book seeks to answer the "why" of Chaucer's early modern reception by exploring the "what" and "how" of that reception. Each chapter offers a Chaucerian lens through which to examine the intercalation of medieval literature and national identity in early modern England. Antiquarian commentary shows that, especially where Chaucer was concerned, in this period national history and literary history were not only intertwined but, often, one and the same. Although many of the figures I examine here advance claims about the medieval past that are at best pedantic and at worst historically inaccurate, the patterns of thought that structure their work reveal much about how antiquarians connected the past with the present and the significant role that Chaucer played in shaping their conceptions of those connections.

These chapters also offer a reappraisal of antiquarian writing itself. Our current disciplinary formations encourage us to treat literary commentary and historiography as wholly separate from the work that they comment upon and presume an easily identifiable division between creative work and scholarly writing. These distinctions are not so clear-cut in the Renaissance. Antiquarian scholarship was collaborative; and scholarly work was deeply concerned with the same questions and anxieties about fragmentation, incompleteness, and loss that shaped more recognizably literary engagement with the past.[32] In Angus Vine's words, antiquarianism was "a dynamic, recuperative, resurrective response to the past. And for this reason it was also an essentially imaginative response to the past," rather than a dry assemblage of facts.[33] This is to say: the writings of John Foxe, John Leland, and other Tudor commentators are a record of an affective engagement with Chaucer and his works, as much as are Spenser's Chaucerian homages or the aureate praises of Lydgate and Hoccleve.

*   *   *

Chapter 1 looks at the ways in which antiquarians shaped the large collected editions of Chaucer's works published between 1523 and 1602. As it does so, it argues that Chaucer's close identification with the English language was key to the temporal doubleness—the ability to signify in both past and present—that made his writings a suitable topic for scholarly inquiry as well as literary appropriation and admiration. This doubleness, I show, played out not only in written commentary but also in visual materials like the dramatic engraving depicting "the Progenie of Geffrey Chaucer" included in the 1598 *Works*. A sense that Chaucer could mark both a special connection to the past and distance from it runs through all folio editions of the *Works* and much of the commentary that derives from them. When this is combined with the fact that, in the Renaissance, Chaucer's contributions to the English vernacular were widely understood as contributions to Englishness itself, it is no surprise that Chaucer emerged as an exceptionally valuable figure for thinking about the medieval past in early modern England.

The following chapters trace specific ways in which this understanding of Chaucer unfolds over the course of the sixteenth century. Chapter 2 turns to early accounts of Chaucer's biography and shows how important this genre was in constructing Chaucer as a writer whose life and works could be known, understood, and valued by later scholarly readers. It begins with the early Tudor antiquarian John Leland's Latin writings on Chaucer, which remained the most important source for biographers until the eighteenth century. Written in the 1530s, Leland's commentary bolsters Chaucer's ability to move between periods by influentially (if spuriously) connecting him to institutions of ongoing importance like the Inns of Court and the universities. At the same time, in a series of Latin poems presented alongside this biographical material, Leland explicitly situates Chaucer in relation to his Greek, Roman, and Italian antecedents. As he draws on both past and present to produce "new" knowledge about the poet's life and works, Leland articulates a humanistic understanding of what a national poet is, or should be. Leland's work was, in turn, a major source for the first extended biography of Chaucer written in English. Prefixed to the 1598 edition of Chaucer's *Works*, the English *Life of Our Learned English Poet, Geffrey Chaucer* was prepared by the volume's editor, Thomas Speght, with assistance from the indefatigable antiquarian John Stow. Written for a less scholarly audience than Leland's Latin account, the *Life of Chaucer* nonetheless shows how influential Leland's understanding of Chaucer as a figure of uncommon poetic and historical significance was for later readers and interpreters of the poet's works.

In Chapter 3, I consider how claims about Chaucer's religious views—specifically, assertions that he was a proto-Protestant—shaped his early modern canon. These claims, popularized in widely read works like John Foxe's *Actes and Monuments*, elevated Chaucer's historical importance by making him integral to the development of English Protestantism. Modern scholars most often discuss these claims in conjunction with the *Plowman's Tale*, an apocryphal anticlerical satire assigned to Chaucer's Plowman and included in editions of the *Canterbury Tales* printed between 1532 and 1721. Here, however, I explore the ways that beliefs about Chaucer's religion shaped the transmission of the genuinely Chaucerian *A.B.C.* (not printed before 1602) and the spurious *Jack Upland*, a Lollard tract that circulated widely under Chaucer's name thanks to its inclusion in Foxe's *Actes and Monuments*.

My fourth chapter looks in greater detail at sixteenth-century views of Chaucerian language as they relate to later forms of literary English. Early Chaucer lexicons, such as the one added by Speght to his edition of the *Works*, illustrate exactly how complex the interplay between Chaucerian language and early modern poetic language could be. I show that Speght's hard word list took some of its strongest cues concerning the treatment of archaic language from the E.K. glosses in Spenser's *Shepheardes Calender* (1579). E.K.'s commentary, written two decades before Speght's edition, invokes Chaucer in order to justify the use of archaic words by the quasi-anonymous "new Poete." This playful, literary engagement with scholarly discourse had surprisingly concrete ramifications for the representation of Chaucer's own *Works* in print. Speght's edition clearly follows the *Calender*'s approach to Chaucer's language, making Chaucer's *Works*, in important ways, a Spenserian text. In both Speght's *Works* and the *Shepheardes Calender*, the introduction of lexicons makes newly visible and newly problematic the particularities of Chaucerian language, framing them as temporally distant even as it insists upon their relevance to contemporary poetic enterprise. The recursivity of this exchange, in which the later poet's writing informs the way his own influences are subsequently presented to readers, emphasizes the degree to which the medieval past is always shaped by its postmedieval interpreters.

Chapter 5 moves beyond language to explore the ways in which scholarly writing situated Chaucer in a wide range of historical discourses, including British antiquities, legal history, alchemy, and heraldry. My focus here is on Francis Thynne (1545?–1608), an active member of the Society of Antiquaries and the son of William Thynne, the courtier who oversaw of the first edition of Chaucer's collected works in 1532. The younger Thynne is best remembered today for his *Animadversions* (1599), an open letter criticizing Speght's 1598 edition of the *Works*. While the *Animadversions* has typically been dismissed as the work of a pedant jealously guarding his father's legacy, it is also a sustained commentary on Chaucer's life and works written by a lifelong scholar deeply involved in London's antiquarian community. This chapter sets the *Animadversions* in the context of Thynne's copious output, including works on heraldry, alchemy, and local history, and even poetry.

In my sixth and final chapter, I consider what I call "coterie scholarship" and explore how antiquarian readers applied knowledge from other areas of study to their reading of Middle English works. I look closely at the annotations, citations, and marginal notations made by three seventeenth-century readers in their copies of the *Canterbury Tales*: the lawyer and antiquarian Joseph Holland (d. 1605), the collector, herald, and astrological enthusiast Elias Ashmole (1617–1692), and the Dutch scholar and philologist Franciscus Junius the Younger (1591–1677). Their notes are in many ways similar across date, professional occupation, national origin, and level of education, and all show relatively little interest in Chaucer's work as poetry. By seeking instead to situate Chaucer's work within the larger scope of historical knowledge, these scholarly annotators both confirm Chaucer's transition from "old" author to historical subject and exemplify the remarkable variety of frameworks in which such a subject might be studied.

Through their broad and varied efforts, early modern scholars played an indispensable role in constructing Chaucer as a poet whose writing both embodies his historical moment and transcends it. As Chaucer's life and works were redefined as subjects for scholarly as well as readerly attention in early modern England, they were inscribed as part of a shared English heritage. At the same time, through a new emphasis on the historical distance of the pre-Reformation past, they were increasingly marked as antecedent to contemporary literary culture. *The Poet and the Antiquaries* shows how antiquarian commentary not only reflected this dialectic but fueled it, transforming Chaucer into a synecdoche not just for earlier poetry but for wide-ranging linguistic, religious, and political dimensions of the English past. The significance granted to Chaucer by these materials extended that influence beyond the poetic realm, shaping the terms in which English nationhood found its cultural voice and making not just Chaucer but commentary upon him absolutely central to Renaissance ways of knowing the medieval.

Approached with this wider bibliographical and historical framework in mind, the Reader's claim in the poem by H.B. with which I began may seem a bit disingenuous. Far from being "unknown" to early modern readers, Chaucer was a versatile figure who stood in for an intricate set of relations between past and present. Moreover, he was known not "only by [his] books," but through a web of comment and commentary that, yes, included the impressive folio editions, but which also ranged from erudite national history to popular poetry and drama. In each of these contexts, Chaucer mattered both because of and in spite of his historical distance from the present. By reading Chaucer in an expanded archive, the following chapters show that Chaucer's status in early modern England depended not just on ongoing enthusiasm for his poetry but on the intertwining and reintertwining of national and literary concerns over a period of several decades. This phenomenon, of course, is not unique to Chaucer in the Renaissance: rather, it is exemplary of the manner in which the literature of the past and the politics of the present speak to one another in surprising and sometimes urgent ways.

CHAPTER I

The First First Folios

Chaucer's *Works* in Print

In 2016, academics and enthusiasts across the globe commemorated the four hundredth anniversary of Shakespeare's death with conferences, exhibitions, and performances. Prominently featured in the celebrations were copies of the 1623 volume *Mr. William Shakespeare's Comedies, Histories, and Tragedies*, or, as it is more commonly known today, the First Folio. In the United States, a "tour" of First Folios set up by the Folger Shakespeare Library that exhibited copies in all fifty states, Washington, D.C., and Puerto Rico was heralded by promotional materials touting a chance to come "face to face" with "the book that gave us Shakespeare."[1] Brought forth from the vault of the Folger to commemorate the death of their author rather than the anniversary of their own publication, the touring folios took on the status of relics, offering an opportunity for Shakespearean enthusiasts to bear witness to an object central to the poet's lasting reputation.

The enduring impact of the Shakespeare First Folio depends on its form as well as its contents. When it was published by Isaac Jaggard and Edward Blount in 1623, it did more than gather together Shakespeare's plays—previously circulating in manuscripts or single-text quartos—into a single, large volume. It also presented a particular version of the author and his works to the world. With its large size and engraved frontispiece depicting the deceased playwright, it staked a claim for the cultural and literary significance of its contents in the English literary marketplace. In its scale and scope, it functioned—and continues to function—as a particularly effective monument to Shakespeare and his literary accomplishments, the scholarly and financial value accorded to it today reflecting Shakespeare's unique place in the English-language literary canon.

The Shakespeare First Folio was not, however, the *first* First Folio.[2] That distinction belongs to *The workes of Geffray Chaucer*, first printed in 1532 by Thomas Godfray and overseen by a courtier named William Thynne. The 1532 volume marked the first attempt to combine all the works of an English-language author into a single, impressively large printed book. Dedicated to Henry VIII, *The workes of Geffray Chaucer* brought together a wide range of Chaucerian texts that had previously only been available in manuscript or in smaller printed volumes. Like the Shakespeare First Folio, the Thynne edition of Chaucer's *Works* set a precedent for later printers: for close to two and a half centuries, until Thomas Tyrwhitt's edition of the *Canterbury Tales* (1775–1777), the folio collected works would be the dominant format for printing Chaucer.[3]

Chaucer was a mainstay of English printing well before the publication of the *Works*, but the books produced by William Caxton, Wynkyn de Worde, and other early printers works were different in both size and scope from the larger volumes that would follow.[4] Pre-1532 editions of Chaucer were either quartos or small folios consisting of a single longer work or several shorter pieces.[5] A transition to more comprehensive collections began in 1526, when Robert Pynson published a series of Chaucerian volumes, each with its own title page, designed to be bound together as a *Sammelband*, giving readers the ability to assemble their own grouping of Chaucerian works.[6] For the first time, buyers had the opportunity to own a large portion of the Chaucerian canon in print in a common format. While these editions—along with manuscripts produced both before and after the arrival of print—continued to circulate in the sixteenth century and beyond, the large folio editions of *Works* produced after 1532 were a bibliographic departure from their predecessors and, in time, would come to outnumber these earlier publications.

Through their contents, their commentary, and their material form, these folio editions demonstrate the persistent link between Chaucer and emerging ideas of "Englishness," as well as Chaucer's role as a privileged innovator in the history of the English language. They also map a crucial phase in the development of English literary and linguistic history and the tools for pursuing it: the 1532 Thynne edition presumes Chaucer's Middle English will be more or less accessible to its readers, but by the end of the century Thomas Speght will append a substantial glossary of Chaucer's "hard words" to his

1598 version of the *Works*. Between these two poles lies a slow evolution of Chaucer's status as a writer and as a historical figure. Chaucer in the Renaissance occupied a middle position between the literary and the scholarly, at once good to read and, increasingly, in need of specialized study.

Caroline Spurgeon's foundational work of bibliography, *Five Hundred Years of Chaucer Criticism and Allusion*, provides ample evidence of wide-ranging and diverse engagement with Chaucer in early modern England.[7] The sixteenth and early seventeenth century produced some of the most celebrated reworkings of Chaucer's verse and stories, including Spenser's *Faerie Queene* and Shakespeare's *Troilus and Cressida*. But Chaucer also figures in works that are not primarily concerned with poetry, such as John Foxe's Protestant historiography, William Camden's topographical history of the British Isles, John Stow's *Annales*, or the Catholic Anglo-Dutch antiquarian Richard Verstegan's *Restitution of Decayed Intelligence*. The diversity of these responses invites several broader questions: How did an increasingly robust body of extrapoetic commentary on Chaucer enable, on the one hand, specific stories about the English past and, on the other hand, new ways of conceptualizing English literary history? How did Chaucer's dual role in poetic and extrapoetic discourses shape the way in which his writings were read and the forms in which they were transmitted?

This chapter addresses these questions, first, by tracing the development of Chaucer's printed *Works* across successive printed editions, from 1532 to 1602. In the middle section of this chapter, I look more closely at several paratextual additions designed to shape the way readers thought about Chaucer and his place in English history: William Thynne's preface to the 1532 *Works*, a woodblock frame depicting the genealogies of the houses of York and Lancaster used in the 1561 *Works* (but originally created for the 1550 edition of Edward Hall's *Union of the two noble and illustre famelies of Lancastre and Yorke*), and an intricate full-page engraving, depicting Chaucer and his genealogy, prepared for the 1598 *Works* by the antiquarian and cartographer John Speed. A final section reflects on the special emphasis given to Chaucer's language in antiquarian commentary and considers how this discourse evolves as Chaucer's Middle English grows ever-more distant from contemporary forms of the English language.

Throughout the chapter, I argue that Chaucer's exceptional status in early modern England was created and secured by a unique sense of his temporal doubleness. For antiquarians and for those who read their work, Chaucer and his language were a site at which they could simultaneously celebrate a connection with the past and measure distance from that past. In the *Works* and in antiquarian commentary alike, this doubleness combined with a sense of Chaucer's special relationship to the English language to make Chaucer an ideal figure with which to think through early modern England's relationship to its medieval past.

Printing Chaucer, 1532–1602

For all its topical and methodological diversity, early modern engagement with Chaucer remained centered on the half dozen folio editions of Chaucer's collected works published between 1532 and 1602.[8] From the early 1500s to the eighteenth century, these black-letter editions were the form in which most readers encountered Chaucer and his works.[9] Each was produced under the supervision of an individual with ties to antiquarian communities: William Thynne (1532, reprinted 1542 and 1555), John Stow (1561), or Thomas Speght (1598, revised 1602, reprinted 1687).[10] As these collections transmitted Chaucer's writings to a new and wider audience, they mediated and shaped readers' understanding of Chaucer and his text. Those responsible for the production of these volumes made decisions about which texts to include and which exemplars to use (if and when multiple sources were available), arranged the works within the volume (the *Canterbury Tales* has always been first), and in some cases bestowed on poems the titles by which they are still known today. At times, they selectively intervened in their text, emending and modernizing and choosing between variants in source material.[11] Their influence—along with that of the stationers with whom they worked—extended to the choice of typeface, the design of the title page, and the addition of introductory and explanatory materials like dedications and, later, glossaries. Regardless of the interests or investments that might lead early modern readers to Chaucer, in them they would find a representation of Chaucer already informed by an antiquarian perspective.

    In content as well as in form, the 1532 *Workes of Geffray Chaucer newly printed* set the pattern for Chaucerian printing for the next two centuries. Drawing on previously printed editions of Chaucer as well as on manuscripts, it dramatically increased the size and scope of the Chaucer book in print, making a bold claim for Chaucer's cultural import as it did so.[12] The book was very much a product of the Henrician court: William Thynne was chief clerk of the kitchen, his collaborator Brian Tuke was treasurer of the chamber, and Thomas Godfray, who printed it, was the recipient of the first royal patent for printing a book in England.[13] Unsurprisingly, the book was dedicated to Henry VIII, and equipped with a fulsome preface addressed to the monarch.

A hefty folio of nearly four hundred pages, Thynne's edition and its successors retained their status as the largest printed volume of English poetry throughout the sixteenth century. The 1532 edition includes the first printed editions of a number of Chaucerian texts, including the *Legend of Good Women*, the *Treatise on the Astrolabe*, and Chaucer's translation of the *Romaunt of the Rose*. In addition, Thynne added—unwittingly or otherwise—a number of non-Chaucerian works; taken together, these apocryphal pieces constitute nearly a quarter of the book's pages.[14] Most of these pass without comment, but in later editions of the *Works*, some, such as Lydgate's "A Balade of good conseile," were identified as the work of their non-Chaucerian authors.

The 1532 *Works* were reprinted in 1542 and again in 1550, after Thynne's death in 1548. The chief textual difference between these editions and the 1532 *Works* is the addition of the spurious *Plowman's Tale*, an antifraternal satire, to the *Canterbury Tales*.[15] (Godfray, printer of the 1532 *Works*, brought out a separate edition the *Plowman's Tale* around 1534 [STC 5099.5], although it appears it was conceived of as a publication separate from the *Works*.)[16] The *Plowman's Tale* does not appear in any earlier printing of the *Tales*, and it is not found in any surviving *Canterbury Tales* manuscript.[17] In the 1542 edition, it appears after the *Parson's Tale*, making it the final element in the *Tales*, while in 1550, it was moved into the penultimate position between the Reeve and the Parson, disrupting the link between these two segments in what was perhaps an attempt to affirm its status as a full part of the *Tales* rather than a supplement. The *Plowman's Tale* was carried forward in this place in subsequent editions of the *Works*.

In 1561 the *Works* were printed again, this time under the aegis of the antiquarian John Stow.[18] The 1561 *Works* mark the first time a Chaucerian text had been printed during Elizabeth's reign (Mary is the only Tudor monarch under whose reign no texts attributed to Chaucer were printed). Stow's edition reproduced the text of the 1542 *Works* with only minor alterations, but it added a series of shorter poems at the end of the volume, most of which were drawn from two fifteenth-century miscellanies (now Cambridge, Trinity

College MS R.3.19 and R.3.20).[19] R.3.20 was compiled by the scribe and bibliophile John Shirley (ca. 1366–1456), an important source for the attestation of many of Chaucer's shorter poems.[20] Of the pieces added by Stow, only *Adam Scriveyn*, *A Complaint Unto His Lady*, and *Against Women Unconstant* and the *Proverbs* remain canonical today. Although Stow's *Works* appeared when he was in his midthirties, he would return to Chaucer almost forty years later, contributing materials related to Chaucer's biography to Thomas Speght's edition of the *Works*.[21]

In 1598, more than sixty years after Thynne's first edition, the *Works* were printed again, under the auspices of schoolteacher Thomas Speght. Speght's edition was revised and reprinted in 1602, and reprinted a third time in 1687 for a consortium of booksellers. The 1598 edition reproduces Stow's 1561 text and adds two previously unprinted apocryphal poems, *The Assembly of Ladies* and *The Floure and the Leafe*. These are included in the 1602 revision, which also adds two more works, both religious in nature: the *A.B.C.*, Chaucer's previously unprinted translation of a French poem in praise of the Virgin Mary, and *Jack Upland*. *Jack Upland*, a proto-Protestant prose polemic, had been previously printed at least twice, once in the 1530s and in the 1550s (in an edition by John Day described by John Bale but now lost). *Jack Upland* was also included—and attributed to Chaucer—in John Foxe's *Actes and Monuments*, beginning with the second edition of 1570.

In addition to these new texts, the Speght editions expanded upon previous iterations of the *Works* by adding a significant amount of paratextual material designed to help readers better appreciate Chaucer and his work. This material places a focus on explanation, rather than simply praise, of Chaucer and his writings. The new front matter included dedication to Sir Robert Cecil and an address to the reader, as well as the prefatory material from the original 1532 *Works*, a substantial life of the poet, and summaries of each of the *Canterbury Tales*.[22] At the back of the volume, Speght added translations for Chaucer's Latin and French phrases, a list of authors cited in the text, and a hard word list—the first significant glossary of Chaucer's Middle English.[23] All of these components, with the exception of the material taken over from the 1532 prefatory materials, were revised and expanded in the 1602 reprint. In some ways—its glossary, its explanation of Chaucer's metrics, and working assumption that readers will find Chaucer's poetry both difficult and distant—the 1598 Speght edition is the first to look forward to modern editions of Chaucer and other Middle English authors. In other ways, however, it is a culmination of the past century's engagement with Chaucer: throughout the paratextual materials, Speght presents Chaucer as a medieval author who anticipates and enables the literary successes of later English poets, while also remaining exemplary of his own historical and literary moment.

The Cultural Work of the *Works*

Although they appeared over a span of seven decades, the Chaucer folios share a number of features that demonstrate the importance of both historical and literary concerns in the production, marketing, and use of the Chaucer book.[24] The sustained run of monumental folio editions from the 1530s onward is a unique feature of Chaucer's early modern transmission: no other author's works were collected, printed, and reprinted on such a scale. No effort was made to gather the writings of John Lydgate, the only other Middle English author with a similarly large and diverse vernacular canon.[25] Of the writings of John Gower, whom admiring fifteenth-century writers often invoked alongside Chaucer and Lydgate as the greatest of English poets, only the *Confessio Amantis* appeared in print (in 1483, 1532, and 1554). The collected editions of John Skelton and John Heywood's writings published later in the century were both smaller in format (octavo and quarto, respectively), as were the works of the Scots poet Sir David Lindsay and the poems of George Gascoigne (both also quarto).[26] The folio edition of the English works of Sir Thomas More, published in 1557, was not reprinted.[27]

While Chaucer's contemporaries in the continental vernaculars— Petrarch, Boccaccio, and Dante, as well as the Frenchmen Chartier, Ronsard, and Marot—were printed more frequently than their English counterparts, they were most often published in small-format books that did not seek to encompass the author's entire canon. In bibliographic terms, the folio Chaucers look less like other literary productions and more closely resemble the large-format legal, antiquarian, and religious productions that would have formed a substantial portion of the libraries of the lawyers and scholars in Chaucer's early modern audience. The heft of these editions helped lend Chaucer an authoritative, scholarly air, but at a certain cost, since folios are less portable and less suited to private, individual reading than smaller formats.

Chaucer's sixteenth-century print history is also remarkable for what it does *not* include: editions of individual works. Despite their large size and significant price tag, the collected *Works* appear to have satisfied market demand for new copies of Chaucer in print. While prior to 1532, editions of the

Canterbury Tales, *Troilus and Criseyde*, and shorter poems issued with some regularity from English presses, after the appearance of the first edition of Thynne's *Works*, there was no further effort to reproduce these texts in the more modest formats. The only works printed under Chaucer's name between 1532 and 1687 were the apocryphal *Plowman's Tale* and *Jack Upland*. Both of these were published as inexpensive pamphlets, clearly intended for readers more interested in the texts' proto-Protestant views than in their poetic value or historical interest.[28]

Although new texts were added and some line readings changed (whether by design or accident), the text of Chaucer remained largely stable across these folio editions. In 1532, Thynne drew from a mix of print and manuscript sources, reflecting the variety of textual witnesses in circulation; two manuscripts and a copy of Caxton's *Boece* used in the preparation of his edition survive today.[29] Subsequent editions of the *Works* relied on the most recent previous edition, with the 1542 printers using a copy of the 1532 *Works*, the 1550 printers using the 1542 edition, and so on. Through this process of enchainment, Thynne's text remained the basis for all printed editions of Chaucer until Thomas Tyrwhitt's 1775–1777 edition of the *Canterbury Tales*, published three hundred years after Thynne's main source for the *Tales*, Caxton's 1477 edition.[30] (Poems and other texts added to the *Works* in later editions generally came from manuscript sources, although Speght took *Jack Upland* directly from the text printed in Foxe's *Actes and Monuments*.)[31] For good or for ill, this stability meant that decisions made in the preparation of one edition of the *Works* continued to shape Chaucer's text as it was encountered by many future generations of readers.

The tendency of one edition to build on the previous through a process of textual accretion affected not just individual passages in Chaucer's text, but the development of his canon as well. Once a text was printed in the *Works*, it was also *reprinted* in the *Works* (this was also true of paratextual elements like Thynne's dedication to Henry VIII, which appeared in every edition of the *Works* until the eighteenth century). As noted above, while the folio editions contain most of the Chaucer canon as we regard it today, they also include a significant number of apocryphal texts, which early readers generally seem to have accepted as Chaucer's own. Thynne's 1532 edition, in particular, introduced several longer apocryphal works—among them Usk's *Testament of Love*, Robert Henryson's *Testament of Cresseid*, and *The Floure of Curtesie*, now attributed to John Lydgate—but new, non-Chaucerian texts were also added at later stages of transmission: the *Plowman's Tale* (1542), most of the poems supplied by John Stow (1561), and three of the four pieces added in Speght's editions (*The Assembly of Ladies*, *The Floure and the Leafe*, and *Jack Upland* are apocryphal; the *A.B.C.* is not).[32]

These spurious works played a significant role in shaping readers' understanding of Chaucer as an author. While the *Plowman's Tale* supported Chaucer's posthumous reputation as a religious reformer, many of the poems added by Stow (most of which do not carry attribution in manuscript) cast Chaucer as a courtly figure by the way they engage with topics of courtly love and *fin amor*.[33] While later sixteenth-century editions of the *Works* sometimes identify certain texts as the work of other writers, it is not always clear whether unmarked new additions—some of which are titled simply "a ballade"—were included on the basis of an amorphous notion of Chaucerian affinity and affiliation, or with the understanding that they were written by Chaucer himself.[34]

As the size of Chaucer's canon expanded, so too did the amount of paratextual material, often antiquarian in nature, that accompanied it. As in the case of the *Works'* literary contents, an additive tendency prevails: once a new element is introduced, it generally appears in all subsequent editions. Thynne's 1532 dedicatory preface to Henry VIII, which I discuss in greater detail below, was included in editions of Chaucer's works long after the demise of its addressee.[35] Later publications carried over other elements from Thynne as well, including a table of contents (which is updated to reflect additions and changes in later editions) and three short non-Chaucerian poems that appear sandwiched between the table of contents and the interior title page for the *Canterbury Tales*. Greg Walker has argued that these three poems—"Eight goodly questyons, with their aunswers" (Digital Index of Medieval English Verse [hereafter DIMEV] 4978), "To the kynges most noble grace, and to the lordes and knyghtes of the garter" (written by Hoccleve, DIMEV 6045), and an untitled fourteen-line excerpt from prophetic verses sometimes attributed to Chaucer and sometimes to Merlin (DIMEV 6299)—were placed there deliberately, forming a kind of bridge between the concerns of the preface and the main body of the text, and that their didacticism offers a model for interpreting the Chaucerian pieces that follow.[36] Like the dedicatory preface, these were reprinted in later editions of the *Works*, even though the specific cultural and political moment they appear to address had passed. Along with the preface, their continued presence in later editions marked Chaucer as a poet who had become, in important ways, a Tudor author as well as a Ricardian one.

Chaucer's Language and the Language of Chaucerian Praise

In the paratextual material associated with the *Works* as well as in other antiquarian contexts, extrapoetic discourse around Chaucer coalesced around a few major themes during the sixteenth century, most significantly the excellence of his language. For many commentators, Chaucer's most noteworthy poetic accomplishments were not his robust characters, his sophisticated engagements with classical and continental sources, or his experiments in meter. They were, instead, his words, which were seen to have a salutary impact on the language as a whole, such that Chaucer could be credited with single-handedly elevating English to the same level of richness and sophistication as the continental vernaculars. (Chaucer, in this sense, occupied a role analogous to that of Shakespeare in the later Anglophone world, a proper name to which wide-ranging claims of linguistic innovation could be attached.) Chaucer's language was important to his poetic admirers from Thomas Hoccleve and Thomas Usk onward, but the collected folio editions of the *Works* were especially attuned to the broader extraliterary significance of claims for Chaucer's eloquence.

The dedicatory preface to William Thynne's 1532 edition of Chaucer's collected *Works* offers what is perhaps the most fully articulated account of this view. Addressed to Henry VIII, the preface underscores Chaucer's potential usefulness to early modern projects of nation building, while also emphasizing the importance of learning and wisdom to good government.[37] For Thynne, eloquence goes hand in hand with other forms of cultural excellence. Discussing the biblical, then the classical past, he writes that "Amonges other / the Grekes in all kyndes of sciences / semed so to prevayle and so to ornate their tonge / as yet by other of right noble langages can nat be perfitely ymitated or folowed." Similarly, "the Latyns by example of the grekes, have gotten or wonne to them no small glorie / in the fourmynge / order / and uttrynge of that tonge." Whatever eloquence these languages now possess is a tale of corruption followed by redemption, an important detail if one is to imagine the eventual perfection of the English tongue. Thynne explains that the Spanish language, "beinge also latyn was by Vandales / Gothes / Moores / Sarracenes / and other so many tymes blemysshed / as marveyle it is to se nowe unto what perfection these two [Italian and Spanish, the two languages that Thynne identifies as being closest to Latin] formed out of the latyn and barbare speches be reduced." He continues, "Next unto them / in symilytude to the latyn is the Frenche tonge / whiche by dilygence of people of the same / is in fewe yeres passed so amended / as well in pronunciation as in writyng / that an Englyshman by a small tyme exercised in that tonge hath nat lacked grounde to make a gramer, or rule ordinary therof."[38] For Thynne, as for most premodern writers on the topic, language and identity were deeply related. Here, "French" refers both to the language and to the "people of the same," whose cohesion as a group stems from their shared language.

The preface suggests that Thynne valued regularity and systematic organization in language, qualities not particularly prominent in early modern English, but also that he saw linguistic improvement and standardization as the result of intentional effort—"dilygence"—on the part of a language's speakers rather than as an organic process.[39] In his comments on German, Thynne praises the language for its similitude to Latin: "Though of trouthe (whiche some shall scarsely beleve) the Germayns have so fourmed the order of their langage / that in the same / is bothe as moche plentie and as nere concordaunce to the phrase of the latyn / as the Frenche tong hath."[40] He concludes, "and veraiyly / lyke as al these and the rest have ben thus vigilant and studyous to meliorate or amende their langages: so hath there nat lacked amonges us Englishmen / whiche have right well and notably endevoyred and employed themselves / to the beautifying and bettryng of thenglyshe tonge."[41]

Chief among those who have worked for the betterment of the language, of course, is Geoffrey Chaucer. Thynne's comments on Chaucer address his style as well as his works, but coming after a lengthy and sweeping discussion of other languages, it is clear that for Thynne Chaucer's significance lies not in his poetry itself but in what his verses prove about the excellence and capability of English, in both the linguistic and national sense of the term. The architect of this excellence must be suitably accomplished. Thus, Thynne praises Chaucer as someone "in whose workes is so manyfest comprobacion of his excellent lernyng in all kyndes of doctrynes and sciences, suche frutefulnesse in words / wel accordinge to the mater and purpose / so swete and pleasant sentences / soche perfection in metre / the composycion so adapted / soche fresshnesse of invencion / compendyousnesse in narration / suche sensyble and open style / lackyng neither majestie ne mediocritie / covenable in disposycion / and suche sharpnesse or quycknesse in conclusyon."[42] Although he begins with Chaucer's learning, Thynne devotes most of this passage to describing Chaucer's writing. Presented as a master of the superlative expression of literary values that Thynne believes his sixteenth-century audience will share, Chaucer sounds very contemporary here. Chaucer's works matter not only because of what their content reveals about their author, but also because they are the evidence of the "beautifying and bettryng of thenglyshe tonge." In this way, according to Thynne, Chaucer was not just a good poet, but an extraordinary one. As Thynne puts it, "it is moche to be marvayled / howe in his time / whan doutlesse all good letters were layde a slepe throughout the worlde / as the thynge, whiche either by the disposycion and influence of the bodies above / or by other ordynaunce of god / semed lyke as was in daunger to have utterly perysshed / suche an excellent poete in our tonge / shulde as it were (nature repugnyng) spryng and arise."[43] From a grammatical perspective, is not entirely clear what "thynge" is in danger of perishing without Chaucer's aid, but what is certain is that in order to be the exceptional poet that Thynne presents him as, Chaucer's poetic achievements must transcend their historical moment, making them temporally as well as literarily exceptional. And, indeed, Chaucer is presented here as a figure not just untimely but unnatural, springing forth despite "nature repugnyng."

As the preface continues it becomes evident that, for Thynne, Chaucer's significance lies not just in the unprecedented eloquence of his English poetry but, as the passage above suggests, more specifically in his ability to reach such heights at an unlikely historical moment. An air of untimeliness floats around Chaucer, whose works "semeth for the admiracion / noveltie / and strangenesse that it myght be reputed to be of in the tyme of the authour / in comparison / as a pure and fyne tryede precious or polyced jewell out of a rude or indigest masse or matere."[44] Rather than emerging from the "indigest masse" of late medieval England, Thynne suggests Chaucer belongs more properly to either the Greek and Roman past or to the Henrician present, the parallels Thynne finds between Chaucer and Greek and Roman exemplars making him appear more like the writers of the sixteenth century than the fourteenth. Thynne continues,

> For though it had been in Demosthenes or Homerus tymes / whan al lernyng and excellency of sciences florisshed amonges the Grekes / or in the season that Cicero prince of eloquence amonges latyns lyved / yet had it ben a thyng right rare and straunge / and worthy perpetuall laude / that any clerke by lernyng or wytte coulde than have framed a

tonge before so rude and imperfite / to suche a swete ornature and composyicion / lykely if he had lyved in these dayes / being good letters so restored and revyved as they be / if he were nat empeched by the envy of suche as maye tollerate nothyng / whiche to understonde their capacite doth nat extende / to have brought it unto a full and fynall perfection.[45]

In this passage, Thynne articulates a view of Chaucer that will be echoed in the works of later writers, including John Leland and Sir Philip Sidney. On the one hand, for Thynne, Chaucer is an extraordinary writer whose accomplishments are all the more remarkable because they occurred during a period when "all good letters were layde a slepe throughout the worlde." Approached synchronically, in his own moment, Chaucer is exceptional. On the other hand, by setting Chaucer apart from his medieval antecedents and contemporaries, Thynne can also construct a diachronic narrative that not only links Chaucer to exemplars of classical eloquence but also imagines his reception (as if a living author) in the Henrician present in which "good letters" are "so restored and revyved" as to make "a full and fynall perfection" of the language possible. Although cut off from both the illustrious past and the glorious future by their medieval moment, Chaucer's writings here are presented both as a continuation of classical learnedness and as something that might draw the "envy" of a lesser sort of contemporary reader. While Thomas Wilson might have had poetry in mind when he complained, in his 1553 *Arte of Rhetorique*, that "the fine Courtier wil talk nothyng but Chaucer," Thynne's preface suggests a variety of reasons why the English courtier—eager to demonstrate both loyalty and eloquence in the rapidly shifting environs of the Henrician court—might have found Chaucer, in particular, a useful focal point for courtly discourse.[46]

(Re)framing Chaucer

While Thynne's preface did much to link Chaucer with the development of the English language (and, through it, Englishness itself), the 1561 edition more vividly shows how bibliographic features like title pages could convey specific ideas about how and why Chaucer mattered in sixteenth-century England. The title pages to the three Thynne editions use relatively sedate architectural

borders, but John Stow's edition of the *Works* introduces a new title page, fea-
turing the Chaucer family coat of arms (thereby emphasizing Chaucer's
social status; see Figure 1), and on several interior title pages makes use of the
extraordinary "tree of Jesse" woodcut frame originally produced for Edward
Hall's *Union of the two noble and illustre fameliers of Lancastre and Yorke*, better known as *Hall's Chronicle* (STC 12723), and used subsequently in Thomas
Marshe's 1555 edition of Lydgate's *Troy Book* (STC 5580) (see Figure 2).[47] The
bottom corners of the frame depict the slumbering figures of John of Gaunt
and Edmund of York, from whose torsos emerge rose bushes, blooming with
the visages of various fifteenth-century luminaries. At the top of the frame,
the two bushes join as Henry VII extends a hand from his bloom to greet his
queen Elizabeth in hers. Above, in a double Tudor rose, Henry VIII presides
over the entire scene. In the 1561 *Works*, where the woodcut prefaces the *Canterbury Tales* and the *Romaunt of the Rose*, it quite literally provides a historical frame for Chaucer's text. The juxtaposition is striking: while the image
quite clearly reflects the contents of *Hall's Chronicle*, there is no self-evident
link between the *Canterbury Tales* and the War of the Roses. Instead, the
woodcut invites the reader to make the link between Chaucer, the historical
figure, and the luminaries depicted in the woodcut, most notably Chaucer's
patron John of Gaunt.

The Hall woodcut provides a visual analogue to what had by the middle
of the sixteenth century become an increasingly historicized and politicized
frame of reference for reading Chaucer. The woodcut's biographical connection to Chaucer depends upon the figure of Chaucer's patron and brother-in-
law John of Gaunt at the bottom left; its appearance here must indicate that
whoever was responsible for the its appearance in this book was aware of the
connection between Chaucer and Gaunt and wished to emphasize this. Joseph
Dane and Seth Lerer have argued that evidence of a stop-press correction of a
typographical error in *Adam Scriveyn* indicates that Stow himself was involved
in the production of the *Works*, perhaps even present in the printing house.[48]
Stow certainly had the necessary historical background to recognize the connection between Gaunt and Chaucer, and he must have known *Hall's Chronicle* as a source for his own historiography.[49] I think it very likely that Stow
himself wanted this image placed in this book.

The use of the Hall woodcut in 1561 anticipates the more explicitly antiquarian orientation of the 1598 and 1602 Speght editions, which actively connect Chaucer's writings to his historical circumstances. The frontispiece of the
1598 *Works* enumerates some of the features and aids for potential readers

Figure 1. Title page, *The woorkes of Geffrey Chaucer, newly printed with divers addicions, whiche were never in printe before* (1561); STC 5076. By permission of the Folger Shakespeare Library.

Figure 2. Interior title page for the *Canterbury Tales* from *The woorkes of Geffrey Chaucer, newly printed with divers addicions, whiche were never in printe before* (1561), sig. A1; STC 5076. By permission of the Folger Shakespeare Library.

and buyers, beginning with the John Speed engraving I will discuss in detail below:

1. His Portraiture and Progenie shewed.
2. His Life collected.
3. Arguments to every Booke gathered.
4. Old and obscure words explaned.
5. Authors by him cited, declared.
6. Difficulties opened.
7. Two Bookes of his, never before Printed.

Notably, neither this list nor the text of the title page as a whole make mention of any of Chaucer's works by title; Chaucer's own name is the selling point here. The frontispiece for the revised edition, which appeared just four years later in 1602, has a similar appearance and emphasis. Readers are advised that they will find that "to that which was done in the former Impression," "much is now added," including:

1. In the life of Chaucer many things inserted.
2. The whole Worke by old Copies reformed.
3. Sentences and Proverbes noted.
4. The Signfication of the old and obscure words proved: also Caracters shewing from what Tongue or Dialect they be derived.
5. The Latine and French, not Englished by Chaucer, translated.
6. The Treatise called *Jacke Upland*, against Friers: and Chaucers A.B.C. called *La Priere de nostre Dame*, at this Impression added.

Taken together, these two lists offer would-be buyers and readers a number of reasons that they might turn to this particular edition of Chaucer. Some of the aids listed here, such as the translation of Latin and French phrases and the glossary of "old and obscure" terms, could potentially help any reader. But taken together, these title pages present "our most learned and ancient English poet" as a figure of biographical and genealogical interest, a source of proverbial wisdom, and a multilingual and intertextual writer. These themes are already present in the Thynne preface, but here it is clear that, in assuming these roles, Chaucer has been made into an object of scholarly labor: arguments are "gathered," words are "explained," and difficulties are "opened," even if, on close examination, the assertion that the "whole worke [is] by old Copies reformed" proves to be somewhat (and somewhat predictably, given the tendency toward hyperbole on early modern title pages) overstated.

Speght's editions make especially visible the hybrid status that Chaucer acquired over the course of the sixteenth century: on the one hand, as a poet whose works are witty and wise, and who can be read for pleasure or for edification; on the other, as a figure from the increasingly distant English past, someone whose life and works require explanation and interpretation so that later readers can fully understand the importance of his contributions. Chaucer's *Works* remain a book to be read, but they are also, increasingly, presented as texts requiring study and careful explication.

Chaucerian Genealogies

A striking, full-page engraving prepared for the 1598 edition of the *Works* visually demonstrates this dual approach to Chaucer (Figure 3). The artist, historian, and cartographer John Speed was best known for his *Theatre of the Empire of Great Britaine* and for the genealogical tables he contributed to the Authorized Version of the Bible, and was well connected in antiquarian circles.[50] Speed's engraving is significant in that it marks the first time a formal author portrait appeared in a printed edition of Chaucer's writings (early editions of the *Canterbury Tales* depict the author/narrator on horseback), but it adds to that portrait a number of features that reflect Chaucer's status as an object of antiquarian fascination. In form and in content, the engraving exemplifies the two distinct, though interrelated, ways of thinking about Chaucer that predominated at the close of the sixteenth century: one literary and laudatory, the other historical. Viewed through the literary lens, Chaucer is a great poet whose poetic achievements are said to transcend his historical moment in ways that allow Renaissance readers to feel particularly close to him. Viewed through the historical lens, Chaucer is of his moment, connected through family and marriage to a range of significant political figures. A tension between historical fixity and literary mobility lies at the heart of claims for Chaucer's exceptional status, a point that the complex visual rhetoric of the engraving makes clear as it navigates between multiple schemata for periodizing Chaucer.

At the center of the image is a large, full-length portrait of Chaucer, modeled on that found in manuscripts of Thomas Hoccleve's *Regiment of Princes*.[51] The caption underneath identifies it as "the true portraiture of GEFFREY

Figure 3. "The Progenie of Geffrey Chaucer," from *The Workes of our Ancient and learned English Poet, Geffrey Chaucer, newly Printed* (1602); STC 5080. By permission of the Folger Shakespeare Library.

CHAUCER / the famous English poet, as by THOMAS OCCLEVE is described who lived in his time, and was his Scholar," touting the picture as an authoritative and authorized image of the poet grounded in firsthand experience.[52] In it, a rotund and goateed Chaucer, looking serious in a smock and wide-sleeved garment, holds a penner in his right hand and a string of rosary beads in his left.

This portrait, which could have easily appeared in a fifteenth-century copy of Hoccleve's poem, introduces familiar tropes of literary laureation, but it is the least elaborate aspect of Speed's engraving. Directly below, Speed depicts the double tomb of Thomas and Maude (Matilda) Chaucer, Chaucer's son and daughter-in-law, shown in situ at the Ewelme parish church. (Notably, Speed does not depict Chaucer's own modest tomb in Westminster Abbey.)[53] The tomb chest features some two dozen shields, representing not only Thomas and Maude's direct ancestry, but the impressive number of baronial families to which the couple—though not Geoffrey Chaucer himself—was related by blood or marriage (the connections are mostly through Maude's family or Philippa Chaucer, née Swynford).[54] Speed has distorted perspective here to show three sides of the tomb and thus maximize the number of shields that can be illustrated; the arms appearing include those of John of Gaunt and Edward, 2nd Duke of York and the son of Edmund, 1st Duke of York. John of Gaunt and Edmund, Duke of York, are two of the key figures in the woodcut from *Hall's Chronicle* used in the 1561 *Works*.

While the tomb occupies the space below the central portrait, an extensive genealogical diagram fills the space above and to the sides. Its circular medallions recall the medieval armorial roles that would have served as Speed's sources and anticipate the genealogical tables that Speed would later produce for the Authorized Version of the Bible.[55] Like the other elements of the engraving, the genealogy bristles with information, presented in a format widely used in antiquarian contexts.[56] These elements not only speak to the new significance that Chaucer and his writings had taken on as objects of historic and antiquarian study by the turn of the seventeenth century but, considered along with the more conventional author portrait, also exemplify the dualism that is central to antiquarian responses to the medieval poet in this period.

This dualism also plays out in the ways the engraving depicts Chaucer's relation to his "progeny": at the center, the Hocclevian portrait recalls the poetic pedigrees and praise for "father Chaucer" familiar to literary scholars. It collapses historical distance and invites viewers to come face-to-face with the author, carrying forward the conventional hallmarks of Chaucerian tribute and memorialization. It cultivates a sense of personal connection to the poet, akin to the firsthand knowledge suggested by the *Regiment of Princes* portrait or the more metaphysical associations implied by Spenser's claims for a spiritual connection to his predecessor.[57] In her discussion of Speght's edition, Stephanie Trigg comments on the ways in which the prefatory materials encourage readers to imagine not only a synchronic "horizontal communion" of Chaucer lovers in the present, but a kind of diachronic "vertical communion" with previous admirers and finally the great man himself.[58] While Trigg imagines this community as centered on printed editions of Chaucer's poetry, this engraving encourages devotion based not around a book but on the author himself. With this sense of connection, however, also comes an awareness of distance; Chaucer is, in fact, no longer present and the reader must make do with the book before him or her. As in religious devotional images, the viewer is visually cued to the fact the encounter is a mediated one, here by looking across the surface of the tomb that appears at the bottom of the engraving, which functions as a casement, arch, or doorway might frame an image of a saint in a Book of Hours.[59] Attending to these qualities of the engraving, Martha Driver aptly describes it as a "Protestant rereading of a medieval devotional image."[60]

The material that surrounds the portrait, by contrast, situates Chaucer in a specific historical moment and represents his historical existence as part of a genealogy that is not at all dependent upon his poetic accomplishments. Although the heading at the top of the frame reads "The Progenie of Geoffrey Chaucer," it is Chaucer's father-in-law, "Payne Roet Knight," who sits atop the family tree. Paon de Roet (or Roelt, Ruet) was a knight from the Low Countries who came to England in the service of Edward III and who was father not only to Chaucer's wife Philippa (identified here merely as "The Daughter of Payne Roet") but also to Katherine Swynford, the mistress and later wife of John of Gaunt.[61] As the left side of Speed's engraving illustrates, through this family connection, Chaucer can be linked to several major figures in fifteenth-century history, including both Henry IV and Henry V. The right-hand margin shows Chaucer's line of descent via his son Thomas, a successful politician in his own right. Thomas Chaucer's only child, Alice, acquired prodigious amounts of wealth and power through a series of impressive marriages; the third and last, to William de la Pole, Duke of Suffolk, resulted in a son, John. John was the father of Edmund de la Pole, the Yorkist pretender to the throne executed by Henry VIII in 1513. Speed thus links Chaucer with the houses of both York and Lancaster and, through them, to networks of power and institutions that continued to shape the world in which Speed's audience lived and read. This is not so much a poetic tribute as a history lesson.

Taken as a whole, Speed's engraving brings together praise of Chaucer as a posthumous but sacrosanct literary figure with a sense that he is, as Helen Cooper writes, "embedded in the great tradition of the nation in part by his close incorporation into the royal and aristocratic history of England."[62] Importantly, this connection is not limited to Chaucer's own lifetime, nor does it only look backward to the classical inheritance (a move that ultimately contemporizes Chaucer for later readers who were themselves ardent students of the Greek and Roman past). Instead, as the genealogies remind us, Chaucer's legacy extends directly to the sixteenth century, which will see "the comparison of him to the great classical authors in the *Works*, the patronage of Henry VIII, the tussle to claim him for each religion, the triumph of his misidentification as a forerunner of English Protestantism, and the erection of his tomb close to those of England's monarchs."[63] All these various claims for Chaucer's lasting import find support in the genealogical framework that Speed provides.

Like the conventions of Chaucer's literary reception, which venerate him as the author *Troilus and Criseyde* and the *Canterbury Tales* while largely ignoring texts like the *Legend of Good Women*, both the portrait and the genealogy that surrounds it are selective, and this encodes a series of value judgments: the stemma depicts only those branches of the family tree that afford Chaucer the most impressive and politically significant connections, and while Speed emphasizes the authority of the portrait by associating it with a named author who lived in Chaucer's time, he calls Hoccleve a "scholar" rather than identifying him as a poet in his own right. In both poetic and historical registers, Chaucer appears *sui generis*, without any representation of his own poetic influences or (relatively modest) parentage. At each of its many levels, the Speed engraving offers a visual example of the representational choices consistently made when presenting Chaucer to early modern audiences. These choices, in both the engraving and in the larger context of the *Works* and related commentary, maximize Chaucer's status and importance not just to literary history but to English nationalism at large.

Antiquarian Readers and the Middle English Past

Although antiquarian readers like Thynne, Stow, and Speght made up only a small part of Chaucer's early modern readership, they played a disproportionately significant role in defining the medieval poet's reputation and constructing his canon. As a result of their work with medieval materials, antiquarians were probably among the best-equipped readers of Chaucer's Middle English in early modern England. The average reader of the *Works* and other printed copies of Middle English verse must have lacked the linguistic facility of an aficionado like John Stow, but the assumption still seems to have been that she or he could read, admire, and appreciate the language of earlier poetry. Indeed, the increasingly palpable antiquity of Middle English could even be a selling point.

This attitude is not limited to Chaucer. Introducing his 1532 edition of John Gower's *Confessio Amantis*, the printer Thomas Berthelette praises the poem's "olde englysshe wordes and vulgars [that] no wyse man / bycause of theyr antiquite / wyll throwe asyde."[64] He juxtaposes Gower's language with "newe termes" that "wryters of later dayes" borrow from foreign languages. Such unfamiliar terms, he writes, impede readers' understanding since "they that understode not those langages / from whens these newe vulgars are sette / coude not perceyve theyr wrytynges." The implication seems to be that Gower's poetry can provide a suitable alternative to this unnecessary borrowing by offering a stock of novel, but still English, words.[65] Robert Braham, in his epistle to the reader in Thomas Marshe's 1555 edition of Lydgate's *Troy Book*, complains at length about the errors in the text introduced by earlier scribes and printers (of Pynson's 1513 edition, he grumbles that "bothe the prynter and correctour, neyther of them as it shoulde seme [were] eyther learned or understandynge englishe"), but presumes that, once the text has been emended, readers will recognize Lydgate as one who "may worthyly be numbred amongest those that have chefelye deserved of our tynge," the "verye perfect disciple and imitator of the great Chaucer."[66] Robert Crowley, introducing his 1550 edition of *Piers Plowman*, faces a more difficult task, since the alliterative vocabulary of Langland's poem differs much more starkly from sixteenth-century English than Chaucer's or Lydgate's language. Yet even he assures readers that "the Englishe is according to the time it was written in, and the sence somewhat darcke, but not so harde, but that it may be understande of suche as will not sticke to breake the shell of the nutte for the kernelles sake."[67] In each case, the commentator acknowledges the difficulty or historical distance of the text he introduces but also articulates a confidence that the sixteenth-century reader will be able to navigate the intricacies of Middle English verse.

This combined sense of connection and distance is also on display in Speght's 1598 Chaucer, the full title of which is *The Workes of Our Antient and*

Learned English Poet, Geffrey Chaucer, as well as in the revised 1602 edition
that follows. Speght's title marks Chaucer as a specifically English poet, but
he is also, for the first time, "antient." Taken together, "antient," "learned,"
and "English" suggest a native author as sophisticated and rich as Latin and
Greek classics. This dynamic finds novel lexicographical expression in the form
of the glossary. Glossaries, like genealogies of the sort offered in the Speed
engraving, provide a path linking an archaic term (or ancestor) with its contemporary equivalent (or descendant). This connection is, importantly, never
quite immediate, and access to the figure of Chaucer is never unmediated: in
Speed's engraving, readers must navigate five generations to move from Geoffrey
Chaucer to Edmund de la Pole. In a glossary like Speght's, readers must move
back and forth between Middle English terms and their definitions, linguistic
difference functioning here as a marker of historical distance.

The distancing effect produced by Speght's title and glossaries might seem
at first primarily negative. After all, at the end of the sixteenth century, as
Speght compiled his list of "old and obscure words" in Chaucer, continental
editions of Boccaccio and Dante came equipped not with glossaries but with
indexes designed to aid the reader as he or she incorporated the language of
the fourteenth-century poets into his or her own writing.[68] The linguistic and
historical alienation that prompts Speght's interventions is not necessarily un-
desirable, however, because it opens up new ways of situating the poet in relation to the more distant past. There might be no glossary in Dante, but similar
lexicons can be found in school texts of Virgil, Seneca, and the like. With their
language marked both as historically distant and foundationally English,
Chaucer's writings become the first English "classics."

Far from bracketing off Chaucer as an antiquarian curiosity irrelevant
to current experiments in form and diction, the increasing unfamiliarity of
Chaucer's language might well have helped to assure his relevance to the major
conversations about language, influence, and national identity in early modern England.[69] On the printed page, Chaucer, viewed from the far side of religious reform and the "new" learning, could look surprisingly like certain
influential Greek and Roman writers. Furthermore, as Lucy Munro demonstrates, the sixteenth century witnessed a sustained poetic engagement with
the idea of archaism in ways that both drew upon and helped to shape antiquarian practice.[70] Archaism, which like antiquarianism was in its early modern form deeply concerned with questions of national identity and England's
relation to its own past, made Chaucer's distant language newly available
for poetic appropriation, perhaps most notably in the writings of Edmund

Spenser.[71] The perceived outdatedness of Chaucer's language—the idea it was now, as Puttenham wrote, "no longer with us"—was precisely what allowed him to serve as Spenser's "well of English undefiled" and to appear as a writer who was, in the words of Speght's title page, both "antient" and "English."[72]

A few conclusions can be drawn from these examples. First, early modern readers and writers were alert to the changing nature of the English language. An awareness of language change in English was not new to post-Reformation England: in the thirteenth century the Tremulous Hand glossed Old English words with their Middle English equivalents, while around 1490, Caxton famously commented on the vagaries of the English tongue in his preface to his *Eneydos* (STC 24769). Throughout the premodern era, scribes and printers silently emended their sources to modernize their form and diction. But in sixteenth-century England, new kinds of changes made the difference between the language of the past and that of the present even more visible.[73] Modifications in pronunciation, orthography, and grammar all played a role, and caused particular challenges when scanning and pronouncing works in verse.[74] Errors proliferated as Middle English texts were copied and recopied by sixteenth-century scribes and compositors. Evolving attitudes toward the past itself—specifically, the notion that there was a "chiaroscuro" contrast between the present and the pre-Reformation past—also contributed to a sense that the language of the past was different and distant, and therefore more difficult to read and comprehend.[75]

Second, despite this change, it is clear that readers retained a real connection to the language and stories of late medieval England. A number of things testify to their ongoing vitality: multiple editions not only of Chaucer's *Works* but also of writings by Gower, Lydgate, and Langland; ongoing references to and adaptations of Chaucer and his contemporaries in poetry, drama, and prose; and the abundant presence of sixteenth- and seventeenth-century annotations both in medieval books and in early printed volumes containing Middle English. Even if readers were increasingly aware of the historical and linguistic distance between themselves and their medieval predecessors, and even if Chaucer's language was manifestly more difficult than it had been a hundred years earlier, the evidence suggests that a significant number of readers retained some ability to comprehend and appreciate London dialects of late Middle English. The ability to read as well as study these older texts, in other words, never disappeared completely.

Beginning in the middle decades of the sixteenth century, many antiquarians also devoted at least some of their energies to the study of Anglo-Saxon, and the degree to which Old English was necessarily treated as a separate language offers an illustrative contrast to late Middle English's proximity to early modern English. For texts written in older forms of the English language, the distinction between historical and literary modes of reading was much more clear-cut than it was for Middle English. (This is not to say Anglo-Saxon could not be deployed for literary purposes: from the sixteenth century to the twenty-first, poets have deliberately engaged with Old English language and poetry, whether translating it or, occasionally, composing new verse.)[76] Early modern readers could at least follow the sense of Chaucer's stories without special training, even if individual words or references might be obscure or a corrupt or poorly edited text caused difficulty. Study of Old English grammar and language, however, was a necessary prelude to further investigation into Anglo-Saxon law, historiography, and religion.[77] Key figures in the development of Anglo-Saxon studies, such as Matthew Parker, understood this and supported the work of grammarians and lexicographers accordingly.[78] By and large, these early scholars turned to the surviving corpus of Old English writing as a source lexical and linguistic insight rather than poetic pleasure.[79] It would not be until the early twentieth century that Anglo-Saxon verse would be seriously studied from a literary, rather than philological, perspective.

Third and finally, as the sixteenth century progressed, Chaucer, in particular, became a site for the commingling of a tradition of readerly enjoyment and a new sense that the English past was worth studying in rigorous ways. This is true of other late medieval authors as well, of course, but the sustained attention given to Chaucer's archaisms is unique and testifies to what I have argued throughout this chapter was Chaucer's exceptional place as a figure primed to index both connection to and distance from the medieval past. Marked by language that was both recognizably English and increasingly historically distant, Chaucer was at once an object of antiquarian fascination and a familiar English writer whose works remained accessible to many readers.

While Chaucer's early modern transmission and reception can and should be understood in a context that included the work of other Middle English writers, Chaucer's especially vaunted position in poetic genealogies from the fifteenth century onward made both the author and his language a privileged site for contemplation of the past in early modern England. As a writer whose language was identifiably English and whose achievements could be favorably compared with both later writers and classical ones, Chaucer represented continuity and historical progression. At the same time, because his language was an earlier form of the vernacular, and because the historical and cultural moment in which he lived was increasingly thought of as "other" to the post-Reformation present, he also signaled the presence of chronological rupture within English history. This doubleness is key to Chaucer's special status in early modern England and the basis for his ability to signify meaningfully in both literary and historical contexts—an ability that is increasingly foregrounded in successive editions of his *Works*.

In their shared concern for Chaucer's poetic legacy and the English past, the work of early antiquarians constitutes the pre-philological beginnings of what we today recognize as English literary history. To adapt Claude Lévi-Strauss's claims about the ceremonial importance of certain foods that are "good to think" if not necessarily "good to eat," Renaissance antiquarians selected Chaucer for a special role because they found him exceptionally "good to think," even if he and his contemporaries no longer remained unequivocally "good to read" as his language became more difficult for everyday readers.[80] The materials I consider in the following chapters show Chaucer's works poised on a permeable boundary between "texts for reading" and "texts for studying": what one reader considers a text for serious scholarly examination in one context may also be read for literary pleasure or moral insight in another.

In the decades since Alice S. Miskimin's landmark 1975 study *The Renaissance Chaucer*, medievalists and early modernists have both done much to map the ways that Chaucer was read in the sixteenth century and beyond. Yet Tudor readers with connections to antiquarian communities have a special and largely untold role to play in this story, since not only do they comment on Chaucer, they play a key shepherding Chaucer's works into print and keeping them there. In the following chapter, I turn to John Leland. Although Leland never edited Chaucer, his antiquarian writings influenced a century's worth of English antiquarians, and any account that seeks to understand antiquarians' influence on Chaucer's transmission must account for the foundational role played by Leland and his commentary.

CHAPTER 2

"Noster Galfridus"

Chaucer's Early Modern Biographies

In 1532, when William Thynne assembled the first edition of Chaucer's collected *Works*, there was no written biography of Chaucer.[1] Chaucer's own writings are reticent about the facts of his life, and what they do say is often mediated through persona and allusion. A few fifteenth-century references mention Chaucer's death, traditionally believed to have occurred on October 25, 1400: the scribe and bibliophile John Shirley calls Chaucer's *Truth* a "Balade that Chaucier made on his deeth bedde."[2] Thomas Gascoigne, in his *Dictionarium Theologicum* (ca. 1434–1458), appears to draw upon the *Retraction* to the *Canterbury Tales* as he describes a penitent Chaucer who dies bemoaning his inability to recall from circulation "those things that I wickedly wrote concerning the evil and truly disgraceful love of men for women."[3] No surviving account from the fifteenth century discusses Chaucer's family, his education, or his travels abroad.

In the sixteenth century, however, that would change, thanks to the rise of antiquarian scholarship and an increasingly robust body of commentary on Chaucer's life and works. In antiquarian writings, especially those with an explicit interest in Chaucer's life, focus shifted from Chaucer's texts themselves to their cultural and historical significance. In these writings, history, language, and English nationalism became conflated in ways that would shape Chaucer's transmission and reception for centuries to come.

Antiquarian interest in Chaucer begins where early modern English antiquarianism itself arguably begins, in the writings of John Leland (ca. 1503–1552), the humanist poet and scholar. As a part of a larger work, *De Viris Illustribus* (On Famous Men), Leland's Latin writings on Chaucer circulated

in manuscript throughout the sixteenth century and beyond and were a continuous and foundational influence on antiquarian scholarship in England.[4]
They were known to both the Protestant polemicist John Bale and the martyrologist John Foxe, and eventually served as the primary source for the first
English-language account of Chaucer's life, printed in Speght's 1598 edition
of Chaucer's *Works*.[5] Reading Speght's *Life of Our Learned English Poet, Geffrey
Chaucer* in light of *De Viris Illustribus*, as I do in this chapter, underscores
how Leland's account shaped subsequent conversations about Chaucerian biography.[6] Leland bequeathed to Speght not just details concerning Chaucer's
life, but an understanding of Chaucer as national poet whose cultural impact
extended beyond the realm of literature and aesthetics into a wider historiographic and nationalistic context. Because Speght's *Life* was written in English, not Latin, and because it circulated in print, not manuscript, it also
made Leland's humanistic view of Chaucer available to a new and wider
audience.

Before this, though, Leland's biography and the texts it influenced restruc-
tured Chaucer's reputation in early modern England, shifting attention away
from the content of his works and toward the author himself. While earlier
poetic tributes focused primarily on the Chaucerian text and its "rhetoric" or
"eloquence," Leland and Speght treated Chaucer as a historical individual
whose writings could be better assessed in terms of their influence on a shared
national vernacular and identity than on their ability to move individual readers or innovate in form or style. Even when praising Chaucer's poems, Leland
directs readers' attention to Chaucer the author who stands outside his own
works. As he does so, he reconstructs Chaucer as an author according to the
discursive norms of early modern England, contributing to the ongoing evolution of what Alexandra Gillespie, following Michel Foucault, calls the
"Chaucer 'effect,'" defined as "the author who is a 'function' of the creation,
circulation, and interpretation of his texts, paratext, and others' texts about
his work."[7]

Leland's biography of Chaucer guided the development of this "Chaucer
effect" in several overlapping and reinforcing ways. First, it created historical
narrative that corroborated one of the key motifs of Chaucerian praise: the
idea that the poet played a unique role in the improvement of the English language and through that, made a lasting contribution to English identity. In
Leland's text and those that follow from it, Chaucer becomes a synecdoche
for national exceptionalism, someone who simultaneously stands for England's
worldliness and its uniqueness. Second, Leland's use of Latin in his account

inaugurated a split between praise of Chaucer and imitation of Chaucer, two strands of reception that had previously been closely linked. When, some sixty years later, Speght wrote his English version of Chaucer's life, the language of Chaucerian commentary returned to the vernacular, but the sense of critical distance introduced by Leland remained. In Speght and in Leland both, praise of Chaucer's works, which in poetic tributes can take on an intimate, deeply affective tone, now reads more like an objective recitation of facts. Third, these biographical writings situate Chaucer's life story in relation to the present, emphasizing the continuities between his historical moment and that of his latter-day readers. Leland and his followers achieved this effect not only by celebrating Chaucer as a poet who both enabled and offered a glimpse of what English poetry would become, but by linking him to institutions and locations, such as the University of Oxford, that signified learning, power, and intellectual significance in the early modern present. These factors combined to reinforce an understanding of Chaucer as not only a source of readerly pleasure but a figure of national importance and a subject fit for scholarly inquiry.

Leland's remarks on Chaucer are best understood not in isolation (as they have been treated by some previous scholars) but as part of the larger scholarly enterprise from which they come. Accordingly, this chapter begins with a discussion of the overall scope, plan, and purpose of *De Viris Illustribus*. In the central sections, I take up Leland's writings on Chaucer directly, including the three Latin poems in praise of Chaucer that appear in *De Viris Illustribus*, and discuss how they present Chaucer and his writings. I also consider his comments on Gower, the only other vernacular poet discussed in the collection. In the final section, I turn to Speght's English *Life of Chaucer* and explore the ways it elaborates on Leland's foundation. Whereas Leland works to situate Chaucer in the context of institutions familiar to his own readers, Speght makes copious use of genealogical material, articulating both continuity and change between the medieval poet and his latter-day readers and marking yet another phase in Chaucer's continually changing postmedieval career.

On Famous Men

John Leland's life and biography reflect the cultural complexity of his historical moment. Like many other Tudor readers with an interest in Chaucer, his relationship to the English past was a complicated one. Born in London and orphaned as a child, Leland studied at St. Paul's School under William Lily before taking his AB from Christ's College, Cambridge in 1522 and pursuing further studies in Oxford and Paris, possibly under the patronage of Cardinal Thomas Wolsey.[8] In Paris, he wrote Latin poetry and developed an interest in ancient texts and manuscripts that would remain with him throughout his career. Sometime before 1529, Leland returned to England, where he continued work as both a scholar and a poet, now cultivating the ascendant Thomas Cromwell as a patron.

Starting in the 1530s, Leland made plans for a number of ambitious projects relating to English history, and in 1533 he apparently received a royal commission "to peruse and dylygentlye to searche all the lybraryes of Monasteryes and collegies of thys your noble realme."[9] Leland, then in his early thirties, spent the next three to four years traveling throughout England, researching and cataloging the holdings of monastic houses, in some cases just months before their official suppression.[10] The commission was, of course, given by Henry VIII, who was himself the major animating force behind the dissolution of the monasteries. Thus, as James Simpson writes, "Leland's *raison d'être* for constructing a British past is in part, then, the fact that the past is undergoing destruction by Leland's own patron. Leland is himself, accordingly, an agent of destruction, and the very object of his attention as antiquary—the past seen as something distant and sharply *different*—is itself a product of Leland's moment."[11] The complex set of motivations behind the visitations notwithstanding, Leland's travels gave him an unparalleled knowledge of the breadth and depth of England's medieval textual and intellectual heritage.

Upon his return, Leland used the materials collected during these journeys to begin working on the massive compendium of the life and works of learned Britons now known as *De Viris Illustribus*.[12] Like Leland's other writings, *De Viris Illustribus* expresses a deep appreciation for the English past alongside loyalty to a Tudor regime that increasingly defined itself against that past.[13] While Leland's antiquarian writings bemoan the destruction of the monastic libraries during the dissolution, his position within the court of Henry VIII meant his critiques were enabled by the patronage of those largely responsible for it.[14] The result is, in Simpson's phrase, "a deeply divided consciousness."[15]

Leland explains the origins and scope of the *De Viribus* project in a kind of prospectus, written in the mid-1540s and published some years later (with interpolations by John Bale) as *The laboryouse Journey and serche of Johan Leylande, for Englandes Antiquitees* (1549; STC 15445). Addressed to

Henry VIII, *De Viris Illustribus*'s prospective patron, Leland explains how the project would bring together records of a "great a numbre of excellent godlye wyttes and wryters, learned wyth the best, as the tymes served, hath bene in thys your regyon," who without such a monument were "lyke to have bene perpetually obscured, or to have bene lyghtelye remembred, as uncerteyne shaddowes."[16] The ensuing book would cover the accomplishments of English writers from pre-Roman times to the present, with the final volume (of four) dedicated solely to the reign of Henry VIII.[17] Leland completed substantial work on *De Viris Illustribus* by the early 1540s, but around the time of Henry's death in 1547 he experienced what Bale calls a "soden fall"—apparently some kind of mental breakdown—that brought an end to his scholarly activities. He died in 1552, having been declared insane two years prior.[18]

In its final yet incomplete form, *De Viris Illustribus* covers nearly a millennium of British intellectual history and presents information on the work of nearly six hundred individuals, from Roman antiquity to the early sixteenth century.[19] That said, *De Viris Illustribus* includes some entries for figures who not only did not write the works Leland attributes to them, but did not exist at all. As James Carley notes, "Leland does tend to be credulous in his enthusiasm for the British past, most notoriously in his accounts of the ancient prophets Aquila (the eagle in Geoffrey of Monmouth's *Historia Regum Britanniae* who prophesied when Shaftesbury was built) and Perdix (a prophetic partridge at the time of King Rivallo) and in the account of Pope Joan."[20]

A typical entry in *De Viris Illustribus* describes its subject's life and education, offers a list of his works—sometimes supplemented by comments about Leland's research in monastic libraries—and concludes with a few words about the subject's death, burial place, and legacy. There is room for significant variation and digression within this format, however: Leland's entry on the fourteenth-century chronicler Ranulf Higden (no. 354), for example, devotes more than half its space to criticisms of Leland's contemporary and nemesis, the Anglo-Italian antiquarian and historiographer Polydore Vergil.[21] The entries are arranged in roughly chronological order, beginning with the Druids and ending with the poet and musician Robert Widow, who died in 1503.[22]

While each entry is discrete and Leland does not provide the kind of contextual historical narrative that John Bale does in his later appropriations and expansions of Leland's work, the various political, religious, and pedagogical links among his subjects form a web of historical connections. Read as a whole, the work constitutes a grand narrative about the transmission of knowledge that stretches back, ultimately, to the Roman occupation of the British Isles and, through that, to the glories of classical civilization. In this way, Leland anticipates the interest in antiquity that marks the work of later antiquaries like William Camden and Sir Robert Cotton, but he also reflects admiration of the Greek and Roman past that characterizes the humanistic beginnings of Renaissance antiquarianism.

As a collection of biobibliographic writings, *De Viris Illustribus* continues a long-standing and wide-ranging scholarly genre that includes works by Jerome, Petrarch, and Boccaccio. The immediate catalyst for Leland's work was the *Liber de Scriptoribus Ecclesiasticis*, written by the German polymath, abbot, and early humanist Johannes Trithemius and printed in Basel in 1494.[23] Trithemius's work includes entries for nearly a thousand writers, including numerous English authors. Leland felt that Trithemius had failed to acknowledge the significance of English writers and their accomplishments, and had unjustly set them apart from their rightful place in a distinctively English intellectual tradition.[24] By researching and writing *De Viris Illustribus*, Leland sought to claim these writers, and many more, for England.

In its awareness of the asymmetry between the reputation of continental writers in England and the reputation of English writers abroad, *De Viris Illustribus* reflects something of the anxiety around English as a cultural and national identity in the sixteenth century.[25] Leland's desire to equip English readers with an intellectual genealogy of their own makes him a historiographical analogue to writers seeking a native alternative to "inkhorn terms" brought over into English from other vernaculars.[26] In the dedication to his English version of Jacopo di Porcia's *De Rei Militari* (1554), for example, the translator Peter Betham makes the case directly: "I take them beste englyshe men, which folowe Chaucer, and other olde wryters, in whyche studye the nobles and gentle men of England, are worthye to be praysed, whan they endevoure to brynge agayne to his owne clennes oure englysshe tounge, & playnelye to speake wyth our owne termes, as others dyd before us."[27] For Betham and other advocates of nativist diction, Englishness and use of the English language tended to go hand in hand. Leland, by contrast, remained a consummately Latinate thinker. Not only is *De Viris Illustribus* written in Latin, the majority of its subjects are learned clerics who—while celebrated here for their English origins—also write in Latin.

In this context, the entries on John Gower and Geoffrey Chaucer stand out as vernacular exceptions to the Latinate rule. While John Bale's later *Catalogus* (which takes Leland as its main source) adds entries for English-language writers like John Lydgate, Walter Hilton, and even the elusive

"Robert" Langland, Gower and Chaucer are the only English-language poets included in Leland's collection.[28] Leland's decision to include Chaucer and Gower in *De Viris Illustribus*—a work that, as *The laboryouse Journey* makes clear, is dedicated to the glories of England—is a bold claim for the importance of their poetry, not just in the field of literary endeavors but in intellectual and learned culture more generally. Their very presence in the project places the two poets at the intersection of English poetics and a largely Latinate intellectual tradition and suggests that their vernacular poetry is an important part of the shared national culture in England, worthy of commemoration at the highest levels. Writing about Middle English poetry in Latin is, in Pierre Bourdieu's terms, an act of consecration that elevates Gower and Chaucer to an elite position within their field of cultural production. It is also a means of spreading their fame as English writers to an audience that extends, at least in theory, far beyond England toward a wider community defined by *latinitas*.[29]

While a tradition of vernacular tribute to Chaucer and his contemporaries continued to flourish among early Tudor poets, Latin praise of English poets was something relatively novel in the 1530s. By the time that Leland set to work on *De Viris Illustribus*, poets like John Skelton and Stephen Hawes had begun to blend an appreciation for Chaucer's achievements rooted in fifteenth-century Chaucerianism with a new sense of the possibilities of English verse. Gower, too, remained a familiar name among the literary cognoscenti, his reputation bolstered, perhaps, by his consummate Ovidianism and Thomas Berthelette's 1532 edition of his *Confessio Amantis* (Leland will misidentify Berthelette as the printer of the 1532 Chaucer).[30] Importantly, however, these tributes almost exclusively take the form of English verse or, in the case of John Shirley's headnotes and the comments of marginal annotators, prose that accompanies Middle English writing attributed to one of the poets.[31] Leland's Latin commentary not only put the work of Chaucer and Gower on the same level as that of Latinate scholars, but in its linguistic shift away from the vernacular it split apart two strains of response—imitation and appreciation—that had previously been closely entwined.

Leland's turn to Latin set a precedent for later scholarly discussions of Chaucer's English eloquence, which—in English or in Latin—were undertaken separately from attempts on the part of the commentator to express eloquence in English himself. In the long run, this split creates a place for vernacular work on Chaucer written in forms of English very different from Chaucer's own. In *De Viris Illustribus*, Leland carries on a long tradition of

English writers praising Chaucer, but—writing in Latin—he does not imitate him. His Latin verses and the accompanying prose present themselves as a sufficient memorial to the author, but there is not one line of English in the entirety of *De Viris Illustribus*. Freed from the near obligation to imitate the master, Leland's account must tell, rather than show, what it is that makes Chaucer special. When this new kind of description, coupled with an interest in Chaucer's biography, filters back into the vernacular later in the century, it begins to look something very like literary criticism.

John Gower, "studiosius quam felicius"

As the earliest attempt to provide a comprehensive biography for both Chaucer and Gower, Leland's accounts lay the groundwork upon which subsequent commentators would build throughout the early modern period. Given Chaucer's close association with the English language, it is unsurprising to find him singled out for special attention in *De Viris Illustribus*. Gower, however, may strike some modern readers as a less obvious subject, especially given the absence of other vernacular writers in Leland's project. Leland does not mention John Lydgate, for example, whose plentiful works he would have almost certainly encountered in the course of his research, nor does he mention William Langland, whose *Piers Plowman* may in fact be the *Petri Aratoris fabula* that Leland lists among Chaucer's writings.

Leland wrote shortly after publication of Thomas Berthelette's first edition of Gower's *Confessio Amantis*, which appeared in 1532, the same year as the first edition of Thynne's *Works*. Like the *Works*, the *Confessio* is a handsome folio volume (albeit not quite as large).[32] Like the *Works*, Berthelette's *Confessio* is dedicated to Henry VIII and furnished with a laudatory preface. The preface is in some ways similar to that found in the 1532 *Works*, which suggests that the figures of Gower and Chaucer could perform similar authorizing cultural work in the 1530s (hence their appearance in Leland), and that, in both cases, their reputations hinged upon their achievements as vernacular authors. Like the preface to the *Works*, Berthelette begins with a classical anecdote (this time drawn from Plutarch) and flattering praise of the sovereign before offering an account of the difficulties and labor involved in bringing the work to press. This work, however, is worth the trouble since readers of the *Confessio* will find it "plentifully stuffed and fournysshed with manyfolde eloquent reasons / sharpe and quicke argumentes / and examples of great

auctorite / perswadynge unto vertue / not onely taken out of the poetes / ora-
tours / history wryters / and philosophers / but also out of the holy scripture."[33]
Berthelette does not credit Gower with the kind of untimely linguistic excellence that Thynne attributes to Chaucer, but he does emphasize that the *Confessio* contains "olde englysshe wordes and vulgars no wyse man / bycause of
theyr antiquite / wyll throwe asyde," words that offer an alternative to those
writers who feel themselves "constrayned to brynge in / in their writynges /
newe termes (as some calle them) whiche they borowed out of latyne / frenche
/ and other langages"[34] Berthelette concludes with a ringing endorsement
of Gower's language, especially its utility in the present: "if any man wante /
let hym resorte to this worthy olde wryter John Gower / that shall as a lan-
terne gyve hym lyghte to wryte counnyngly / and to garnysshe his sentencis
in our vulgar tonge." The Latin verses included in the *Confessio*, and Gower's
other major works in Latin (*Vox Clamantis*) and French (*Mirour de l'Omme*)
are not discussed.

Given this framework, and the fact that Berthelette, like Leland, was
closely associated with the Henrician court, it is less surprising to find Leland
acknowledging the work of the poet in *De Viris Illustribus* and emphasizing
his contributions to the English vernacular. Although he acknowledges that
Gower wrote in Latin as well as in English, Leland makes a strong claim for
Gower's contributions to the vernacular, asserting that he was "the first to pol-
ish our native language" (*primum patriae linguae expolitorem*) and that, "before his time the English tongue was cultivated and almost completely
unformed. Nor was there anybody who could write any work in the vernacular [*vernaculo idiomate*] fit for a cultured reader. . . . He wrote a great deal in
his mother tongue, both in verse and prose, which is carefully read by scholars even in this our blossoming age."[35]

Apart from this singular fact, Leland's knowledge of Gower's work appears to be limited. His comments on the poet's three major works later in
the entry have the vague air of a learned person discussing books he has not
read, even though he asserts that Gower's works are "carefully read by scholars even in this our blossoming age." He writes that, "among his longer works
the most important is his *Speculum Meditantis*, the second his *Vox Clamantis*,
and the third his *Confessio Amantis*. A fastidious reader may not perhaps consider that it is elegance that determines these titles. Yet there is something mysterious in them and a certain concord, as if one depended on the other."[36] If
Leland ever read the French *Mirour de l'Omme* (*Speculum Meditantis*) or Latin
Vox Clamantis, it is not at all apparent here. In addition to these major works,

Leland also mentions Gower's English poem "In Praise of Peace," but he mis-identifies its dedicatee as Richard II, when in fact the first lines of the poem reveal the addressee to be Richard's successor Henry IV (this despite the fact that Leland also quotes verbatim a Latin couplet from the end of the poem, another indication of his linguistic preferences).

In general, Leland has little to say about French in England (although he mentions French translations of the Latin works of English writers on several occasions and asserts that Chaucer wrote excellently in French), and he is consistently dismissive of the literary qualities of medieval Latin throughout *De Viris Illustribus*. Leland's attitude toward most medieval writing—a mark of his high humanist moment—sets him apart from later antiquaries like William Camden, whose work demonstrates a robust knowledge of Anglo-Latin writing, or even John Foxe, who includes a more detailed account of Gower's tomb (including its incorporation of three books representing the poet's major works, in each of the three languages of late medieval England) than that offered by Leland.

In many ways, including his praise of innovation and poetry in the vernacular, Leland's entry on Gower is a preview of the much longer entry on Chaucer that follows. In the remaining portion of his entry on Gower, he emphasizes the poet's use of the same classical sources admired by later scholars, his association with the legal profession, and—what is clearly of greatest interest to Leland—his purported mentorship of Chaucer. In *De Viris Illustribus*, Gower functions as a sort of John the Baptist, crying out in a literary desert to prepare the way for a poetic messiah.

While Berthelette's preface places Gower on similar footing to his contemporary Chaucer, it is clear from the length, specificity, and enthusiasm of Leland's entry on Chaucer (the only place in *De Viris Illustribus* where Leland incorporates his own Latin verses), that Leland feels the eloquent Englishmen of the sixteenth century owe their greater debt to Chaucer. Framed as part of a long tradition of learnedness and scholarship, rather than vernacular poetry, Chaucer's presence in *De Viris Illustribus* testifies to the way his particular brand of cultural significance could be transposed from the discourse of vernacular literature to that of English cultural accomplishments writ large.

Leland's admiration for Chaucer can be thought of as an extension of two closely related strands of fifteenth-century praise for the poet. First, there is a tradition of special appreciation for Chaucer's language, in which literary admiration frequently bleeds over into a sense of pride grounded in Chaucer's status as a specifically English author, as in Henry Scogan's praise of Chaucer as "this noble poete of Brettayne."[37] This gives Chaucer a special place in the English intellectual tradition, broadly construed, that is Leland's focus in *De Viris Illustribus*. Second, there is the frequently voiced appreciation for Chaucer's "eloquence" and "rhetoric." Christopher Cannon argues that the standard vocabulary for Chaucerian praise privileges terms abstract enough to adapt to the aesthetic needs of the moment, even as literary tastes and the English language itself continue to evolve.[38] As Cannon observes, "such early definitional terms matter very much because they actually sketch out a typology into which almost every subsequent definition of Chaucer's achievement fits," and this flexibility encourages the repetition of earlier praise, keeping Chaucer's close association with the English language intact.[39] This flexibility also creates a space for Leland—who does not seem to have been particularly fond of vernacular writing—to discover in Chaucer's English poetry an eloquence that is consistent with his own Latinate taste.

The asymmetry of Leland's interest in Chaucer and Gower—rooted in a sense that it is Chaucer who makes the transformative contribution to the English language—presages the divergence of the writers' reputations in the decades to come and shows the impact of Chaucer's already exceptional status.[40] In the fifteenth and early sixteenth centuries, Chaucer frequently shared the spotlight with both Gower and John Lydgate as part of a triumvirate of Middle English poets. Over the course of the sixteenth century, however, as judged by the relative number of contemporary references and the frequency of printed editions of their works, their reputations began to differ and as Chaucer's stock rose, that of the other two did not. The reasons for this are varied: the *Confessio Amantis* may have been superseded by the availability of other Ovidian works better suited to contemporary tastes and more readily available to readers, while Alexandra Gillespie argues that the majority of the works of "Dan John [Lydgate], monk" were an unappealing business prospect for printers in an age of Protestant polemic.[41] Yet, judged on the content of his writings alone, Chaucer should not be immune to similar charges. His work contains religious content (especially if the non-Chaucerian religious poems included in the 1532 *Works* are taken into account), and his classical themes, from Statius's *Thebiad* to Ovid's *Heroides*, are later taken up by Tudor writers using style and language more amenable to sixteenth-century readers. But precisely because they are celebrated for their linguistic qualities as well as their poetic acumen, Chaucer's works are never really consigned to the past on the grounds of form or of content. Looking closely at Leland's writings on Chaucer reveals a poet uniquely situated at the intersection of literary history

and a sweeping, at times propagandistic, account of the formation of Englishness itself.

"Noster Galfridus"

Leland's entry on Chaucer consists of three principal parts: an account of his
life, a list of his works, and four poems in praise of Chaucer. Three of these
poems are Leland's own work, while the third is the epitaph for Chaucer commissioned by William Caxton and written by the Italian poet Stephanus
Surigonus. Leland's writings on Chaucer have a clear influence on the poet's
reception in the sixteenth century and beyond: later scholars accept Leland's
conclusions, often unquestioningly, and the *De Viris Illustribus* account is the
basis for all subsequent biographies of Chaucer until the 1800s. Less apparent—
but no less important—are the ways Leland's use of Latin shaped Chaucer's
trajectory in the years and decades ahead. Like the rest of the work, the entry
for Chaucer is written entirely in Latin, save for the title of the *Romaunt of the
Rose*, which Leland renders in French as the *Roman de la Rose*. This marked
an important shift away from earlier English encomiums to the poet, which
self-consciously deployed the same poetic vernacular that they charge Chaucer
with creating. Leland's Latin text provides a model for writing *about* Chaucer
without writing *like* Chaucer.

In his account of Chaucer's life, Leland presents his readers with a mixture of tradition, extrapolation, and hearsay that adds up to something quite
different from the London-born son of a vintner known to modern biographers. In the process, he crafts an image of the poet that might have looked
reassuringly familiar to his sixteenth-century readers. This is not because
Chaucer's life story was already widely known, but because Leland's version
of Chaucer's life sets the poet amid educational, social, and cultural institutions that would have held meaning and resonance for many Latinate English
readers. In some ways, this does echo earlier praise of Chaucer. Leland followed in the footsteps of those earlier admirers who, as David Lawton has argued, tended to project onto Chaucer an idealized relation between poet and
sovereign.[42] Thus, we find Leland asserting that Chaucer "was known to
Richard of Bordeaux, king of England, and was dear to him on account of
his virtues, so too he was held in high regard for the same reasons by Henry
IV and his son, who triumphed over the French."[43] Leland spent most of his
career under the patronage of Henry VIII or highly placed figures in his

court; the idea of a poet in close proximity to the sovereign would certainly have been meaningful to him and to other literary and scholarly courtiers in his audience.

Leland also writes that Chaucer, whom he calls "a young man of noble birth and the highest promise," was a student at the University of Oxford and that he emerged from that institution "an acute logician, a sweet-toned orator, a sparkling poet, a weighty philosopher, an ingenious mathematician . . . as well as a devout theologian."[44] This claim that Chaucer attended the University of Oxford would stand unchallenged until the eighteenth century and was rooted in Chaucer's references in the *Treatise on the Astrolabe* to the Oxford-based mathematicians John Somer and Nicholas of Lynn, whom Leland identifies in *De Viris Illustribus* as Chaucer's teachers.[45] For Leland, Chaucer's alleged time at Oxford provides the needed explanation of how a noncleric came by his Latinate learning. A university education provides a new context for claims like Hoccleve's that Chaucer was a "Universel fadir in science," second only to Aristotle in "philosophie," and bolsters assertions like William Thynne's that Chaucer's writing displays "manyfest comprobacion of his excellent lernyng in all kyndes of doctrynes and sciences."[46] To have attended Oxford (Leland says only that he studied there, not that he received a degree) signals a familiarity with Latin culture that Chaucer's English poetry alone cannot demonstrate, even if readers might infer it through his translation of Boethius, his glib use of scholarly sources in the *Nun's Priest's Tale*, or his claims to have translated *Troilus and Criseyde* from his "auctor" "Lollius."[47]

A claim about Chaucer's education is a claim about language as well as learning: the litany of scholarly accomplishments that Leland ticks off here strongly implies that Chaucer had the ability to write in Latin, but merely *chose* not to. Latinity is at the heart of Leland's understanding of poetic production, even as he celebrates Chaucer's work as an English poet. Chaucer here is not an untutored, native genius, as some later commentators might suggest. Rather, he is a sophisticated scholar whose command of learned disciplines places him on a par with those other much-admired elevators of vernacular literature, Dante and Petrarch, to whom Leland compares Chaucer later in the entry.

James Simpson has argued that, in the early modern period, historical research into the lives of medieval notables could serve an overtly periodizing purpose by fixing them in a past that is defined in opposition to the present.[48] As a figure perceived as at once both medieval and modern, Chaucer is an important exception to this tendency. While Leland's account clearly locates

Chaucer in a pre-Reformation, pre-humanist, pre-Tudor past, it also takes pains to emphasize his participation in institutions and traditions of importance to an early modern audience, including the Inns of Court (where Leland claims both Chaucer and Gower studied), the universities, and the court itself. In this framework, Chaucer's antiquity signifies not because his life and works appear on the "wrong" side of a historical gap, but because it places him at an early stage of literary and historical genealogies still vital in the early modern present.

The same sort of reasoning informs Leland's treatment of Chaucer's language. At first, it might seem that Leland's preference for Latin leaves both Chaucer and Gower outside the scope of *De Viris Illustribus*. But what are the Latin alternatives to vernacular poetry in the Middle Ages? For Leland, there were none. Despite what James P. Carley calls Leland's "clear admiration for the glories of the monastic world," Leland almost always characterizes its literary output as an artistic failure, lacking both the eloquence of the past and the rhetorical sophistication of the present.[49] When it comes to Gower and Chaucer, Leland explains these stylistic failures not as a lack of talent but as an inevitability of the historical and cultural contexts in which those writers lived. In his entry on Gower, Leland writes that Chaucer's friend "wrote many [poems] in Latin, imitating Ovid rather more studiously than felicitously [*studiosius quam felicius*]. This must not be thought surprising, especially in a semi-barbarous age, since even in our own flourishing times there are few who can fittingly express Naso's [i.e., Ovid's] abounding fruitfulness in verse."[50] If Latin was not a viable means for poetic expression in the hands of medieval monks and schoolmen, it nevertheless served as an important link between past and present. In *De Viris Illustribus*, the Roman occupation of Britain is a benign or even beneficial force, insofar as it provides the vehicle through which Latin learning arrives in Britain. In its wake, according to *De Viris Illustribus*, "a high standard of learning prevailed in Britain, the great contribution of the Romans who had made it a province; and the nobles were notable for their practice of eloquence and the other usual arts."[51]

For Leland, the English tongue serves as an imperfect memorial of Roman greatness, even in an age of overall cultural decline. Earlier in *De Viris Illustribus*, he links Latin with the vernacular, writing that "before the arrival of Caesar, [the British language] was partly Hebrew and Greek and partly barbarian," but under Roman rule it "was gradually transformed halfway to Latin in the same way that the Gallic island, by long habit, was reduced, albeit with difficulty, to a province."[52] In Leland's view, this is improvement, not colonization. It is analogous to Chaucer's comparison of his own work to classical sources, a juxtaposition that elevates English poetry by linking it with Latin and Greek models even as it also adopts a position of ostensible humility. Although he does not cite it, Leland would have likely known Chaucer's instructions to his "litel book" in *Troilus and Criseyde*, wherein he implores it to "kis the steppes where as thow seest pace / Virgile, Ovide, Omer, Lucan, and Stace."[53] In Leland's formulation, the English language itself performs a similar obeisance to the Latin model.

When it comes to Chaucer, Leland is very clear about the purpose of his English poetry. It is not a means of literary expression but rather a vehicle through which Chaucer can accomplish his nationalistic goal of improving the English language. Leland writes,

> Now, indeed, the order of my discourse demands that I show clearly Geoffrey's goal in his studies. Indeed, *the single aim of his studies was to make the English language as polished as possible in all respects*, for he had seen what good progress Gower had made in the same task, although much was left to be done. Therefore, he thought he should leave no stone unturned in order to reach the highest degree of success. And since he always admired poetry above all things, had loved and cultivated it religiously, it seemed most convenient to him to make his way towards the very heights of expression through poetry.[54]

In Leland's view, poetry is a convenient and authoritative medium through which to improve the English language, an enterprise already authorized by Gower's earlier work along similar lines. Ultimately, however, poetry is merely the setting; the words themselves, which can be appropriated and redeployed to any number of rhetorical ends, are where value truly lies.

This emphasis on words rather than entire works is, perhaps, why Leland never quotes from Chaucer's poems directly. His most extended engagement with Chaucer's poems comes in the form of a list of titles, translated into Latin from the 1532 printing of William Thynne's edition of Chaucer's *Works*.[55] Leland lists twenty-two works, including two collective titles ("Fabulae Cantianae" and "Cantiones," minor poems), one piece he identifies as spurious (*The Floure of Courtesy*, or "flos humanitatis, qui libellulus a multis, tanquam nothus, reiicitur,"—a small book that many reject as spurious), and something he calls the "Tale of Piers Plowman" (*Petri Aratoris fabula*), which he claims was suppressed because of its anticlerical tone ("quia malos sacerdotum mores vehementer increpavit, suppressa est").[56] This is apparently Langland's *Piers Plowman*, which Leland has confused with the apocryphal *Plowman's Tale*, which is absent both from Thynne's edition and from earlier printed copies of the *Canterbury Tales*. Leland also describes an early collected edition of Chaucer produced by Caxton; no bibliographical evidence supports this claim, and Alexandra Gillespie surmises that Leland had encountered pre-1532 editions of the *Tales* and other poems bound together, which he mistook as a more deliberately unified production.[57]

When Leland lists the titles of Chaucer's works, he is not simply quoting the titles or incipits from Latin works as in the case of most of his other subjects, but translating an English text (here, not Chaucer's own words but rather titles assigned to his works in Thynne's edition) into Latin. In this, Leland anticipates a tendency to classicize and Latinize Chaucer that will become increasingly prominent over the sixteenth and seventeenth centuries. It will take forms as varied as Robert Greene's ventriloquizing of Chaucer and Gower in order to discuss Horatian poetics in *Greenes Vision* (ca. 1590; published 1592), Gabriel Harvey's annotations identifying classical analogues in his copy of the *Canterbury Tales* (ca. 1600), and Sir Francis Kynaston's translation of *Troilus and Criseyde* into Latin hexameters (1635).[58] Leland explains that he has provided his list of Chaucerian titles "so that readers may be able, as the saying goes, at least to measure the lion by his claws."[59] The phrase, which has classical antecedents and is also found in Erasmus, is not entirely apt, since Leland never offers readers even a single claw's worth of Chaucerian English. Chaucer's poems are twice mediated here: once because they are referred to only by their titles (which are generally editorial rather than authorial), and a second time because these titles are Latinized. Paradoxically, Chaucer's language becomes most occluded at the moment it becomes most central to Leland's claims.

Nevertheless, Leland retains his focus on Chaucer's language throughout the entry, a contrast to his comments on Gower, which mention his language only in passing. When Leland compares Chaucer with French and Italian writers, it is also in terms of the ways these poets shaped their respective vernaculars. Once again, he frames Chaucer's achievements in linguistic but not necessarily literary terms. Discussing Chaucer's models, he writes that "Petrarch was flourishing in Italy at the time [at which Chaucer wrote], by whose efforts the vernacular tongue of that land [*lingua ibidem vernacula*] had been brought to such a point of refinement that it was competing with Latin itself for the prize in eloquence. A certain Alain [Chartier] had likewise polished the French language in an infinite variety of ways."[60] In both cases, the works of Chaucer's continental analogues are framed in national-linguistic terms. Leland takes a schematic approach in his celebration of Chaucer's writing, and especially of his works as a translator, viewing the medieval poet's work structurally and holistically rather than attending to the finer details of its contents. He describes the progress of Chaucer's career in the following terms:

> It was thus under favourable auspices that [Chaucer] applied
> himself to the work he had begun, now translating books written
> elegantly, ornately, and eloquently in the French language into his
> native speech; now rendering Latin verse into English, learnedly,
> aptly, and harmoniously; now committing to enduring parchment
> many of products of his own imagination, which equalled Latin
> authors in their aptness of expression; now striving with all his
> strength to be of use to the reader, and alternately taking sedulous
> care to delight him. He did not desist until he had raised our
> language to such purity, such eloquence, such concision and grace,
> that it could justly be ranked among the cultured languages of the
> nations.[61]

In Leland's framing, the goal—linguistic improvement—remains the same in the case of both Chaucer's translations and his original works, even as Leland's choice of adverbs in this section (e.g., *docte, apte, canore*; sweetly, ornately, elegantly) recall the aureate diction of fifteenth-century Chaucerians.

A similar emphasis on language and national identity marks the three poems by Leland that appear in the second half of the entry. While Leland was a prolific poet, these are the only examples of his own verse that appear in *De Viris Illustribus*.[62] Their appearance here both situates Leland's work in a long history of poetic tributes to Chaucer and reemphasizes his commitment to Latin as the language of serious intellectual labor, including poetry. Accordingly, these verses—like the entry as a whole—leverage the prestige and cultural connotations of Latin even as they argue for the cultural importance of Chaucer's vernacular poetry. Like the list of titles, these poems can only pro-

vide indirect proof of Chaucer's poetic excellence: as Latin verses about a vernacular poet, they can describe, but not demonstrate, the linguistic and poetic
achievements that are their raison d'être.

Leland himself recognizes the mediated nature of these tributes. He writes
that he wishes "our language [that is, English] were known to the Latin poets;
then they would easily—I say easily—accede to my opinion [of Chaucer].
But since what I want is scarcely possible, I wish at least that having been
prevailed upon they would have some faith in me as a lover of Latin literature
in this matter."[63] While it is difficult to say whether the Latin poets that
Leland has in mind are ancient or his sixteenth-century contemporaries, his
comment suggests that both a linguistic gap and a historical gap separate the
medieval poet from those best able to appreciate his works.

The first poem presented by Leland, a short epigram, sets three pairs of
poet and place in relation to one another:

> Praedicat Aligerum merito Florentia Dantem,
>   Italia et numeros tota Petrarche tuos;
> Anglia Chaucerum veneratur nostra poetam,
>   Cui veneres debet patria lingua suas.

> (Florence rightly trumpets Dante Alighieri
>   And all Italy your verses [*numeros*], Petrarch;
> Our England reveres the poet Chaucer,
>   To whom our native tongue owes its beauties.)

Here, Leland transposes Chaucer's achievements in language from the individual to the collective realm. (Chaucer never claims to be a national poet,
so later writers must make this connection posthumously, beginning with
Lydgate's interpellation of his predecessor as the "chiefe Poet of Britaine.")
The verb (*veneratur*) indicates that "our England" (*anglia . . . nostra*) the subject, is in the present, but it and Chaucer share a "native tongue" (*patria lingua*) as do Dante and Florence and Petrarch and Italy. Although Leland's
aim here is to increase Chaucer's poetic reputation among Latinate readers,
he also articulates a significant connection in the form of a language shared
between English-speaking collectivities in the present and Chaucer himself,
making the poet a focal point not only for England's literary reputation
among readers of Latin, regardless of nationality, but also establishing him as

the founding figure of an English-language tradition that carries on into the present.

The second poem opens with an allusion to Virgil's *Eclogues*, comparing poetic fame to the natural affinity of animals to their native habitats:

> As long as the boar love the mountain ridges, the merry bird the
>   branches,
>   And the scaly fish the limpid waters,
> Homer, the most renowned author of the Greek tongue,
>   Will always be first in Aonian song.
> So, too, will Virgil always be the greatest glory of the Roman muse,
>   If Apollo himself is the judge.
> No less will our Geoffrey Chaucer always be
>   The fairest ornament of the British lyre.
> The former, of course, were born in fortunate times,
>   Yet the latter, great as he was, was born at a barbarous hour.
> If he had lived when the muses flourished,
>   He would have equaled or surpassed his famous predecessors.[64]

Like the epigram that proceeds it, this poem links Chaucer with a larger, transhistorical collectivity: comparing the enduring fame of Homer (whom Leland refers to here as Maeonides) and Virgil to these natural affinities, Leland writes that "Nec minus et noster Galfridus summa Britannae / Chaucerus citharae gratia semper erit" (No less will our Geoffrey Chaucer always be / The fairest ornament of the British lyre). Whereas the first poem compares Chaucer with his contemporaries, this poem uses classical writers. This second juxtaposition suggests a kind of *translatio imperii* that links England with ancient Greece and Rome through the shared greatness of their principal poets, but also reminds readers of Chaucer's belated historical moment. In a passage that resonates strongly with the preface to the 1532 *Works*, Leland concedes that Homer and Virgil were, "of course, were born in fortunate times," yet Chaucer, "great as he was, was born at a barbarous hour." Had he "lived when the muses flourished," Leland writes, Chaucer "would have equaled or surpassed his famous predecessors." As elsewhere in *De Viris Illustribus*, the temporal infelicity of medieval writing is used to explain away any unfavorable comparisons between Chaucer and his classical antecedents. Chaucer might be a vernacular poet living in Leland's Latinate world, but, according to the poem, his significance, like Homer's and Virgil's, will always endure. Emphasizing this point, each of the three couplets describing the individual poet's fame ends with the same phrase—*semper erit*, always will be.

In his third and final poem, Leland articulates more directly the notion of *translatio linguae* implied in the previous piece.[65] Just as *translatio studii*, the transmission of learning, is linked to *translatio imperii*, the movement of imperial power from East to West, so too Leland suggests that excellence in learning is naturally accompanied by excellence in language itself. The poem, the longest of the three, describes the development of the Greek language, then that of Latin, before turning to the role of "eloquent Chaucer" who was

> The first in proper conciseness
> Who cast our native language into such a form,
> That it might shine with much beauty and charm,
> With much wit and grace,
> Like Hesperus among the lesser stars;
> And yet did not arrogantly reproach
> Any other language for barbarity.[66]

In the lines before this passage, Leland attributes the improvement of the Greek language to "Atticus" and the Latin tongue to "Quirinius" (another name for Romulus).[67] Although both figures are allegorical rather than historical, Leland fits Chaucer into their company as naturally as he does that of Dante and Petrarch. The invocation of Chaucer in their presence puts forth a different view of the poet than that offered by either of the two preceding pieces. In their company, Chaucer assumes a mythic status closer to that of the Druids and Arthurian figures found in the early entries in *De Viris Illustribus* than to the Italian poets mentioned in the first poem, or even Homer and Virgil in the second. Here, Chaucer's role is as a founder of language in the most abstract sense. While this contrasts with Leland's interest in the particulars of Chaucer's life (his education at Oxford, his burial in Westminster), it is also a logical extension of his claims for Chaucer's significance as a poet whose work both elevates literature within English and raises the status of the English language in a transhistorical and interlinguistic framework.

All three poems celebrate Chaucer's poetic and aesthetic value, but that value is always understood in relation to a shared intellectual tradition and national identity. Rather than echo earlier poets who present Chaucer's writings as the apex of English poetry, Leland's poems transform him into a foundational figure whose importance is best understood not in terms of individual poetic genius but in terms of his linguistic (and therefore national and even imperial) significance. As a result of this emphasis on Chaucer's foundational status rather than his ongoing influence, there is a new sense of distance here. In this last poem, in particular, we see a burgeoning sense of Chaucer as a revered ancestor rather than the recently deceased kinsman lamented by Hoccleve and Lydgate.

Thomas Speght's *Life of Chaucer*

Leland's account circulated widely in antiquarian circles throughout the Tudor and Stuart eras, and at the end of the sixteenth century, it served as the basis for the first full-fledged English-language biography of Chaucer. First published in the 1598 edition of Chaucer's *Works*, the *Life of Our Learned English Poet, Geffrey Chaucer* includes sections on Chaucer's origins, education, marriage and children, and professional activities, as well as a discussion of his poetic accomplishments and influence.[68] Written by Thomas Speght, who was also responsible for most of the other explanatory materials added to this edition, the treatise supplements material that originated with Leland with references to popular scholarly works like William Camden's *Britannia* and archival materials provided by the antiquarian John Stow who, Speght writes, "helped me in many things."[69] Though *De Viris Illustribus* was not Speght's only source, it was his main one, and he agrees with his predecessor on all major points.

Speght appears to have known Leland's writings through the work of the antiquary's friend and literary executor John Bale. Although Bale is perhaps best remembered today for his dramatic writings, his activities as a radical Protestant polemicist extended from the stage to the more sedate world of scholarly publishing. His *Illustrium Majoris Britanniae Scriptorum* (1549, revised 1557) is a massive compendium of biobibliographical data intercalated with accounts of papal and European history. Leland's *De Viris Illustribus* forms the nucleus of this Latin work, which Bale initially compiled while in exile during the 1540s and extensively revised and expanded for its second publication in 1557. Bale's presentation of literary history *as* salvation history played a crucial role in the reimagination of the medieval past in the wake of the dissolution of the monasteries and the destruction and dispersal of medieval textual culture.[70] These printed books provided a vehicle through which Leland's writings on Chaucer might reach a broader audience than that of *De Viris Illustribus*, although Leland's manuscripts continued to circulate in antiquarian networks. Bale readily acknowledges his reliance on Leland, and when Speght cites material taken from *Illustrium Majoris Britanniae Scriptorum*, he names Leland, not Bale, as his ultimate source.[71]

In tone, form, and content, Speght's *Life of Chaucer* is a celebration of the medieval poet. It demonstrates how, by the end of the sixteenth century, Chaucer was "established as an important father for English history: a suitable object of veneration and recuperation for a nationalist humanism seeking to rival the Italian discovery of the Latinate past as an antecedent for its contemporary poetics."[72] Indeed, it shows that Chaucer had become a father for English history in a general sense, a figure whose importance was not limited to literary discourse but who signified meaningfully in nationalist narratives about the development of English cultural identity on multiple fronts.

At first glance, Speght's account, with its use of multiple outside sources, seems markedly more scholarly than Leland's. Whereas Leland's assertions about Chaucer's biography are not backed with any evidential claims, Speght cites a variety of secondary archival and historiographical sources. In the 1598 version of the *Life*, for example, Speght's discussion of the source and antiquity of the Chaucer family coat of arms includes references to "the opinion of some Heralds," historical facts that "as by Chronicles appeareth," "the Records of the Tower," "the Records of the Exchequer," and "the Roll at Battle Abbey."[73] At times throughout the *Life*, Speght cites specific locations within the patent rolls and quotes from them at length; these are the same sources cited by the modern *Chaucer Life-Records*.[74] Bolstered by references like these, Chaucer's life appears as a matter of historical fact, whose details have been recovered through assiduous archival research.

In other ways, however, Speght's biography is much like Leland's, especially in its willingness to treat Chaucer's words themselves as a historical source. Like Leland in *De Viris Illustribus*, Speght takes a dominant idea from the Chaucerian tradition—specifically, the notion that there is something fundamentally English about Chaucer's language—and expounds on it in a scholarly way. The result is a body of commentary, separate from Chaucer's writing, that models a specific way of reading and judging the Chaucerian text. In the *Life*, for example, Speght uses Chaucer's language to rebut historical sources that (correctly) indicate that Chaucer's progenitors were comparatively recent arrivals in England. Speght invokes the purity of

Chaucer's language to argue for both the antiquity and status of Chaucer's family:

> But wheras some are of opinion, that the first coming of the
> Chaucers in England was, when Queene Isabell wife to Edward the
> second, and her sonne Prince Edward with Philip his new married
> wife, returned out of Henault into England, at which time also
> almost three thousand Straunger came over with them (as by
> Chronicles appeareth) I can by no meanes consent with them; but
> rather must thinke, that their name and familie was of farre more
> auncient antiquitie, although by time decayed, as many more have
> been of much greater estate: and that the parents of Geffrey
> Chaucer were meere English, and he himselfe an Englishman
> borne. *For els how could he have come to that perfection in our
> language, as to be called, The first illuminer of the English tongue, had
> not both he, and his parents before him, been born & bred among us.*[75]

In this passage, beliefs about Chaucer's contribution to the English language trump the testimony of the chronicles. If the chronicles place his ancestors on English soil later than Speght feels is appropriate for the progenitors of the "first illuminer of the English tongue," then the chronicles, not Chaucer's reputation, must be inaccurate. Chaucer's words do more than simply ensure his reputation: they become the evidence upon which the *Life* justifies its claims for Chaucer's biography. Even though Speght has already noted that Chaucer's family were vintners, he cannot divorce his assessment of their social standing from his perception of Chaucer as a national poet with a special relationship to the English language.

For Speght, language can also function as a guarantor of authenticity in Chaucer's writings. In the "His Bookes" section of the *Life*, Speght lists the titles of books he believes were written by Chaucer but that are "besides those books of his which he have in print."[76] In this same section, Speght writes of poems that "I have seene without any Authours name, which for the invention I would verily judge to be Chaucers, were it not that wordes and phrases carry not every where Chaucers antiquitie." Here, Speght makes a judgment based not on the apparent age of the manuscript or the contents of the verse, but on "wordes and phrases" that carry (or fail to carry, in this instance) evidence of "Chaucers antiquitie." As Leland's emphasis on Chaucer's lexis reminds us, "wordes and phrases" are exactly what Chaucer's early modern reputation is based upon. In Speght, as in Leland's earlier work, the same criteria used in aesthetic valuations of Chaucer are applied to the ostensibly more objective task of assembling an accurate canon.

Like Leland before him, Speght drew heavily on Chaucer's own writings when constructing his biography of the poet. Because the Chaucer canon that Speght knew included numerous apocryphal works, this strategy can sometimes backfire. For example, Speght correctly asserts that Chaucer was born in London. He does so, however, based on statements made in the *Testament of Love*, a Boethian allegory in prose written by Londoner Thomas Usk in the 1380s. The *Testament of Love* was first printed in the 1532 edition of the *Works*, and generally accepted as Chaucer's own until the eighteenth century. The *Testament* may also be behind Speght's claim that Chaucer fell into "some daunger & trouble" during the earlier years of the reign of Richard II, "by favoring some rashe attempte of the common people" and that, because "as he was learned, so was he wise," he "kept himself much out of the way in Holland, Zeland [*sic*] and France, where he wrote most of his books."[77] While the *Chaucer Life-Records* contains no support for such a claim, the speaker in the *Testament of Love* writes from prison, in a position of great personal and political distress, such as might necessitate a self-imposed exile (in fact, Usk was executed on March 4, 1388, for his role as an informant in conspiracies concerning the election of the Lord Mayor of London). In the absence of other biographical material, this may have been enough to lead Speght to conjecture that Chaucer left England for a time. In the case of both Chaucer's London origins and his putative exile, Speght reports traces of what might be construed as biographical disclosure in Chaucer's canon as though they were straightforward historical fact.

Like *De Viris Illustribus*, and unlike modern biographies of Chaucer, the *Life* concerns itself primarily with the professional details of Chaucer's life and does not attempt to integrate biographical events with the composition and reception of the literary works for which its subject is chiefly remembered.[78] Although the *Life*'s title page, like the title page of the *Works* as a whole, identifies its subject as a poet (see Figure 4), only two sections ("His Friends" and "His Books") explicitly address the production of poetry. When specific works are invoked, it is often as sources for certain biographical details, as is the case with Chaucer's connection with John of Gaunt, for which the *Book of the Duchess* is cited as evidence.

Like Leland, Speght emphasizes Chaucer's relation to institutions, individuals, and locations recognizable to latter-day readers, especially those with

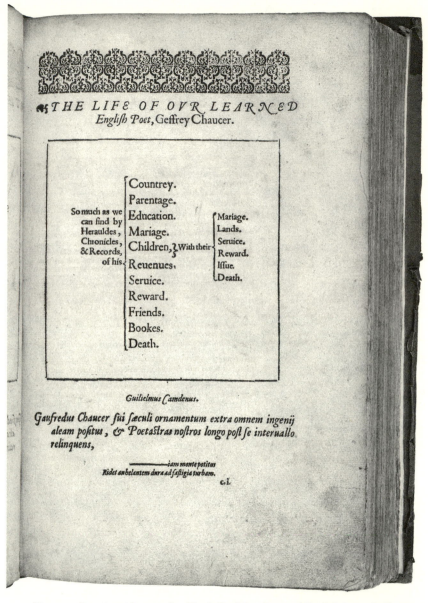

❧THE LIFE OF OVR LEARNED
English Poet, Geffrey Chaucer.

So much as we can find by Herauldes, Chronicles, & Records, of his	Countrey. Parentage. Education. Mariage. Children, Reuenues, Seruice. Reward. Friends. Bookes. Death.	With their ⎰ Mariage. Lands. Seruice. Reward. Issue. Death.

Guilielmus Camdenus.

Gaufredus Chaucer sui sæculi ornamentum extra omnem ingenij
aleam positus, & Poetastras nostros longo post se interuallo
relinquens,

————— *iam monte potitus*
Ridet anhelantem dura ad fastigia turbam. c. I.

Figure 4. Interior title page for *The Life of Our Learned English Poet, Geffrey
Chaucer* from *The Workes of our Antient and Learned English poet, Geffrey
Chaucer, newly Printed* (1598), sig. C1; STC 5079. By permission of the
Folger Shakespeare Library.

legal, antiquarian, or scholarly backgrounds. While Speght gives more attention than Leland to the linguistic and cultural differences between Chaucer's
day and his own historical moment, he also elaborates on the institutional
framework in which Leland situated Chaucer. Now, instead of merely attending Oxford, in Speght's account Chaucer studied "by all likelihood in Canterburie or in Merton Colledge with *John Wyckelife*, whose opinions in religion
he much affected" a supposition that both derives from and reinforces previous claims for Chaucer's proto-Protestantism.[79] (The reasons for and implications of this claim are explored in Chapter 3.) Now, instead of studying and
working alongside Gower at the Inns of Court, Chaucer is installed in the
Inner Temple where, Speght writes, he was arrested and fined for beating a
Franciscan friar in Fleet Street.[80] This anecdote, conveniently, ascribes to
Chaucer both a social and religious disposition in line with that of many of
his early modern admirers.

While both Leland and Speght are eager to connect past and present,
Speght, in particular, also takes pains to show that relation as mediated. The
Works as a whole makes prominent use of interpretive devices that convey a genealogical relationship between present and past. These include John Speed's
genealogical engraving and a full-page woodcut of Chaucer's coat of arms, used
as a title page in Stow's 1561 edition and repurposed here as an interior title
page.[81] In the *Life*, Speght's interest in Chaucer's "progeny" leads him to take
up the successful political career of Chaucer's son Thomas (apparently unknown to Leland, Bale, and Foxe) and the rather spectacular trio of marriages undertaken by Thomas's daughter Alice. Chaucer's descendants are
described narratively in the section of the *Life* entitled "His Progenie and Their
Advancement" and in a full-page Latin stemma, accompanying this section,
prepared by the herald Robert Glover (Figure 5). Like the John Speed engraving also prepared for this edition, Glover's stemma is not centered on Chaucer, but rather on Thomas Chaucer and his wife Maude (Matilda), the couple
whose tomb, decked with baronial arms, Speed also depicts. The point of the
Glover stemma is to illustrate Chaucer's familial connections to historically
significant individuals, and not to celebrate his poetry, but it also provides essential context for a historical reading of that poetry.

These Chaucerian genealogies, which unfold over time and culminate in
figures whose historical import easily overpowers Chaucer's own, run parallel
to the accounts of Chaucer's influence on later writers found in the section on
"His Death." Despite the finality of Speght's subtitle, both the genealogy and
the poetic tributes are oriented toward a future that is, for readers, already past:

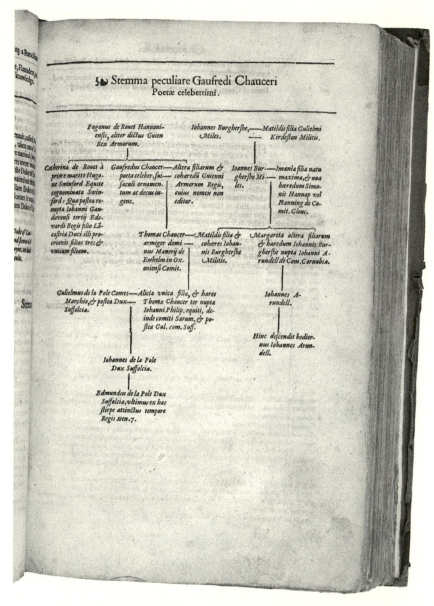

Figure 5. "Stemma peculiare Gaufredi Chauceri Poetæ celeberrimi"
from *The Workes of our Antient and Learned English poet, Geffrey Chaucer,*
newly Printed (1598), sig. B4; STC 5079. By permission of
the Folger Shakespeare Library.

in Speght's formulation, which evokes Leland's, Chaucer's true literary import and historical significance are revealed not in his own day but rather by
the individuals who carry on his lineage after his death. In Speght, this shows
up in two distinct ways that reflect Chaucer's dual significance for antiquarian readers: through family connections (in the Speed engraving, this can be
traced by following the presence of Chaucer's arms in the heraldry of later generations) or through later writers' use of Chaucerian language. It is in order
to trace this second kind of lineage that Leland and Speght need to focus on
the lexical rather than rhetorical dimensions of Chaucer's poetry: like arms,
which can be bisected and quartered, and quartered again, incorporating traces
of new alliances and allegiances while containing within the identifying mark
of the original grantee, Chaucer's lexicon is available for recombination and
reappropriation with new words and in new contexts, while still retaining its
identity as "Chaucer's English." Chaucer's literary achievements of narrative,
genre, and characterization lack this mobility and adaptability; they are objects of study, while, at least potentially, Chaucer's words remain objects of
both study and use.

Like Leland, Speght clearly believed his vernacular subject to be worthy
of both scholarly consideration and literary appreciation. Echoing and ampli-
fying the sentiments expressed in the 1532 editions of Chaucer's *Works* and
Gower's *Confessio Amantis*, Leland's entries on Chaucer and Gower in *De Viris
Illustribus* assert, by their mere presence, that vernacular literature is part of
what makes English culture great. Speght's attention to Chaucer's biography
carries on this tradition, elaborating Leland's account and, by transposing it
into English, making it available to a wider variety of readers. Crucially, this
movement back into the vernacular does not preclude a reading of Chaucer
that, like Leland's, privileges historical and biographical concerns rather than
poetic details. Rather, it reinforces it.

Leland, writing in the 1530s, and Speght, working circa 1598, bookend an
important phase in Chaucer's early modern reception. During this period, interest in Chaucer's late medieval contemporaries faded, while Chaucer was
widely and repeatedly identified as *the* individual founder of English poetry,
the only poet of his era capable of authorizing and legitimizing an ongoing
tradition of English verse. The biographical narratives of Leland and Speght
both bolster and affirm this view, stressing Chaucer's outsize eloquence and
exceptional contributions to the English language.

It would be a mistake, however, to overlook the fact that their writings
shifted emphasis away from the content of Chaucer's poems and onto their

cultural and linguistic impact. With Chaucer's work framed in lexical terms
and explicitly linked to the development of English as a national identity, his
influence was no longer limited to the realm of poetry; he became a cultural
force on the broadest possible scale. In their biographical writings, Leland
and Speght produce new knowledge about Chaucer's life and works that
supports their claims for the poet's widespread significance. The historical narratives they provide offer a foundation for the sense of temporal doubleness,
of simultaneous connection and distance, that I argued in the previous chapter was an essential part of Chaucer's exceptional status in early modern
England. Their work offers us a view of Chaucer that is in some ways quite different from the one known to modern scholars, but at the same time crafts a
figure uniquely well suited to the needs and desires of sixteenth-century
Chaucerians.

CHAPTER 3

"For Every Man to Read That Is Disposed"

Chaucer the Proto-Protestant

Geoffrey Chaucer was "a right Wiclevian, or els was never any," declares the martyrologist John Foxe in the second edition of *Actes and Monuments*, published in 1570.[1] This strident, even polemical claim is fitting for the monumental work of Protestant historiography in which it appears, but it should strike modern students of both Chaucer and Wycliffe as rather off the mark. While Chaucer's religious views are difficult to pin down, it seems clear that he was *not* in fact a Wycliffite—that is, a follower of the English theologian John Wycliffe—at least not in the sense that Foxe implies.[2] Nonetheless, Foxe's assertion, echoed and amplified, made its way into the Chaucer print tradition via the biography of the poet that appeared in the 1598 and 1602 editions of Chaucer's collected *Works*.[3] This *Life of Chaucer* also states that Chaucer was a student at Oxford (a claim originally advanced in the writings of John Leland), where he studied "by all likelihood in Canterburie or in Merton Colledge with *John Wyckelife*, whose opinions in religion he much affected."[4] Speght's supposition both derives from and reinforces Foxe's claims for Chaucer's proto-Protestantism, transposing it out of the realm of religious historiography and into a literary historical context.

This chapter seeks to understand how, as consensus built around the idea of Chaucer as proto-Protestant—a consensus promoted by Foxe and further shaped by his publication of a Lollard tract, *Jack Upland*, as Chaucer's own work—the scope of the Chaucerian folio canon changed to fit this consensus. In it, I argue that the confidence with which both Foxe and Speght make their claims about Chaucer's religion can only be fully understood by reflecting on the secure place of certain apocryphal texts, several of Wycliffite origin, in Chaucer's early modern canon. These texts encouraged certain narratives about Chaucer's life and work and foreclosed upon others. They offered a context for reading and interpreting other pieces in the Chaucerian canon and helped to create a particular cultural and religious space for the idea of Chaucer in the centuries after his death. Thomas J. Heffernan writes of the Chaucerian apocrypha that, "prior to the end of the [nineteenth] century, the judgment whether a text was genuine or not was often indebted to extra-textual biases: the complex political, social, moral and religious beliefs which informed the editor's historical imagination."[5] This chapter not only looks at the influence of "extra-textual biases" on the formation of Chaucer's canon, but demonstrates how the evolving Chaucerian canon shaped those biases in the first place. When it came to Chaucer and religion, canon and commentary influenced each other recursively, creating a set of mutually reinforcing claims about author and work.

This chapter begins by considering how the martyrologist John Foxe presented Chaucer—both the book and the man—within the context of his *Actes and Monuments*, taking up both his use of Chaucerian sources and his commentary on the medieval poet and his writings. The apocryphal prose treatise *Jack Upland*, along with the better-known (though also apocryphal) poem the *Plowman's Tale*, is a central part of this story, especially where the question of Chaucer's religion is concerned. I then turn to Thomas Speght's 1598 and 1602 editions of Chaucer's *Works*, the first editions published after the *Actes and Monuments*. Speght's *Works* offer a perspective similar to Foxe's, not only at obvious moments like the passage from the *Life of Chaucer* cited above, but more subtly in the way that the 1602 edition introduces two texts with religious themes, *Jack Upland* and the genuine *A.B.C.*, into the folio canon.

Actes and Monuments

John Foxe's *Actes and Monuments* is a monumental production, both technically and ideologically, offering a sweeping account of salvation history stretching from the early church to the reign of Mary Tudor. An epic work of English and European history written from an explicitly and propagandistically Protestant point of view, it proudly touts its use of primary sources. According to the title page of the 1563 edition, the material contained within had been "gathered and collected according to the true copies and wrytinges certificatorie, as wel of the parties themselves that suffered, as also out of the Bishops Registers, which were the doers thereof."[6] As it took its place in many parish churches, as well as in private and institutional collections, *Actes and Monuments* became, in the words of one scholar, "the most successful piece of Protestant propaganda ever printed in England."[7] Unlike books aimed at a more limited scholarly or antiquarian audience, *Actes and Monuments* reached a broad audience in both individual and group settings, as well as through frequent use by preachers.[8] By the late seventeenth century, it was circulating in more than ten thousand copies.[9]

The first edition of *Actes and Monuments* appeared in 1563, without references to Chaucer. Plans to revise and expand the book were under way as early as 1565, however, bolstered by Foxe's desire to respond to Catholic attacks against the first edition.[10] With this revision, not only the scope but also the detail of the work increased, since "demonstrating the existence of 'Protestantism' before Luther not only demanded that the chronological range of the book be increased but that its documentary base be expanded as well."[11] In both the original 1563 edition and the revisions that followed, Foxe acted as "author-compiler," drawing on printed books and manuscripts from England, a range of continental sources, and the personal accounts of those who had witnessed more recent events firsthand.[12] For more historically distant events, Foxe referred to English chronicles and histories, some of which he read in manuscript.[13] He received his sources from a network of antiquarian colleagues, including John Bale, Archbishop Matthew Parker, and John Stow, whose edition of Chaucer had appeared in 1561, two years before the first edition of *Actes and Monuments*.[14] Foxe's work, especially the sections of the text that dealt with the medieval past, could not have been accomplished without significant contact with these collectors and scholars.

The revised 1570 version added two passages on Chaucer, commentary that would shape the way readers thought of the poet and his religion for many years to come.[15] If Leland, by including Chaucer and Gower in his *De Viris Illustribus*, sought to make a place for vernacular poetry in an intellectual history of England, then Foxe, by incorporating Chaucer (and, to a lesser extent, Gower) into *Actes and Monuments*, claimed a place for him in the genealogy that connects the early church with the Protestant religion. At the same time, because Foxe's understanding of the history of Christianity was intimately bound up with English religion and politics, he followed Leland and other predecessors in using Chaucer's name and reputation in the service of a wider set of claims about England's past. Foxe, however, sought a wider audience than that reached by the scholarly writings of Leland and Bale. By rendering portions of his predecessor's Latin writings into English, Foxe anticipated the vernacularization of Chaucer's life undertaken in Speght by more than two decades.

Actes and Monuments is arranged chronologically, which means that the logical place for commentary on Chaucer would be the sections dealing with the late fourteenth century. This is not, however, where Chaucer appears. Instead, Foxe placed his discussions of Chaucer in book 4, which treats English history from William the Conqueror to John Wycliffe, and book 7, which addresses events of the early sixteenth century. As Holly Crocker argues in an essay with important ramifications for our understanding of Chaucer's relationship to temporality in early modern England, this displacement makes Chaucer an untimely figure in *Actes and Monuments*, a historical personage whom Foxe cannot contain within the chronological structure of the book as a whole.[16] In this sense, Chaucer functions in Foxe as he does in many contexts throughout the sixteenth century. He is a figure *from* the past who retains his importance precisely because he is perceived as not being fully *of* the past. Instead, Chaucer prefigures what is still to come, both prophetically *in* his writing and historically *by* the act of writing such poetically and ideologically advanced material at an early date.

In both of his Chaucer passages, Foxe used previously printed texts and antiquarian commentary to construct an extraliterary argument for the significance of Chaucer and his works. His commentary offers a snapshot view of what Chaucer could have meant to Protestant readers in the later sixteenth century, but it also shows how that meaning was constructed from a variety of textual sources already circulating. Foxe had access to at least three sources on Chaucer: a copy of the Lollard treatise *Jack Upland* that attributed the piece to Chaucer, an edition of the *Works* containing the apocryphal *Plowman's Tale* (this excludes the 1532 edition, which does not have it), and Leland's commentary on Chaucer. Most likely, Foxe knew the Leland material through John Bale, who drew heavily on Leland's *De Viris Illustribus* in his own bibliobiographical writings. Taken together, these sources demonstrate Chaucer's significance within both narratives about English literature and broader narratives of religious, social, and cultural identity.[17] The available canon and archive shaped Foxe's ideas about Chaucer. In the concluding section of this chapter, I will argue that his claims informed the way that Chaucer and his writings were presented in subsequent editions of the *Works*, even in the absence of explicit religious framing.

Antifraternal Chaucer: *Jack Upland* and the *Plowman's Tale*

Chaucer first appears in book 4 of *Actes and Monuments*, in a section devoted to the rise of the mendicant orders. After describing the major orders of friars in detail, Foxe provides a long list of other religious orders, drawn primarily from the historical material found in Bale's *Catalogus*. He also prints a prophecy taken from the *Scivias* of the twelfth-century German mystic Hildegard von Bingen, which he frames as a prognostication of the fall of the Roman church. Following this, he prints the Lollard treatise *Jack Upland*, "compiled by Geoffray Chawcer." Ascribed to Chaucer, the piece functions both as a historical document and as antifraternal propaganda. In an introductory note, Foxe explains his reasons for including it:

> For so much as mention is here [in *Actes and Monuments*] made of these superstitious sectes of Fryers, and such other beggerly religious, it shall not seme much impartinent . . . so now to annexe also to the same, a certayne other auncient treatise compiled by Geoffray Chawcer by the way of a Dialogue or questions moved in the person of a certaine uplandish and simple ploughman of the countrey. Which treatise for the same, the author intituled Jack Upland: wherin is to be sene and noted to all the world, the blynd ignorance and variable discord, of these irreligious religions, how rude & unskilful they are in matters and principles of our Christian institution.[18]

Foxe goes on to invoke the language of *Jack Upland* as proof of its association with Chaucer and, by extension, evidence of the venerability of the antifraternal position in England: "As by the contents of this present dialogue appeareth, the wordes wherof in the same olde english, wherin first it was set forth, in this wise do proceede. Wherin also the mayst see, that it is no new thinges that their blasphemous doings hath by divers good men in the olde time bene detected as there are many and divers other old bookes to shewe."[19]

For Foxe, the "olde english" of the treatise is a sign of the "olde time" in which it was written. The antiquity of the text having been established by its language, the contents are proof that "good men" have always "detected" the "blasphemous doing" of the friars.

These comments draw attention to the linguistic specificity of Chaucer's historical moment and use it to emphasize the importance of the polemical *Jack Upland*. As in the case of E.K.'s comments in the *Shepheardes Calender*, published in 1579 (nine years after Foxe), Foxe places particular emphasis on Chaucer's association with "olde english" language, signifying both historical distance ("olde") and continuity with the present (visibly different but still "english").[20] In keeping with the historiographical and religious focus of the work as a whole, Foxe expresses little interest in Chaucer as a poet—though he assumes his readers will recognize Chaucer's name and his significance— and yet even he seems drawn to Chaucer's words themselves, which here serve as an important register of date and historical context.

In book 4, Foxe prints *Jack Upland* in its entirety before returning to his historical narrative, which picks up with the reign of the Holy Roman Emperor Frederick II. He adds marginalia throughout the piece that highlight and summarize key points, for example, "All Friers found liars."[21] Interestingly, while Foxe often uses marginal quotation marks alongside work taken directly from other sources, they are not used here. Renaissance quotation marks were, in Margreta de Grazia's words, "originally notices in the margin intended to catch a reader's attention . . . *to quote* was *to mark* in the double sense of making a mark but also of heeding or minding it."[22] It is possible, then, that the lack of quotation marks in this passage, attributed as it is to the closest thing medieval English literature had to an *auctor*, reveals some skepticism or uncertainty about the origins of the piece.

Such uncertainty would be well-placed given that *Jack Upland* was, of course, not written by Chaucer but rather by an anonymous fifteenth-century Lollard. On the basis of its allusion to Wycliffe's attack against the doctrine of the Eucharist, P. L. Heyworth dates it to sometime after 1390, but probably before 1420.[23] A prose treatise of approximately three hundred lines, it poses a series of pointed questions about clerical abuses, including covetousness, false doctrine, and exploitation of the poor.[24] The questions pile up on one another, without an opportunity for response on the part of the fraternal addressee. Interrogating his antagonist, the rustic speaker wastes no time getting down to business:

Frere, hou many ordris ben in erthe, and which is moost perfight
ordre?

Frere, of what ordre art thou and who made thin ordre? What
ben thi rulis, and who made thi cloutid rulis, sith Crist made hem
not ne noon other a thousende yeere aftir that Crist stighe into
hevene?

Frere, is ther ony ordre more perfighte than Crist Hym-silf
made?

Frere, if Cristis rule is moost perfight, whi rulist thee not
theraftir?

Whi schal a frere be more punyschid if he breke the rulis that
his patroun made, than if he breke the heestis that God Hym-silf
made? For brekynge of youre rulis ye ben prisonyd ofte.[25]

The piece's rather leaden style and lack of theological sophistication helps to
explain general disinterest in the text on the part of either Chaucerians or students of Lollard writing. Heyworth, its modern editor, characterizes it as "co-
lourless and rather flaccid prose," and notes its "generally unlearned quality,"
heightened by a reluctance or inability to use Latin.[26]

Nevertheless, by the time that Foxe wrote, *Jack Upland* had been circulating under Chaucer's name for at least forty years. Ideologically if not stylis-
tically, the text is a natural companion to the *Plowman's Tale*, another example
of late medieval satire written in the voice of a rural laborer that found a place
in Chaucer's canon in the early sixteenth century, and which certainly would
have been known to Foxe.[27] Although the title "Jack Upland," used in previous printed editions of the tract, evokes rural origins and the tradition of plowman satire, the text itself never identifies its speaker as a plowman or other
laborer. Foxe in his headnote is the first to call him "a certain uplandish and
simple *plowman*"—effectively a double for the speaker of the *Plowman's Tale*—
but he makes no explicit claims about *Jack Upland*'s relation to either the
Plowman's Tale or to Chaucer's other writings.

As it appears in the early folio editions, the *Plowman's Tale* is an anticlerical satire of about fourteen hundred lines, stitched onto the *Canterbury Tales*
by means of a brief prologue added some time after the composition of the
poem.[28] In the prologue, the Plowman leaves off his labors at midsummer and
joins the pilgrims on their journey to the shrine of Thomas Becket.[29] The Host
requests the Plowman tell the assembled group "some holy thynge," and the

Plowman responds with "a good preachynge" that he once heard from "a prest in pulpit," carefully situating his story within the legitimate scope of Christian teaching. It soon becomes clear that the Plowman's story is more radical than this introduction suggests. It is unapologetically antagonistic toward the established church, setting "popes, cardynals, and prelates / parsons, monkes, and frères fell / priours, abbottes of great estates" against the "poore and pale," "caytyffes sore a-cale" who are "i-cleped lollers and londlese."[30] He introduces two speakers, the Pelican, who argues on behalf of the "lollers," and the Griffin, who takes the opposing side. The Pelican, who speaks at much greater length than his popish counterpart, articulates many conventional anti-papal and antifraternal arguments, accusing the pope and priests of a litany of abuses against the poor "caytifs" and "lollers" who bear the brunt of clerical exploitation. Though the poem is staged as a dialogue, the Griffin is given only a perfunctory opportunity to rebut the Pelican's claims, and their exchange ends with the Pelican claiming victory and pronouncing a death sentence on the Griffin. An avenging Phoenix appears, in the manner of a deus ex machina, and swiftly dispatches the offending Griffin in the poem's final lines. The tale concludes with a reminder that readers should attribute its polemical positions to the Pelican, and not to the Plowman. This protestation notwithstanding, if Chaucer's Host really does "smell a Loller in the wind" on the way to Canterbury, any reader of the *Plowman's Tale* would sensibly conclude that it is the Plowman he detects, not the Parson.[31]

Using linguistic evidence and textual allusions, Andrew Wawn dates the *Plowman's Tale* to around 1400, with the prologue and several other interpolations added near the end of the fifteenth century.[32] The lack of any fifteenth- or early sixteenth-century witnesses implies it did not circulate widely, if at all, with the *Tales* in the fifteenth century. By contrast, the apocryphal *Tale of Gamelyn* appears in more than two dozen fifteenth-century *Tales* manuscripts yet never makes the transition into print.[33] Rather than emerging during the period of the *Tales'* greatest fluidity in the early fifteenth century, the *Plowman's Tale* finds a place in Chaucer's canon primarily as a result of later political and religious concerns.

Since the *Plowman's Tale* introduces a perspective similar to that of *Jack Upland* but claims a plausible place within the scope of the *Canterbury Tales*, it seems likely that the Chaucerian attribution of *Jack Upland* followed from the ascription of the *Plowman's Tale* to Chaucer. Today, *Jack Upland* survives in two manuscripts, British Library MS Harley 6641, a fifteenth-century theological miscellany, and Cambridge University Library (CUL) MS Ff.vi.2, copied in the sixteenth century.[34] In the Harley manuscript, the text is not attributed to any author, but in the Cambridge manuscript the word "Chaucer" is inscribed in a sixteenth-century hand at the beginning of text. While the texts in these two manuscripts are closely related, both differ significantly from that found in the later printed editions, suggesting that the treatise circulated in both print and manuscript during the early Tudor period—perhaps even more widely than the *Plowman's Tale*.[35]

Like the *Plowman's Tale, Jack Upland* was initially printed apart from the collected *Works*. A 1536 edition by John Gough survives in two copies; John Bale, in his *Index Britanniae Scriptorum*, describes a second edition of *Jack Upland* published by John Day in the middle of the century, which does not survive.[36] (Bale assigns the text to Wycliffe rather than to Chaucer, and he does not specify what attribution, if any, Day's edition carried.)[37]

In preparing *Actes and Monuments*, Foxe took his text of *Jack Upland* from Gough's edition or something similar to it. As such, it is worth considering how Gough framed the text in his edition. The title page of his edition plays upon the celebrity of its purported author, announcing that the text was "compyled by the famous Geoffrey Chaucer" (Foxe will also describe the text as "compiled").[38] The first page contains an introductory note, explaining that "These be the lewed questions of Freres rytes and observaunces the whych they chargen more than Goddes lawe, and therfore men shulden not gyve hem what so they beggen, tyll they hadden answered and clerely assoyled these questions."[39] This introduction—a similar note is found in Foxe and later reproduced in part in Speght's edition of the *Works*—is significantly shorter than the prologue found in the surviving manuscripts and omits a description of the Antichrist at work in all levels of society.[40] Whether Gough altered the text himself or took it from his exemplar, this printed prologue frames the text as an overt antifraternal polemic. Lacking the broader social and spiritual context afforded by the prologue, the friars become a particular evil to be expelled rather than a symptom of larger social imbalance. Gough's edition did not herald *Jack Upland*'s wholesale incorporation into the Chaucer canon. Unlike the *Plowman's Tale*, the piece does not appear in any edition of Chaucer's collected works until Speght adds it in his revised edition of 1602.

Because it circulates with the rest of the Chaucerian canon, the *Plowman's Tale* might be the expected source for Foxe's views on Chaucer and religion, and, as we shall see, he does indeed turn to that poem elsewhere in the *Actes and Monuments*. His primary interest in book 4, however, lies with the more direct and confrontational *Jack Upland*. As he introduces the treatise, Foxe

frames the text for maximum polemical impact by emphasizing its critique of
the friars and leveraging its association with the well-known figure of Chaucer. By attributing the text to Chaucer, Foxe makes the text available for
deployment in a well-worn rhetorical maneuver: as a part of the Chaucerian
canon, *Jack Upland* can be used to provide historical grounding for a sixteenth-
century concern—namely, Foxe's position against the friars.

John Foxe on "Chaucer" in Print

Chaucer appears again in book 8 of the 1570 *Actes and Monuments*, which
focuses on the sixteenth century. Here, Foxe pauses in the middle of a discussion of John Colet, founder of St. Paul's School, to digress on several famous pairs of learned men, including Gower and Chaucer. Moving on from
his discussion of early English humanists (in addition to Colet and William
Lily, the first master of St. Paul's School, he discusses the scholars William
Latimer and William Grocyn, as well as the physician Thomas Linacre and
diplomat Richard Pace), Foxe segues to the medieval writers by writing that
he thinks it "not out of season" to discuss their relationship here. Although
Hildegard, too, provided "season" for Foxe to turn to Chaucer, the turn of
phrase in this passage more directly suggests a heterogenous temporal progression in which Chaucer and Gower fit in better with men who lived in the
early sixteenth century than with their own contemporaries. In this passage,
Foxe praises both Chaucer and Gower as individuals, but he goes on to emphasize the importance of Chaucer's books as the means by which his putatively reformist views reach the present. For Foxe, the publication of Chaucer's
works in print offers both proof of Chaucer's exceptionalism and evidence of
a divine hand guiding and preserving the Protestant cause in England. It
constitutes a kind of bibliographic expression of the temporal mobility—the
ability to signify meaningfully in narratives about both past and present—
so valued by other early modern commentators on Chaucer.

In assembling his discussion of Gower and Chaucer, Foxe drew from
Leland's account of the friendship between the two poets in *De Viris Illustribus*.
As discussed in my second chapter, they are the only vernacular writers included in Leland's compendium, which contains entries for more than five
hundred theologians, scholars, and chroniclers. Foxe does not discuss Gower
in the same degree of detail that Leland does. However, perhaps extrapolat-
ing from the close connection between the two poets described his sources,

Foxe appears to have regarded Gower as a fellow proto-Protestant and includes him, alongside Chaucer, on a list of "faithful witnesses" in the time of John Wycliffe.[41] Foxe gives no further details here and does not mention Gower's religious views in the section dealing with Gower and Chaucer.

Like Leland (and unlike Bale, who adds entries for John Lydgate and "Robert" Langland, as well as expanded entries for figures like Walter Hilton and Richard Rolle), Foxe's interest in medieval literary figures is fairly circumscribed. He does not mention Lydgate, who as a monk and as the author of numerous devotional works, may have appeared too closely aligned with traditional religion to be successfully incorporated into the *Actes'* Protestant historiography. More surprising is the lack of any mention of *Piers Plowman*, a work that had been most recently printed in 1561 and which had gone through a notable three editions in 1550, all printed by Foxe's friend Robert Crowley. Crowley's epistle to the reader and the printed marginalia in his editions appear especially sensitive to what could be considered *Piers*'s prophetic content, as well as its proto-Protestantism. This would seem to make *Piers* an even better analogue than *Jack Upland* to the Hildegard prophecy printed in book 4. One possible reason for the absence of *Piers Plowman* is a lack of a strong, historicized authorial figure attached to the text; the particulars of Langland's biography remain mysterious even to contemporary scholars.

Foxe frames the relationship between Chaucer and Gower not in terms of politics, faith, or literary interests, but in terms of their accomplishments in learning and righteous living. He stresses the untimeliness of their achievements; Chaucer and Gower anticipate the intellectual norms of a later age. "Both," Foxe writes, were "notably learned, as the barbarous rudeness of that tyme did geve, both great friends together and both in like kinde of study together occupyed, so endevoring themselves, and employing their tyme, that they excelling many other in study and exercise of good letters did passe forth their lyves here right worshipfully & godly to the worthye fame and commendation of their name." Foxe marvels that laymen Gower and Chaucer were "so industrious & fruitfully occupied" in "liberall studies" in an age that was, for him, chiefly distinguished by the "idle life" of the clergy. In another moment that signals both temporal distance and the collapse of that distance, Foxe writes that, though Chaucer and Gower are "much discrepant from [Colet and Erasmus] in years," they are worthy to be matched with them.[42]

Foxe then moves from the past to the sixteenth-century present. Though he does not list exact death dates for Gower and Chaucer, he offers descriptions of their tombs in St. Mary Overie and Westminster Abbey as they appeared near the middle of the century, noting that a new tomb for Chaucer was installed in Westminster in 1556.[43] These sepulchral descriptions—similar accounts are found in both Leland and Bale—locate the memory of the medieval poets in a contemporary urban landscape, much as Foxe's other comments situate certain of Chaucer's works amid contemporary political and religious controversies.

For Foxe, however, the poets' most significant monuments are not their tombs but their books. Chaucer's books, specifically, extend his role in Foxe's salvation story from the past to the present. While Leland praised Chaucer's language and while both Leland and Bale offered full catalogs of Chaucer's writings in their accounts, Foxe subordinates Chaucer's poetic achievements to the role of his (attributed) texts in salvation history, naming only those works (the *Plowman's Tale*, *Jack Upland*) in which he finds evidence for reformist views.[44] Although Foxe notes that "Chaucers woorkes bee all printed in one volume, and therefore known to all men," his commentary makes it clear that the real story is not the existence of this volume (though it does speak to the particular impact of the folio format also used by Foxe) but the divine providence that allowed those works and their ostensibly Protestant message to reach later generations of English readers.

To support this narrative, Foxe first reminds his readers how Chaucer's works demonstrate a reformed religious perspective and then explains how the preservation and transmission of those works down to 1570 involved divine guidance. On both points, apocryphal texts are key to this new narrative of Chaucer's life and legacy. Foxe begins with the claim that that Chaucer "saw in Religion as much almost, as even we do now, and uttereth in hys works no lesse, and semeth to be a right Wiclevian [i.e., Wycliffite], or els was never any."[45] Indeed, he writes, "all his workes almost, if they be throughly advised, will testifie (albeit it bee done in myrth, and covertly)."[46] The actual examples he cites as evidence of this claim, however, are somewhat more circumscribed than "all his workes almost." The first item Foxe cites in support of this idea is book 3 of Thomas Usk's *Testament of Love* (first printed as Chaucer's work in 1532, and reprinted as such up through the eighteenth century). The *Testament of Love* lacks the polemical force of the other pseudo-Chaucerian pieces cited in Foxe and is today more usually thought of as a work in the Boethian tradition influenced by Chaucer's *Troilus and Criseyde*.[47] Nonetheless, according to Foxe, in it "purely he [Chaucer] toucheth the highest matter, that is, the Communion: Wherin, excepte a man be altogether blynde, he may espye him [Chaucer the "right Wycliffite"] at the full."[48] While the *Testament of*

Love does discuss the Eucharist in passing, it does not do so in an exceptionally polemical or detailed way. Its contents become important to Foxe because he seeks evidence for a Protestant Chaucer, and, viewed from a certain angle, the *Testament* can provide it.

The second piece of Chaucerian apocrypha cited here by Foxe is the *Plowman's Tale*. Considering the *Plowman's Tale* and what it reveals about Chaucer's religious views, Foxe offers readers a string of rhetorical questions:

> For to omitte other partes of his volume, whereof some are more
> fabulous than other, what tale can bee more playnely tolde, then
> the talke of the ploughman? or what finger can pointe out more
> directly the Pope with his Prelates to be Antichrist then doth the
> poore Pellycan reasonyng agaynst the gredy Griffon? Under whiche
> *Hypotyposis* or Poesie, who is so blind that seeth not by the Pellicane,
> the doctrine of Christ, and of the Lollardes to bee defended agaynst
> the Churche of Rome? Or who is so impudent that can denye that
> to be true, which the Pellicans there affirmeth in describyng the
> presumptuous pride of that pretensed Church? Agayne what egge
> can be more lyke, or figge unto an other, then ye words, properties,
> and conditions of that ravenyng Griphe resembleth the true Image,
> that is, the nature & qualities of that which we call the Church of
> Rome, in every point and degre?[49]

These unrelenting questions—like those of the Pelican against the Griffin in the *Plowman's Tale*—permit little opportunity for a reply, especially since anyone who fails to read the *Plowman's Tale* as he does must be, in Foxe's words, "blind." Foxe's choice of the term "hypotyposis" to describe the tale's allegory may carry prophetic connotations; while the term in its classical sense refers to any vivid description, especially of the distant past, mid-sixteenth century commentators gave it added force.[50] The term is most often used in explicitly Protestant contexts. In William Alley's *Ptochomuseion: The poore mans Librarie* (1565), for example, "hypotyposis" is defined as "a figure to shew forth a mater before the eies, as it wer done in deede," but Alley also notes that "such sightes are often geven to the Prophetes, and they are brought forth, not as true histories, or as formes and playne examples to teach and shew the thinges, as it were before the eyes."[51] The idea of Chaucer as a prophetic writer is not wholly without analogue: the eight-line prophetic poem beginning "When faith faileth in priests saws" (DIMEV 6299) is associated with Chaucer in some manuscripts and printed with the prefatory material of the *Works* (albeit without explicit attribution to Chaucer) from 1532 onward.[52]

Foxe valued Chaucer's writings not just for their prescient views, but also because of what he believed to be the providential way in which they were preserved and transmitted to future generations. In this same passage, he marvels "how that the Bishoppes condemnyng and abolishyng all maner of English bookes and treatises, which might bryng the people to any light of knowledge, did yet authorise the woorkes of Chaucer to remayne still and to be occupied."[53] This is a reference to the 1543 Act for the Advancement of True Religion, which greatly circumscribed the legal readership for the Bible in the vernacular and as well as all books printed before the 1540 except those "entituled Statues, Chronicles, Canterbury Tales, Chaucer's books, Gower's books, and stories of men's lives."[54] According to Foxe, "the Bishops" failed to recognize what they had in Chaucer, since "belike, takyng hys workes but for jestes and toyes, in condemnyng other bookes, [they] yet permitted his bookes to be read." This is not lucky chance, but divine providence. Foxe continues: "So it pleased God to blinde then they eyes of them, for the more commoditie of his people, to the entent that through the readyng of his treatises, some fruite might redounde therof to his Churche, as no doubt, it did to many." While this blinding of the eyes of ecclesiastical authorities would have occurred in the 1540s, Foxe adds a personal grace note when he assures readers that "I am partlye informed of certeine, whiche knewe the parties, which to them reported, that by readyng of Chauser workes, they were brought to the true knowledge of Religion. And not unlike to be true."[55] If this observation has grounding in fact, and writing attributed to Chaucer did shape readers' religious development, it is a striking testament to the authority associated with Chaucer's name in early modern England.

Foxe is especially interested in the absence of the *Plowman's Tale* from "copies of Chaucers workes," which might include manuscripts as well as pre-1542 printed editions. Given the *Tale*'s contents, he writes that it was "no great marvell, if that narration was exempted out of the copies of Chaucers workes: whiche notwithstandyng now is restored agayne, and is extant, for every man to read that is disposed."[56] For Foxe, the *Plowman's Tale*'s absence (which he construes as removal, apparently believing it had one time circulated with the rest of the *Tales*) is proof of just what a powerful criticism that poem offers.[57]

The bibliographic evidence tells a slightly different story than Foxe's account of presence, suppression, and eventual restoration: in fact, the *Plowman's Tale* is absent from all surviving manuscripts and pre-1532 printed editions of the *Canterbury Tales*, as well as from William Thynne's first edition of the *Works*.[58] There is no decisive evidence that connects its circulation to the *Canterbury Tales* prior to the 1542 *Works*, where it was inserted after the *Parson's Tale* (the *Retraction*, it is worth noting, is not included with any edition of the *Canterbury Tales* printed between 1532 and 1721).[59] When the *Works* were reprinted a third time around 1550, the *Plowman's Tale* was moved between the *Manciple's Tale* and the *Parson's Prologue*, with "Manciple" changed to "Plowman" in the link at the beginning of the *Parson's Prologue*, a move that implies a desire on the part of someone involved in the edition to mark the *Plowman's Tale* as fully canonical. The *Plowman's Tale* remained in this position until 1775, when Tyrwhitt removed it from his edition of the *Tales*.

In the meantime, its presence in the most widely available printed editions of Chaucer's *Works* became central to claims, like Foxe's and later Speght's, that Chaucer was a proto-Protestant. Inclusion in the folio editions seems to have conferred legitimacy on the *Plowman's Tale*. In the second half of the sixteenth century, there was no controversy whatsoever about its Chaucerian origins; Spenser and Sidney, for example, accept its authorship without question. Spenser, discovering both a poetic and spiritual forefather in Chaucer, even incorporated lines from the *Plowman's Tale* in the *Shepheardes Calender* in the eclogues for Februarie (line 149) and Aprill (line 99), and imitated it in the anti-papal Julye eclogue (lines 169–204). Though Spenser does not invoke Chaucer by name at these moments, E.K.'s commentary draws attention to them as Chaucerian allusions. (Spenser's own Protestantism, of course, might have made him particularly predisposed to accept a text such as the *Plowman's Tale* as Chaucerian.)[60]

While Sidney, Spenser, and Foxe all knew the *Plowman's Tale* through the *Works*, sixteenth-century readers could also have encountered the *Plowman's Tale* in several other forms, apart from the rest of the Chaucer canon. The *Plowman's Tale* was printed on its own three times: by Thomas Godfray around 1535 (STC 5099.5), by William Hill in about 1548 (STC 5100), and by George Eld in 1606 (STC 5101). These separate printings are unusual, as no stand-alone editions of the *Canterbury Tales*, *Troilus and Criseyde*, or any other of Chaucer's poems were published during this period. These three editions mean that—although both Hill and Eld's edition emphasize their connection to both Chaucer and the *Canterbury Tales*—the *Plowman's Tale* circulated (like *Jack Upland*) *without* other Chaucerian texts, and thus had the ability to reach a different audience from that of the folio Chaucers published in this period.[61] The texts of all three editions are similar and related to the text found in the

Works, indicating later editions were set from previously printed exemplars rather than manuscripts.

Godfray's edition from the 1530s, which survives today in a single, incomplete copy at the Huntington Library, is of special interest, because Godfray also printed the 1532 *Works*. Like the *Works*, his edition of the *Plowman's Tale* is a folio in sixes, and, also like the *Works*, it uses an unusual bâtarde typeface.[62] Because the Huntington copy lacks its title page, it is impossible to say exactly how it was presented to readers, but Joseph Dane argues that the congruency in format and type demonstrate that the *Plowman's Tale* was meant to be circulated alongside the *Works*.[63] As Alexandra Gillespie notes, however, although the format is the same, the Godfray *Plowman's Tale* is of a smaller size than the *Works*. This means that, even if the two were linked in some way, it is unlikely Godfray meant for it to be bound within the 1532 *Works*.[64]

Although the evidence leaves room for some uncertainty, it would seem the *Plowman's Tale*—like the 1532 *Works* as a whole—had currency as a piece of pro-Henrician propaganda. John N. King argues that the Godfray *Plowman's Tale* was intended as a way to smuggle this Lollard work into the Chaucerian corpus and therefore to a wider audience.[65] There is evidence that Godfray had reformist sympathies: he had previously printed *The prayer and complaynt of the Ploweman unto Christ* (STC 20036.5), another work in the plowman satire tradition, and several of his explicitly Protestant prints were banned in 1546.[66] At the same time, the middle years of the 1530s were a time when, far from wanting to repress the anticlerical sentiment expressed in the *Plowman's Tale*, the Tudor propaganda machine, ginning up support for Henry's divorce, would have welcomed and potentially benefited from it.[67] Importantly for this line of reasoning, the third and final portion of the *Plowman's Tale* (lines 702–1276) dwells at length on the institutional church's inappropriate use of its authority. As Thomas Heffernan notes, in this the poem picks up on a major polemical theme of the Henrician Reformation, pitting a foreign Catholic influence against a native strain of "true" Christianity.[68] (Godfray also printed an English translation of Lorenzo Valla's *On the Donation of Constantine* [STC 5641] in 1534.) Godfray may also have had a particularly close a connection with Thomas Berthelette, printer to Henry VIII. Berthelette's preface to his 1532 edition of Gower's *Confessio Amantis* warmly praises Godfray's Chaucer, and the two printers make use of the same ornaments. Although Peter Blayney disputes this view, Wawn speculates that Godfray may have taken on additional work commissioned or requested by Henry that Berthelette lacked the capacity to publish on his own.[69] The fragmentary nature of the sole surviving copy makes it difficult to draw a firm conclusion about exactly when, why, and from whom Godfray printed the *Plowman's Tale*, but it is clear that the association with Chaucer helped to spread the Plowman's message.

The *Plowman's Tale* was printed a second time by William Hill (or Hyll) in an octavo edition of 1548 (STC 5100) that takes its text from the 1542 edition of Chaucer's *Works*.[70] Hill, who was active only in 1548 and 1549, also printed works by John Calvin, William Tyndale, and Miles Coverdale, along with the first two English editions of the *Examinations of Anne Askew* (STC 851 and STC 852). Although the *Plowman's Tale* was already available to readers of the 1542 *Works*, Hill's edition would have cost significantly less than that large folio. His anticipated reader, then, seems to be a consumer of cheap print primarily interested in the work's antifraternal message.[71] The attribution to Chaucer on the title page and the connection to the *Canterbury Tales* made in the colophon ("thus endeth the boke of Chaunterburye Tales") both locate the text and its claims in a particular time, place, and social stratum, creating a historical basis for the religious and political stances advanced in both the *Plowman's Tale* and in Hill's other publications.[72]

Finally, in 1606, George Eld produced a quarto edition of the poem (STC 5101), with text taken from Speght's 1602 edition of the *Works*. Eld's edition is unique among printings of the *Plowman's Tale* in that it offers a significant amount of printed marginalia interpreting the text as a prophecy of the Gunpowder Plot. Drawing on the glossary and other commentary found in Speght, it also offers a "short exposition of the words and matters" addressed to the "simpler sort of reader," once again suggesting a more down-market audience than that sought by the magisterial folio editions.[73] By emphasizing and extending the views, ostensibly Chaucer's own, expressed in the *Plowman's Tale*, the anonymous commentator makes claims for Chaucer's religious modernity that parallel, and so draw strength from, claims about his poetry.

The print histories of the *Plowman's Tale* and *Jack Upland* invert the trajectory of canonical texts like the *Canterbury Tales* and *Troilus and Criseyde*. In the more general case, poems were printed in individual volumes prior to 1532 and afterward appeared only within the context of the collected works. In the case of the *Plowman's Tale* and *Jack Upland*, there is little evidence for fifteenth-century circulation of the texts as Chaucer's, and these works continue to circulate apart from the rest of the canon throughout the sixteenth century. There is also a question of size: Gough's edition of *Jack Upland* is in octavo, and the later editions of the *Plowman's Tale* are in quarto (Eld) and octavo (Hill). In this sense, these apocryphal publications more closely resemble Robert Crowley's 1550 quarto editions of *Piers Plowman*, another Middle English work embraced by Protestant reformers. By contrast, the 1555 edition of John Lydgate's *Troy Book*, a work that directly invokes the narratives of national origin and self-legitimization that also weave through the paratext of the *Works*, was printed in the larger folio format used for the collected editions of Chaucer, as were the 1532 and 1554 Berthelette editions of Gower's *Confessio Amantis*, which include their own nationalizing dedication to Henry VIII.[74] In general, publications intended to shore up national identity received the folio treatment, while more polemical materials that advanced the Protestant cause found their way into smaller—and cheaper—formats.

The belief in Chaucer's proto-Protestantism articulated in Foxe and reflected in the publication of *Jack Upland* and the *Plowman's Tale* shaped Chaucer's fate in early modern England in specific ways. First, as England came to define itself as a Protestant nation over the course of the sixteenth century, Chaucer's putative beliefs helped to secure his position as a figure able to testify to the antiquity of Englishness itself—not just in its linguistic and cultural dimensions, but now in its religion as well. This, in turn, helped to preserve Chaucer's visibility as a writer and, consequently, to construct a sense of singularity around his writing. These two points came together as early as the 1543 Act for the Advancement of True Religion, which both curtailed the circulation of much medieval writing on religious grounds and explicitly excused Chaucer's writings from censure, on the apparent presumption that the religious content of his works was unobjectionable.

From the *Works* to *Actes and Monuments* and Back to the *Works*

Commentary like Foxe's no doubt helped to naturalize the *Plowman's Tale* as a Chaucerian piece, but the assumption that Chaucer "saw in Religion as much almost, as even we do now" informed the treatment of other texts as well. Belief in Chaucer's proto-Protestantism shaped the folio canon, offering justification for the inclusion of apocryphal texts in the *Works* and creating new contexts for reading pieces containing more traditional religious content. Speght's second edition of 1602, which prints for the first time both the genuine *A.B.C.* and the apocryphal *Jack Upland*, illustrates this point particularly well. While *Jack Upland* is an antifraternal prose treatise of Lollard origin, the *A.B.C.* is Chaucer's Middle English translation of a French poem in praise of the Virgin Mary. In their origin, form, and outlook, the two pieces are very different. Despite their divergent tone and content, with *Jack Upland* pointing toward the Protestant Chaucer found in Foxe and the *A.B.C.* recalling more traditional modes of piety, Speght clearly approached the two pieces in tandem. Their resulting presentation in the *Works* was shaped in concrete ways by prevailing attitudes—derived in large part from Foxe—concerning Chaucer and religion.

Speght's editions were the first published after the appearance of *Actes and Monuments*, and they reflect the growing consensus that Chaucer was a proto-Protestant. In the *Life of Chaucer*, for example, Speght synthesizes claims for Chaucer's Protestantism with ideas about his education that had been in circulation at least since Leland.[75] Like Foxe discoursing on the friendship between Chaucer and Gower, Speght (perhaps working in conjunction with John Stow) takes a received narrative about Chaucer's life and adds a Reformation twist that underscores Chaucer's Protestant credentials. According to the *Life*:

> His bringing up, as *Leland* saieth, was in the University of Oxford, as also in *Cambridge,* as appeareth by his owne wordes in his booke entituled *The Court of Love:* and in Oxford by all likelihood in Canterbury or in *Merton* Colledge, with *John Wickliffe,* whose opinions in religion he much affected; where besides his private studie, he did with great diligence frequent the publique schooles and disputations: *Hinc acutus Dialecticus, hinc dulcis Rhetor, hinc lepidus Poeta, hinc gravis Philosophus, ac sanctus Theologus evasit. Mathematicus insuper ingeniosus erat à Johanne Sombo, &c.* Hereupon, saith Leland, he became a wittie Logician, a sweet Rhetorician, a pleasant Poet, a grave Philosopher, and a holy Divine.[76]

While Leland describes Chaucer as a "sanctus Theologus," he does not connect him with Wycliffe or pro-reformist views in any way. The claim that Chaucer was at Canterbury or Merton College with Wycliffe (Wycliffe had connections with both colleges, as well as Balliol) is articulated for the first time by Speght in 1598 and emerges only *after* the publication of the *Plowman's Tale* and *Jack Upland*, as well as Foxe's comments in *Actes and Monuments*. Since the text of the *Life* neither cites nor alludes to additional sources for this claim, it seems likely that Speght made an inference here, conditioned by what Foxe and the apocrypha say about Chaucer's life and writings.

If a reader were to notice this claim, and take it seriously, it could have radical implications for the way Chaucer and his writings are understood: for example, the *Friar's Tale* and the *Summoner's Tale* no longer seem like particularly witty salvos at common satirical targets, but instead read like comparatively tame expressions of a general orientation against the established church. Certainly, a belief that Chaucer had studied with Wycliffe would help to make not only the *Plowman's Tale* but also *Jack Upland* appear a credible part of the Chaucerian canon and lend new significance to the *Testament of Love*. It would also make it easier to understand why, in Speght's revised and expanded edition of 1602, *Jack Upland* finally appeared in print alongside the rest of the Chaucerian canon.

Thanks to its inclusion in the popular *Actes and Monuments*, *Jack Upland* was among the works most frequently printed under Chaucer's name in sixteenth-century England. By contrast, the *A.B.C.* was not printed before 1602, although it is strongly connected with Chaucer in manuscript. By adding *Jack Upland* and the *A.B.C.* to his 1602 text, Speght continued the tradition of what Seth Lerer calls the "omnivorous character of sixteenth-century Chaucer editing."[77] Adding these two texts *together*, however, necessitated that Speght engage in a complex set of editorial mediations among the received folio canon, the new works he added to the canon, and his understanding that Chaucer was, in Foxe's words, a "right Wycclevian." While the 1602 *Works* puts the two texts on equal footing, prior to this their circulation history had been very different.

Although it does not include either text, the 1598 version of the *Life of Chaucer* mentions *Jack Upland* and the *A.B.C.* together in a printed marginal note, which states that "Jack Upland is supposed to be his," followed by the considerably more confident assertion that "the A.B.C. called *Priere de nostre Dame*, is certainly Chaucers doing."[78] The contrast between the emphatic attribution of the *A.B.C.* to Chaucer and the more qualified ("supposed to be his") connection with *Jack Upland* is revealing: though it had been nearly thirty years since Foxe first printed *Jack Upland*, little notice seems to have been taken of the text among Chaucerian commentators. References to the text as Chaucer's own can be found in *World of Wonders* (1607; an English version of Henri Estienne's *Apologie pour Herodote*) and the controversialist Simon Birkbeck's *The Protestants Evidence* (1634), but both were written after the publication of Speght's *Works. Jack Upland* and the *A.B.C.* are linked again on the title page to the 1602 edition, which announces "the Treatise called *Jacke Upland*, against Friers: and Chaucers A.B.C. called *La Priere de nostre Dame*, at this Impression added," phrasing that highlights the religious content of both works. Paired together on the title page and printed alongside one another at the back of the book *Jack Upland* and the *A.B.C.* coexist uneasily.[79]

In the accompanying headnotes in 1602, Speght offers contrasting explanations as to the origin of each text. As context, it is useful to briefly consider Speght's commentary on the *Plowman's Tale*, which had been printed with of Chaucer's works for more than half a century by 1598. In his headnote, Speght describes the poem as "a complaint against the pride and covetousnesse of the Cleargie: made no doubt by Chaucer, with the rest of the Tales," and notes that "I have seene it in written hand in John Stowes Librarie in a booke of such antiquitie, as seemeth to have been written neare to Chaucers time."[80] Derek Pearsall reads some ambivalence about the canonicity of the *Plowman's Tale* in Speght's "no doubt."[81] This is a suggestion worth taking seriously because, while Speght accepts Foxe's presentation of Chaucer as a robust proto-Protestant, he elsewhere displays some skepticism about his sources. In the "His Bookes" section of the *Life of Chaucer*, for example, Speght writes of "[other poems] I have seene without any Authours name, which for the invention I would verily judge to be Chaucers, were it not that wordes and phrases carry not every where Chauceres antiquitie."[82] (In 1602, he added "in the hands of M. Stow that painfull Antiquarie" after "Authours name," perhaps thinking of specific materials shown to him by Stow.[83]) It is not clear whether the books that Speght refers to here are manuscripts or printed books, but these remarks together seem to articulate an interest in determining an authentic Chaucerian canon based on linguistic and manuscript evidence. This makes Speght's choice to add *Jack Upland*—drawn from a printed book and without special comment on its un-Chaucerian diction—especially notable. It is a reflection, perhaps, of the stature of Foxe's compendium and *Jack Upland*'s place in it that Speght makes use of it even in the apparent absence of any corroborating manuscript evidence.

Like Foxe's handling of *Jack Upland*, Speght's presentation of the text is linked with the canonical position of the *Plowman's Tale* and extends and amplifies the work that poem does toward securing Chaucer's Protestant bona fides. Speght took his text of *Jack Upland* from Foxe, and while the title page in 1602 notes that this treatise is "against Friers," the headnote to the piece in

the 1602 *Works* uses Foxe's phrasing to construct a more complicated genealogy for the piece, one that connects it with the *Plowman's Tale*:

> In this Treatise is set foorth the blind ignoraunce and variable
> discord of the Churchmen, how rude and unskilfull they were in
> matters & principles of our Christian institution. This is thought to
> bee that Crede which the Pellican speaketh of in the Plowmans tale
> in these words:
>> Of freers I have told before,
>> In a making of a Crede,
>> And yet I could tell worse and more,
>> But men would werrien it to rede.[84]

It seems more likely that what the author of the *Plowman's Tale* refers to here
is a work known as *Piers the Plowman's Creed*, another fifteenth-century satire that was printed in the sixteenth century, but never attributed to Chaucer.[85] Nevertheless, Speght's claim here piggybacks on the canonical status of
the *Plowman's Tale* and uses it to craft a justification for *Jack Upland*'s inclusion that is literary as well as ideological. This identification of *Jack Upland* as
the Plowman's "Crede" appears to be Speght's own invention, since neither
Foxe nor Gough makes a similar assertion.

Speght's headnote explains Chaucer's relationship to *Jack Upland* in a
highly mediated way: it identifies the piece as a text alluded to by a character
(the Pelican) in a story told by yet another character (the Plowman) in a larger
framework of which Chaucer himself is the narrator (the *Canterbury Tales*).
This is a contrast with Speght's headnote to the *Plowman's Tale* itself, which
restricts itself to evidence for the poem's authenticity or, at least, its date. Even
as Speght gives it a place in the canon, *Jack Upland* takes on a liminal status,
presented as the work of a Chaucer writing in the voice of one of his pilgrims,
but outside the framework of the *Tales*. One possible explanation for this me-
diation is stylistic: while a connection to the *Tales* helps to secure *Jack Upland*'s
place in the canon, a more specific link with the rustic Plowman explains the
text's rough style and lack of rhetorical sophistication.

Perhaps due to its close association with a particular set of political and
religious circumstances, *Jack Upland*'s stay in the canon was comparatively
short: after the 1602 *Works*, it appeared in print as Chaucer's just two more
times, in the 1687 reprint of Speght and in the 1721 edition of *Works* edited by
John Urry.[86] Even in that volume, skepticism abounds: Thomas Dart, author

of a new biography of Chaucer written for that edition, suggests that Chaucer was sympathetic to Lollardy, but wrote that he could not "go so far as to suppose [Chaucer] scurrilously reviled the Established Religion of those times, and therefore cannot think that either the *Plowman's Tale* or *Jack Upland* were written by him."[87] *Jack Upland* was omitted from later editions of Chaucer's works, and when it was finally printed again, in Thomas Wright's *Political Poems and Songs Relating to English History* (1861), its previous association with Chaucer was mentioned only in passing.

Jack Upland is a work whose attribution to Chaucer can only be explained by the religious and political contexts in which his writings were read in the sixteenth century. Its presence in the 1602 edition demonstrates how the idea of a Protestant Chaucer might shape his canon beyond the *Plowman's Tale*. The late appearance of the *A.B.C.* in that same edition shows how questions about religious identity might also preclude or delay the presentation of Chaucerian works more familiar to modern readers.

While a few shorter poems are added to the print canon in the nineteenth century, the *A.B.C.* is the last Chaucerian poem of any significant length to appear in print.[88] An acrostic prayer to the Virgin Mary, it takes as its source an equivalent passage in Guillaume de Deguileville's *Pèlerinage de la vie humaine*.[89] In Chaucer's English version, as in the French original, each stanza begins with a successive letter of the alphabet and meditates on a particular devotional image or theme. The first stanza, for example, begins with an *A* and focuses on the intercessory power of the Virgin:

> Almighty and al merciable queene,
> To whom that al this world fleeth for socour,
> To have relees of sinne, of sorwe, and teene,
> Glorious virgine, of alle floures flour,
> To thee I flee, confounded in errour.
> Help and releeve, tho mighti debonayre,
> Have mercy on my perilous langour!
> Venquisshed me hath my cruel adversaire.

The versification here is careful and deliberate, and uses the same form— eight-line stanzas in decasyllables—that Chaucer would later use in the *Monk's Tale* and several shorter poems. While the poem is a translation, it is also one that is carefully crafted, and which works well at the level of English poetics.

The lack of sixteenth-century references or witnesses to the *A.B.C.* contrasts with the evidence for its transmission and reception in the fifteenth century. Sixteen manuscripts of the *A.B.C.* survive, all dating from before 1500, pointing toward early popularity and widespread transmission (*Troilus and Criseyde* also survives in sixteen manuscripts).[90] Four of these explicitly name Chaucer as the author.[91] On this evidence, John Thompson concludes that, "*An ABC* was a well-regarded text which quickly gained a place and reputation among Chaucer's writings."[92] In the early fifteenth century, it was certainly known to John Lydgate, who in his own translation of the *Pèlerinage* refers to "my mayster Chaucer" who

> . . . in hys tyme
> affter the Frenche he dyde yt ryme,
> Word by word, as in substaunce,
> Ryght as yt ys ymad in Fraunce,
> fful devoutly, in sentence,
> In worshepe, and in reverence
> Off that noble hevenly quene,
> Bothe moder and a maydë clene.[93]

These claims are in keeping with Chaucer's early reputation as a "grand translateur," and Lydgate further asserts that the work was translated "fful devoutly" as Chaucer's own praise of the Virgin, aligning the speaking voice of the poem with Chaucer himself.

Speght's exemplar for the poem in 1602 was the large fifteenth-century collection that is now Cambridge University Library MS Gg.4.27.1, and overall, he is faithful to his source.[94] As the first editor of the poem, Speght gives the *A.B.C.* not just a printed text but also a printed title, "Chaucers A.B.C. called *La Priere de nostre Dame*."[95] Speght devoted some thought to his titles and was not averse to altering them, as demonstrated by his decision to retitle the poem that Thynne had called "The Dreame of Chaucer" as the *Book of the Duchess*, and to use the title "Chaucers dreame" instead for the poem now known as the *Isle of Ladies*.[96] Speght's chosen title for the *A.B.C.*, incorporating both English and French, appears on the frontispiece of the 1602 *Works*, in the table of contents, and in the title to the poem itself.[97]

Wherever the title appears, it performs interpretive work that situates Chaucer in relation to the poem's devotional content. Its second half, *La Priere de nostre Dame* draws attention to the poem's French sources and thus to its status as a translation, while the English title "Chaucer's A.B.C." carries pedagogical overtones (the poem's Marian subject matter is, tellingly, expressed in the French half of the title rather than the English).[98] The atomization of letters in the English title emphasizes Chaucer's special associations with the development of the English language, an emphasis that echoes throughout the materials added by Speght. Here, it also provides an alternative generic frame to *priere*—useful for readers who would not pray to *nostre Dame* and who might also be uncomfortable with the idea of Chaucer doing so. In effect, Speght's double title, unique in the *Works*, encapsulates two alternative ways of reading the poem and, by extension, Chaucer: one religious and moral, the other focused on questions of text, language, and translation.

Speght also includes an "argument," or headnote, for the *A.B.C.* In this case, Speght's note elides Chaucer's responsibility for the poem's content, stating that it was in fact a commission. He writes that the poem was "made, as some say, at the request of Blanch [*sic*], Duchesse of Lancaster, as a praier for her privat use, being a woman in her religion very devout."[99] Although no such note is found in the CUL manuscript or the related Pepys manuscript, Derek Pearsall suggests that Speght's "gossipy" comments might draw on material from one of the four folios now missing from Gg.4.27 and could ultimately derive from "an authentic tradition" but equally "may go back no further than Stow (imitating Shirley)" and the claim about an elite commission "certainly fits suspiciously well with the increased emphasis on Chaucer's aristocratic connections in the Speght 'Life.'"[100] Regardless of its veracity, the claim that Blanche of Lancaster, wife of John of Gaunt, was a patron of the *A.B.C.* fosters the courtly image of Chaucer as a well-placed favorite of high-born and powerful women. Although Speght offers no specific evidence of Blanche's patronage, she is a logical candidate for this role, since the *Book of the Duchess* links her to Chaucer.[101] (The historical record contains several examples of Blanche's religious gestures, including petitions made with her husband to the pope, and Speght may have been aware of this.)[102]

By explicating the context of the poem's production, Speght's note for the *A.B.C.* puts Chaucer back in his historical moment, shifting focus away from the poet's personal religious beliefs. While Speght's claims here are ultimately nothing more than speculation, his comments are also a turn away from the untimely Chaucer of *Actes and Monuments*, and toward a more particularized and historicized understanding of Chaucer's work. No longer a transcendent figure, the poet is of his time and place. Naming a patron minimizes Chaucer's spiritual involvement in the poem; the *A.B.C.*, Speght is careful to note, was for "privat" use, not written from Chaucer's own perspective but translated for the devotion of another. Speght's account of the *A.B.C.*'s composition allows him to accept the poem as canonical, even if appears to be at odds with the reformist enthusiasm expressed in other work ascribed to Chaucer. As in the *Life*, Speght uses historical details to anchor Chaucer's text at a specific point in the past, but he interprets those details in ways that do not trouble the received notion of a Protestant Chaucer.

Speght's characterization of the poem as an act of translation rather than a poetic composition in its own right has long-term echoes in the *A.B.C.*'s critical reception. Writing in the late nineteenth century, Walter Skeat asserts that the *A.B.C.* "is not strictly 'made,' or composed, but only translated."[103] Accepting the association with Blanche first articulated in Speght, Skeat dates the piece between 1359 and 1369 and posits a probable composition date of 1366, which would make it one of Chaucer's earliest surviving compositions. Skeat comments further that "it may well stand first in chronological order, being a translation just of that unambitious character which requires no great experience."[104] Subsequently, scholars have tended to tread lightly over the *A.B.C.*, either echoing Skeat's views or avoiding discussion of it entirely. This unusually quiet scholarly history of the poem prompts William A. Quinn to suggest that "the critical neglect of Chaucer's *Priere* entails an opposition between Catholic and non-Catholic perspectives that can be traced all the way back to the Reformation."[105] More recent critics have reassessed the merits of the *A.B.C.*, finding it to be much more than the barely competent translation described by Skeat. Kay Gilliland Stevenson, for example, draws attention to the poem's theological "extravagance," which amplifies and extends upon the French original.[106] Read in conjunction with *Jack Upland* in 1602, Speght's comments on the *A.B.C.* work to make the poem compatible with received understandings of Chaucer as a proto-Protestant, but the later critical history of the poem also reflects how Speght's subordination of the poem as "just" a translation endured long after the idea of Chaucer the Wycliffite had been laid to rest.

Taken together, the *Plowman's Tale*, *Jack Upland*, and the *A.B.C.* demonstrate three interrelated points. First, their overlapping history shows the wide variety of contexts and conversations in which Chaucer figured meaningfully during the sixteenth century, from religious polemic to the self-consciously literary presentation of the 1602 *Works*. Second, the particular use of Chaucer in *Actes and Monuments* shows how Foxe, as a religious chronicler working alongside Protestant antiquarians, brought together both literary sources and antiquarian commentary as he constructed a version of Chaucer that best fit his purposes. His way of reading Chaucer cultivates the same sense of doubled historical and contemporary import found in other antiquarian commentary on Chaucer. Third, Speght's use of Foxe and his related treatment of *Jack Upland* and the *A.B.C.* reveal the ways—explicit and implicit—that extraliterary engagement with Chaucer shaped the representation of his canon.

Reading *Actes and Monuments*, the Chaucerian apocrypha, and Speght's *Works* together shows how commentary and publication decisions related to Chaucer's religion reshaped the medieval poet and his works, once again remaking literary history in ways that reflected the desires of his early modern readership. Similar to the evolving biographical narratives I discussed in Chapter 2, during the sixteenth century the discourse around Chaucer's religion shifted in ways that had little explicit connection to literary or aesthetic concerns. Instead, it was guided by concerns about identity on a collective scale. Cast as a proto-Protestant, bolstered by appropriate textual attributions, and still bearing his special relation to the English language, Chaucer both represents an idealized version of the past and connects that past to the present. In the following chapter, I turn to Chaucer's language—a mainstay of poetic praise of the author as well as a subject of increasing antiquarian interest—and its treatment in both antiquarian contexts and literary ones, mostly notably in Edmund Spenser's *Shepheardes Calender*.

CHAPTER 4

"Difficulties Opened"

Confronting Chaucer's Archaism in Spenser and the 1598/1602 *Works*

In the later decades of the sixteenth century, the distance between Chaucer's English and contemporary language became increasingly visible to critics and admirers alike. Rather than consigning Chaucer to obsolescence, however, the archaic qualities of his words became central to celebrations of Chaucer as a foundational figure whose antiquity was a dominant part of his enduring appeal. This chapter looks at the unique intersection of poetic and antiquarian responses to Chaucer that shape both Edmund Spenser's *Shepheardes Calender* (1579) and Thomas Speght's 1598 and 1602 editions of the *Works*. More specifically, it argues that Speght's treatment of Chaucer's language was directly informed by Spenser's, making the *Works*, in surprising ways, a Spenserian text.

Examining the way Chaucer and his language are handled in both the *Calender* and the Speght *Works* allows us to trace, first, how a preexisting concept of Chaucerian language was leveraged by Spenser at the beginning of his career and, second, how Spenser's treatment of Chaucer in turn influenced Speght's work. In the *Shepheardes Calender*, Spenser's poet-shepherds deliver eclogues studded with archaisms that the accompanying glosses and commentary at times identify as explicitly Chaucerian. This commentary is attributed to a mysterious commentator called "E.K." (possibly Spenser himself, and certainly someone known to the poet) who is also responsible for the epistle addressed to Gabriel Harvey that prefaces the *Calender*.

E.K.'s comments, while sometimes useful, are often oblique or enigmatic; Speght's, by contrast, are more straightforward. In the *Works*, the archaic qualities of Chaucer's language are praised in prefatory epistles and made dramatically visible through the inclusion of glossaries and "hard word" lists alongside his poems. Though the glossary is now a standard component of most editions of Middle English poetry, Speght's use of a "hard word" list for Chaucer was an innovation when it was first published in 1598. By separating out Chaucer's words from their contemporary synonyms, Speght opened up a linguistic and cultural gap between verse and reader, even as he claimed to mediate that gap through his commentary. This sense of historical distance, as well as the new space for commentary and criticism that it creates, reverberates throughout the *Works*, borrowing from both the form and content of the equivalent materials in the *Calender*. In both the *Calender* and the *Works*, when treated as a matter of lexicographical fact, Chaucer's old words became a metonym for the antiquity of the English poetic tradition and Englishness itself, even while they are also used to align Chaucer with certain figures from Greek and Roman antiquity.

Chaucer, Spenser, and Speght

Speght's 1598 edition and its revised counterpart, published in 1602, marked the first publication of Chaucer's poems alongside materials designed not simply to praise them but to explain them to a potentially uncomprehending or unappreciative audience. Chaucer's language is a prominent theme throughout these materials, especially in the introductory epistles written by Speght and his associate, the jurist Francis Beaumont, and in the hard word list. The Speght editions were also the first to be published after the publication of Spenser's *Shepheardes Calender* (1579) and the *Faerie Queene* (1590/1596). While the *Faerie Queene* is a more ambitious work than the *Calender* and, at the end of the sixteenth century, the more widely known and celebrated one, it appears to have been the *Calender*, and its presentation of Chaucer, that most influenced the *Works*. Although Speght's approach to Chaucer is in many ways consistent with earlier commentators, reading the paratext of his edition alongside the epistles and glosses that accompany the *Shepheardes Calender* shows that Speght's approach to both Chaucerian language and the figure of the poet himself was deeply marked by the way that Spenser's text engages with these same topics.

Its use of Chaucer is just one aspect of the *Calender*'s complex poetic conceit. The work, which in structure and appearance resembles an almanac, consists of twelve eclogues assigned to the months of the year, each with an accompanying woodcut and motto. In each case, the speaker or speakers of the eclogue are identified as part of a group of shepherds who interact in various combinations across the poems. The *Calender* is Spenser's first major work (like Virgil, he begins with eclogues before undertaking epic), and it was initially published anonymously, with an address to the book foregrounding this fact appearing on the verso of the title page. Even in its first printing, however, it included a significant amount of prose, all attributed to one "E.K." (Though much critical ink has been spilled on the topic, the exact identity of E.K. is not important here; the point is that, as with Speght's Chaucer, the combination of obscure text with learned commentary creates a bibliographic package that is both consciously abstruse and purportedly self-explanatory.)[1]

Throughout the book, Spenser and E.K. brilliantly exploit the ability of Chaucer's language—and, by extension, the figure of Chaucer himself—to register as both "ancient" and English. First, Spenser uses words that, in E.K.'s glosses, are marked as Chaucerian (and less frequently as Lydgatian). According to E.K., the poet's use of archaisms here is sanctioned by Cicero (but also, perhaps, the inevitable result of what E.K. describes as the "sunburn" obtained by the poet in his reading of early English poetry). Like the dedication to Henry VIII in the 1532 *Works*, this treatment of language on a word-by-word basis marks Chaucerian words as historical, not contemporary, while also demonstrating their contemporary usefulness. Second, in the *Calender* Chaucer's distance from the present is presented in ways that invite comparison and even conflation of the English poet and classical writers. This picks up on the classicizing treatment of Chaucer that can be found, for example, in the preface to the 1532 *Works*, but the *Calender* offers a more sustained and complex comparison of Chaucer to the Roman poet Virgil through their mutual identification with the figure of Tityrus, the recently deceased poetic master of Spenser's shepherds. Ultimately, however, the goal of the *Calender* is not to celebrate Chaucer so much as it is to draw attention to the skill of the "newe poete": by marking Chaucerian words as archaic and by linking Chaucer with poetic figures from antiquity, E.K.'s commentary uses Chaucer to show how Spenser carries on both Latin and vernacular poetic traditions.

Scholars have long recognized Chaucer's influence on Spenser, but Spenser's influence on the presentation of Chaucer in print has been largely overlooked.[2] The *Shepheardes Calender* provided Speght with a model both for thinking about Chaucer in relation to the classical past, and for dealing with Chaucer's archaic language in a scholarly way. The figure of Chaucer in Speght's

Works is, in many ways, that of the "good old poet" in the *Calender* who enables and authorizes the efforts of the "newe poete."

As it seeks to promote Chaucer and his poetry, the Speght *Works* becomes, in surprising ways, a Spenserian text, disrupting any tidy or linear narrative of literary history. Remarks in the apparatus make it clear that Speght and his colleagues knew the *Shepheardes Calender*, and that they were familiar with E.K.'s commentary on it. Rather than dismissing E.K.'s comments as an attempt to claim for the "new Poete" the authority more usually ascribed to classics like Chaucer, Speght appears to have taken E.K.'s apparatus as a model, at least in part, for his own scholarly commentary. There is a significant difference in that, while E.K. explicates a text that is merely designed to appear medieval through its use of archaisms, Speght's undertaking involves actual medieval poetry. Nonetheless, the Spenserian commentary provides Speght with a distinctly sixteenth-century, distinctly English understanding of both poetic tradition and archaic language.

Archaism, Classicism, and Novelty

In the *Shepheardes Calender*, the annotations attributed to E.K. offer a quasi-scholarly counterpoint to the pastoral voice of the "new Poete" and his textual alter ego, Colin Clout. This commentary takes the form of an epistle addressed to Gabriel Harvey, an essay on the history of the eclogue, and a series of notes keyed to individual words and phrases in the text of the *Calender*, printed after each eclogue under the heading "Glosse."[3] E.K.'s explicatory gaze is wide-ranging: he devotes substantial attention to apparently obscure English words and phrases, but also discourses at length, and with varying degrees of clarity, upon many of the poem's classical allusions and allegorical devices.

Because they frequently emphasize the *Calender*'s use of conventions from classical eclogue, and because their presence evokes early modern commentaries on authors like Virgil and Petrarch, E.K.'s glosses have been understood as an attempt to situate the work within preexisting literary genealogies and claim for Spenser's debut the authority and gravitas more commonly ascribed to already canonical texts.[4] Whether or not the reader engages with E.K.'s comments, their presence on the page helps portray the text as worthy of serious scholarly attention, a sort of "instant classic."[5]

E.K.'s glosses serve this purpose not only because of their role in the *Calender*'s mise-en-page but also because they draw attention to the poet's

archaisms. As E.K. explains in his epistle to Harvey, the very act of incorporating such old words is authorized by classical literary theory and found in the
works of Livy and Sallust. What distinguishes the *Calender* from these classical examples is not the relative age of the words it uses, but their origin, which
E.K. takes pains to mark as explicitly English but nonetheless "auncient." He
warns readers, "I know [it] will seeme the straungest, the words them selves
being so auncient, the knitting of them so short and intricate, and the whole
Periode and compasse of speache so delightsome for the roundesse, and so
grave for the straungenesse. And firste of the wordes to speake, I graunt they
be something hard, and of most men unused, yet both English, and also used
of most excellent Authors and most famous Poetes."[6] Significantly, the antiquity of these English words, and therefore their compatibility with classical
precedent, is established not by orthography or morphology, but by their appearance in texts ascribed to "excellent Authors" and "famous Poetes," In
other words, E.K. suggests that language—like history itself—can be broken up into periods, and that these periods are distinguished not by ruler or
epoch, but by the authors the words are associated with.

In his glosses, E.K. identifies several words as having been used by Chaucer or by Lydgate: of "gride," E.K. writes, "perced: an olde word much used
of Lidgate, but not found (that I know of) in Chaucer."[7] He defines "clincke"
as "a key hole. Whose diminutive is clicket, used of Chaucer for a Key."[8] Although slight, these references to medieval texts distinguish E.K.'s "glosse"
from earlier, topically limited English lists of hard words and terms of art and
anticipate the supporting quotations found in early modern dictionaries like
those published by the Estienne family.[9] As commentary that evokes the lat-
est in humanistic lexicography, these glosses have a twofold authorizing function, identifying the antiquity and source of the words used in the verse and
signaling the learnedness of the commentator, as well as the worthiness of the
text upon which he comments.

E.K.'s use of Lydgate as a linguistic model is somewhat surprising, given
that by the middle of the century, Chaucer was more commonly paired with
John Gower. While Spenser likely knew the *Confessio Amantis*, the *Calender*
never mentions Gower by name and R. F. Yeager writes that Gower's influence on Spenser "remains an open question."[10] By contrast, Spenser seems to
have known several works by Lydgate, including his translation of Deguileville's *Pèlerinage de la vie humaine*, *The Assembly of the Gods*, and his translation of Guido delle Colonne's *Historia destructionis Troiae*, known as the *Troy
Book*, which, along with Chaucer's *Troilus and Criseyde*, could be thought of

as a model for the kind of vernacular epic Spenser will seek to construct in the *Faerie Queene*.[11] Two of the three glossed terms that E.K. associates with Lydgate ("gride" from Februarie and "dead at mischiefe" from September) can be found in the Middle English *Pèlerinage*; "welk" from November can be found in the *Troy Book*.

Spenser likely knew the *Troy Book* through the 1555 edition printed by Thomas Marshe (STC 5580). (Marshe was also responsible for the octavo edition of John Skelton's works published in 1568.) The preface to Marshe's *Troy Book*, attributed to one Robert Braham, shows how Chaucer and Lydgate might be thought together at the middle of the sixteenth century, with Chaucer praised as the pioneering figure and Lydgate valued for his ability to follow faithfully in Chaucer's footsteps. The preface clearly takes the Chaucer *Works* as a model for presenting the work of a medieval author in print, praising Thynne's work as an editor and borrowing language from the 1532 preface.[12] It also celebrates Lydgate as one who "prevayled in this our vulgare language, that havynge his prayse dewe to his deservynges, may worthyly be numbred amongest those that have chefelye deserved of our tunge" yet notes that Lydgate does so "as the verye perfect disciple and imitator of the great Chaucer, the onely glorye and beauty of the same."[13] Chaucer, clearly, retains the preeminent position, but Lydgate gains significance because of his relation to him. If Lydgate is understood as imitating Chaucer, and Chaucer is understood as a linguistic innovator, then it follows that some of Chaucer's innovation must filter into Lydgate's texts, making them available for appropriation under the aegis of Chaucerianism.

By identifying certain words, like "perced" and "clincke," as both old and English, E.K. lays the groundwork for a broader application of classical rhetoric to the language that originates closer to home—the language of the English past. Newly identified as archaic, Chaucerian and Lydgatian words equip the poet with the language needed for his vernacular application of classical literary precepts to English verse. E.K. praises the aesthetic effect produced by the poet's use of "old words and harder phrases," declaring that, although such "olde and obsolete wordes are most used of country folke," when applied according to rules of proportion and decorum, "they bring great grace and, as one would say, auctoritie to the verse."[14] In support of this, he cites Cicero's *De Oratore*: "For if my memory fayle not, Tullie in that booke, wherein he endevoureth to set forth the paterne of a perfect Oratour, sayth that ofttimes an auncient worde maketh the style seeme grave, and as it were reverend: no otherwise then we honour and reverence gray heares for a certein religious regard, which we have of old age, yet nether every where must old words be stuffed in, nor the commen Dialecte and maner of speaking so corrupted therby, that as in old buildings it seme disorderly and ruinous."[15] This passage mixes bodily and architectural metaphors for language, comparing archaic words to first to gray hairs and then (when overused) to the "disorderly" incorporation of previously used materials in old buildings. In it, E.K. argues that the *Calender*'s use of old English words constitutes adherence to "Tullie"'s policy of limited archaism. The glosses necessarily play an integral role in this aspect of the project, since readers cannot be expected to recognize the poet's archaisms as fidelity to Cicero and other Latin writers unless they can first properly identify the "auncient" words within the English text.

As E.K. describes it, however, the *Calender* is more than a simple vernacular homage to classical models. It is also a work in which the poet "hath laboured to restore, as to theyr rightfull heritage such good and naturall English words, as have ben long time out of use and almost cleare disherited."[16] In this sense, the glosses have a more immediate purpose: to educate English readers about their own linguistic past. E.K. explains,

> Hereunto have I added a certain Glosse or scholion for thexposition of old wordes and harder phrases: which maner of glosing and commenting, well I wote, wil seeme straunge and rare in our tongue: yet for somuch as I knew many excellent and proper devises both in wordes and matter would passe in the speedy course of reading, either as unknowen, or as not marked, and that in this kind, as in other we might be equal to the learned of other nations, I thought good to take the paines upon me, the rather for that by means of some familiar acquaintaunce I was made privie to his counsell and secret meaning in them, and also in sundry other works of his.[17]

As E.K. describes his glosses here, their intended effect is not to classicize the text directly (though "scholion" has associations with Latin and Greek scholarship) but rather, by drawing readers' attention to the "old wordes and harder phrases" found in the *Calender*, to raise these English readers' understanding of their own language to that of "the learned of other nations." Given that the words that E.K. defines may be either "unknown" or "not marked," his purpose here should be understood as twofold: glosses can explain unfamiliar words to readers or alert readers to the antiquity of words still in regular use and hence "not marked" in the "speedy course of reading." E.K.'s phrasing here highlights the fact that not all "old words and harder phrases" are immediately recognizable as such. In the case of the *Calender*, readers must be taught to recognize the antiquity of certain words, not only in order to be better educated about their own language, but also to better appreciate the eclogues' fidelity to classical models.

E.K.'s understanding of the *Calender* as a text that draws on intersecting classical and vernacular literary traditions is demonstrated in the glosses themselves, which juxtapose explanations of classical allusions with explications of difficult English words. The gloss for August, a typical example, begins as follows:

Bestadde) disposed, ordered.
Peregall) equall.
Whilome) once.
Rafte) bereft, deprived.
Miswent) gon a straye.
Ill may) according to Virgile. Infelix o semper ovis pecus.
A mazer) So also do Theocritus and Virgile feigne pledges of their strife.
Enchased) engraven. Such pretie descriptions every where useth Theocritus, to bring in his Idyllia. For which speciall cause indede he by that name termeth his Æglogues: for Idyllion in Greke signifieth the shape or picture of any thyng, wherof his booke is ful. And not, as I have heard some fondly guesse, that they be called not Idyllia, but Hædilia, of the Goteheards in them.
Entrailed) wrought betwene.
Harvest Queene) the manner of country folke in harvest tyme.
Pousse.) Pease.

In the *Calender*, English words and classical allusions are generally treated in separate annotations, tied to a specific word or phrase from the verse, but the standardized typography and format of the glosses place the two on equal footing (Figure 6).

For E.K., as for Speght some years later, the act of glossing also asserts distance between the everyday linguistic world of the present and the putatively obscure language of the text. Spenser may or may not have expected

Iulye.

Morrell.
Ah good *Algrin*, his hap was ill,
but shall be better in time.
Now farewell shepheard, sith thys hyll
thou hast such doubt to climbe.

Palinodes Embleme.
In medio virtus.

Morrells Embleme.
In summo fœlicitas.

GLOSSE.

A Goteheard] By Gotes in scrypture be represented the wicked and reprobate, whose pastour also must needes be such.

Banck] is the seate of honor.

Alsfordo. Clymbe] spoken of Ambition. Michle] much.

necta his verse. Deciunt cella graviore lapis.

The sonne.] A reason, why he refused to dwell on Mountaines, becaue there is no shelter againft the scorching sunne, according to the time of the yeare, whiche is the whoteft moneth of all.

The Cupp and Diademe] Be two signes in the firmament, through which the sonne maketh his course in the moneth of Iuly.

Lion] Thys is Poetically spoken, as if the Sunne did hunt a Lion with one Dogge. The meaning wherof is, that in Iuly the sonne is in Leo At which tyme the Dogge starre, which is called Syrius or Canicula reigneth, with immoderate heate casting Pestilence, drought, and many diseases.

Ouerture] an open place. The word is borrowed of the French, & used in good writers To holden chair] to talke and prate.

A Loorde] was wont among the old Britons to signifie a Lorde. And therefore the Danes that long time usurped theyr Tyrannie here in Bryanie, were called for more dread and dignitie, Lurdanes, Lord Danes. At which time it is sayd, that the insolencie and pryde of that nation was so outragious in thys Realme, that if it fortuned a Briton to be going over a bridge, and sawe the Dane set foote upon the same, he must retoorne back, till the Dane were cleane over: or els bydde the peyce of his disfeisure, which was no lesse, then present death. But being afterwarde expelled that name of Lurdane became so odious vnto the people, whom they had long oppressed, that euen at this daye they vse for moft reproche, to call the Quartane ague the Feuer Lurdane.

Recks much of thy swine] cowns much of thy paynes. VVecclesse] not vnderstode.

S. Michels

S. Michels mount] is a promontorie in the VVeft part of England.

Abul] Parnassus afforesayd. Pan Christ. Dan] One trybe is put for the whole nation per Synecdochen

VVhete Titan] the Sonne. VVhich story is to be redde in Diodorus Syc. of the hyl Ida; from whence he sayth, all night time is to bee seene a mightye fire, as if the skye burned, which toward morning beginneth to gather into a rownd forme, and thereof ryseth the sonne, whome the Poetes call Titan:

The Shepheard] is Endymion, whom the Poets fayne, to haue bene so beloued of Phœbe, the Moone, that he was by her kept asleepe in a caue by the space of xxx. yeares, for to enioye his companye.

There] that is in Paradife, where through error of the shepheards understanding, he sayth, that all the sheatds did vse to feede they flocks, till one, (this is Adam by hys follye and disobedience, made all the reft of hys offspring be debarred & shute out from thence.

Synah] a hill in Arabia, where God appeared.

Our Ladyes bowre] a place of pleasure so called.

Faunes or Sylvanes] be of Poetes feigned to be Gods of the VVoode.

Medway] the name of a Ryuer in Kent, which running by Rochester, meeteth with Thamys, whom he calleth his elder brother, both becaue he is greater, and also falleth sooner into the Sea.

Meyn] mingled. Melampode and Terebinth] be herbes good to cure diseased Gotes. Of these speaketh Mantuane, and of the other Theocritus.

Night heauen] Note the shepheards simplenesse, which supposeth that from the hylls is nearest waye to heauen.

Leau] Lightning, which he taketh for an argument, to proue the nighnes to heauen, becaue the lightning doth comenly light on hygh mountaynes, according to the flying of the Poete. Feriuntque summos fulmina montes.

Lorell] A lorell. A borrell] a playne fellowe. Narre] nearer.
Hale] for hole. Yede] goe. Frowye] musfye or moffie.
Or yore] long agoe. Forewente] gone afore.

The firste shepheard] was Abell the righteous, who (as scripture sayth) bent hys mind to keeping of sheepe, as did hys brother Cain to tilling the grownde.

His keepe] hys charge of his flocke. Lowred] did honour and reuerence.

The brethren] the twelue sonnes of Iacob, by which were the pemisfters, and jwed oue lye thereupon.

Whom Ida] Paris, which being the sonne of Priamus king of Troy, for his mother Hecubas dreame, which being with child of hym, dreamed fhe brought forth a firebrand, that set all the towre of Illium on fire, was caft forth on the hyll Ida; where being fostered of the shepheards, he was in time became a shepheard, and lastly came to knowlege of his parentage.

Alisfe] Helena the wyfe of Menelaus king of Lacedemonia, was by Venus for the golden Aple to her geuen, then promised to Paris, who thereupon with a forte of luftye Troyanes, stole her out of Lacedemonia, and toke her in Troy, which was the caufe of the tenne years warre in Troy, and the moft famous ciye of

H.i.

the *Calender*'s intended readership to find the language of the poems confusing, but E.K. often responds as if the eclogues' readers come from that class of Englishmen who what they "understand not, they streight way deeme to be sencelesse, and not at al to be understood."[18] The glosses are E.K.'s response to this problem, whether it is a real one or simply a convenient rhetorical construct (comments on Chaucer's language in sources contemporary to the *Calender* suggest that either option is a possibility). Their presence speaks to a belief that the full meaning of words and allusions is both available to the editor and essential to the readers' understanding of the work.

E.K.'s annotations lay out a paradigm for the use and explanation of archaic forms of English that will later be adopted by Speght in his *Works*. Equally relevant to the plan of Speght's *Works* is E.K.'s understanding of Chaucer as an authorial figure. The glosses mention Chaucer by name more than a dozen times, often citing him as a source for words used by Spenser. As we have seen, Lydgate is also invoked as a lexical authority of this sort, but Chaucer's preeminent status—the status necessary to elicit a monumental production like the *Works*—is reflected in the sustained comparison of Chaucer to Tityrus, Virgil's poetic persona in the *Eclogues*, that runs throughout E.K.'s commentary.

This comparison first appears in the opening lines of the epistle to Harvey. What seems at first a fairly straightforward statement echoing the incipit of Immeritô's prefatory poem, itself a twofold reference to Chaucer's *Troilus and Criseyde* ("Goe little booke: thy selfe present / As child whose parent is unkent . . ."), immediately foliates into a thicket of reference and citation: "Uncouthe unkiste, Sayde the olde famous Poete Chaucer: whom for his excellencie and wonderfull skil in making, his scholler Lidgate, a worthy scholler of so excellent a maister, calleth the Loadestarre of our Language: and whom our Colin clout in his Æglogue calleth Tityrus the God of shepheards, comparing hym to the worthines of the Roman Tityrus Virgile."[19] In a single sentence, E.K. invokes no fewer than four poets (Chaucer, Lydgate, the author of the *Calender*, and Virgil), four texts (*Troilus and Criseyde*, *Fall of Princes*, the *Calender*, and the *Eclogues*), and two textual personae (Colin Clout and Tityrus).[20] Lydgate (identified here as a "scholler" rather than a poet in his own right, a designation consistent with the way Lydgate is presented in the *Troy Book* preface) reflects Chaucer's aureate glow back upon him and provides a foundational insight that will structure the work's treatment of Chaucer: namely, that his most significant role is as the "Loadestarre of our Language." No sooner has this claim been made, however, than E.K. shifts his focus to the *Calender*'s yoking of Chaucer and Virgil in the figure of Tityrus.

According to the epistle to Gabriel Harvey and the gloss on the Januarye eclogue, Colin Clout is the name under which the ostensibly anonymous poet "secretly shadoweth himself" (the name is borrowed from John Skelton, whose work, especially *Garland of Laurel*, also queries the boundaries between past and present in vernacular poetry).[21] He is identified as a speaker in the Januarye, June, November, and December eclogues. E.K. explains in the epistle that the *Calender*'s author adopts this pastoral persona in imitation of Virgil, who calls himself Tityrus in his eclogues.[22] "Tityrus" also appears within in the *Calender*, first in the Februarie eclogue as the shepherd from whom Thenot "cond" the fable of the Oak and the Briar while "keeping his sheepe on the hils of Kent."[23] He appears a second time at line 81 of the June eclogue as Colin's teacher, the "God of Shepheardes" whose death Colin laments. Though in both cases context seems to indicate a native and, especially in Februarie, a specifically English referent, E.K.'s opening remarks in the epistle remind us that the name also registers as a measure of the *Calender*'s debt to the Virgilian exemplar.[24] The layering of these three—Tityrus, Virgil, and Chaucer—suggests that, while already well established as a model for vernacular poets, Chaucer is being recognized here an exemplar who can sit comfortably alongside, and is indeed in some sense interchangeable with, Virgil himself. This points in turn to a new sense of compatibility between vernacular writing and ancient texts.

In his comments to the eclogues themselves, E.K. treats Tityrus solely as a referent for Chaucer. In his glosses for the Februarie eclogue he writes that by Tityrus, "I suppose he meane Chaucer, whose prayse for pleasaunt tales cannot dye, so long as the memorie of hys name shal live, and the name of Poetrie shal endure," and describes Thenot's tale "as learned of Chaucer."[25] (Thenot says in the eclogue that he "cond" it from Tityrus.) Similarly, in the June eclogue, E.K. writes "that by Tityrus is meant Chaucer, hath bene already sufficiently sayde."[26] Although E.K. does not mention Virgil by name in his comments to the eclogues, his glosses sustain the relationship between Chaucer, Spenser, and Virgil as sketched in the opening lines of the epistle to Harvey. In his capacity as "Tityrus" to Spenser's Colin Clout, Chaucer is both English (like Spenser) and "ancient" (like Virgil), and thus capable of authorizing the *Calender* both as a vernacular work and one with a substantial classical pedigree. Neither Virgil nor Chaucer is mentioned within the verse itself; as Colin Fairweather notes, the articulation of these literary historical relationships is left to E.K. In this sense, the *Calender*'s recuperation of the

English past and promotion of English poetry depend not on the poet but on the editorial figure, whose distance from both the text and its sources allows him to make explicit a connection that, if named within the verse itself, would disrupt the conceit of artistic intimacy between Chaucer/Tityrus and Spenser/Colin.[27] It is in E.K.'s annotations that Chaucer comes into his own as "our poet," a figure who functions meaningfully as a sign of both historical distance and the ability of the later poet to overcome that distance through judicious appropriation.

In annotating Spenser's archaizing text for both its Chaucerian language and its classical allusions, E.K. models editorial strategies that Speght will bring to bear directly on Chaucer's poems. In the *Calender*, as in the *Works*, the prominent presence of commentary signals a desire that the poetry it accompanies be accepted as canonical. Both E.K. and Speght treat Chaucer as a foundational figure in English poetry but, more unusually, Speght also follows E.K. in presenting Chaucer as heir to a classical literary inheritance. The glosses to the *Calender* make little distinction between the ancient and modern poetic inheritance; in the *Works*, these categories merge even further, and verse from the more recent English past is discussed in terms usually applied to works from the distant Latinate past. This lexicographical "gallimaufray or hodgepodge" (to borrow E.K.'s terms for the English language itself) marks both Spenser's *Calender* and Speght's edition of Chaucer as enterprises that consider poetic influence and accomplishment as, necessarily, a hybrid of ancient and native traditions.[28] In the following section, I assess Speght's approach to the "good old Poete" in light of the analytical and interpretive strategies deployed by E.K. on the work of Spenser's "newe poet."

Our Antient and Lerned English Poet, Geffrey Chaucer

In the *Arte of Englishe Poesie*, published in 1589, George Puttenham offers a piece of advice that would seem to place the *Calender* squarely outside the bounds of poetic propriety. "Our maker therfore at these dayes," he writes, "shall not follow *Piers plowman* nor *Gower* nor *Lydgate* nor yet *Chaucer*, for their language is now out of use with us: neither shall he take the termes of Northern-men, such as they use in dayly talke, whether they be noble men or gentlemen, or of their best clarkes all is a matter."[29] Puttenham's comments, and others like them, have prompted several scholars to conclude that language difficulties were a key cause of declining interest in Chaucer's poetry at the close of the sixteenth century. While Chaucer was still widely revered as the proverbial father of English poetry, according to Alice Miskimin, "the increasing obscurity of [Chaucer's] language at first parallels, and then outruns, the reverence of posterity."[30] The linguist Johan Kerling also espouses this view, arguing that "the relative absence of comments upon the incomprehensibility of Chaucer's language in the first half of the sixteenth century is significant—as is also the gradual increase in the second half in the number of comments in which Chaucer's language is said to be 'out of use,' 'no longer with us,' etc.: during the century Chaucer clearly became increasingly difficult to understand. The very fact that Spenser used a considerable number of Chaucerian words, *with glosses*, shows that these words—and, by extension, Chaucer's language—had become difficult to understand."[31] While Kerling aptly characterizes a trend in comments on Chaucer's language, it is important to remember that comments like Puttenham's, as well as E.K.'s glosses, have a prescriptive as well as descriptive dimension. Whatever practical help they may offer, by labeling Chaucer's language as antique, E.K. makes a rhetorical intervention that situates Chaucer in a specific literary and historical context. Though certainly reflective of real changes in the English language, the linguistic otherness attributed to Chaucer in the sixteenth century was also constructed in critical discourse and subsequently took on the appearance of self-evident fact in glossaries, lexicons, and word lists.[32] E.K. reveals as much, when he explains that he has provided explanations not only for words that might be "unknown" to readers, but also for those whose antiquity might be "not marked" in the usual course of reading. Likewise, Speght's hard word list includes words in contemporary usage, like "belt," that would have been more likely to pass "unmarked" than appear "unknown," since they are commonly used in early modern English. In both books, glossaries and annotations not only explain the text but insist that the text *needs* explanation.

Both in the *Calender* and in the *Works*, words identified as Chaucerian are treated as a genuinely older form of English, not as a poetic conceit. In the *Calender*, such language provides linguistic material for Spenser's shepherds; in the *Works*, linguistic antiquity becomes a sign of the durability of the English poetic tradition. The commentary on it, accordingly, highlights Chaucer's chronological distance from sixteenth-century readers, as well as the cultural rupture that separates them. The *Works'* treatment of Chaucer's language places him in a very particular version of the past—his own past, the Age of Chaucer *avant la lettre*—that is both distinguished from the present and made accessible and connected to that present through the efforts of learned commentators like Speght.

In the dedicatory epistle to the revised 1602 version, which includes an expanded glossary, two new texts, and several other enhancements, Speght surveys the changes from the 1598 edition and concludes, "I have reformed the whole Worke, whereby Chaucer for the most part is restored to his owne Antiquitie."[33] Insofar as "Antiquitie" implies historical distance, Speght's claim to return Chaucer to it seems at odds with the interpretive materials that Speght tells readers he has labored to perfect and that are presumably there to make the poetry they accompany more accessible to readers. Restoring Chaucer "to his owne Antiquitie" is, however, a crucial step in the "reform[ing]" of Chaucer's works at the turn of the seventeenth century, one that creates a version of the past best suited to the needs of the present.[34]

More so than earlier, less precise forms of commentary, the *Works'* scholarly apparatus provides Speght with the opportunity to define what, exactly, constitutes Chaucer's "owne Antiquitie" by selecting aspects of his poems that are both in need of and suited to further explication. For example, Speght includes a list of the Greek and Latin authors cited by Chaucer, but no measure of his references to saints or engagement with the liturgical calendar.[35] To restore Chaucer "to his owne Antiquitie" is to exile him from the present and yet by doing so create an opportunity to bring him back to that present in a specific capacity that serves current needs and values. Ultimately, the "Antiquitie" to which Speght claims to restore Chaucer is as much a product of the sixteenth-century understanding of the past as it is of Chaucer himself.

This dynamic is clearly visible in the address to the reader that follows the dedication to Sir Robert Cecil in both the 1598 and 1602 versions of the *Works*. In the address, Speght explains Chaucer's writing in terms of classical rhetoric, placing his emphasis less on lexis than on syntax and morphology. Speght's discussion transforms the alterity of these elements of Chaucer's verse from evidence of obsolescence into a symptom of the poet's own anticipation of the future of English poetry.[36] Speght acknowledges that Chaucer's poetic sophistication may be less than self-evident to his readers, and he begins his address accordingly, warning readers in the 1602 version that they "must not condemne in [Chaucer] as a fault" the corruption of Latin and Greek names. Instead, he writes, Chaucer's nonstandard spelling should be considered *metaplasmus*, or "metaplasm" (Richard Mulcaster benignly defines the rhetorical term as "alterations of the words form and favor").[37] Speght thus transforms erratic transliteration (and possible errors in transmission) into a sophisticated poetic device authorized by classical precedent, neatly sidestepping the near-synonym *barbarismus* and its potentially negative connotations.[38] This justification by appeal to classical rhetorical precept is analogous to E.K.'s Ciceronian explanation for Spenser's archaisms in the epistle to Harvey. Even more remarkably, Speght identifies Chaucer's double negatives as imitative of constructions found in ancient Greek (a language Chaucer did not know): "it is his manner likewise, imitating the Greekes, by two negatives to cause a greater negation: as, I ne said none ill."[39] In both cases, Speght explains Chaucer's "old and obscure" words not by stressing their connection with present-day English, but by arguing that Chaucer's verse represents an English writer's contribution to an ancient tradition.

This formulation keeps Chaucer at the head of an English poetic tradition by attributing to the medieval writer the artistic mastery to which his sixteenth-century successors aspire, in the terms in which they aspire to it. Although Speght sees the language of Chaucer's text as outdated, he treats the authorial figure behind it as very much present. Chaucer, once again, carries with him a certain untimeliness or temporal slipperiness that allows him to be both historically distant and, especially when it comes to the affective bonds that link him to his later readers, close to the present. As a result of this affective proximity, Speght can write of Chaucer as though he approaches language in the same way a contemporary poet might, treating obvious differences from prevailing linguistic norms as though they are deliberate and fall under the scope of Chaucer's poetic prerogative.[40]

The presentist perspective that views Chaucer's work as more or less equivalent to that of a contemporary poet extends to issues of versification as well. Later in the address, Speght writes that the "skilfull Reader" of Chaucer's lines can "scan them in their nature" and find appropriate meter in them. Any irrefutable irregularities are the result not of Chaucer's error or linguistic change but of textual corruption due to the "negligence and rape of Adam Scrivener."[41] In support of his claim, Speght cites Chaucer's own words from the fifth book of *Troilus and Criseyde*:

> And for there is so great diversitie
> In English, and in writing of our tongue,
> So pray I God, that none miswrite thee,
> Ne thee mismetre for defaut of tongue, &c.[42]

According to Speght, these lines are proof "how fearfull [Chaucer] was to have his works miswritten, or his verse mismeasured." The possibility of textual corruption, raised by the poet himself, enables Speght to imagine an idealized Chaucerian text that is perfectly and perpetually metrical.[43] If the surviving text fails to measure up to these ideals, then Speght has recourse to Chaucer's own prophetic prediction of future textual corruption to explain the deficiency. The utility of this is clear: Speght's transforms his editorial interventions, intended to undo the "injuries of time, ignorance of writers and negligence of Printers," into an act of fidelity to Chaucer himself.[44] With the specter of corruption raised by *Adam Scriveyn* at the forefront of the reader's mind, the emendations made by Speght and other later editors can be justified on the grounds that they are what Chaucer himself would have wanted.

Speght closes the epistle in 1602 by committing "to your wonted favor this our Poet, and what here is done, for the Poets sake."[45] Speght frames his labor as an attempt to return Chaucer to the age in which he rightfully belongs, an age that is constituted by the fact that he belongs in it. To restore Chaucer to *his own* antiquity through glossaries, biographies, and other interpretive devices does more than "restore antiquity to Britaine, and Britaine to her antiquity," as antiquarian William Camden sets out to do in his *Britannia*. In Speght's formulation, Chaucer does not stand in synecdochically for a broader body of vernacular literary production, but rather becomes the literature of that period *in toto* (so, too, his canon steadily expands in the Renaissance, absorbing more and more writing now attributed to his contemporaries or considered anonymous).[46] The chief literary production of the Age of Chaucer, as Speght tautologically presents it, is the work of Geoffrey Chaucer. In his dedication and address to the reader, Speght claims a privileged understanding of this work, much as E.K. presumes to speak on behalf of the anonymous poet of the *Shepheardes Calender*.

Vinewed Words

Speght is the addressee, rather than the author, of the third and final prefatory epistle, written by his college friend Francis Beaumont.[47] Beaumont's ostensible purpose is to exhort Speght to publish his work on Chaucer, but he takes this opportunity both to defend Chaucer's writing and to examine the role Speght's commentary might play in improving opinions of it. Like Speght, Beaumont emphasizes the relationship between Chaucer's language and that of the Greek and Latin past and stakes his strongest claims for Chaucer's significance on his ability to measure up to ancient models. These models also provide the material for rebuttals to two criticisms, both involving language and style, that Beaumont hopes Speght's efforts will counteract by offering readers more guidance in their encounter with Chaucer. These are, first, "that many of [Chaucer's] words are become (as it were) vinewed [moldy] & hoarie with overlong lying" and, second, "that some of his speeches are somwhat too broad & plaine; and that the worke therfore should be the lesse gratious."[48]

Beaumont addresses this first concern by drawing a schematic distinction between languages "contained in learning" and vernaculars used in daily speech. According to Beaumont, in the "learned tongues," meaning is fixed and static, since "they having *Testamentario jure* [i.e., the ability to be used in a court of law], their legacies set downe by them that be dead, words must be retained and continued in them in such sorte as they were left, without alteration of the Testators willes in any thing." In the "languages of common practice," by contrast, "choise of words are, and ever will be subject unto change, never standing at one stay, but somtimes casting away old words, sometimes renewing of them, and alwaies framing of new."[49] Beaumont concludes that, when it comes to vernacular language, "no man can so write in them, as that all his words may remaine currant many yeeres." Linguistic mutability is inevitable in vernacular tongues; language change is outside the control of individual actors.

In a move that recalls the twinned epigraphs from Chaucer and Ovid that grace the 1598 title page (Figure 7), Beaumont supports his claims about language with a two-pronged appeal to Chaucerian and classical authority. First, he cites Horace's *Ars Poetica*, in which the Latin poet "declareth that wordes in common tongues, like unto leaves must of necessitie have their buddings, their blossomings, their ripenings, and their fallings."[50] Following this, he cites *Troilus and Criseyde* 2.22–26 as it appears in Speght:

> I [*sic*] know that in fourme of speech is chaunge
> Within a hundreth [*sic*] yeere, and words tho
> That hadden price, now wonder nice and straunge
> Thinke we them, and yet they spake them so,
> And sped as well in love, as men now do.[51]

Chaucer is referring here to the longer evolution of Latin into vernacular tongues, but Beaumont reads this as testimony concerning inevitable change within vernaculars after "so long a time" (he takes his quotation from Speght or another early edition, which describes the time passed as a century, rather than the millennium indicated in modern editions and the authoritative manuscripts). By juxtaposing Chaucer's own words with those of Horace, Beaumont presents a poet who imitates the ancients, anticipates the moderns, and so provides a link between the two.

Somewhat surprisingly given his earlier comments regarding the fixity of the learned tongues, Beaumont goes on to describe Chaucer's linguistic obscurity as a fate shared by many Latin writers. "Impossible it was," he writes,

> that either *Chaucer* could, or any man living can keepe words of unlearned tongues from falling after so long a time. And this hath happened amongst the Latine writers themselves when theirs was a spoken tongue, as ours now is, who though they first made their owne words, and gave them their allowance, yet diverse of *Cecilius, Statius, Ennius* and *Plautus* were by later Latinists rejected: and now againe many of them, by the last writers of all (though before, as it were by Proclamation, put downe for basenesse) are upon a new touch warranted for good, and pass abroad as sterling.[52]

As it further classicizes Chaucer, this comparison reinforces a sense of historical distance between the medieval poet and the early modern reader by aligning his fate with that of the Latin writers. The boundary between Beaumont's present and the past writ large is, in this formulation, much less fluid than the boundary between Chaucer's past and antiquity. Beaumont's epistle also, rather remarkably, deposes Latin from its position as the fixed pole against which the mutability of vernacular languages can be measured, raising unanswered questions as to whether linguistic permanence is, in the absence of editorial assistance, an attainable ideal. Neither Beaumont nor Speght ever describes Chaucer as having made use of archaic words, as E.K. explains the *Calender*'s poet has done. Instead, Beaumont does E.K. one better, casting Chaucer not as an imitator of the ancients, but as one who shares in their obsolescence (and, presumably, in their fortunate restoration at the hands of humanist scholars and latter-day poets).

Although he emphasizes the connection between Chaucer and classical writers, Beaumont does not neglect Chaucer's relationship to English poets. In a passage that evokes the opening lines of E.K.'s epistle to Harvey, and even mentions Spenser by name, Beaumont begins by noting, "so pure were

Figure 7. Title page, *The Workes of our Antient and Learned English poet, Geffrey Chaucer, newly Printed* (1598); STC 5079. By permission of the Folger Shakespeare Library.

Chaucers words in his daies, as *Lidgate* that learned man, calleth him The Loadstarre of the English language."[53] Beaumont regards Chaucer's purity as both transhistorical (Beaumont never considers that Lydgate might mean something different than he does by "the English language") and well suited to emulation.[54] Significantly, he locates this purity not in the form or subject of Chaucer's writing, but in his words. Of these, Beaumont writes in the epistle that, "so good they are in our daies, as Maister *Spencer* (following the counsaile of *Tullie* in his third book *De Oratore*, for reviving of auncient wordes) hath adorned his stile with that beautie and gravitie, that *Tullie* there speakes of: and his much frequenting of *Chaucers* auncient words, with his excellent imitation of diverse places in him, is not the least helpe that hath made him reach so hie, as many learned men doe thinke, that no Poet either French or Italian deserves second place under him."[55] While this passage credits Chaucer with Spenser's success to a remarkable degree, Beaumont's own writing owes a debt to the *Shepheardes Calender*, insofar as E.K. has influenced his own views on Chaucer. In this passage, Beaumont's choice of allusions, phrasing, and argument are all drawn from E.K.'s comments in the epistle to Harvey, although he does not quote it directly.[56]

Beaumont does not mention Cicero by name, either, but the precepts of "Tullie" nevertheless are crucial to his account, as they are in E.K.'s assessment of Spenser's verse. In the *Calender*, Ciceronian rhetoric justifies the use of archaic words, which are treated as broadly Chaucerian. By juxtaposing one of Chaucer's contemporaries (Lydgate) with a sixteenth-century writer (Spenser) and a classical *auctor* (Cicero), Beaumont sketches out a narrative of Chaucerian reception that extends both forward toward the present and, anachronistically, backward into the past. Here, as in the *Calender*, Cicero proleptically authorizes Spenser's use of Chaucer. This narrative, which emphasizes Spenser's debt to Chaucer, is at odds with the teleological emergence of the "new poet" as described by E.K. and is perhaps intended to rebut it. In the 1598 version of Beaumont's epistle, which appeared before Spenser's death in 1599, Beaumont drily notes that Spenser's use of "Chaucers auntient speeches" has caused "many to allow farre better of him, then otherwise they would."[57] The 1602 version, though more moderate in its claims, also identifies Spenser as "much frequenting" Chaucer's words. While few readers familiar with the *Calender* would question this, and while Beaumont is clearly championing Chaucer in this epistle, the fact that Beaumont makes this reference to Spenser at all represents a shift from praise of Chaucer in absolute terms to a more presentist, relational view that sees value not just in his

influence on but in his usefulness to later writers. While careful not to dis-
lodge Chaucer from his foundational place in literary history, Beaumont understands Chaucer's significance in light of what his work has enabled later poets
to do.

A particular regard for the antiquity of Chaucer's language, along with
its excellence, distinguishes the praises of Beaumont and Speght (along
with other late sixteenth-century commentators such as Sidney) from earlier
encomiums to the poet's words. Their view, in turn, made it newly possible to
contemplate the ways that Chaucer's poetics might be seen as compatible with
classical poetic strategies. Such a development could have been sparked earlier in the century by the efforts of earlier humanist admirers of Chaucer like
the poet and antiquary John Leland (whose Latin poetry compares Chaucer
with the mythical founders of the Greek and Latin tongues, as well as with
Dante and Petrarch). Significantly, however, it was only after Spenser had
brought together the classical and the Chaucerian, and won wide recognition
for it, that commentators like Speght and Beaumont began to search for, and
find, these rhetorical and poetic devices in Chaucer's writing. Their desire
to find traces of antiquity in the writings of England's most famous native
poet mirrors the interest that William Camden's *Britannia*, that paradigmatic
work of sixteenth-century English antiquarianism, takes in uncovering the
ancient inhabitants of the British Isles.

In his letter to Speght, however, Beaumont looks not only backward to
classical antecedent, but forward to the present, ultimately casting Spenser as
the poetic epitome of "our daies," whose stature goes unquestioned at a time
when Chaucer's fame appears to be waning. Though Beaumont writes in praise
of Chaucer, his reliance on E.K. as he theorizes Chaucer's literary achievements
hints at concern about the ongoing relevance of medieval poetry to contemporary literature. The use of Spenser in his letter suggests that, by 1598,
Chaucer had as much to gain from linguistic association with the "newe" poet
as Spenser did from successfully linking himself to the "well of English undefiled" some twenty years earlier.[58]

Beaumont addresses the second major criticism, "the incivilitie *Chaucer* is
charged withall," with a more direct comparison to the classics, finding Chaucer to be no more offensive than his received test of Virgil ("in his *Priapus* . . .
worse by a thousand degrees"), Ovid, Horace, Catullus, or the elegist Tibullus.
Furthermore, if Chaucer shares the vices of the Latins, he also partakes of their
virtues: according to Beaumont, the "low" language of certain pilgrims in the
Canterbury Tales derives only from Chaucer's desire to observe decorum, after the

fashion of the Roman comedians.[59] Beaumont discovers proof of the author's artistic intent in his own words, invoking Chaucer's exculpation of his broad speech in the *General Prologue* as he asks permission of the reader to "plainly speake" of his subjects, and citing as well the *Manciple's Tale*'s quotation of the Platonic dictum that "the word must cosin be to the working."[60] Here, as in E.K.'s epistle in the *Calender*, an appeal to decorum is used to explain the author's deviation from what would seem to be standard poetic practice.

Like Speght's treatment of Chaucer's rhetoric in the address to the reader, Beaumont's understanding of Chaucer's decorum implies a temporal scheme in which the Chaucerian past is firmly separated from the present by virtue of its language, even as that same language, in its fidelity to precedent established by Greek and Latin texts, transcends the divide between the two. For Beaumont, the obscurity and obscenity of the "low" language of characters like the Reeve and Miller is a symptom of the rudeness of the majority of people living in the time at which Chaucer wrote of higher (i.e., ancient) subjects like Troilus and Criseyde. Beaumont muses that "no man can imagine in his so large compasse, purposing to describe all Englishmens humors living in those daies, how it had been possible for him to have left untouched their filthy delights; or in discovering their desires, how to have exprest them without some of their words."[61] Though these rude words are used, rather than invented, by Chaucer, their presence in his writing contributes to a respect for decorum that links Chaucer and the great writers of the Latin past.[62]

Beaumont sees Chaucer as a writer who combines the sententiousness and gravity of the classical tradition with wholly original English elements, making him "the pith and sinowes of Eloquence, and very life itselfe of all mirth and pleasant writing."[63] In Beaumont's view, Speght's edition of the *Works* is important because it recognizes and communicates this to readers, along with a better understanding of the text itself, imbuing the volume with the potential to advance powerfully the interests of English writing in a multilingual literary world.[64] With this in mind, Beaumont poses a further challenge to Speght, asking whether, "seeing not onely all Greeke and Latine Poets have had their interpretours, and the most of them translated into our tongue, but the French also and Italian, as *Guillaume de Salust*, that most divine French Poet; *Petrarke* and *Ariosto*, those two excellent Italians . . . shall onely *Chaucer*, our ancient Poet, nothing inferiour to the best, amongst all the Poets of the world, remaine alwaies neglected, and never be so well understood of his owne countrie men, as Strangers are?"[65] The concern that Chaucer might be overlooked and underinterpreted, not only in comparison to Greek and Latin writers, but also to the best writing in contemporary vernaculars, recalls the nationalistic emphasis of the dedicatory preface to the 1532 *Works* (reprinted in Speght between the end of the *Life of Chaucer* and the beginning of the *Canterbury Tales*). Here, Beaumont suggests that estrangement from Chaucer's poetry severs a link with the literary past that is necessary if English is to achieve the same status as Greek, Latin, and Romance languages, a link that has already been described by E.K. in the *Calender* and that had been addressed in John Leland's Latin commentary as early as the 1530s. Like E.K., Beaumont's anxiety is that Chaucer's language may be passed over as "unknowen, or as not marked." Beaumont retains a deep investment in the presentation of Chaucer as a viable and accessible poet, and he views both the *Works'* classicizing measures and its linguistic explications as steps toward this goal. As in Speght's notes, however, the content of Chaucer's poetry remains largely elided: ultimately, for Beaumont, the point of Speght's edition is not the reproduction of the text at all. Rather, its significance lies in its presentation and annotation of a national poet's works, identifying and praising in the poems of the "old poete" many of the same features that E.K. finds so appealing in the *Calender*.

The attention given to Chaucer's language in the biographical sketch that follows these epistles is one measure of how central the poet's use of the English language was to assessments of his enduring importance. In the *Life of Chaucer*, the poet appears not just as a passive "well of English undefiled" but as the deliberate architect of a national vernacular. Speght writes,

> Chaucer had alwaies an earnest desire to enrich and beautifie our
> English tongue, which in those daies was very rude and barren:
> and this he did, following the example of *Dantes* and *Petrarch*, who
> had done the same for the Italian tongue; *Alanus* for the French;
> and *Johannes Mena* for the Spanish: neither was Chaucer inferior to
> any of them in the performance hereof: And England in this
> respect is much beholden to him, as *Leland* well noteth:
> > *Anglia Chaucerum veneratur nostra poetam,*
> > *Cui veneres debet patria lingua suas.*[66]

This passage brings to the fore the comparative, vernacular dimension of the *Works'* treatment of Chaucer's language. By detailing the ways in which Chaucer adapts classical standards of eloquence and rhetoric to vernacular poetry, Speght and Beaumont (as well as Stow) are also arguing for the poet's significance in comparison to the leading poets in other vernaculars. Although Speght's editorial apparatus suggest he recognizes Chaucer's debt to Latin and French models, here, Chaucer's imitation of other "great authors" such as Dante is carefully distinguished from lexical borrowing, in order to allow for the dual fantasy of Chaucer's "pure" English and his direct, linear imitation of classical literature.[67]

The final section of the *Life of Chaucer* collects a variety of epigraphs and other verses in praise of Chaucer, beginning with Lydgate and Thomas Hoccleve and ending with Spenser. Speght's summary of Spenser's debt to Chaucer is of particular note because it demonstrates how deeply Spenser is implicated in the *Works'* own understanding of Chaucer's relevance to contemporary English poetics:

> Master *Spenser* in his first Eglogue of his Shepheards Kalender, calleth him *Titirus*, the god of Shepheards, comparing him to the worthinesse of the Romane Titirus Virgil. In his Faerie Queene . . . he termeth him, Most renowmed and Heroicall Poet: and his writings, The works of heavenly wit: concluding his commendation in this manner:
> > Dan Chaucer, Well of English, undefiled,
> > On Fames eternall beadrole worthy to be filed.
> > I follow here the footing of thy feet,
> > That with thy meaning so I may the rather meet.[68]

Significantly, the passage refers to Spenser's use of Tityrus as a figure for both Chaucer and Virgil. As discussed above, this comparison takes place not in the verse, but in E.K.'s commentary, meaning that those preparing Chaucer's poetry for publication in the 1590s were familiar not just with the *Faerie Queene* and the *Shepheardes Calender*, but with the paratextual apparatus as well.

Glossing Chaucer's Hard Words

Previous editions of the *Works* assumed that, given an accurate text of Chaucer's poems, readers would be able to interpret his poems without help. Speght's editions did not make this assumption. Instead, they began to claim Chaucer's writings as the province of the scholar, fit for the more general reader only after they had been outfitted with a significant amount of explanatory material. This

explanatory material appears necessary, in part, because of the increased historical distance that the Speght *Works* attribute to Chaucer, especially
where language is concerned. But the glosses and annotations introduced by
Speght also have a role to play in constructing the very sense of historical difference that they purport to resolve.

The discussions of Chaucer's language described above show this dynamic
in action, as does the glossary, a now-familiar feature of printed editions of
Chaucer that was first introduced in Speght. No longer do Chaucer's archaisms pass unglossed (or, in E.K.'s term, "not marked"). By appending a list of
"hard words" and explaining them with contemporary synonyms, Speght anticipates an influential and long-lasting lexicographic emphasis in Chaucerian scholarship, but he also inherits a Spenserian sensitivity to archaic words
within English.[69] Like E.K.'s glosses, Speght's list of hard words focuses on a
subset of language distinguished neither by its occupational use (as in lists of
terms of art) nor by cultural associations (as in canting pamphlets or glossaries of foreign words). Instead, the distinguishing feature of the terms in
Speght's list of hard words is their purported status as archaic English, signaled by their appearance in the Chaucerian text.

The hard word list appended to Speght's *Works* is a substantial undertaking by any measure, running to forty-two folio columns in the 1598 version
and sixty-six in the expanded and revised 1602 version. Other collections of
Middle English "hard words" do exist, at least one of which, printed on the
final leaf of a 1560 edition of the anonymous fifteenth-century poem *Pierce
the Plowmans Crede*, antedates both the *Shepheardes Calender* and Speght's
Chaucer.[70] That glossary, however, includes fewer than fifty headwords, far
fewer than the scores of notes on archaic language in E.K.'s glosses or the thou-
sands found in Speght.

In its original 1598 form, Speght's list of "the old and obscure words of
Chaucer, explaned" contains approximately two thousand entries, each glossed
with one or two contemporary synonyms, and an adjacent "annotations and
corrections" section with additional explanatory material and a few textual
notes. The glossary seems to have been somewhat hastily prepared: the alphabetization, generally by the first and second letter only, is not without errors,
and there are often multiple headwords for variant spellings of the same word.
This is true although, as Johan Kerling notes, the representative distribution
of entries across the alphabet suggests the compiler was working somewhat
systematically from the text.[71] The 1602 revision improves the alphabetization,

removes duplicates, incorporates the annotations and corrections (many supplied by Francis Thynne, whose criticism Speght acknowledges in the revised dedicatory epistle), and adds more than four hundred new entries to the list. Small initials are also added to some entries, to mark those words "that either are, by nature or derivation, Arabick, Greek, Latine, Italian, French, Dutch, or Saxon," bringing the characteristic antiquarian analytical mode of etymology to bear on Chaucer's language and, as Camden does in his *Britannia*, stressing the hybrid nature of the English tongue.[72] Although the average gloss in Speght is much shorter than those found in the *Calender*, a revised and expanded number of annotations (printed in a separate section in 1598) are now incorporated into the word list. Visually, the overall effect is not unlike E.K.'s glosses (compare Figures 7 and 8).[73]

Speght's lists predate Robert Cawdrey's *A Table Alphabeticall* (1604), often regarded as the first English dictionary, but they play a significant role in shaping perceptions of the history of English for decades to come. As Jürgen Schäfer has demonstrated, terms drawn from Speght constitute the bulk of the archaic words marked in John Bullokar's *English Expositor* (1616; the words taken from Speght are distinguished by an asterisk) and John Minsheu's *Ductor in Linguas* (1617; the words are labeled as "Chaucerian").[74] Furthermore, as Johan Kerling has shown, through an often-unmarked process of borrowing and reworking, a corpus of Speghtian words make their way into dictionaries published as late as 1696. Speght's decisions about what words to gloss and how to define them, then, continue to influence readers very far removed from the *Works'* initial audience. New "old words" were added to later dictionaries over time, but much as Chaucer himself remained the central figure in the Middle English literary canon, so too his words remain central to later understandings of the Middle English lexicon. As in the sixteenth century, perceptions about Chaucer's language and perceptions about his literary historical importance work to reinforce one another.

Like E.K.'s glosses, the lexicon in the Speght *Works* directs the readers' attention to particular words used in the main text and, as in the *Calender*, the accompanying paratextual material alerts readers to the importance of such words. In the *Works*, the dedication to Cecil, address to the readers, and letter from Beaumont all argue that Chaucer's language expresses a particular set of literary values and that it should be valued and studied because of this. In the *Calender*, E.K.'s epistle to Harvey and glosses to the eclogues emphasize the poet's complex engagement with his poetic forefathers and his skilled

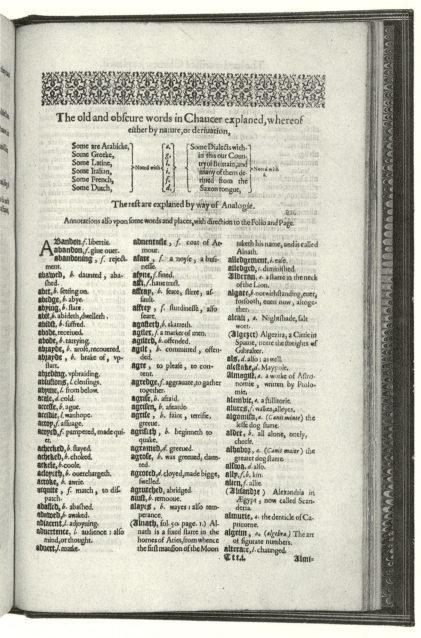

Figure 8. "The old and obscure words in Chaucer explaned," from *The Workes of our Ancient and learned English Poet, Geffrey Chaucer, newly Printed* (1602), sig. 3T1; STC 5080. By permission of the Folger Shakespeare Library.

use of archaisms. Although Speght's commentary deals with a medieval text and E.K.'s addresses a text that merely *looks* medieval, both volumes stage historical distance between the language of the presumed reader and the language of the text itself, while directing attention to the editorial figure as a means of bridging this gap. This gives that editorial figure an opportunity to interpret, frame, and praise the work upon which he comments. Should the reader encounter these texts unawares, both E.K. and Speght's commentary announces the linguistic challenge posed by archaic language and insists upon the difficulty of the poetry at hand. At the same time, however, in both cases they posit that difficulty and the historical distance that it signals (or seems to signal, in the case of Spenser) as easy enough to overcome through humanistic editorial practices. The crucial difference between the two is that while E.K. presumes to annotate words that have been chosen by the poet as archaic, Speght sets out to annotate words that were contemporary when Chaucer's poems were written, but whose significance has shifted over time and whose present importance hangs as much on their perceived antiquity as on their poetic value.

Unlike E.K., who provides a mixture of one-word synonyms and longer comments that better fit the heading of "glosse," Speght's list generally presents one Chaucerian word (in black-letter) and one contemporary alternative, with occasional additional exposition. The one-to-one correspondence between Chaucer's words and the contemporary synonyms that the glossary supplies would seem to reflect a fairly strict distinction between Chaucer's English and the English of Speght's day, but the fact that one signifier can merely substitute for another also suggests the two forms of the language are imagined as quite congruent even if separated. Derek Pearsall is careful to note that, while the glossary itself was certainly helpful to the reader, Speght's commentary rarely goes beyond the level of detailed knowledge that could be expected of any well-educated person.[75] Such well-educated readers, like the men with whom Speght and Beaumont attended Cambridge, would seem to be the principal market for the *Works*, and they would be unlikely to lack the resources to discern the allusions pointed out by Speght, or to require translation of Chaucer's Latin and French phrases, as Speght offers in the 1602 folio.[76]

An annotated edition of Chaucer's *Works* would have, no doubt, appeared at some point, but Speght's is formed and shaped by the *Calender*'s precedent. And yet, as much as Speght's annotations may owe to them, E.K.'s teasing glosses these are not: whereas E.K. often tantalizes the reader by highlighting what it is that will *not* be revealed, the glossaries and Speght's commentary in general emphasize what has already been announced on the title page—that Chaucer is an ancient, learned, and, yes, English poet, both in language and origin. The real function of the glossary and the related commentary on Chaucer's language is to insist upon the legibility of these characteristics in Chaucer's verse, specifically in his words. In this way, Speght's glossary can be understood as part of a larger effort to situate Chaucer's writings within an increasingly dense and multifaceted matrix of knowledge about language, history, and the poet himself, an effort inspired, in part, by Spenser's use of Chaucerian language.[77] In the *Works*, this endeavor extends to other parts of the apparatus, including the biography, depictions of Chaucer's coat of arms and family tree, and references to Chaucer in chronicle histories, but Chaucer's language remains at its center. Indeed, if one follows the claims made by Speght and Beaumont in the prefatory materials, the legibility of the entire project depends upon the proper exposition of his words.

*　*　*

Habits of literary analysis often presume an easy distinction between the primary text and commentary upon it, and between poetic and scholarly writing. Viewed in light of one another, the *Shepheardes Calender* and Speght's *Works* suggest that these distinctions are less clear-cut than they may at first appear, and that they can be manipulated by both poet and editor. While Spenser's use of Chaucer has always been recognized, a tendency to limit our concept of influence to the composition of texts rather than their presentation and re-presentation has led us to overlook the ways that Spenser shaped the ways that Speght and his antiquarian contemporaries understood Chaucer. Commentary shapes the self-conception of editors as much as their understanding of their subjects: E.K. provides Speght with not only a model for writing about Chaucer's text but a model for understanding his own role as commentator. While Speght's edition, recognizably similar to our own critical text, may lead us to hail him as an early practitioner of textual scholarship, a closer examination of the debt he owes to E.K. and the *Calender* reveals the poetic grounds of his literary history.

If Spenser's work in the *Shepheardes Calender* and Speght's efforts in the *Works* show how a poetic enterprise (whether authorial or editorial) might shade into antiquarianism, the writings of the herald and antiquary Francis Thynne, to which I turn in the next chapter, tell us something about what this flexible boundary might look like from the perspective of a scholar.

Responding to Speght's edition of the *Works*, Thynne's *Animadversions* takes Speght to task for a litany of perceived scholarly faults, but a consideration of Thynne's long and prolific career and his writings in both prose and verse show his antiquarian efforts and poetic investments to be deeply and sometimes surprisingly intertwined.

CHAPTER 5

Chaucer's Herald

The Work of Francis Thynne

Francis Thynne (ca. 1545–1608) was an antiquarian, herald, and the son of William Thynne, the courtier who oversaw the first collected edition of Chaucer's *Works*. The younger Thynne was a prolific, if not particularly gifted, writer on a wide array of antiquarian subjects, including Chaucer. His best-known work, *Animadversions uppon the Annotacions and Corrections of some imperfections of impressiones of Chaucers workes (sett downe before tyme, and nowe) reprinted in the yere of oure lorde 1598*, is a long open letter addressed to Thomas Speght that outlines a variety of oversights and errors that Thynne perceived in the 1598 edition of the *Works*. From the perspective of modern literary criticism, the *Animadversions* is a failure: it is myopic, pedantic, and frequently factually incorrect. For all its shortcomings, however, the *Animadversions* makes it clear that Thynne regarded Chaucer's writings as a subject of serious historical, scholarly inquiry. Like Camden's *Britannia* or Holinshed's *Chronicles*, Thynne's work on Chaucer can be understood as an attempt to recover a previously unclaimed part of British history and thereby construct a common past that meets the needs of the present. While the full commentary on Chaucer that Thynne hoped to undertake was never realized, the records we have of his career in antiquarian circles provide ample context for understanding the scholarly stakes of his writing on Chaucer.

Thynne's life and career intersected with those of a several of well-known antiquarians, including John Stow, Abraham Fleming, and William Camden. His collection of emblems and epigrams, compiled the year after the *Animadversions* in 1600, contains a number of poems that offer insight into Thynne's community of fellow antiquarians and their shared interests. These poems also provide a more expansive context for the two poems by Thynne included with the revised 1602 edition of Speght's *Works*, "On the Picture of Chaucer" and "Of the Animadversions upon Chaucer." These more expressive articulations of literary and scholarly affinity overlap in tone and theme, if not in form, with Thynne's written comments on Chaucer in the *Animadversions*. Thynne's commentary there applies the habits and practices of antiquarian scholarship to Chaucer and his writings, as well as to Speght's annotations on them. Considered as whole, Thynne's writings show how, by treating Chaucer as a subject of history, antiquarian commentary worked effectively to secure his lasting reputation as an author.

Thynne's interest in Chaucer was admittedly personal, given the family connection, but his work nonetheless represents a sustained effort to think about the ways that other kinds of knowledge—linguistic, historical, numismatic, geographical—can improve understanding of Chaucer and his texts. For Thynne, commentary like the *Animadversions* was not only a necessary but also a deeply meaningful way of preserving Chaucer for future readers, one that actively sought to knit Chaucer's Middle English text to an increasingly dense web of knowledge about the English past. Thynne's writings on Chaucer show a willingness to question sources that is new to the scholarly response to Chaucer's life and works, and represent the very beginning (or perhaps the prehistory) of a scholarly approach to Middle English writers and texts. Thynne's version of Chaucer scholarship, more critical and more invested in secondary sources than earlier commentators, in certain ways looks much like our own. His approach was not a conscious innovation, however, but rather was the result of a lifetime of antiquarian study, a deep familiarity with the norms and practices of early modern English historiography, and two hundred years of celebration of Chaucer's place in English poetry.

As the acknowledged head of the English poetic tradition, Chaucer was a natural literary subject for an antiquarian. The preface to William Thynne's edition of the *Works* and Leland's commentary in *De Viris Illustribus* both celebrate Chaucer not only as a great poet, but as an indispensable figure in the development of English language and identity. John Stow's 1561 edition of the *Works* shows that Chaucer could fit into an active scholarly career devoted to antiquarian pursuits. Speght's 1598 edition, with its glossary and explanatory materials, hazarded something like a scholarly edition of the Middle English text. Francis Thynne's work built on all of this.

However lofty his ambitions may have been, Thynne's efforts were not wholly altruistic. According to the *Animadversions*, in the 1590s the younger

Thynne planned to produce an updated version of his father's text and, as Thomas Speght puts it, "had a purpose . . . to set out Chaucer with a Coment in our tonge, as the Italians have *Petrarke* and others in their language."[1] Unfortunately, in 1598 Speght preempted those plans by publishing a new edition of the *Works*. Speght's interpretive aids, while not quite up to the level of Italian editions of Petrarch, addressed many of the most salient issues regarding Chaucer's text and certainly obviated the need for a new edition. The *Animadversions* was Thynne's response.[2] In it, he praises the work of his father who made Chaucer "most acceptable to the worlde in correctinge and augmentinge his woorkes" and implies that, in producing a new edition, Speght has deprived him of his rightful patrimony as a Chaucerian editor.[3] He describes, often in minute detail, more than fifty errors he finds in Speght's edition, most of which occur not in the text itself (which had been reset using the 1561 edition), but in the biographical sketch, genealogical diagrams, and hard word lists that accompany them. Speght appears to have received Thynne's corrections graciously but not unreservedly and incorporates many of them, but not all, in the revised 1602 version of the *Works*.

Thynne's missive would likely have been forgotten entirely had he not presented a copy to Sir Thomas Egerton, Lord Ellesmere, in December of 1599. (The letter is framed as a New Year's gift, a common way to seek patronage and one also used by John Leland when seeking support for his own antiquarian activities.)[4] This manuscript, originally a part of the Bridgewater collection, survives at the Huntington Library in San Marino, California. In 1865, George H. Kingsley edited it for the Chaucer Society and the Early English Text Society (EETS), and in 1875, EETS published a new edition prepared by Frederick Furnivall.[5] The ease of access afforded by the EETS volume, along with Furnivall's emphasis on Francis's claims to have owned some twenty-five Chaucer manuscripts, including one (Thynne says) with the notation "examinatur Chaucer," has ensured lasting interest in the treatise among Chaucerians. Despite Furnivall's enthusiastic commentary, assessments of the *Animadversions* have not been kind, and it is typically dismissed as the work of a bitter would-be scholar jealous of his father's reputation. Derek Pearsall, for example, concludes that, Thynne's "judgment is poor, his understanding of context unsound, and he lacks all sense of the difference between important and trivial matters. He is, in fact, the perfect pattern of the pedant, and the tone of his letter, which ranges from the patronizing to the irascible, is in accord."[6]

My goal here is not to dispute Pearsall's characterization, but rather to set the *Animadversions* in its wider scholarly context. The *Animadversions* exists not because of Thynne's love for Chaucer, or even his love for his father's edition of Chaucer. Thynne wrote it because he saw, in response to Speght, an opportunity for scholarly self-promotion. While the *Animadversions* offers little in the way of new readings of Chaucer's poetry, it nevertheless reveals much about Thynne's attempts to integrate the study of Chaucer's life and works with the historical and antiquarian scholarship by which he hoped to make his reputation. Thynne's reading is an inverse to Spenser's use of Chaucer in his own poetry: while in the *Shepheardes Calender*, Spenser adapted the tropes of antiquarian scholarship to literary conceits, Thynne took what was commonly seen as a literary text and excavated its antiquarian concerns. Both Thynne's and Spenser's work depends on an understanding that these two sets of concerns intersect when it comes to Chaucer. In writing as one ostensible lover of Chaucer to another, Thynne partook in a form of coterie scholarship that evokes traditions of Chaucerian reading from John Shirley to John Stow, but he used a distinctively antiquarian set of rhetorical and discursive conventions to make his claims.

Thynne's Antiquarian Ambitions

Francis Thynne was probably born around 1545; his father, William, died in 1546. Records of his early life are scarce, although he is listed as a student at the Tonbridge School under its first master, John Proctor. Without a university education and with only a brief sojourn at Lincoln's Inn, Francis Thynne's study of English history, the law, and related topics would have been largely self-directed.[7] Manuscript evidence suggests that his first scholarly interests were alchemical; his collections on the topic date to the early 1570s, when he was in his late twenties.[8] Thynne lacked the resources to pursue such studies independently, however, and around this same time he began to court the patronage of William Cecil, Lord Burghley, Elizabeth's adviser, who would become a supporter of major antiquarian works like Holinshed's *Chronicles* and Camden's *Britannia*.

Thynne married in 1564, apparently quite unhappily.[9] Disagreements with his wife's guardian led to a period of financial distress in the mid-1570s (perhaps also precipitated by the cost of applied studies in alchemy), and Thynne's troubles culminated in more than two years of imprisonment for debt in the White Lion prison in Southwark.[10] Though Thynne claims, in the *Animadversions*, to have inherited from his father some twenty-five manuscripts of

Chaucer, he also says he sold off many around this time.[11] Thynne's penury is a lifelong motif in his correspondence with friends and family members, and there is a particularly sharp contrast between his fortunes and those of his cousin John Thynne, who built Longleat House out of a former Cistercian priory in Wiltshire. Thynne lived there, in "this out-nook of the little world," for a period of time following his release from prison (in another stroke of bad luck, he was apparently evicted upon John's death in 1580).[12]

By 1580 Thynne had returned to London and was living in Poplar. By 1582, he had begun work on the enterprise that should have established his reputation as a historian, the expanded 1587 edition of Holinshed's *Chronicles*.[13] How Thynne became attached to the project is something of a mystery: he had no prior reputation as a historical writer, and there is no evidence that his earlier historiographic and genealogical works dedicated to Cecil and Lord Cobham had been particularly well received.[14] Under the leadership of Abraham Fleming, Thynne's primary responsibility was revising and updating the material on Scotland, but in the end he contributed a dozen substantial passages scattered throughout the *Chronicles*. Unfortunately, in February 1587 the Privy Council ordered cuts to the new version of the *Chronicles*, eliminating the bulk of his additions.[15] Though he was the contributor "most directly embarrassed" by the censorship of 1587, Thynne repackaged some of this material in deluxe manuscripts presented to patrons, several of whom had sat on the Privy Council at the time of the excisions.[16]

Despite its suppression, Thynne's work on Holinshed's *Chronicles* secured a place for him in London antiquarian circles, and he became a regularly contributing member of the Elizabethan Society of Antiquaries around 1591.[17] While the majority of papers presented to the society are no longer extant, eight of Thynne's papers are published in Thomas Hearne's eighteenth-century compendium of the society's papers, *A Collection of Curious Discourses Written by Eminent Antiquaries Upon Several Heads in Our English Antiquities*. The topics of Thynne's papers range from the origin of sterling money ([1590]), to the history of the houses of law (1591), to the historical role of the earl marshal (1603). The unusually high number of papers attributed to Thynne indicates especially regular participation and probably also high regard by his peers.[18]

Thynne would later borrow from research undertaken for meetings of the Society of Antiquaries in his commentary in the *Animadversions*; in addition, his involvement with the group facilitated his access to primary sources for historical research. His manuscripts indicate he had access to the papers and books associated with midcentury antiquarians like John Leland, Laurence Nowell, and Matthew Parker, as well as to the collections of his contemporaries John Stow and Joseph Holland, both of whose libraries contained important literary manuscripts.[19] For David Carlson, Thynne's use of this material "reflect[s] an ongoing exchange of documents and information with other members of the Society," an exchange of which Thynne was very much a part.[20]

The final phase of Thynne's career was dominated by heraldry and genealogical research. Although Thynne produced armorial manuscripts throughout his career, official recognition of his expertise was slow in arriving. His correspondence indicates that he sought appointment as a herald as early as December 1588; he wrote to Burghley a second time in 1593, asking for recommendation to the College of Arms and stressing his extensive learning, "even in the deepest pointes of Armorye, which cannott be knowed with oute the mysteries of Philosophye and the judygmente of histories."[21] On April 22, 1602, with great ceremony, he was finally created Lancaster Herald, and his later works are all on heraldic topics.[22] Membership of the Society of Antiquaries overlapped heavily with that of the College of Arms, and it is not surprising that someone with Thynne's interests should be involved with both. The society's founder, William Camden, served as Clarenceux King of Arms from 1597 until his death in 1623, and the antiquaries met in the rooms of William Dethick, the Garter King at Arms. Thynne likely died in 1608, as his successor in the position of Lancaster herald was installed in November of that year, without Thynne having previously surrendered his patent.[23]

Ultimately, the ambitions of Francis Thynne far outstripped his accomplishments. What we know of his personal life, marred by persistent financial problems, an unhappy marriage, and "that cruell Tyraunt, the unmerciful goute," suggests it was not a pleasant one.[24] In his professional life he was marginally more successful, but despite the zeal with which he pursued his studies in the fields of alchemy, arms, and British antiquities, he published no major works of his own, and it would be possible to write a history of any of these fields in early modern England without special reference to his contributions. Nevertheless, if not an innovator like his friends William Camden and Sir Robert Cotton, Thynne was a solid, contributing citizen of his milieu, whom an admiring Furnivall described as "at least high in the second rank of antiquaries of his day."[25] While it is possible to view Thynne, as Pearsall does, as "one whose entire career consisted of being put upon," by the end of his life he had achieved at least a measure of the professional recognition that he craved. Sir Robert Cotton took pains to preserve his manuscripts and Camden referred to him in *Britannia* as "that skilfull Antiquary," "who with exceeding great commendation hath travelled very much in this Studie of Antiquities."[26]

At his death, Thynne left writings in manuscript on historical, genealogical, and alchemical topics, in addition to his contributions to various printed volumes. Today, more than fifty survive.[27] These manuscripts suggest a scholar who, though of diverse interests, sought to understand the past in all its related dimensions. In the words of Thynne's bibliographer Carlson, "no single contemporary figure better than Francis Thynne, both by the nature of his various interests and by the ways in which he combined the kinds of knowledge he acquired, confirms that all the forms of Elizabethan science, in the broad sense of the term, embodied a single, unified way of thinking about things."[28]

Many of Thynne's projects emphasize the importance of origins—of words, technologies, practices, and ideas. The search for origins also motivated heraldic research, with its focus on genealogy and the interwoven histories of noble families; it was equally central to many of the papers that Thynne and his colleagues presented to the Society of Antiquaries. A belief that to understand the present one must understand its origins in the past stood at the heart of celebrated works of Tudor scholarship like Camden's *Britannia* as well as earlier antiquarian works including Polydore Vergil's *De inventoribus rerum* (1499) and historiographic manuals like Jean Bodin's popular *Methodus ad facilem historiarum cognitionem* (1566, revised 1572). It is also central to understanding the increasing value placed on Chaucer as part of a shared cultural heritage.

It its outlook and emphases, Thynne's work is characteristic of early modern antiquarian scholarship. The place of medieval poetry is, overall, small. Apart from the *Animadversions*, his scholarly interest in literary, philosophical, and aesthetic matters is modest; he prefers to focus on historical, genealogical, and antiquarian affairs. He offers no aesthetic comment on the many epitaphs he transcribed during his visits to churches and graveyards, for example, and he treats Gower's Latin poem *Vox Clamantis*, which he would have known in manuscript, only as a corroborating witness to events of the 1380s.[29] Even Thynne's own poetry, which I discuss in the following section, frequently focuses on historical, genealogical, and antiquarian topics and, when it turns to literary themes, relies on tropes and structures of thought borrowed from antiquarian practice. His engagement with Chaucer, then, is best understood not as a self-conscious foray into literary criticism, but rather as an extension of his other forms of interest in the English past.

Emblemes and Epigrames

Although Francis Thynne clearly aspired to a scholarly profession, he also wrote poetry throughout his career. Around 1573, Thynne composed two lengthy poems on armorial subjects, one devoted to explicating the Burghley family coat of arms, and another explaining his self-devised coat of arms for alchemists, and he added short prefatory verses to many of his prose works.[30] On December 20, 1600, a year after he presented the *Animadversions*, he offered up a collection of emblems and epigrams consisting of 140 short poems as a New Year's gift to his patron Sir Thomas Egerton. These verses reveal that, wherever Thynne's artistic strengths lay, it was probably not in poetry, but they also provide a framework for his engagement with Chaucer and further insight into the antiquarian milieu at the turn of the seventeenth century. In addition to these materials, the two anonymous prefatory poems added to the 1602 edition of Speght's *Works* can be attributed to Francis on the basis of drafts in his hand found his copy of the 1598 *Works*.[31]

A number of the poems in *Emblemes and Epigrames* take up scholarly matters (heraldry is an especially prominent theme, perhaps a reminder to Egerton that Thynne was at this time still seeking an official appointment in the College of Arms), but many deal with classical, moralizing, or observational topics (the pleasures and perils of wine, the supposedly inevitably duplicitous nature of women) that do not otherwise figure prominently in his writings.[32] As Thynne describes them, the poems are "naked (for soe I doe terme them, because they are not clothed with engraven pictures) emblems and Epigrams, whatsoever they be, partlie drawen out of histories, and partlie out of Phisicall Philosophie, but tending to moralitie, and for the most part endinge in necessarie precepts, and perswatione to vertue."[33] The collection includes two poems on the antiquarian luminaries John Leland, by then deceased for half a century, and William Camden, still very much alive in 1600 (Leland's own Latin epigrams, some of which were printed in 1589, may have served as a model for Thynne).[34] It also includes a poem on Spenser's *Faerie Queene*. This is a rare reference to contemporary poetry in Thynne's work, albeit one that appears slightly less unexpected when considered in the context of the *Works'* concern with the relationship between Chaucer and Spenser, discussed in the previous chapter.

Though the manuscript itself is small and plain, the *Emblemes and Epigrames* was clearly a patronage-seeking project designed to win its author financial reward. Despite the difference in status between author and dedicatee, the spirit in which Thynne presents the work to Thomas Egerton evokes the masculine collegiality that Stephanie Trigg sees as characteristic of Chaucerian reading communities in early modern England (it bears mentioning that the famous Ellesmere manuscript of the *Canterbury Tales* came into the possession of the Egerton family around this time, and that the manuscript bears a pressmark in the hand of John Egerton, Thomas's son).[35] Thynne writes that, in addition to the moral and philosophical poems in his collection, "some of them are composed of thinges donn and sayed by such as were well knowne to your Lordshipp, and to myself in those yonger yeares when Lincolns Inn societie did linke us all in one cheyne of Amite; and some of them are of other persons yet living, which of your Lordship are both loved & liked."[36] (Thynne's association with Lincoln's Inn was apparently brief, and he never entered the legal profession.)[37] The collection, then, is meant to affirm and record the affective ties among a particular group of men of which Thynne and Egerton have both been a part, a gesture that recalls similar comments in the Beaumont epistle at the beginning of Speght's *Works*. As in that case, Chaucer triangulates the scene: in the closing lines of the preface, Thynne writes that his "slender poems" "may be equalled with Sir Topas ryme in Chaucer."[38] Though on the surface self-deprecating, this remark aligns Thynne with Chaucer and Egerton with Chaucer's patrons (according to Leland, these included no less a personage than Richard II).

The choice of Chaucer as an analogue here (in a work that is, by and large, not about Chaucer) seems to reflect the particular valence that the poet and his work had in legal and antiquarian circles: the joke becomes subtler, and more flattering to Egerton, the greater the knowledge of Chaucer one brings to it, since Chaucer's patrons were presumed to be among the most consequential political figures in late fourteenth-century England.[39] Thynne makes a similar comparison between his poetry and *Sir Thopas* in his Epigram 51, "To Humfrie Waldronn." Interweaving references to Chaucer with classical allusions and references to the Elizabethan translator Arthur Golding, Thynne writes:

A Foolishe Cherill I maye seeme to bee,
    that shame not to present unto thy sight

Sir Topas ridinge rime not meet for thee,
Nor Gouldings learned vewe, that famous wight,
whose hawtie verse, with sugredd words well knitt,
bereaves the same of *Chawcers* flowing witt.
Then frendlie take in gree this frendlie verse I frame,
and thinke, to his *Perithous*, that *Thesius* writes the same.[40]

Here again the reference serves to affirm what the two men have in common (in this case, an understanding of Chaucer), while downplaying their differences (the perceived gap between Thynne's skills as a versifier and those of his friend) and aligning Thynne himself with Chaucer, who is, after all, the speaker as well as the author of *Sir Thopas*.[41] As this passage illustrates, Thynne favored oblique references even in cases where a more straightforward expression might suffice ("Cherill" is Cherillus, or Choerilus, a poet whose inferior poems in praise of Alexander the Great garnered appropriately scanty reward). Thynne mixes classical and Chaucerian allusions here, as E.K. and Spenser do in the *Shepheardes Calender*, and as Thomas Speght and Francis Beaumont do in the prefatory materials to the 1598/1602 *Works*. Together, these examples show how Chaucer could function as a part of antiquity, as conceived by late Tudor Englishmen, as well as part of their imagined English past.[42]

Chaucer appears in his capacity as the founder and standard-bearer of English poetry in Emblem 38, "Spencers Fayrie Queene." Although antiquarian readers like Thynne might have seen ideological parallels to their own work in the *Faerie Queene*'s investment in British mythology and national identity, Thynne focuses here on Spenser's literary achievements. In the poem, he addresses his contemporary directly:

Renowmed Spencer, whose heavenlie sprite
ecclipseth the sonne of former poetrie,
in whome the muses harbor with delighte,
gracing thy verse with Immortalitie,
Crowning thy fayrie Queene with deitie,
the famous *Chaucer* yealds his Lawrell crowne
unto thy sugred penn, for thy renowne.[43]

As in the prefatory materials to the 1598 and 1602 editions of his *Works*, Chaucer serves as a literary yardstick from which to measure the greater poetic heights scaled by later luminaries like Spenser. The use of "yealds" to describe

Chaucer's giving way to Spenser implies an ongoing cultural presence and, perhaps, some residual agency for the medieval poet even as he abdicates his preeminent position among English authors. "Sugred penn," meanwhile, evokes the aureate praises of Chaucer that, in the first half of the fifteenth century, knit his language to the notion of Englishness itself.[44]

In the second half of the poem, Thynne attributes to Spenser the same immortality through poetry that previous admirers ascribed to Chaucer:

> Noe cankred envie cann thy fame deface,
> nor eatinge tyme consume thy sacred vayne;
> noe carpinge Zoilus cann thy verse disgrace,
> nor scoffinge Momus taunt thee with disdaine,
> since thy rare worke eternall praise doth gayne;
> then live thou still, for still thy verse shall live,
> to unborne poets, which light and life will give.[45]

His words here echo Leland's assertion that "noster Galfridus summa Britannae / Chaucerus Musae gratia semper erit" (our Geoffrey Chaucer will always be the greatest ornament of the muse of Britain).[46] In Thynne's formulation, the praise of later poets is proof of the medieval writer's poetic immortality. An unbroken tradition of admiration can transcend the ravages of time and the depredations of jealous critics.

On the basis of this poem alone, Thynne appears to favor Spenser over Chaucer. However, the poem's last two lines are either drawn from or reused in Thynne's poem "Upon the Picture of Chaucer," which appears in the 1602 edition of the *Works* opposite John Speed's genealogical engraving. The mobility of this particular expression of poetic immortality shows Thynne thought about Spenser and Chaucer in structurally analogous terms and suggests a more fluid, less linear narrative of English literary history than indicated by the first stanza of the epigram. Not only does Thynne mix Chaucerian and classical allusions, his praise of a contemporary author can apply to Chaucer too, reflecting Chaucer's exceptional temporal fluidity. If the *Works'* plentiful references to Spenser serve as a guide, the multifaceted connections between Chaucer and Spenser would have been readily apparent to antiquarian readers like Thynne.

Thynne introduces an alternative basis for lasting fame in "Mr Camdens Britania," a poem in praise of the groundbreaking chorographic history of the

British Isles. First published in 1586, the Latin *Britannia* was in its sixth edition by 1600. Thynne would have known Camden personally through their mutual involvement in the Society of Antiquaries. The thirty-six-line poem, which contains endorsements such as "Buy then this worke! doe reade and read againe!" must have been written in hope of finding a place among the prefatory poetry included with the ever-popular and ever-expanding *Britannia*; it was not, however, so published. In the poem, Thynne praises

> learned *Camden*, with his searching witt,
> whose deepe studie, by travells carefull payne,
> hath from errors and mace [maze] of *Dedalus* pitt,
> (for Cuntries love,) drawne unto light agayne
> worthye Antiquities, wherof before
> none sayed the like, or shall doe anie more.[47]

Here, Thynne tropes on a sense of sharp contrast between the dark past and the illuminated present. This is a characteristic scholarly metaphor, particularly prominent in English antiquarian writings, and its appearance here shows how, even while his own antiquarian writing seldom looks beyond concrete specificities, Thynne was aware of the broader currents that shaped historiographic thought in sixteenth-century England, especially where periodization was concerned.[48]

In his second antiquarian poem, "Leylands rightefull ghost," Thynne weighs in on a controversy that roiled scholarly and heraldic circles at the end of the seventeenth century, involving Camden and Ralph Brooke, the York Herald. Brooke was a litigious and combative individual who was nonetheless an important force for reform within the College of Arms. In a 1599 pamphlet, *A discoverie of certaine errours published in print in the much commended Britannia* (STC 3834), Brooke accused Camden of borrowing both the plan and much of the material in the *Britannia* from the work of John Leland without giving proper credit. The final leaf of Brooke's pamphlet features a poem entitled "Leylands supposed Ghost." The first three stanzas deal with attacks levied at Leland by the Italian historian Polydore Vergil after Leland had criticized Vergil's assault on the historicity of the Arthurian narrative as recorded in Geoffrey of Monmouth; in the last stanza, the speaker considers the fate of Leland's works and reputation in the present and regrets that they are "drownd in such a thankless *Denn*"—presumably, a reference to the *Britannia*.[49]

As an aspiring herald, Thynne had good professional reason to side with Camden, then Clarenceux King at Arms, rather than with the upstart Brooke. Thynne comes to Camden's defense in his epigram, writing in the voice of Leland's "rightefull" ghost, rather than the "supposed Ghost" of Brooke's poem. In Thynne's version, Leland rebuts the insinuations made in Brooke's poem:

> My name, my fame, my labors, and my penn,
> my indisgested worke of highe conceit,
> came not to be obscur'd in thanklesse *Denne*
> For he (whome skillesse malice through deceit
> sekes to entrapp with hooke of scorning beyt)
> doth gratefullie receive my buryed name,
> which otherwise had perished to my shame.[50]

Like Chaucer yielding his laurels to Spenser, the earlier scholar Leland acknowledges the superiority of Camden's work while noting that the accomplishments of successors like Camden would be impossible without his contributions. Leland's ghostly voice offers praise of Camden and his patriotic efforts:

> By him I live, by him the world doth knowe,
> by him the heavens and humane Lawes doe finde
> that he hath, farr beyond my broken shewe,
> his Cuntries glorie in one worke combinde,
> with gratious style, and sprite of heavenlie minde,
> which both to mine and his immortall praise,
> in spite of spite, will honnored bee allwaies.[51]

As in the poem on the *Britannia* itself, Thynne stresses Camden's patriotism and assures readers that the fame of both text and author will endure. The fact that both Thynne and Brooke write in Leland's voice using English, rather than the Latin he used for most of his scholarship and poetry, suggests a sense of connection and proximity to the antiquary; Leland is not an abstract textual authority, but an individual whose reputation has been impugned (or not) by Camden's work. Thynne's treatments of the epic *Faerie Queene* and the scholarly *Britannia* are quite similar: both are praised on the grounds that they exceed earlier work, and both are assured of enduring audience and fame. These are not unusual claims in and of themselves, but they align poetry and historiography in ways that remind us how, for the sixteenth-century antiquarian reader, Chaucer might fall into both categories.

Thynne's Verses in the 1602 *Works*

Emblemes and Epigrames provides a snapshot of Thynne's interests around 1600. Presented to Egerton as a bid for patronage, it forms a part of Thynne's efforts to fashion himself as a professional scholar and intellectual worthy of financial remuneration. Around the time he was compiling *Emblemes and Epigrames*, Thynne also wrote two poems that appear in the revised 1602 edition of the *Works*, "Upon the Picture of Chaucer" and "Of the Animadversions upon Chaucer." Like the poem on Camden's *Britannia*, these appear to have been written for publication with the book they discuss. Thynne's aim, it would seem, was that these poems would secure a place for himself in the printed records of antiquarian labors and in a community of readers who love and appreciate Chaucer.

"Upon the Picture of Chaucer" refers to the genealogical engraving prepared by John Speed, and it is on the back of this leaf that Thynne writes the poem in his copy of the 1598 *Works*. The title is rather disingenuous, since the poem focuses on Chaucer's literary legacy rather than the genealogical relations that are prominently featured in the "picture." As it appears in the 1602 *Works*, the poem reads as follows:

What *Pallas* citie owes the heavenly mind
Of prudent *Socrates*, wise Greeces glorie;
What fame *Arpinas* spreadingly doth find
By *Tullies* eloquence and oratorie;
What lasting praise sharpe witted Italie
By *Tasso's* and by *Petrarkes* penne obtained;
What fame *Bartas* unto proud France hath gained,
By seven daies world Poetically strained:

What high renoune is purchas'd unto Spaine,
Which fresh *Dianaes* verses do distill;
What praise our neighbor Scotland doth retaine,
By *Gawine Douglas*, in his *Virgill* quill;
Or other motions by sweet Poets skill,
The same, and more, faire England challenge may,

By that rare wit and art thou doest display,
In verse, which doth *Apolloes* muse bewray.
          Then *Chaucer* live, for still thy verse shall live,
          T'unborne Poëts, which life and light will give.[52]

Much as John Leland does in his Latin poems on Chaucer, and just as Speght
and Francis Beaumont do in the prefatory letters in the *Works*, Thynne
favorably compares the English poet with both classical figures (Cicero and
Socrates) and more recent vernacular writers, finding him a more than ade-
quate match in both cases.[53] In "Upon the Picture of Chaucer," this competition
includes the Italians Petrarch and Torquato Tasso, the French poet Guillaume
de Salluste du Bartas, and the Scot Gavin Douglas, whose translation of the
Aeneid Thynne specifically mentions.[54] (Only Tasso is not invoked elsewhere
in the prefatory materials.) Unlike Leland, who compares Chaucer with his
approximate contemporaries, the trecento triumvirate of Dante, Petrarch, and
Boccaccio, Thynne measures Chaucer's accomplishments against sixteenth-
century poets like Tasso, Du Bartas, and Douglas.[55] These are claims that
emphasize Chaucer's place in a linguistically diverse field of vernacular literature, and not just his historical significance.

"Upon the Picture of Chaucer," like Thynne's poem on Spenser, emphasizes Chaucer's ability to measure up to the (implicitly greater) work of later
poets, including and especially across national and linguistic boundaries.
Thynne's assessment here inverts the comparison to Chaucer typically found
in the writing of the poet's fifteenth-century admirers: for poets like Hoccleve and Lydgate, Chaucer's status was cemented by the fact that no later writer
had reached his level of excellence, but in Thynne's formulation, Chaucer now
strives for the standards set by other, later authors. While a desire to claim
Chaucer as an explicitly English poet remains consistent across these tributes,
Thynne's formulation reflects a growing cultural space for vernacular literature across Europe and an increasingly powerful identification between nation
and language. In this, Thynne's work also represents a progression from the
views expressed in Leland's *De Viris Illustribus*. Although the classical comparison does not drop out entirely, Thynne combines the classical and vernacular in a single poem, while Leland treats them in separate pieces. Perhaps
in part because he lacked Leland's erudition and familiarity with Latinate culture, Thynne appears more willing than Leland to consider vernacular works
alongside Greek and Latin sources.[56]

In his comparisons, Thynne also selects one writer each from a number of linguistic, and hence national, traditions.[57] In his own poems included in *De Viris Illustribus*, Leland chose poets that early sixteenth-century humanists like himself believed best represented the potential quality of vernacular literature; that they are all Italian has less to do with political relations between Italy and England at the time than with a more general interest in humanism and in Italian culture. By contrast, Thynne's poem on Chaucer makes reference to specific political entities—France, Spain, Scotland—over which Tudor England sought to assert political and military hegemony. In writing, he presents the poetic efforts of these nations as a literary-political offensive whose influence "fair England challenge may" by wielding "that rare wit and art" found in Chaucer. A similar conflation of Chaucer and Englishness may be found on the title pages of Speght's editions, which celebrate him as "our antient and learned *English* poet."

While only "Upon the Picture of Chaucer" is attributed to Thynne in the *Works*, the poem that appears below it on signature B1, "Of the Animadversions upon Chaucer," also appears in Thynne's hand and with his revisions in his copy of the 1598 edition at the Houghton Library, making it clear that Thynne was the author of both pieces.[58] In the poem, the insight provided by "the helpefull notes explaining *Chaucers* mind" leads Thynne to proclaim "*Speght* is the child of *Chaucers* fruitfull breine."[59] Thynne's assertion makes scholarly explication an explicit component of Chaucerian tradition. Like "Upon the Picture of Chaucer," the poem's conceit rests on the dual assumption that progeny (whether literary or scholarly) are necessary to preserve text and reputation over time and that, in order to claim their status as heirs, later generations must carefully preserve and memorialize their origins. Thus, Thynne writes,

> In reading of the learn'd praise-worthie peine,
> The helpefull notes explaining *Chaucers* mind,
> The Abstruse skill, the artificiall veine;
> By true Annalogie I rightly find,
> *Speght* is the child of *Chaucers* fruitfull breine,
> Vernishing his workes with life and grace,
> Which envious age would otherwise deface:
> Then be he lov'd and thanked for the same,
> Since in his love he hath reviv'd his name.[60]

The poem's conclusion recalls the comment in the 1602 version of the Beaumont epistle that Speght has "restored" Chaucer, "both alive againe, and younge againe."[61] While an important rationale for commentary and editorial criticism, the idea that Chaucer requires reviving and rejuvenation ignores the ongoing popular reception of Chaucer: Caroline Spurgeon's *Five Hundred Years of Chaucer Criticism and Allusion* actually records an uptick in Chaucer references during the second half of the 1590s. People were still talking about Chaucer, whether or not they were reading him with the same ease they had earlier in the century. As with Speght's hard word list, however, claims such as Thynne's form part of the process by which Chaucer's writing is transferred from the province of the general reader to the specialized realm of those already initiated into the arcana of Chaucer's "antient" writing.

Thynne's poetry testifies to the permeable boundary between the spheres of antiquarian study and literary reception at the end of the sixteenth century and to Chaucer's position at the flexible border between them. Thynne's writings are a reminder of Chaucer's ongoing utility as an archetype of English eloquence and enduring poetic fame and as a site of shared affection through which commentators can affirm the bonds between groups of masculine readers, as Stephanie Trigg's study of Chaucerian reception shows. For Thynne, Chaucer was an "antique" writer who could blur the boundaries between the vernacular and Greek or Latinate past, as he does in his turn as Tityrus in the *Shepheardes Calender*. This blurring makes him a particularly appealing figure to humanist readers eager for a connection to both the English past and more distant antiquity. Thynne, like many sixteenth-century commentators, figures his accomplishments in patriotic terms. In Thynne's case, his admiration for Chaucer is analogous to his appreciation for William Camden's antiquarian achievements. Thynne's poem on the portrait of Chaucer in the 1602 *Works* underscores Chaucer's importance as a specifically *English* poet, while the verses addressed to Speght claim a new place for the commentator in the ongoing work of preserving and presenting Chaucer to new generations of readers.

The *Animadversions* and the 1602 *Works*

In the *Animadversions*, written the year before the *Emblemes and Epigrames* and around the same time as the two poems that appear in the 1602 *Works*, we see Thynne's efforts to present himself as a Chaucerian initiate not through poetry but through a critical assessment of Speght's edition. While the

Animadversions offers little in the way of new readings of Chaucer's poetry, it nevertheless documents Thynne's attempts to integrate the study of Chaucer's life and works with historical and antiquarian scholarship.

As critical reviews go, Thynne's *Animadversions* is not an especially positive one, but, expanding and rephrasing many of Thynne's handwritten notes in his own copy of the 1598 *Works*, it does seem to represent Thynne's honest scholarly opinion of the text. In its surviving manuscript (an additional copy presumably reached Speght), the text begins with an address to Thynne's friend and patron Sir Thomas Egerton. Like Leland's *Laboryouse journey*, written a half century earlier, it invokes the custom of a New Year's gift, a practice that Thynne tells us has, like language and laws, eventually made its way from ancient Rome to the "litle worlde of Brytannye."[62] This leads to a flattering suggestion that both Thynne's learning and Egerton's patronage of it are based on classical models. An obvious analogue is Speght's use of classical poetic examples in the *Works*' dedication to Robert Cecil, but while Speght compares Chaucer's verse with classical models, Thynne highlights the resonances between scholarship and patronage in the past and in the present.[63]

The letter itself is addressed to Thomas Speght. Ever mindful of Chaucer's reputation, Thynne assures Speght that he is acting out of familiarity with and respect for "oure famous poete Geffrey Chaucer." Thynne then turns to the conventional identification of Chaucer with the English language to reframe this mutual affection in nationalistic terms. He writes that anyone who loves "our Countrye" and reveres learning has, as a result, a duty to "suche a singuler ornament of oure tonge as the woorkes of Chaucer are," a formulation that recalls the comments on Chaucerian language in the preface to his father's edition.[64] As Trigg notes, when Thynne emphasizes that "the work of the fathers—Father Chaucer, Father Thynne—must be protected and constantly policed," he also articulates the often implicit link between early modern celebrations of Chaucer's language and emergent English identity grounded, at least in part, by a shared language. Furthermore, as Trigg observes, "embedded within this discourse is also a strong sense of the linguistic instability of the English language, which renders Chaucer progressively more illegible to his sixteenth century readers, and the philological support offered by the editor increasingly necessary, increasingly elaborate."[65] This sense of instability creates space and urgency not only for Speght's apparatus, but for Thynne's criticism of that apparatus as well.

At a more personal level, Chaucer mediates any tension between Thynne and Speght. Thynne can assure Speght that he offers correction not out of animosity but out of "the duetye and love whiche I beare to Chaucer," making the poet both the passive conduit through which Thynne's feelings toward Speght may be channeled and a buffer against any criticism of his project.[66] Thynne's claims of duty toward his subject ring a bit hollow, since—apart from his notes in the *Works* demonstrating familiarity with Chaucer and Gower, as well as Boccaccio, the *Roman de la Rose*, and Petrarch's *Trionfi*—his writing suggests little in the way of an ongoing interest or "love" toward Chaucer or literature more generally. Indeed, as many readers of the *Animadversions* have noted, Thynne's strongest sense of obligation appears to be not toward Chaucer but to the legacy of his father, William Thynne, the man who, in his son's words, "made [Chaucer] most acceptable to the worlde in correcting and augmentinge his woorkes."[67]

Accordingly, the first topic Thynne addresses in the *Animadversions* is the relationship between Speght's *Works* and William Thynne's edition. Although this discussion accounts for little more than a tenth of the text, it has drawn the most attention from modern readers of the *Animadversions*, especially those interested in Thynne's edition of the *Works* and its possible sources. The younger Thynne offers a confusing account of the origins of his father's edition, involving a supposed "commissione to serche all the libraries of Englande for Chaucers Workes" given to William Thynne by Henry VIII, with the result that "oute of all the Abbies of this Realme (which reserved anye monumentes thereof) [he was] fully furnished with multitude of Bookes."[68] Such a commission, if it ever existed—and there is no evidence to suggest that it did—would have predated Henry's similar charge to John Leland by several years.

There are other factual problems with Francis Thynne's account of his father's efforts. According to the *Animadversions*, the first collected edition of the *Works* was a single-column, single-volume production containing, along with other previously unpublished Chaucerian texts, the *Pilgrim's Tale*, an anticlerical poem that Francis describes as "a thinge moore odious to the Clergye, then the speche of the plowmanne."[69] This edition, according to Francis, was completely suppressed after an incensed Cardinal Wolsey, having learned of the objectionable poems, demanded the entire edition be destroyed and reprinted with the offending material excised.[70] Only Henry VIII's favor and personal intervention saved William Thynne from bodily harm. While the *Pilgrim's Tale* is a real poem, a reference to the Pilgrimage of Grace in the *Pilgrim's Tale* indicates that it could not have been written before 1536, meaning that this supposedly suppressed first edition (and there is no evidence for such an edition) would need to have been published *after* the 1532 edition.

This story, while demonstrably apocryphal, lionizes both Chaucer and William Thynne as defenders of a Protestant version of truth and history against a decadent ecclesiastical establishment, creating yet another kind of Chaucerian community.[71] Thynne's account, which emphasizes Henry's interest in his father's work, also imagines an updated, scholarly analogue to the poetic golden age invoked by fifteenth- and sixteenth-century Chaucerians, a misty vision of a time when sovereigns knew and protected their antiquarian subjects.[72] Like Leland and Speght before him, Thynne makes Chaucer the basis for a community of readers connected both in the present and across time. The association here is especially poignant and powerful: Francis Thynne is, through Chaucer, linked with his father, who died when the younger Thynne was two, and his father is, through Chaucer, linked with Henry himself.[73] Moreover, the *Animadversions'* account of the lost first edition of the *Works* makes William Thynne a witness to an abuse of clerical power that evokes of the misuse of ecclesiastical office decried in the *Pilgrim's Tale* and the *Plowman's Tale* (both treated by Francis Thynne as authentic works). In his desire to publish the spurious tale in the face of opposition, then, William Thynne shares in Chaucer's status as a reformist *provocateur*.

Questions about the first edition of the *Works* aside, the younger Thynne views the 1542 printing, which includes the *Plowman's Tale* (not present in the 1532 edition) as the fullest expression of his father's work, rather than the initial 1532 printing or the reprint that appeared around 1550, after his father's death in 1546.[74] Thynne also explicitly excludes from his discussion "the second edition to one inferior persone then my fathers editione was."[75] The "one inferior persone" must be John Stow and the "second edition" his 1561 version of the *Works*. The source of Thynne's animosity toward Stow is unclear; Thynne could have perceived his publication of Chaucer as presumptuous (a grudge Thynne would have carried for nearly forty years by 1599). Thynne and Stow's mutual involvement in the Society of Antiquaries would have provided other opportunities for conflict and, apparently, reconciliation, as Stow refers to Thynne in his additions to the 1587 revision of Holinshed, and Thynne makes use of Stow's writings in other works.[76]

Collecting and connoisseurship—a field Stow knew well—emerge in the *Animadversions* as both a major part of antiquarian scholarship and part of the work of the transtemporal coterie responsible for preserving Chaucer and his reputation. For Thynne, his father's authority as an editor of Chaucer rests on his use of an apparently remarkable collection of manuscripts, of which Francis Thynne claims to have inherited more than two dozen. And indeed,

William Thynne does seem to have used a number of manuscripts and early printed volumes, brought together using a loose form of collation.[77] Francis says that William "made greate serche for copies to perfect [Chaucer's] woorkes," but as proof of these labors he cites only the note printed at the end of the 1542 *Squire's Tale*, which reads "there can be founde no more of this foresayd tale, whiche hath ben sought in dyvers places."[78]

Francis also claims, tantalizingly, that his father made use of a manuscript that was "subscribed in divers places with *examinatur Chaucer.*"[79] Whether true or not, this claim exceeds the more common assertion that the best text of Chaucer's poetry comes from manuscripts and not from the printed editions, which are, as both Thynnes emphasize, subject to the depredations of unlearned printers (not to mention the sloppy scribes who came before them). By asserting that his father owned and made editorial use of a manuscript at least examined by Chaucer, Francis Thynne can make the claim that his father's work is, at least in part, taken *ad fontes*. This claim functions (at least within the *Animadversions*) as the basis for a comparative assessment of Thynne and Speght's work as editors. Because William Thynne had better manuscripts, Francis seems to say, his edition is necessarily more faithful to what Chaucer wrote than Speght's and therefore to be preferred.

Though, in his 1598 address to the reader, Speght includes a disclaimer explaining that the *Works* went to press before editorial work could be completed, Francis Thynne takes at face value Speght's assertion that his text is "by old Copies corrected." He worries accordingly that the "old copies" used by Speght are not the right ones, but inferior examples of their type. In Thynne's view, his awareness of the fact that not all Chaucer manuscripts are created equal grants him a privileged perspective on Speght's edition. Such awareness is born of personal experience, and genealogical right, in the form of the "some fyve and twentye" manuscripts he claims to have inherited from his father.[80] The fate of this collection is unclear. Some of these manuscripts, Thynne says, he was forced to sell (perhaps an unsuccessful attempt to avoid imprisonment for debt?), while others he gave (or perhaps sold) to Stephen Batman, the agent for Archbishop Matthew Parker's book collecting enterprises.[81] Still others he claims were later stolen from his house in Poplar.[82] The collection having been so dispersed, Thynne muses, "yt maye happen soome of them to coome somme of your frendes handes," and thus to Speght.[83] This is potentially a problem, since the dispersal put certain "copies ymperfect," both with and without William Thynne's corrections, into circulation. Francis lectures Speght that "yf by anye suche written copies you have corrected Chaucer, you maye as well offende as seme to do good."[84] While Francis Thynne's suggestion about how these manuscripts might be detected—"I knowe yf I see agayne"—is highly subjective, his warnings speak quite sensibly to the risks of editorial intervention in the absence of a system for identifying and tracking manuscripts and assessing their relative importance. Thynne notes sagaciously that among the *Canterbury Tales* manuscripts, there are "manye false copyes, whiche Chaucer shewethe in writinge of Adam Scrivener."[85] In addition to demonstrating how quickly Chaucer's *Adam Scriveyn* had become a byword for textual corruption since its first printing in 1561, the claim underscores Chaucer's position as source of the authentic canon (the true original behind the "false" copies). Simultaneously, however, Thynne's reading of *Adam Scriveyn* imagines Chaucer as anticipating future failures of transmission, thereby proleptically authorizing the editorial enterprise in which Thynne and Speght are both engaged.

Francis Thynne's desire to collapse the distance between himself, his father, and Chaucer runs counter to the more detached, scholarly approach found elsewhere in the *Animadversions*, as well as in his own reading notes to the *Works*. In the sections that follow, Thynne moves quickly from his role as apologist for his father's "perfectest" edition of the *Works* to that of a critic well versed in the historical and political particulars of fourteenth-century England. Not surprisingly, given his expertise in heraldry and genealogical research, Thynne casts an especially sharp eye on the description of Chaucer's family and descendants in the *Life of Chaucer* added in the 1598 edition and seizes upon the opportunity it gives him to discuss Speght's edition not with the special love of the Chaucerian, but with the specificity and attention to small detail characteristic of the antiquarian scholar.

A number of the corrections to Speght suggested in the *Animadversions* derive from Thynne's own projects, making his commentary on Chaucer both a methodological and a topical extension of his earlier antiquarian work. One topic that Thynne does seem to have researched specifically for the *Animadversions*, however, is Chaucer's family background. He cites material from the patent rolls ("Dorso Rotulor") apparently unnoticed by Speght or Stow, concerning damages claimed by one John Chaucer, whom Thynne identifies as Geoffrey's father, in a 1301 court case.[86] This material provides corroborating evidence for Speght's claims concerning the long tenure of the Chaucer family in England, in support of which Speght had previously cited only the excellency of Geoffrey Chaucer's English.[87] While Thynne's evidence supports this aspect of Speght's work, it is also a rebuttal of Speght's claim that Chaucer's father was Richard Chaucer, a vintner. Thynne does not dispute the evidence concerning Richard's occupation, but he does wonder whether Richard Chaucer may have been some other relation to Chaucer besides his father (thus maintaining the possibility of a more gentlemanly family background for the poet), and whether the thousand-pound damages claimed by one John Chaucer might mean that he, and by extension the family, was of more than modest means. Ultimately, both Thynne and Speght are wrong in some particulars, but Thynne is on the right track here: Chaucer's father was indeed named John (although not the John named in the suit cited by Thynne) and Richard was John's half-brother.[88] Both men were prosperous wine merchants.

After a detailed discussion of the etymology of the surname Chaucer and the French roots of the family (both Thynne and Speght believe that the Chaucer name appears on the rolls at Battle Abbey; Furnivall suggests this might come from a bad line reading), Thynne moves to another field in which he has considerable expertise, heraldry.[89] The Chaucer family coat of arms appears on both the tomb of Chaucer installed in Westminster Abbey in the mid-sixteenth century and on the fifteenth-century tomb of Thomas Chaucer at Ewelme, as well as in a fifteenth-century book of arms, now British Library MS Harley 2169.[90] For sixteenth-century readers, the Chaucer coat of arms could convey a variety of information about the poet, perhaps most importantly his social standing, and those responsible for putting the *Works* into print were clearly sensitive to this fact: the woodcut depicting the Chaucer family crest that appears on the title page of Stow's 1561 edition of the *Works* was apparently created specifically for this publication. In Speght's editions, this same woodcut appears at the beginning of the *Canterbury Tales*, placed opposite the opening of the *Knight's Tale*, a juxtaposition that links this symbol of Chaucer's identity with his highest-ranking pilgrim. The Chaucer arms also appear in the "His Parentage" section of the *Life of Chaucer* and are worked into John Speed's genealogical engraving. In the *Animadversions*, Thynne moves to defend these "mean armes," writing that "Chaucers armes are not so meane, eyther for coolour, Chardge or particione as some will make them," although it is not clear who has lodged such criticism.[91]

While ready to uphold the antiquity and rank of the arms themselves, Thynne quite sensibly moves to discredit Speght's suggestion that Chaucer invented them and took their design from Euclid.[92] Thynne does not dispute Chaucer's skill in geometry (indeed, he emends the *Nun's Priests Tale* to be more mathematically accurate, as he believes Chaucer must have intended), but he notes that all heraldic devices that are not "Anymalls or vegitalls" are based on geometry, making them extremely familiar even to those without special mathematical knowledge.[93] Thynne's expertise in heraldry also informs his argument that the arms of the merchants of the Wool Staple, found in the windows of the house at Ewelme associated with Geoffrey Chaucer (it in fact belonged to his son Thomas), are insufficient proof that his ancestors were merchants. Because the merchants did not receive arms until after the death of Chaucer's parents, he writes, they must have been added to the windows at a later point.[94]

When it comes to Chaucer's own occupation, Thynne affirms Speght's view that Chaucer, along with John Gower, was involved in the legal profession, a claim that ultimately derives from Leland's *De Viris Illustribus*. Here, as elsewhere, Thynne ultimately displays a relatively detailed knowledge of Gower's life and works that goes beyond the material available in Leland and Bale. In the *Animadversions*, Thynne corrects Speght's misquotation of the *Confessio Amantis* and draws attention to the dedication to "moral Gower" at 5.1856 of *Troilus and Criseyde*, which Speght appears to overlook when discussing the relationship between the two poets. Thynne recognizes this oversight as a mistake originating not with Speght but in material carried over, without attribution, from Bale's *Catalogus*.[95] The extraliterary, antiquarian origins of Speght's material are clear, as are Thynne's command over these same sources and his willingness and ability to offer critique when it is warranted (and sometimes when it is not).

Thynne also notes that Speght errs, following Bale again, in identifying Gower as "a Yorkshire man." Thynne emphasizes this in part because it allows him to score an easy point against Speght. He can prove that the John Gower who wrote the *Confessio Amantis* was from another family than the Gowers of Yorkshire, because the two families bear different coats of arms. In this case heraldry provides more concrete and specific historical information than can surname alone.[96] These coats of arms are for Thynne dense sites of meaning capable of conveying historical facts above and beyond those found in written records.[97] In addition to providing Thynne with an opportunity to demonstrate the utility of his specialized knowledge, this comment is a more pointed challenge to the schoolteacher Speght who, Thynne says, knows no more of heraldry than he needs (that is, not much).[98]

The overlap between Thynne's role as Chaucerian commentator and his contributions to the Society of Antiquaries comes to the fore again when Thynne discusses Speght's claim that Chaucer was fined for beating a friar in Fleet Street while a resident at the Inner Temple.[99] Although Thynne, following

Bale and ultimately Leland, shapes Speght's belief that Chaucer practiced law, he writes that the poet could not have been a student at the Inner Temple since, as he understands it, it was not established until near the end of Edward III's reign (Edward died in 1377), by which time Chaucer would have already been "a grave manne, holden in greate credyt, and employed in embassye" and therefore too old to be engaging in boisterous activities such as the assault of clergy.[100] Thynne had researched the establishment of the London schools of law for a paper delivered at a 1591 meeting of the Society of Antiquaries, and it seems probable that either research for that paper or a paper given by another member at that meeting is the basis for his claim here.[101]

Thynne offers here a sound and logical argument based on his understanding of the establishment of the Inner Temple. This is Thynne at his most sensible and least polemical, and his claim here shows how a working knowledge of medieval English history, while not explicitly literary, might nevertheless shed light on the life and career of the poet. In this sense, at least, Thynne intuitively grasps what will become the basis for modern historicist studies of medieval literature. Moreover, Thynne demonstrates here a willingness to disprove an anecdote that, left unexamined, could have been marshaled in support of a strong proto-Protestant view of Chaucer, thereby strengthening Thynne's own account of Wolsey's suppression of the first edition of the *Works*.

If there is a common thread to Thynne's various corrections for Speght's *Life of Chaucer*, it is that Speght is too credulous in his adaptation of sources, especially Bale, and that Thynne's broader antiquarian and heraldic learning provides him with access to the documentary evidence that a proper historical account of this important material requires. In general, Thynne prizes historical accuracy, or what he believes to be historical accuracy, even at the expense of decorum. In the *Animadversions*, as in his own copy of the *Works*, he reproves Speght because his stemma of Chaucer's family (actually prepared by Robert Glover) fails to note that Katherine Swynford's children by John of Gaunt were born "longe before that marriage" (*ante nupitas,* in Thynne's handwritten note to his copy) and had to be legitimized by the pope.[102] Nor does he shy away from engaging with the heavyweights of Tudor antiquarianism: in addition to his criticism of Bale, he points out two errors Speght takes from William Camden, both concerning the Burghersh family of Ewelme, of which Thomas Chaucer's wife was a member.

That said, it is not clear how much independent research Thynne actually undertook when writing the *Animadversions*: for example, like his predecessors, he remains unable to discover the name of Chaucer's wife (Philippa), despite being exceptionally well positioned to do so.[103] He provides a great deal of information, however, about the de la Pole family, to whom the Chaucers were connected by the third marriage of Geoffrey's granddaughter Alice. This material is drawn from Thynne's history of the chancellors of England, presented to Egerton in 1597 and based on material originally intended for the 1587 revision of Holinshed.[104] Like his discussion of the Gower arms, the material on the de la Pole family features prominently because it allows Thynne to seize upon a tangential connection to his own work and use it to display his erudition and learning. In the case of the de la Pole material, Thynne's enthusiasm is so great that he eventually digresses completely from Speght's material in order to discuss Thomas of Walsingham's claim that Michael de la Pole was a merchant.[105]

As this overview makes clear, the bulk of the *Animadversions* focuses on Speght's apparatus to Chaucer's poems, not the poems themselves. Thynne does offer a few corrections to Speght's "arguments," or summaries, to the poems, mostly corresponding to his handwritten notes in the *Works*, and points out some errors in identification and attribution. Spurious works, he writes, should be distinguished within the volume, and he lists among them the *Testament of Cresseid*, the *Letter of Cupid* (both also printed in his father's edition), and the ballad "I have a lady, whereso she be" (added by Stow).[106] These comments show that Thynne was aware of the presence of non-Chaucerian texts in the *Works* and imply that he regarded apocryphal pieces *not* singled out this way to have been written by Chaucer himself. Nowhere does Thynne indicate he would like to see these apocryphal pieces removed from the *Works*. Instead, his comments indicate both awareness that the authorial Chaucer canon is more limited than the contents of the *Works* and ongoing interest in a more broadly defined canon of what might be called Chauceriana.

Most of Thynne's remaining comments on Chaucer's poetry involve language, either as it is explicated in the hard word list at the back of Speght's volume or as it is emended within the body of the text. In general, Thynne approves of Speght's treatment of Chaucer's language. Still, he writes, "In the expositione of the olde wordes, as you shewe great diligence and knowledge, so yet in my opynione, unleste a manne be a good saxoniste, french, and Italyane linguiste, (from whence Chaucer hathe borowed manye woordes) he cannott well expounde the same to oure nowe understanding."[107] This statement shows that Thynne—like other early modern commentators on later Middle English poetry—saw the English language as subject to both continuity and change, and assumed that Speght thought similarly. Moreover, Thynne's words here suggest Chaucer's language could and should be situated in the context of a number of different vernaculars, and that it could be usefully explicated using techniques borrowed from the rapidly developing field of lexicography—a field that, as Hannah Crawforth has shown, is intimately bound up with emerging notions of both nationhood and periodization, and which, through its interest in etymology, deeply inflects the literature of the early modern period.[108]

Thynne, one presumes, saw himself as ready to shoulder this large linguistic burden, and the last and largest section of the *Animadversions* is composed of Thynne's notes on Speght's hard word list and the list of annotations that in 1598 follows it. Many of these corrections find their way in to the 1602 revision, meaning that Speght not only received them, but took them seriously (Thynne is also probably responsible for the addition of small letters to some definitions in the glossary, indicating the linguistic origins of the headword). In most cases, Thynne focuses on words related to his areas of specialty: alchemy, heraldry, and British antiquities. In 1598, for example, Speght defines "Besant" as a ducat, citing Hollyband's English-French dictionary as his authority. Drawing on papers on the history of sterling money, including his own, presented to the Society of Antiquaries in 1590, Thynne explains that although the coin in question was used by both the Saxons and Normans, its origin is Greek, not English.[109] In the revised 1602 edition of the *Works*, Speght incorporates Thynne's comments and cites William of Malmesbury as his authority, just as Thynne does in the *Animadversions*. Elsewhere, Thynne corrects Speght's claims about the currency used in Chaucer's day. The Society of Antiquaries papers are again the likely immediate source, though Thynne is careful to point out that his information ultimately derives from exchequer records.[110]

While the connection between his Society of Antiquaries presentation on sterling money and his comments on currency is clear, Thynne's scholarly interests inform his comments in Speght's edition in other, less direct ways. His fierce devotion to the herald's office doubtless inflects his somewhat scandalized objection to Speght's emendation of "harlottes" to "heralds" at *Romaunt of the Rose* folio 144 (line 6068 in modern editions). Heralds, he writes, "wolde mightily be offended to have them holden of the conditions of 'false semblance'" as Speght's line has it.[111] Thynne strengthens his claim with reference to his own work on the office of the Earl Marshal, explaining that the marshal was expected, among other things, to keep unseemly women away from the court, and thus was known at times as the "Rex Ribaldorum," or king of harlots.[112] In 1602 Speght adopts Thynne's correction, with something less than a *mea culpa*, writing in the expanded hard word list,

> *Harrolds*, fol. 144, whereas in some bookes it is, 'my king of Harrolds shalt thou be'; it is now corrected thus (my king of Harlots shalt thou bee.) For so it is in the French Moralization of [Jean] Molinet 149, where hee is called *Roi des Ribaulds*, which is the king of harlots, or wicked persons: an office of great account in times past, and yet used in the court of Fraunce. Of this office speaketh *Johannes Tillius* in his second booke *De rebus Gallicis*, under the title *De Praefecto pretorio Regis*.[113]

Speght concludes this observation with the note, "but more hereof when time shall serve in M. F. Thins comment." This remark is generally dismissed, with the understanding that such "comment" was never executed. The annotations in Thynne's copy of the 1598 *Works*, which are especially dense in the *Romaunt*, could be evidence that such a project was indeed under way when Speght wrote in 1602.[114]

Terms related to alchemy also draw Thynne's attention in this final section. He corrects Speght's definition of "fermentation," explaining that it is a term of art, borrowed from baking but most relevant to alchemy, and "citrinatione," which he describes as both "a coolor and parte of the philosphers stoone."[115] Thynne's critical interest in these terms is heightened by his belief, shared with many English scholars in the sixteenth century, that Chaucer was expert in "that abstruce scyence," and therefore could be expected to comprehend and deploy such terms in their obscure sense.[116] This view persists and even flourishes despite the anti-alchemic satire in the *Canon's Yeoman's Tale*; as Thynne explains, in it Chaucer "enveye[s] againste the sophisticall abuse" of the alchemic arts, out of his respect for genuine practitioners.[117] Thynne may even have drawn upon his own alchemical collections when preparing the *Animadversions*: his identification of the poison used in the *Pardoner's Tale* as "resagor," or arsenic, rests on the alchemical treatise "De Phenice," which appears in Thynne's hand in British Library MS Additional 11388.

As a herald and as an alchemist (albeit one better versed in theory than in practice), Thynne is also particularly sensitive—at times oversensitive—to certain kinds of symbolism. He provides a long argument in favor of his father's reading of "ceriall" over Speght's "unserial" in the description of Emily's garland in *Anelida and Arcite*. Thynne argues that serrial, or green, oak is more appropriate to Emily since she sacrifices to Diana who, he explains, is also known as Hecate. According to a number of authorities, Hecate was crowned with green oak, making it the best choice for Emily, her devotee.[118] (He also notes that, by contrast, there is a reference to the "oke serriall" in the "Flower and the Leaf," where it may indeed be appropriate for the chaplets worn by trumpeters.) This is a small point, and Thynne belabors it, but his comments show awareness of the way that variant readings may change not just the meaning of a line, but the allusive and poetic qualities of the text as well.

Thynne is also attuned to obscure words of other origins. Thynne and Speght both appear to struggle to define certain religious words and do so in ways that reveal a Protestant bias. The problems Thynne finds with certain annotations, in particular, suggest that declining knowledge of medieval religious life may have posed a challenge for some early Protestant readers of medieval poetry. In one case, Thynne corrects Speght's misidentification of "vernicle" as a brooch depicting the instruments of Christ's crucifixion, noting that it is in fact the cloth "wherein was the printe of [Christ's] face" (the 1602 edition reflects this correction).[119] In both his written marginalia and in the *Animadversions*, Thynne takes note of Speght's entry "begyn and Bigott," a reference to the *Romaunt of the Rose*.[120] The allusion is to the Beguine order of lay religious women, but Speght, apparently unfamiliar with them, glosses "begyn" from context as "superstitious hypocrites." Thynne, marginally better informed, responds that he is partially correct and clarifies that "begyns" are specifically *women* of this type, as indicated by references in the *Romaunt of the Rose*.[121] He describes the Beguine order as one of "nuns" and refers Speght to Matthew of Paris and Matthew of Westminster on their history.

For Francis Thynne, there may be no real jump between Beguines as he understands them and the "superstitious hypocrites" in Speght's gloss. Both Speght and Thynne approach Chaucer with a reflexively Protestant worldview increasingly hostile to female religious. But absent in this anti-Catholic sentiment is the strong sense of radical polemic that shapes the accounts of mid-century commentators like Bale and Foxe. Still, for Speght and Thynne and others in their intellectual and social circles, Protestantism has become the default lens through which to view the English past.[122]

Thynne's concern for the historical specificity of Chaucer's words extends from the lexicographical to the orthographical and linguistic. His regard for

Chaucer's writing as the product of a particular set of cultural, political, and linguistic circumstances is evident, for example, in his comment on Speght's decision to emend the name Campaneus to the more classical Capaneus.[123] Thynne's justification for this change is substantially more complex than a stubborn resistance to any alteration to his father's text, though he is aware his criticisms of Speght may come across as such.[124] Arguing in favor of the nonclassical orthography, Thynne also demonstrates knowledge of non-Chaucerian poets when he writes, "all the writers of Englande in that age call him 'campaneus,' as Gower 'in confessione amantis,' and Lidgat in 'the historye of Thebes' taken out of Statius, and Chaucer hym selfe in many other places."[125] While Thynne's authorities do not quite constitute "*all* the writers of Englande in that age," his claim shows how emerging notions of periodization—medieval England as something that is both after the classical past and prior to the humanistic recovery of that past—are beginning to inflect the way that literary texts are read. Thynne understands that Chaucer has contemporaries, and they are linked by a common form of the English language that is different from the one shared by Thynne and Speght. Thynne continues, "Wherefore, since yt was universallye received *in that age*, to call him 'Campaneus,' lett us not nowe alter yt but permytte yt to have free passage accordinge to the pronuntiatione and wrytinge *of that age*, since, in deducinge woordes from one language to one other, there ys often additione and substractione of letters, or of Sillabes, before, in the middle, and in the ende of those wordes."[126] Indeed, Thynne at times seems to glory in the potential of language to change: suggesting that Speght reinstate "maketh" for his emendation of "waketh" in the *Summoner's Tale* line 1833 ("this maketh the fend"), he notes that, though "waketh" makes better sense when the line is read according to contemporary subject-verb-object syntax, "fend" is in fact the subject of the verb. Such transposition occurs, he writes, "by a true conversione after the dialecte of oure tonge, whiche withe beawtye useth such transmutacione as I colde gyve you many pretye instances."[127] Occasionally, he even ventures some systemic comment on unfamiliar aspects of Chaucer's English. In a note on the *Nun's Priest's Tale*, for example, he writes "in many olde inglyshe woordes, this syllable (be) is sett before to make yt moor signyficante and of force," and thus its unexpected appearance should be taken as a mark of emphasis, not a scribal error.[128]

For Thynne, an enthusiastic if sometimes inaccurate copyist of medieval texts, Chaucer's poetry has its own historical standard and ensuing kind of linguistic integrity. His access to this integrity is hampered, however, by the absence of any procedure for determining the most authoritative examples among manuscript witnesses. In cases where the manuscripts provide more than one reasonable reading of a line, Thynne is often content to let both stand. In response to Speght's substitution of "Russye" for "Surrye" in the *Man of Law's Tale*, he writes "true yt is, that some written copies have 'Russye' and some 'Surrye.' And therefore indifferent after the wrytten copies, and some auncient printed copies before my fathers editione."[129] In a later note on the *Merchant's Tale* he observes that "that may not saye naye" and "there may no wighte say nay" are "boothe founde in written coppyes."[130] While emphatic that the authoritative text of Chaucer comes from manuscripts, Thynne has no criteria for deciding between variant readings, apart from what seems to him to make the most sense given context or that which has "that energye, sprite or lyfe, whiche have Chaucers woordes."[131] On the one hand, Thynne's perspective anticipates the appreciation of variance offered by postmodern critics like Bernard Cerquiglini and Paul Zumthor; on the other, it demonstrates a pragmatic acquiescence to the realities of textual instability in a manuscript culture.[132] Either way, in this passage we see Thynne confronting the kinds of challenges that textual scholars continue to face today, while also demonstrating a blind faith in the excellence of Chaucer's language characteristic of early modern readers.

Thynne's comments, however pedantic, cast light on what at least one contemporary reader saw as being at stake in the paratextual apparatus and textual emendations found in Speght's Chaucer. They also show how the historical and antiquarian practices of the late sixteenth and early seventeenth century could be applied to the study of vernacular medieval texts. While it is not my intention to claim for either Speght or Thynne a kind of full-fledged literary historicism, their work—Thynne's especially—shows how much overlap there could be between the study of Chaucer and the scholarship fostered in institutions like the Society of Antiquaries and the College of Arms. Like the study of Chaucer, research into sepulchral arms or the ancient boundaries between shires insists upon a historical distance between the object of study and the present, and uses that distance to argue for the antiquity and authority of a tradition identified as distinctively English. More specifically, I believe Thynne's overall approach and his particular interest in the hard word list stems from its affinity with discourses delivered to the Society of Antiquaries, which often began with a discussion of the etymology of key terms related to the topic, a practice borrowed from French legal scholarship.[133] More generally, we can see how Thynne's practice, both in his own notes on Chaucer and in the *Animadversions*, involves extensive reference to secondary sources, the same sources he used in his antiquarian and historical writing.

In the closing lines of the *Animadversions*, a text almost entirely concerned with the past, Thynne looks toward the future of Chaucerian editing. He offers his comments to Speght, he writes, "to the ende Chawcers Woorkes by muche conference and manye judgmentes mighte at leng[t]he obteyne their true perfectione and glorye," reprinted, corrected, and annotated "after the manner of the Italians, who have largelye comented Petrarche."[134] Like Camden's *Britannia* or Holinshed's *Chronicles*, Thynne's work on Chaucer is an attempt to "recover" a previously unclaimed part of British history and so construct a common past for the present. While this full commentary never did appear, Thynne left records of his engagement with Chaucer that illustrate how the scholarly climate of late Tudor England could and did shape the ways in which medieval literature was read, and the uses to which it was put.

Chaucerians and other scholars who read the *Animadversions* in an isolated context have been put off by its cantankerous tone and apparently petty stakes. But the detailed, often accurate, comments proffered by Thynne are both representative of his writing more generally and indicative of a new place for Chaucer and his writing in scholarly discourse. Thynne's work on Chaucer is interdisciplinary, seeking to better understand the text by recourse to legal history, alchemy, and heraldry.[135] This interdisciplinary approach characterizes medieval studies today, too.

The *Animadversions* is also perhaps the first work on Chaucer identifiable as the response of one secondary critic to another, the beginning of a kind of scholarly publishing. While the impetus for Thynne's involvement with Speght's project is no doubt the legacy of his father's *Works*, his treatise and the handwritten notes he took while preparing it represent a real effort to use the historical insights of early modern scholarship to better understand Chaucer and his writing. Viewed within the broader context of Thynne's career, his comments on Chaucer assume their greatest significance not when dismissed as a jealous retort, but rather when understood as a testimony to the close affiliation of English historical and literary scholarship at a formative stage in their development.

Throughout his work, in his poetry as well as in his prose, Thynne anchors Chaucer's writings in the English past but also argues for their importance to intellectual and historical work of the present. Like the glossaries discussed in Chapter 4, Thynne's writings both insist on Chaucer's historicity and offer readers templates—some scholarly and ostensibly objective, others more forthrightly subjective—for relating his works to their own moment. Thus, it is by making Chaucer a subject of history, that Thynne and other early modern antiquarians lay the groundwork for Chaucer's lasting reputation as an author.

CHAPTER 6

Chaucer's Scholarly Readers in Seventeenth-Century England

The revised Speght edition of Chaucer's *Works* published in 1602 marked the beginning of an eighty-five-year hiatus in Chaucerian printing, the longest gap in the poet's history. It did not, however, signal an equivalent pause in antiquarian engagement with Chaucer's works. This final chapter considers a trio of seventeenth-century scholarly readers of Chaucer. Each reworked his book to suit his own particular interest and needs, relying in part on the paratextual apparatus of Speght's 1598 and 1602 editions. These readers—the lawyer and manuscript collector Joseph Holland (d. 1605), the antiquarian, astrologer, and collector Elias Ashmole (1617–1692), and the Dutch philologist Franciscus Junius the Younger (1591–1677)—each worked, to a greater or lesser extent, within the antiquarian traditions responsible for transmitting Chaucer's text in the sixteenth century. Although no edition of the collected *Works* was published between 1602 and 1687, when a booksellers' reprint of Speght's edition appeared, the commentary left by Holland, Ashmole, and Junius shows how the considerations that informed responses to Chaucer in the sixteenth century continued to guide antiquarian engagement with the poet well into the seventeenth.[1]

More than just readers, each annotator left evidence of a distinctive material engagement with the Chaucerian text. Holland used Speght's *Works* to repair and expand an important fifteenth-century manuscript. Ashmole added the apocryphal *Tale of Gamelyn* to the *Canterbury Tales* and recorded both classical allusions and astrological observations in his copy of the 1532 edition of the *Works*. Junius, the most accomplished scholar of the trio, applied his formidable philological and lexicographical skills to the production of a substantial glossary of Chaucerian language.

Just as their approaches differed, so too did the materials they used. Holland worked with a medieval manuscript, the Chaucerian miscellany that is now Cambridge University Library MS Gg.4.27. Ashmole owned a copy of the 1532 Thynne edition, but added to it using the 1598 Speght edition and at least two additional manuscripts. Junius, living in Leiden during the final years of his life, read his copy of the 1598 Speght *Works* alongside a 1553 printed edition of the *Eneados*, Gavin Douglas's early sixteenth-century Scots translation of the *Aeneid*. In addition, the similarities between Ashmole's and Junius's notes suggest that—despite working three decades apart and on opposite sides of the North Sea—the two may have made use of a common set of notes on Chaucer that contained material not found in Speght's commentary. Working with individual copies rather than preparing material for a larger public, these readers produced personalized books that met their specific needs.

Like previous Chaucerians, the readers I consider here were committed to commemorating Chaucer and improving his text. In the address to the reader in his 1598 edition, Thomas Speght asserts that his purpose is to make Chaucer more accessible to a present-day audience of gentlemen and friends. He writes that, "some few years past, I was requested by certaine Gentlemen my neere friends, who loved Chaucer, as he well deserveth; to take a little pains in reviving the memorie of so rare a man, as also in doing some reparations on his works, which they judged to be much decaied by injurie of time, ignorance of writers, and negligence of Printers."[2] Holland, Ashmole, and Junius shared Speght's investment both in "reviving the memory" of Chaucer and in providing some "reparations" to his text.

While marginalia can be difficult to interpret, assessing these "used books" within the context of their owners' broader antiquarian interests lets us see how they both relied upon and departed from an existing tradition of scholarly Chaucerianism in their reading and annotation practices.[3] I discuss their work in the order it was undertaken: Holland is the eldest of the group and dated his manuscript in 1600; Ashmole signed his copy of Chaucer with the date 1642; and Junius—though more than twenty-five years older that Ashmole—began to work on Chaucer in the late 1660s, near the end of a remarkably long and productive career. This arrangement also allows me to move chronologically through their source material: Holland's manuscript, Ashmole's unglossed 1532 edition, and Junius's copies of Speght's editions. Together, these readers form a chronological and methodological bridge with later scholarship, looking forward to the more sophisticated editorial approach of Thomas Tyrwhitt and the great Victorian Chaucerians like Skeat.[4] They show how, increasingly, Chaucer was the province of the scholar rather than the general reader, and how an antiquarian approach to the Chaucerian book created new scenes of reading and interpretation.

Joseph Holland

Joseph Holland (d. 1605) was a lawyer, member of the Inner Temple, and active participant in the Elizabethan Society of Antiquaries.[5] He delivered at least twenty papers to the group, making him one of the society's most active members.[6] His involvement would have put him in regular contact with many antiquarian stalwarts, including Robert Cotton, who cofounded the society with his former teacher William Camden.[7] Cotton, whose manuscript collections were unrivaled in both size and scope in early modern England, famously disbound and rebound volumes in his possession, forming new affiliations between previously separate texts and divorcing materials that had been joined together in earlier bindings.[8] Like Cotton, Holland intervened in the arrangement and contents of his medieval book and, like Cotton, his engagement shows how print shaped his thinking about the medieval manuscript. In Holland's case, his understanding of what his fifteenth-century Chaucerian book should contain was deeply mediated by later printed collections.

Sometime before 1600, Holland became the owner of the large and stately poetic miscellany that is now Cambridge University Library MS Gg.4.27 (hereafter referred to as Gg).[9] Though Gg contains Lydgate's *Temple of Glas* and several anonymous shorter poems, most of its contents are Chaucerian. Its text of the *Canterbury Tales* bears a close relationship to that of the Ellesmere manuscript, and its copy of the *Legend of Good Women* includes the unique "G" version of the prologue.[10] The manuscript also includes the *A.B.C.*, *Lenvoy de Chaucer a Scogan*, *Truth*, *Troilus and Criseyde*, and the *Parliament of Fowles*, all by Chaucer.[11] In their facsimile edition of the manuscript, Malcolm B. Parkes and Richard Beadle date Gg to the second half of the first quarter of the fifteenth century, making it one of the oldest surviving Chaucer manuscripts and placing it among the first attempts to bring together a significant portion of Chaucer's writings in a single codex.[12] The book's patrons and earliest owners are unknown, but it seems to be the product of a workshop outside the ambit of professional London scribes and was probably made in East Anglia.[13] The text was written by two scribes, operating cooperatively; the scribe responsible for the main portion of the text—Parkes and Beadle's Scribe A—is distinguished by his unusual and eccentric orthography, a feature that might have caused the language of the manuscript to appear especially distant and unfamiliar to its early modern readers.[14] Holland apparently had the manuscript cleaned, removing fifteenth-century readers' marks and other evidence that might have given clues to its early provenance.

Though a high-quality manuscript, Gg was significantly damaged by the time it came into Holland's possession. Originally, Gg's text of the *Canterbury Tales* featured a series of pilgrim portraits, similar (though less extravagant) to those found in the Ellesmere manuscript, as well as a unique set of allegorical illustrations in the *Parson's Tale*.[15] It also featured full-page miniatures at the beginning of both the *Tales* and *Troilus and Criseyde*. In the later fifteenth or early sixteenth century, these full-page illustrations, along with the majority of the pilgrim portraits, were removed (the illustrations in the *Parson's Tale* remain intact).[16] This mutilation deprived the book of both the illuminations and the text on their verso, with significant impact on the readability of the *Canterbury Tales*, the first long work in the manuscript and one likely to draw the attention of any reader.

In response to this damage, Holland could have undertaken a simple repair job, supplying the lost passages and perhaps updating some of the more difficult spellings.[17] Instead, he worked with a professional scribe to both mend the book and to supplement its original contents using Thomas Speght's 1598 edition of Chaucer. In doing so, he made changes that expanded the text of the manuscript beyond its original scope, incorporating several new works and adding material drawn from the paratext of Speght's edition. While Speght's edition would have been the newest one available, there is also good reason to believe that Holland and Speght knew each other personally, if not at the time Holland acquired Gg, then shortly thereafter, since the text of the *A.B.C.* printed in 1602 is copied from Gg and the manuscript came into Holland's possession no later than 1600.[18]

Through the introduction of material taken over from Speght, Gg becomes an object retroactively shaped by its own reception, with the late sixteenth-century printed *Works* serving as a model for Holland's treatment of his fifteenth-century manuscript. While some of the additions to Gg were determined by the nature of its damage, others reflect an attempt to bridge the gap between the bibliographic or codicological idea of "Chaucer's works" as embodied in Gg and in Speght. While Holland clearly recognized Gg as a comprehensive collection of Chaucer's writings, his understanding of what such a collection "should" look like was informed in significant ways by Speght's 1598 edition.

Ultimately, thirty-five new leaves were added to the manuscript while it was in Holland's possession. Though originally bound with the manuscript, these additional leaves were removed from the manuscript when it was rebound under the supervision of the Cambridge librarian Henry Bradshaw in the late nineteenth century.[19] They are now bound and cataloged separately as Gg.4.27.1(b) (fragments of a fourteenth-century manuscript containing a portion of the early Middle English romances *Floris and Blanchefleur* and *King Horn* were also bound with the manuscript when it was in Holland's possession and are now cataloged as Gg.4.27.2).[20] All the added pages are vellum of approximately the same size as the sheets used in the original manuscript. Paper would have been more readily available in 1600, and the use of vellum here suggests investment in maintaining the visual and material unity of the book. Most of the pages are written in the hand of Holland's scribe, whose elegant italic script also appears in several other books once owned by Holland, including British Library Cotton MS Vespasian E.v and MS Harley 7026.[21] This scribe also wrote the name of his employer and the date 1600 in capital letters on what is now the manuscript's first folio. Today, Holland's name and the 1600 date have been expunged by a later owner or conservator, placing Holland's role in the transmission of the text and its contents under an uncommonly literal form of erasure.

Overall, Holland's aim seems to have been to improve the readability and utility of the manuscript. (I refer here to Holland but, of course, decisions about the manuscript could have been made by the scribe or someone else in his employ.) His decision to supply the passages lost when the illustrations were removed supports the idea that he regarded Gg as a book to be used and read. Although they are now a separate codex, the leaves containing the missing passages from the *Canterbury Tales* and *Troilus and Criseyde* (now Gg.4.27.1(b) fols. 11–29) were initially inserted into the manuscript at the points where the missing lines would have originally appeared. The scribe also added incipits and catchwords to the surviving fifteenth-century manuscript in order to clarify transitions where the connecting text had been lost due to the removal of illustrations. Along with the use of vellum, the presence of the same hand in both the older portion of the manuscript and on the new pages creates a visual and textual continuity. Inserted into the body of the manuscript, the intercalated leaves minimized the aesthetic disruption caused by the excisions and allowed for continuous reading of both *Troilus* and the *Canterbury Tales* for the first time since the mutilation of the manuscript.

While Holland and his scribe generally placed the missing passages at the point in the manuscript at which they would have originally appeared, there is one exception: the penitent *Retraction* to the *Canterbury Tales,* in which Chaucer apologizes for most of his secular works and asks readers, on the basis of his more moral writings, to pray for the salvation of his soul. At the time new materials were added to Gg, the *Retraction* was placed at the end of the volume, after Lydgate's *Temple of Glas* and just before the abridged version of Speght's hard word list. Gg very well might have originally included the *Retraction*, since the *Parson's Tale* concludes on the verso of folio 443 and the *Legend of Good Women* picks up on the following page (now folio 445) without any loss of text, despite the stub of a missing leaf.[22] If the manuscript did once contain the *Retraction*, in this way it would have differed from the folio editions of the *Works* known to Holland, none of which include it. Holland's scribe copied the *Retraction* from Caxton's 1483 edition of the *Canterbury Tales* (STC 5083), one of several pre-1532 editions that contain it.

While the *Retraction*'s addition is consistent with other choices that bespeak a desire to improve Gg's text of the *Canterbury Tales*, its placement at the back of the volume is an odd choice. There is no clear need or reason to separate the *Retraction* from the rest of the *Canterbury Tales*, nor is there any evidence that the *Retraction* was ever copied separate from the rest of the *Tales* in fifteenth-century manuscripts. Its placement at the end of the volume could indicate that Holland, like some other early readers, considered the *Retraction* a kind of closing statement that applied not only to the *Tales* alone, but to the Chaucerian corpus more generally.[23] Alternatively, it may reflect ambivalence or uncertainty about the relationship of the *Retraction* to the rest of the *Tales*, an uncertainty shared by other later readers of the *Tales*.[24] In either case, the placement of the *Retraction* seems to reflect its status in the early modern Chaucer canon—liminal at best—rather than its probable appearance and original position in the fifteenth-century manuscript.

Not only is the placement of the *Retraction* unusual, so is its text, in ways that suggest further ambivalence about its relation to the Chaucerian corpus. The version of the *Retraction* found in Gg omits the opening lines of the piece, in which Chaucer solicits the prayers of his readers. As it continues, it effectively excises all references to Catholicism from the text. The conclusion in Gg reads:

But of the translacion of Boece de consolacione, and other books, as of legendys of Sayntes, and omelyes, moralitie, and devotion; that thanke I of our Lord Jhesu Crist, besechynge hem that from hensforth unto my lyvys ende, he sende me grace to bewaylle my gyltes; that it maye stande unto the salvacion of my soule: and graunt me grace of very repentaunce, confessyon and satisfaction to doe in this present lyfe thrugh the benygne grace of hem that is King of Kinges, and preest of all prestys; that bought us with the pretious blood of his herte; so that I may bee one of hem at the day of dome that shal be savyd: *Qui cum patre, et Spiritu sancto, vivit et regnat Deus, pro Omnia secula seculorum Amen.*[25]

In Caxton's text and in manuscript versions of the piece, by contrast, the speaker thanks not only Jesus Christ, but also "hys blessyd moder, and alle the sayntes of heven."[26] These changes to the text take Chaucer out of the penitential economy of intercessory prayer and reshape the *Retraction* in ways that are more consistent with the early modern understanding—derived from a mix of apocryphal texts like the *Plowman's Tale* and statements about Chaucer's biography in Foxe and Speght—that Chaucer had been a religious reformer.[27]

The remaining early modern leaves contain material adapted from the 1598 Speght edition of the *Works*. Folios 1–7 in the current MS Gg.4.27.1(b) were originally inserted at the beginning of the fifteenth-century manuscript, while MS Gg.4.27.1(b) folios 29–35 were placed at the back of the manuscript (this includes the leaf containing the *Retraction*, now fol. 29). In form and in content, these additions are clearly modeled on Speght, and they represent the most radical shift away from the manuscript's original design and toward the model offered by printed collections of Chaucer. They make it clear that as Holland reworked his manuscript, he did so with the idea of Speght's edition of the *Works* in mind.

Like other printed collections, Speght's *Works* offers the reader a more comprehensive Chaucerian canon than any manuscript could. Gg is missing several longer poems that would have been familiar to readers of printed collections, perhaps most notably the *Book of the Duchess* and the *House of Fame*. (It does contain the *Parliament of Fowles*.) Holland's scribe did not add any of these pieces, but, on a single leaf at the back of the volume, he copies over three short poems included in Speght. These are "Bon Counsail" (in Speght, the poem appears under the title "A Saying of Dan John" [sig. O2v]; John Shirley also attributes the poem to John Lydgate in manuscript),[28] "Chaucer to his emptie purse," and "Chaucers words to his Scrivener." All three of these were first printed in John Stow's 1561 edition of Chaucer, and all appear together again the 1598 Speght edition. All three (if we take the speaker in "Bon Counsail" to be Chaucer himself) appear to offer some personal insight into the poet, and thus might reflect a special interest in Chaucer's authorial persona and a desire to update the selection of works in Gg accordingly.[29]

More striking than these canonical changes, however, is the addition of material drawn directly from the 1598 paratext. The most dramatic addition to Gg is, without a doubt, a copy of the genealogical engraving produced by John Speed for the 1598 *Works*, which has been tinted in full, with additional details in gilt, displaying Holland's heraldic skills to maximal effect (Figure 9).[30] The engraving, which depicts Chaucer, the tomb of his son and daughter-in-law Thomas and Maude Chaucer, and an elaborate family tree, is a distinctly later production than the manuscript. Its appearance here disrupts the fantasy of codicological and temporal unity that other elements of the volume seem to cultivate: the Speed image traces Chaucer's "progenie" down to the sixteenth century, and the engraving itself is produced using a technology that did not exist when Gg was created. The only printed material in what is otherwise a handwritten production, its presence in the manuscript was noticed in the eighteenth century by the poet Thomas Gray, who describes it in a letter to Horace Walpole as "a pretty old print . . . neatly colored."[31] Inserted following the title page, the engraving pulls in two different temporal directions: like the other paratextual information copied over from Speght's *Works*, this image conveys important historical information, anchoring Chaucer at a particular moment in a narrative of English history that links past and present. At the same time, the lavish embellishment exceeds the purely informative. It responds to the engraving's monumental, memorializing function, and recalls the deluxe and colorful illustrative program put in place by the manuscript's fifteenth-century creators.[32] In Chapter 1 I argued for a kind of devotional quality to this image, and its appearance here, along with tinting and other embellishment, suggests that for Holland, the manuscript constituted a more appropriate site for veneration than the printed book from which it came.

The engraving was originally bound so that it appeared opposite a handwritten page with material drawn from Speght's *Life of Chaucer*. The passage in question discusses the poet Hoccleve, whom the Speed engraving identifies as the source for its portrait. Holland (or, rather, his scribe) writes:

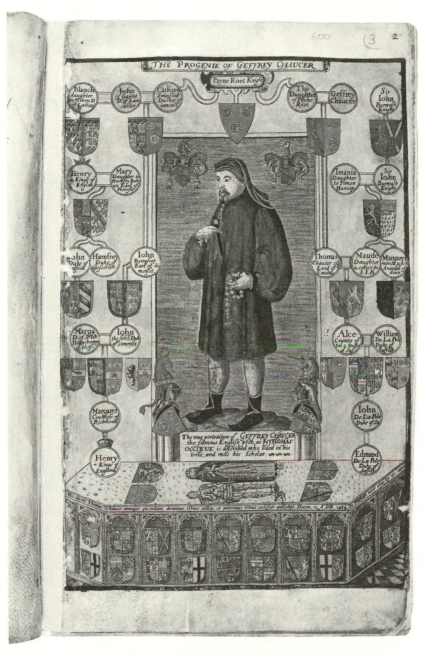

Figure 9. "The Progenie of Geffrey Chaucer," Cambridge University Library MS Gg.4.27.1(b), fol. 1. Reproduced by kind permission of the Syndics of Cambridge University Library.

Thomas Occleve of the office of the privye seale, somtime Chaucers
Scoller, for the love he bare to his master Caused his picture to be
truly drawen in his booke de REGIMINE PRINCIPIS dedicated
unto kinge Henry the fift; according to the which this folowinge
was made by John Spede: And the sayde Occleve in that booke
where he setteth downe CHAUCERS picture addeth these verses:

> Although his life be queint, the Resemblaunce
> Of him hath in me so fresh lifelines;
> That to put other men in remembraunce
> of his person, I have here the likenes
> doe make to the end in sothfastnes
> That they that of him have lost thought and minde
> By this peinture may agayne him finde.[33]

He continues:

The same Author agayne in the same Booke in Comendation of
CHAUCER

> My deare maister, God his soule quite;
> My fader Chaucer, faine wold have me taught;
> But I was younge, and leered lite or nought:
> But welaway so is mine hart woe,
> That the honour of English tongue is deed,
> Of which I wont was counsayle have and reed;
> O master dere, and fader reverent,
> My master Chaucer, flower of Eloquence,
> Mirror of fructious entendement,
> O universall fader of science;
> Alas that thow thine excellent prudence
> In thy bed mortall, mightiest not bequeath.[34]

Holland's version of this second passage actually combines and transposes
two longer quotations from the *Regiment of Princes*, both of which are quoted
in full in Speght.[35] The juxtaposition of the engraving and these lines from
Hoccleve in Holland's own manuscript create an opening in which praise
of Chaucer appears on one leaf and the engraved portrait on the opposite,
just as in Speght. Once again, Gg looks forward and backward, evoking
both the combination of praise and portraiture in fifteenth-century *Regi-*

ment of Princes manuscripts and Speght's late sixteenth-century imitation of the same.

After this decorative and celebratory opening, Holland's scribe has crafted a manuscript title page that mimics the language of the elaborate 1598 title page. His heading, "Here foloweth the works of our Antient, And learned English Poet GEFFREY CHAVCER," follows the wording and orthography of the Speght frontispiece, down to the use of a classicizing *v* in "Chavcer." The use of the term "Works" on this page clearly situates this book in the tradition of monumental efforts to memorialize Chaucer in a single volume. Below this heading are three short verse excerpts, all of which are found in Speght's *Works*. Together, they function as epigraphs for the Gg collection as a whole. These include the opening lines of the *Parliament of Fowls*, the beginning of the Chaucer/Merlin prophetic poem printed without attribution in the prefatories to the *Works*, and a passage from Lydgate's *Fall of Princes* quoted in Speght's *Life of Chaucer*. Taken together, the elements on this page point toward an assiduous reader who judiciously selected material from the *Works* and who took pains to craft his book in the image of Chaucer as he was understood at the end of the sixteenth century, emphasizing his Englishness, his role in the development of vernacular poetics, and his increasing "antiquity."

Below the short epitaphs is a longer passage of seven lines, taken from Lydgate's *Fall of Princes*, in praise of "My maister Chaucer," the "loadsterre" of the English language. In Gg, these lines are introduced with the following note: "John Lidgate a munk of Burie, an excellent poet, And Chaucers scoller; amongst divers others in those days, wrote in Comendation of Chaucer."[36] The same Lydgate passage appears in Speght's *Life of Chaucer*, but while Lydgate is mentioned several times in the paratextual materials to the *Works*, he is never called a "scoller" of Chaucer.[37] For an analogue, one must look to the Speed engraving, which Holland clearly knew well and which names Hoccleve as Chaucer's "Scholar." More tantalizingly, one might also look to the epistle to Gabriel Harvey in Spenser's *Shepheardes Calender* (1579), which does identify Lydgate as Chaucer's "scholar." William Kuskin has argued, in the context of Spenser's text, that this designation denies Lydgate creative agency while at the same time positioning him as an "authentic" witness to Chaucer's genius.[38] It is in this sense that Holland deploys the term as well. The representation of both Hoccleve and Lydgate as "scollers" constructs a genealogy of Chaucerian students or scholars, admirers who are not just imitators and fellow poets. This distinction not only helps to isolate Chaucer as a singular poetic genius without contemporary equals, but also creates a tradition of Chaucerian study in which Holland, Speght, and other nonpoet readers of Chaucer's works can also take part.

A brief summary of Speght's *Life of Chaucer* follows. The Gg abridgment zeros in on details that would interest a late-Tudor antiquarian like Holland: it emphasizes that Chaucer was born in London, was educated at Oxford (Holland's summary includes Speght's claim that Chaucer studied with John Wycliffe), and practiced as a lawyer at the Inner Temple—where, not coincidentally, Holland himself was also a member. The Gg version also includes the detail, originating in Leland and repeated by Speght but not widely referenced elsewhere, that Chaucer "flourished in fraunce, and got himself great commendation there, by his diligent exercise in lerninge," suggesting an interest in Chaucer in a European context, not just an English one. Holland also records Chaucer's traditional death date, October 25, 1400, and offers a brief description of Chaucer's gravesite in Westminster Abbey. His comments offer a plausible firsthand account of the tomb as it appeared at the end of the sixteenth century, although, as Joseph Dane and Alexandra Gillespie have noted, it is difficult to account for the variation among early modern descriptions of Chaucer's tomb and its inscriptions.[39]

The final leaf in this prefatory section of the manuscript contains material taken from the concluding portion of Speght's *Life*, which concerns posthumous tributes by later poets. Holland's account reads:

> Amongst divers lerned men that of late tyme have written in
> commendation of CHAVCER as mr William Thynne in his Epistle
> to Kinge Henry the Eight, Mr Ascham, Mr Spencer, Mr William
> Camden, mr Frauncis Beaumont and others: we may conclude his
> praises with the Testimony of the most worthiest gentilman that
> the Court hath afforded of many years, Sir Phillip Sydney knight;
> In his Apologie for poetry, sayth thus of him: Chaucer undoubt-
> edly did excellently in his Troylus and Creseida; of whom truly
> I know not whether to mervaile more; either that he in that mistie
> time could see so clearly, or that wee in this cleare age, walke so
> stumblingly after him.[40]

Holland's work thus reproduces, in miniature, the key features of Speght's prefatory material: an impressive title page, information about the poet's life and tomb, and a collection of tributes attesting to the poet's ongoing importance. Together, these work (in Gg as in the printed *Works*) to situate Chaucer in relation to the present and to secure his status as an author of stature equal to the great classical and continental writers.

More leaves were added at the back of Gg, most of which (with the exception of the leaf containing the *Retraction*) also contain material drawn from Speght's *Works*. The most significant addition here is an abridged version of Speght's list of "hard words." In Speght, Middle English terms are printed in blackletter while their modern synonyms are given in roman type. In Gg, Middle English terms are written in an italic hand, and their contemporary synonyms in secretary hand, an arrangement that imitates Speght's typographic distinction between older and newer forms of English (see Figure 10). Most of the definitions come directly from Speght, with occasional modifications, and a few new entries are added, perhaps in response to specific challenges posed by the unusual orthography of the manuscript.

On the following folios, which constitute the last of the added leaves, someone (not Holland's scribe) has copied over the arguments section of the 1598 *Works* (the argument for the *General Prologue* to the *Canterbury Tales* was copied over separately and inserted in the body of the manuscript just before the *General Prologue* at folio 132). Since folio numbers have been added in the margins, this section functions as a kind of annotated index; however, here again the materiality of the medieval manuscript and its printed successor butt up against one another. The arguments follow the order and selection of the texts as they appear in Speght. This means that the list includes texts, like the *Romaunt of the Rose* and the *Boece*, that do not appear in Gg, and that those texts that do appear in both Gg and the *Works* are listed in a different order than they are found in the manuscript. Thus, the index, even as it brings Gg closer in line with the functionality and appearance of Speght's printed book, underscores the differences between Gg and the printed *Works*.

Ultimately, Joseph Holland was a careful and enthusiastic custodian of Gg.4.27. Using the best resources available, he and his scribe attempted to remedy deficiencies in its text, supplement its canon with additional works, and ensure that future readers of the manuscript were equipped with the interpretive tools needed both to read Chaucer's works and to understand their cultural import. At the same time, Holland's understanding of how his book could best fulfill its objective as a collection of Chaucerian pieces was clearly derived from later printed editions. The result of this "reverse transmission"

A		
Abaued: Abashed	Awhaped: amased	Bid: a boone made request
Abraid: arose retorned	Awreketh: revengeth	Bigami: twise maried
Abrayd: breake of	Axes: the ague	Bineme: bereave
Abyme from below	Ay: an egge	Bint: bonns
Abent: a steepe place		Bismare: curiositye
Aboune: a request		Bitressed: deceved
Acale: cooled		Blend to blind ons
Accoy: asswage		Blent: blind
Adventaile: roat armour		Ble: sight view
Agipe: a coate full of plays	**B**	Blyn: ceast
Agrise: astonished	Barbicans: watch towers	Blyth: glad
Agrose daunted	Bayne: bath	Blo: blew
A lay: a songe	Bith: both	Blne to swell
Aledge: case	Barme: lap	Boles: bulles
Algates: notwithstanding ever or altogether	Bargarett: a ballad	Boodeth: sheweth
Als: also	Bawsin: bigge	Boot: helpe
Alyres: walked	Baulke: to crosse	Bordels: brothelhouses
Allaundes: greyhoundes	Baudrick: a sword girdell	Boure: rest
Ametised: quenched	Bartele: brave or refuse	Brani: reward
Anteu: song	Bandon: company sort	Brawdery: graven workes
Arblasters: crosebowes	Baudry: braverie	Bronke: desire enioy
Arrere: a part or a syde	Baselardes daggers	Burnet: wollen
Ariste: a rose	Bay: seeke	Burnets: hooded attyre
Arite: a rest or staye	Barbe: maske or visard	Buxumnes: lowliness
Argoile: clay	Bede: offer	Burdon: a deepe base
Arten: constrayne	Bet: better	Burlace: to tarry a dead man to bury
Arke: compasse	Belt: a girdell	Burled: armed
Ascaunce: to looke asyd	Belchose: faire thinge	Bumbeth: soundeth
Astert: let passe	Belchier: good countena= :nce	Byker: a fray
Atterly: extremely	Belamy: faire frend	Bywopen: made speechless
Athroted: cloyed	Bement: lamented	
Attwyte: blamd sharply	Bemes: trumpetts or instruments of musicke	
Avaunt: a bragge or before	Benison: blessinge	
Avenant: agreeble	Bend: a muffler feather or rawse	
Aver: bribery	Benes: bones	
Aumener: cubbord	Benimmeth: bereaveth	
Autentike of antiquity	Bewrecke: revenged	
Autremite: another attire	Bereint: sprinkled	
Auntreth maketh adventure	Betrassed: deceved	
	Behight promised	

Figure 10. Hard word list, Cambridge University Library MS Gg.4.27.1(b), fol. 30. Reproduced by kind permission of the Syndics of Cambridge University Library.

was that, in Holland's pursuit of the ideal Chaucerian book, the fifteenth-century object was remade in the image of its sixteenth-century descendant.

Elias Ashmole

Elias Ashmole (1617–1692) was an antiquarian, astrologer, and alchemic enthusiast.[41] He was also an avid collector of early manuscripts, many of which are today housed at the Bodleian Library (his alchemical collections include several of Francis Thynne's manuscripts).[42] In the words of Bruce Janacek, "Ashmole was an immensely learned and curious individual and brought numerous perspectives to any single issue or text. In addition to antiquarianism and the occult, he was also very interested in botany, medicine, numismatics, heraldry, political and ecclesiastical history and local antiquarian history."[43] For Janacek, Ashmole's wide-ranging interests and accomplishments place him in the company of other learned virtuosos like Kenelm Digby and Athanasius Kircher, but Ashmole is perhaps best remembered for his ongoing interest in alchemy. This interest led to the 1652 publication of *Theatrum Chemicum Britannicum*, a collection of English writings on alchemy that, notably, includes Chaucer's *Canon's Yeoman's Tale*, nominally a satire *against* the casuistry and duplicitousness of alchemists.

Before he undertook these more ambitious projects (and the second marriage that funded them), Ashmole annotated a copy of Thynne's 1532 edition of Chaucer's *Works*, now Bodleian Library MS Ashmole 1095. Ashmole's signature in the book is dated 1642, and most of the annotations appear to have been made around the same time. If Ashmole did indeed make use of the book primarily in 1642, then it is likely he did so during his stay in Smallwood, Cheshire, after the sudden death of his first wife at her family home there in December 1641.[44] While Ashmole was not the first owner of this volume, he was its most active and enthusiastic annotator, supplementing the printed volume with additional material drawn from Speght's later editions and at least two manuscripts in his possession. The book had already been thoroughly used before it came into Ashmole's hands: two other readers, a Thomas Ashall (or Ashill) and a Thomas Gerarde, left their signatures on its pages and the book preserves marks in at least three additional hands.[45]

While Holland used printed texts to bring Gg.4.27 in line with the appearance of the published *Works*, creating a manuscript that in effect anticipates its printed successors, Ashmole updated his book by looking both back to manuscript sources and forward to Speght's editions. Holland's additions focus most closely on improving the text and making it more accessible through paratextual additions like a table of contents. Ashmole was, similarly, interested in access, but he also shared some of the exegetical concerns of later commentators Thomas Speght and Francis Thynne and used material drawn from Speght to hone and clarify his own reading of Chaucer's writings. The detailed nature of his notes testifies to the attention Ashmole devoted to the text: he approached Chaucer not as—or not only as—a source of readerly pleasure, but an object of antiquarian and scholarly inquiry. At the same time, his addition of the apocryphal *Tale of Gamelyn* to the 1532 *Works* reopens questions of canonicity otherwise settled much earlier (following William Thynne in 1532, the folio collected editions of the *Works* all base their text of the *Canterbury Tales* on Caxton's first edition of 1477, which does not include it). Ashmole's copy, like Holland's, is a kind of remix that selectively incorporates new material to make a more useful book. Ashmole's most striking addition to the *Works* is *Gamelyn*, which he had copied by a professional scribe and inserted on a series of sheets following the incomplete *Cook's Tale* (fols. 8–12 in the book's current foliation; see Figure 11). *Gamelyn* is a fourteenth-century outlaw narrative, the tale of a youngest son's efforts to regain his rightful patrimony from an evil brother after the death of his father. The tale appears in twenty-five manuscripts of the *Canterbury Tales*, where it follows the *Reeve's Tale* and functions—as it does in Ashmole—as a substitute for the incomplete *Cook's Tale*. It did not, however, appear in any printed edition of the *Tales* until Urry's 1721 edition of the *Works*, where it was presented as an alternative to the *Cook's Tale*.[46] Its inclusion then was sharply criticized by both Timothy Thomas (who completed work on Urry's edition after his death) and Thomas Tyrwhitt (who removed it from his own edition of the *Canterbury Tales*). *Gamelyn* thus differs from most of the early modern Chaucerian apocrypha in two ways: first, it has a strong association with Chaucer in manuscript; and, second, it does not appear in any of the early printed texts or folio editions.[47]

While it is difficult to believe that earlier Chaucerians were unaware of *Gamelyn*'s presence in numerous manuscripts, Ashmole was ahead of the editorial curve in recognizing this important idiosyncrasy.[48] Ashmole presumably had *Gamelyn* copied from a *Canterbury Tales* manuscript, though his source has not been traced. In his copy of the *Works*, a note in a later hand directs the reader to MS Ashmole 45, an early sixteenth-century manuscript containing the Middle English romance the *Erle of Tolous* and a translation

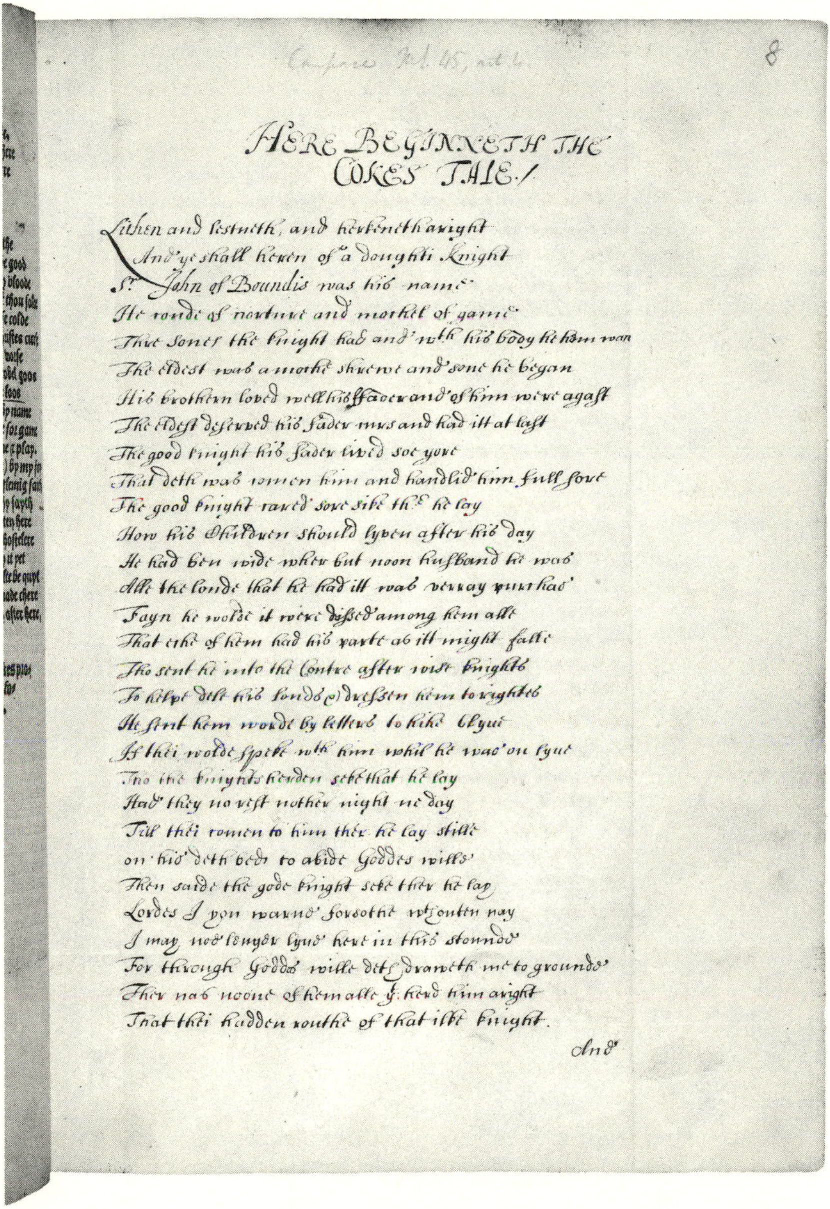

Compare fol. 45, col. 2.

HERE BEGINNETH THE
COKES TALE /

Lithen and listneth, and herkneth aright
And ye shall heren of a doughti Knight
Sᵗ John of Boundis was his name
He could of norture and mokel of game
Thre Sones the knight had and with his body he them won
The eldest was a mokel shrewe and sone he began
His brethern loved well his ffader and of him were agast
The eldest deserved his fader curs and had itt at last
The good knight his fader lived soe yore
That deth was comen him and handlid him full sore
The good knight raued sore sike there he lay
How his Children should lyben after his day
He had ben wide wher but noon husband he was
Alle the londe that he had ill was verray purchas
Fayn he wolde it were dissed among them alle
That eche of hem had his parte as itt might falle
Tho sent he into the Contre after wist knights
To helpt dele his londes and dressen hem to rights
He sent them word by letters to hem blyue
If thei wolde speke with him whil he was on lyue
Tho the knights herden seth that he lay
Had they no rist nother night ne day
Till thei comen to him ther he lay stille
on his deth bed to abide Goddes wille
Then saide the gode knight seth ther he lay
Lordes I you warne forsothe whouten nay
I may no longer lyue here in this stounde
For through Goddes wille deth draweth me to grounde
Ther was noone of hem alle if I herd him aright
That thei hadden routhe of that ilke knight.

Andᵉ

Figure 11. Ashmole's copy of the *Tale of Gamelyn*, identified as the *Cook's Tale* (Oxford, Bodleian Library MS Ashmole 1095, fol. 8). By permission of the Bodleian Libraries.

of Vegetius's treatise *De Re Militari*. To this had been added a second booklet, copied in the seventeenth century, containing Chaucer's incomplete *Cook's Tale* and *Gamelyn* (identified as "The Cook's Tale"), as well as a third containing eight books "of Poetical Astrologie" in verse by John Glanvill and dated 1613.[49] The text of *Gamelyn* that appears in MS Ashmole 45 is written in the same hand that copies the text for inclusion in his copy of the *Works*. (The manuscript also includes a version of the Chaucerian *Cook's Tale*, apparently copied from an untraced manuscript, written in this same hand.)[50] While this second copy provides no further clues as to the context in which Ashmole first encountered *Gamelyn*, its presence in a volume containing other examples of Middle English romance suggests that, while *Gamelyn*'s ostensible place in the *Canterbury Tales* was the primary reason for Ashmole's interest in the poem, he also recognized its affiliation with other, non-Chaucerian works in Middle English.

Ashmole's engagement with *Gamelyn* can tell us a few things about his approach to Chaucer. First, it indicates that Ashmole was reading manuscripts alongside, and comparing them to, his printed copy of the *Works*. Second, the decision to add it to the *Works* indicates that Ashmole believed in the possibility of authentic Chaucerian pieces not yet in print, and that he shared with other antiquarian readers of Chaucer a desire to enlarge and complete the Chaucerian canon. In accepting *Gamelyn* as Chaucer's work and placing it in his volume, Ashmole made a material contribution toward the enlargement of the Chaucerian canon (even if only in his own copy), participating in both the humanist enthusiasm for the discovery of new texts in manuscript and the antiquarian delight in the recovery of the English past.[51] Third, the appearance of a second copy of *Gamelyn* in Ashmole's collections, in MS Ashmole 45, reminds us that Ashmole's interest in medieval poetry was not confined to Chaucer alone. This is a shift away from the single-author focus found in the printed *Works*, but is consistent with the use of a wide variety of medieval texts in chronicles and other early modern historiographic writing.

While Ashmole added *Gamelyn*, he did not go to the trouble of adding the apocryphal *Plowman's Tale* to his copy of the *Works*. (The 1532 Thynne edition is the only one of the Chaucer folios that does not contain it; Ashmole would have had access to it in his copy of Speght.) He did, however, make note of its absence in his copy. At the end of the *Manciple's Tale*, he added the following comment,

> In the latter Impressions of this Author [i.e., the later folio editions], it is thus

> *By that the Plowman had his Tale ended &c*:
> For in this place the Plowmans Tale should have ben incerted, but
> omitted purposely because the Tymes (when this Edition was printed)
> would not beare a thing of so greate abuse against the Clergie, as this
> Tale is throughout.[52]

This assumption—that the 1532 edition omitted the *Plowman's Tale* because
of its anticlerical content—will be repeated up through the end of the twentieth century, although neither Speght nor Francis Thynne make explicit claims
to this effect.[53] The confidence with which Ashmole comments on its absence
indicates that, by the middle of the seventeenth-century, clerical interference
was an accepted explanation for the absence of the *Plowman's Tale*. There is
nothing in Ashmole that indicates discomfort with or skepticism about the
tale's place in the Chaucerian canon.

Not only did Ashmole not find it necessary to replicate material already
in print, when he had the opportunity to draw on manuscript sources instead
of printed ones, he took it. When he needed to replace lines missing from his
text of the *Ballade of Fortune* (in 1532 titled the "Balade of the vyllage without payntyng") due to a tear in the page, he copied them not from another
printed edition, but from the manuscript now Bodleian MS Ashmole 59, an
early fifteenth-century miscellany compiled by the scribe and bibliophile John
Shirley. Using the same manuscript, Ashmole also copied Shirley's headnote
to a short poem that Thynne calls "Scogan unto the lordes and gentylmen of
the kynges house" (DIMEV 3645). Shirley's characteristically detailed annotation offers some appealing particulars, describing the poem as "a moral
balade to my Lord the Prince, to my Lord of Clarence, to my Lord of Bedford, and to my Lord of Gloucestre, by Henry Scogan at a souper of feorthe
[worthy] merchande in the vyntre of London, at the hous of Lowys Johan."[54]
Ashmole copied this note over its entirety, and also changed the running title
in his copy of the *Works* from "To the lords and gentylmen / of the kynges
house" to the more specific "To my foure Lordes the Kynges sones / To the
Kynges Sones." Tracing this poem also lets us see that Ashmole once again
cross-referenced his manuscript and printed sources: in a margin opposite
Shirley's headnote in Ashmole 59, Ashmole writes that the piece was "printed
toward the end of Chaucer's works."

Whereas Holland used his printed copy of the *Works* to expand the contents of his manuscript, Ashmole appears to have been more interested in using his book to record material *not* available to him in later printed sources.

Ashmole's copy of *Gamelyn*, the text of the *Ballade of Fortune*, and the note to the Scogan ballade all show him giving primacy to manuscript evidence. Unlike Holland, Ashmole did not add any of the shorter poems that appear in later editions, though he clearly compared the assortment of poems that conclude his 1532 *Works* with the text found in other sources. Ashmole, in other words, was interested in the limits of what the printed editions of Chaucer could convey, and what new materials might lie, as yet undetected, in surviving manuscripts.

Ashmole also supplied annotations throughout the book, and for this he did rely on the apparatus provided by Speght. Although the 1532 title page is still intact, MS Ashmole 1095 opens with a facsimile of the 1598 frontispiece, erroneously dated 1590, written in the same hand that copies out *Gamelyn*. Like the actual Speght title page (and also like the manuscript version of the 1598 title page added to Cambridge, University Library MS Gg.4.27), this facsimile offers readers an abbreviated reference list of the paratextual materials found in the Speght edition. The presence of both a facsimile title page and annotations within the text indicate that, for a reader like Ashmole, a copy of Chaucer that offered some annotation and explicatory materials might well be preferred to the largely unadorned text offered by Thynne. Notably, Ashmole also had some familiarity with the 1602 edition, which he cites specifically when he notes that "Mr Spight in his addicion printed 1602" identifies the poem that Thynne calls "Consyder wel every cyrcumstaunce" (DIMEV 1070) as "A balade of good Councell, translated out of Latin verses into English, by Dan John Lidgate, cleped The Monke of Bury."[55]

Relying heavily on Speght, the annotations added by Ashmole offer textual correction and marginal commentary throughout the book, mixing explanatory details with more general reading notes (for example, Ashmole marks the descriptions of each of the three temples in the *Knight's Tale*). Longer annotations were written on separate sheets and subsequently bound with the book, while shorter notes were copied into the upper and lower margins. These notes appear throughout the book, but most frequently in the *Canterbury Tales*, then as now Chaucer's most popular work and the first to appear in the volume. While the majority of the annotations correspond to notes found in Speght, and are clearly drawn from his edition, they are not usually copied word for word. For example, the Ashmole copy includes Speght's identification of "Scholler's Hall" with Clare College, Cambridge, alongside the appropriate passage in the *Reeve's Tale*. The note in Ashmole 1095 reads,

Schollar hall or University hall.
Founded 1326. United to the foundacion of
The lady Eliz. De Burgs, Countess of Clare
& called Clare Hall.[56]

In Speght, the note offers slightly more detail: "Sollar hall, *read*, Schollars hall, or Universitie hall, founded by the Chauncelour and Masters of the Universitie, *Anno* 1326. But since united to the foundation of the Lady Elizabeth *de Burgo*, Countesse of Clare, and called Clare hall."[57] The note was probably condensed due to the limited marginal space available, but the adaptation also shows detailed consideration of the original rather than rote copying from one context to another.

Within the *Tales*, Ashmole was most likely to add notes where Chaucer's text touches on one of his extraliterary interests. Foremost among these are astronomy and astrology, which Ashmole developed an interest in during the 1630s that he pursued throughout the rest of his life. Almost every celestial reference in Chaucer's text is marked with an astrological sign, often Mars or Venus. When Ashmole offers additional information at such points, his annotations are often based in classical sources. Alongside the *General Prologue*'s observation that the Physician "was grounded in Astronomie," for example, the following note appears keyed to the sign for Jupiter:

♃ For he was grounded in Astronomie.
He that wil be a Phisitian according to Homer's perscrition vizt: equivalente to any, ought to be skilfull in Astronomy & Magick naturalle: For if by Astronomy he be not able to Judge in what state the Heavens stood, & what their Aspectes were, when his Patient sickned: And by Magick naturall to calculate his Nativity, thereby to know which of the heavenly bodies ruled most in his Birth, he shall hardly or but by chance conjecture to what end his sicknes will sort.[58]

These comments do not correspond to anything in Speght, but below this note, Ashmole has transcribed Speght's comment on the following line, "in houres by his Magike naturelle":

♂ In howers by his Magick naturelle—
He meaneth this Phisitian was skilfull, in Astrologie, & coulde make his election of fortunate howres, wherein to minister

his Potions to his Patientes: & likewise that he was practiced in Magick Naturalle, as in making of Sigilla or Characters stamped in mettall in their due tymes, fitted in that signe, that governed the parte of the Body, wherein the malady was: as the stampe of Aries for the disease in the head, & of Leo for the reynes &c; Hereof he speaketh in the 3ᵈ: Booke of Fame. And Clerkes eke which cone well All this Magick naturalle &c.[59]

By adding these notes to his copy of Chaucer, Ashmole foregrounds the astrological and magical content of the *Works* and makes a selection of Speght's annotations—otherwise clustered together at the end of the volume—a part of the reading experience of the text itself.

In several cases Ashmole's notes cite other texts besides Speght, and these offer some insight into the literary and historical contexts in which he approached Chaucer. At times, he notes classical sources and analogues. In the *Nun's Priest's Tale*, for example, Ashmole inserts a reference to the Latin writer Valerius Maximus, citing a specific location within his text (book 1, chapter 7) that describes "This story of two Arcadians travelling to Megera."[60] An annotation on the verso of that same leaf notes that the history of the Greek poet Simonides can also be found in Valerius, but that Chaucer expands it.[61] In the *Franklin's Tale*, he notes that "Aulus Gellius reported this woful story" of the "eyght maydens of Melyse [Miletus]," but he does not elaborate further on the link between the Latin writer and Chaucer's story.[62]

In other places, Ashmole's annotations reference more recent scholarship. A note in the *Second Nun's Tale* observes that "Cecile was martyred anno 230, in which yeare Pope Urbane was also martyrid," naming the French classicist Isaac Casaubon (1559–1614) as a source. Ashmole also adds a reference to Camden's *Britannia* to Speght's gloss on the "camysed nose" of the miller's daughter in the *Reeve's Tale* (Camden discusses the use of the prefix *cam-* in Cornish place names).[63] In the *Squire's Tale*, Ashmole identifies Gawain, referenced at line 95 of the *Squire's Tale*, as "sisters son to Kinge Arthur," adding that "Anno 1012 at Rose in Wales his Sepulchure was found, & his body affirmed to be 14 feet long," a comment originally taken from William of Malmesbury and repeated by Holinshed, but not found in Speght.[64] These references testify to a broad familiarity with antiquarian writings, brought to bear on Chaucer's poetry. As with Ashmole's other notes on Chaucer's sources, they suggest that, for Ashmole as for other early modern readers, Chaucer's writings were a subject of both literary and historical interest.

Ashmole also attended to the history of Chaucer in print. In addition to his comment on the *Plowman's Tale*, a note in the bottom margin of sig. A3 observes that

> Mr W[illiam] Thynne in his first printed Booke of Chaucers works
> (with one Colume on a side) had a Tale called the Pilgrims Tale,
> which is more odious to the Clergie then the Plowmans. It began
> thus:
>   In Lincolnshire fast by a fenne:
>   Standeth a religious house who doth it kenne. &c.

The *Pilgrim's Tale* is, of course, not a Chaucerian text and it was never printed as Chaucer's. It is, instead, the early sixteenth-century political poem cited by Francis Thynne and others eager to make a claim for Chaucer's reformist tendencies. This account of a single-column edition of the *Works* containing it echoes Thynne's claims in the *Animadversions*, which also cites the incipit of the *Pilgrim's Tale*. Thynne's assertion, however, is not found in either of the Speght editions. The appearance of this claim in Ashmole's copy suggests that he had access to some additional material on Chaucer, either through written or oral traditions—a possibility I will explore later in this chapter.

While Speght's commentary was a clearly valuable resource for Ashmole, as it was for other seventeenth-century readers, its utility would have been diminished by the fact that it appears at the beginning and end of the book, rather than in the text's margins (although the 1602 revision added marginal manicules for *sententiae*), and none of Speght's notes contain page or folio references.[65] To transpose Speght's annotations from the back of the 1598 *Works* to their appropriate places in the 1532 edition, as Ashmole did, would require a considerable degree of coordination. A reader could work through Chaucer's text systematically, checking regularly to see if Speght's notes contained related material. This would require frequent switching between the front and back portions of a large folio, an inconvenient (if not impossible) reading arrangement, or working with two different copies of the *Works* (Ashmole seems to have had access to a copy of the 1602 edition as well as the 1532 printing in which he made his notes). Alternatively, a reader could begin with the apparatus in Speght's edition and proceed either by copying over commentary either when he or she recognized a reference to a specific passage or by hunting for the corresponding lines. This process would be more fluid but would require a thorough knowledge of Chaucer's writings, enough to locate specific words and images within the corpus. In either scenario, the transposition of end-notes to the margins of the book would require a significant investment of time and readerly energy.

Ashmole's signature in his copy of the *Works* dates his use of the volume to 1642, more than ten years before the publication of his *Theatrum Chemicum Britannicum*. Although the *Theatrum Chemicum Britannicum* includes the *Canon's Yeoman's Tale*, there is nothing in Ashmole's notations to the 1532 edition to suggest he used it when preparing the text for print (the printed text is taken from Speght's 1602 edition). If we look forward to the *Theatrum Chemicum Britannicum*, however, we see that Ashmole's treatment of Chaucer there follows the historicizing route taken by many antiquarians. On the verso opposite the title of the *Canon's Yeoman's Tale*, Ashmole prints an engraving of the Purbeck marble altar tomb installed in Westminster by Nicholas Brigham in 1556.[66] The title itself notes that it was "written by our Ancient and famous English Poet, *Geoffrey Chaucer*." The wording here echoes the title of Speght's edition, but *Theatricum Chemicum Britannicum* makes no mention of the larger context of the *Canterbury Tales*, or any of Chaucer's other works (that is, the importance of Chaucer's fame has outstripped the reasons for that fame). In yet another instance of temporal scrambling in Chaucer's reception, Chaucer's sixteenth-century tomb provides a witness that authenticates the fourteenth-century poet for a seventeenth-century audience.

Franciscus Junius

The third and final scholarly reading of Chaucer that I consider here is that of the philologist Franciscus Junius (1591–1677), who, in the last decade of his life, compiled an extensive glossary of Chaucerian language using the 1598 Speght *Works*.[67] Today, Junius is best known as a philologist of Anglo-Saxon and Germanic languages and for the collection of manuscripts he bequeathed to the Bodleian Library upon his death. Junius owned several Middle English manuscripts, including the Ormulum (MS Junius 1) and a *Prick of Conscience* manuscript (now MS Junius 56), and his hand appears in the Leiden Lydgate manuscript (now Vossius Germ. Gall. Q. 9), which also contains Chaucer's *Ballade of Fortune*.[68]

Junius was born in Heidelberg and educated in Leiden, but he maintained significant connections with England throughout his career and was in regular contact with the leading lights of seventeenth-century antiquarianism. His first publication, a work of art criticism called *De pictura veterum* (1637, translated and published in 1638 as *On the Painting of the Ancients* [STC 7302]), was dedicated to Charles I, and for two decades, he lived and worked in the Oxfordshire household of Thomas Howard, Earl of Arundel, serving first as a tutor and then as librarian. In his copy of Sidney's *Defence of Poesie*, which he annotated in the 1630s while working for Arundel, Junius underlined Sidney's comments on Chaucer.[69] (Holland also makes note of these comments, a measure of the influence Sidney's poetic treatise had in securing Chaucer's status as a figure from the past whose writing helped to define the literary standards of the Renaissance present.) After leaving Arundel's household, Junius moved between England and the Low Countries for the remainder of his life.[70] He published in a variety of scholarly fields, including the history of art, translations from Old English and Old High German, and the lexicography of several Old Germanic languages. In the 1650s he began work on a monumental etymological dictionary of English that was posthumously published as *Etymologicum Anglicanum* (Oxford, 1743).

Junius's work was not limited to the earlier forms of the language, but extended to Middle English and, more specifically, to Chaucer. In an important essay, Rolf H. Bremmer Jr. situates Junius's study of Chaucer in the context of a long and robust scholarly career, concluding that "Junius, it would seem, was as fully at home with Chaucer as he was, for example, with the Old English poems contained in the Caedmon Manuscript."[71] In this he was not alone; Bremmer cites, among others, the sixteenth-century Anglo-Dutch Catholic antiquarian Richard Verstegan as a forerunner of Junius.[72] Verstegan's *A Restitution of Decayed Intelligence*, published in Antwerp in 1605, argues for the Germanic origins of the English people and the English language; Verstegan acknowledges Chaucer's reputation while criticizing him as a "mingler" of English and French.[73] Bremmer also identifies the Anglo-Saxonist Johannes de Laet as another example of a Dutchman who owned books by both Chaucer and more recent English writers, and Marcus Zuerius Boxhorn and Jan van Vliet (a friend and correspondent of Junius) as other Dutch scholars who took an interest in, or were at least familiar with, Chaucer's writings.[74] So Junius's interest in Chaucer reflects the concerns of his Dutch scholarly community as well as his English one.

Junius was trained in the philologist Joseph Justus Scaliger's principles of *ad fontes* editing, and with a scholarly background in Germanic languages and linguistics, he represents a more formal approach than that taken by Holland and Ashmole. Nonetheless, Junius clearly shared many concerns with these earlier commentators. Like them, Junius approached questions of literary and linguistic development through the study of specific words and their sources. Despite the intensity of his lexicographical interest in Chaucer's writings, he never attempted to formulate a paradigm or grammatical model for Chaucer's Middle English; like most antiquarian readers of Chaucer, his interest lay squarely with Chaucer's words, their uses, and their sources rather than with grammar or language in a broader sense.

Junius took up Chaucer late in life, at least partly out of frustration with other philological projects.[75] More specifically, Junius turned to his study of Chaucer after 1665, after the long-delayed publication of his edition of the Gothic and West Saxon Gospels.[76] As an accomplished philologist, Junius easily recognized the shortcomings in the available printed editions of Chaucer and the need for a critical edition. As "a true member of the Leiden school of text editors," he further recognized that this could only be accomplished through collation of the printed copies with the oldest and best manuscripts. Unfortunately, given his advanced age and ongoing tensions between Great Britain and the Netherlands, travel to England from his home in The Hague was impractical. "Hence," Bremmer writes, "the only alternative for emending what he thought were nonsensical passages was conjecturing improvements, conjectures sometimes based on his familiarity with English, whether Old, Middle or contemporary, or simply based on intuition and common sense."[77] Thus, even if Junius, as a trained philologist and lexicographer, was in a better position than his predecessors to understand what the editing of Chaucer *required*, his actual approach is rooted in common sense and context, and in this way not so different from that of Holland, Ashmole, or those involved in the production of folio editions of the *Works*.

Junius's work on Chaucer was never published (indeed, much of his extensive work on historical English linguistics remains in manuscript), but it is possible to reconstruct his method. Four volumes related to this project survive today, all cataloged as a part of the Junius collection of manuscripts in the Bodleian Library (correspondence relating to this project is in Leiden). Junius MS 6 is Junius's own handwritten glossary of Chaucerian language. Junius MS 9 is a copy of the 1602 edition of the *Works*, still the most recent edition available in the 1660s. Junius MS 54 is a copy of Gavin Douglas's *Eneados*, a Scots translation of the *Aeneid* completed in 1513 (Junius used William Copland's edition of 1553).[78] Unlike other earlier adaptations of classical material into English, the *Eneados* is self-consciously faithful to its Latin source, meaning that it can be used to determine the Scots equivalent of

Latin words. MS Junius 114 is another handwritten glossary, this time referring back to Douglas's translation.

In February of 1668, Junius explained his approach to Chaucer's language in a letter to the English Anglo-Saxon scholar Sir William Dugdale. He wrote,

> for a chaunge I took your archpoet Chaucer in hand; and though
> I thinke that in many places he is not to bee understood without the
> help of old manuscript copies, which England can afforde manie,
> yet doe I perswade my selfe to have met with innumerable places,
> hitherto misunderstood, or not understood at all, which I can
> illustrate. To which work I hold the Bishop of Dunkel [Gavin
> Douglas] his Virgilian translation to be very much conducing, and
> in my perusing of this prelate his book (to say so much by the way)
> I stumbled upon manie passages wherein this wittie Gawin doth
> grosly mistake Virgil, and is much ledd out of the way by the
> infection of a monkish ignorance then prevailing in Church and
> common wealth; yet is there verie good use to be made of him.[79]

The shortcomings of Douglas's translation notwithstanding, Junius could compare the *Eneados* with Virgil, and by doing so confirm the definitions of a number of terms used by Douglas. These definitions could then, in turn, be used to clarify passages in Chaucer that made use of words also found in Douglas.

Junius's ingenious decision to put Douglas and Chaucer together shows that, in the absence of manuscript access, printed editions (however flawed) could still help to establish a rigorous study of the Middle English language.[80] Junius prepared his copies of both Chaucer's *Works* and Douglas's *Eneados* by dividing the columns into three sections (*infra*, *media*, and *supra*, marked i., m., and s.) and, in the *Works*, numbering the columns consecutively throughout the book. The paratextual materials at the back of the *Works* were removed (possibly for easier cross-referencing while marking up the book) from Junius MS 9, and a set of Latin notes were bound in in their place.

The two glossaries (Junius 6 and Junius 114) consist of booklets that were compiled separately and bound together. Junius 6, which deals with Chaucer, is assembled mostly from long slips of paper pasted onto larger blank sheets. The *Eneados* glossary appears to be a working notebook, less carefully arranged and complete than the larger Chaucer glossary. It contains far fewer explanations and notes than Junius 6. In both books, the layout of entries is generally the same: a headword and a short definition, followed by a list of quotations drawn from one or more sources. In some cases, there is a headword but quotations are noted only by page reference or absent entirely; in a smaller number of cases, Junius offers some discursive commentary on the word under consideration, written in Latin. Junius's entry on "a perse" in the Chaucer glossary is a good example of this longer format (see Figure 12). He defines the phrase, used in Henryson's *Testament of Cresseid* (which is included in the *Works* and which he apparently accepted as Chaucer's own), as a term used to describe special power, talent, or other attractive and admirable qualities.[81] He then quotes two longer passages, one of which describes Criseyde as "the floure and A perse / of Troy and Grece" and another, also describing Criseyde, in which the narrator asserts that "right as our first letter is now an A, / In beaute first so stode she makelees."[82] In this second passage, Junius writes, we may hear Chaucer himself explain the meaning of this phrase ("Chaucerum semet ipsum explicantem audiamus"). He goes on to cite a passage from Douglas's Scots text that also uses "a perse" and adds to this passages from Martial (in Latin) and the book of Revelation (in Greek) that make literary (and, in the case of Revelation, eschatological) plays on the first letter of the alphabet.[83] Drawing on a deep well of literary and linguistic knowledge, Junius moves outward from a single use of "a perse" in Chaucer to offer a perspective that situates his work, and that of Gavin Douglas, in a long and multilingual tradition.

While both of the glossaries draw on multiple sources, all of the notes left by Junius in the printed text of the *Eneados* refer to either Chaucer's writings or to Virgil's Latin text, affirming that Junius used the Scots text as an aid in mapping the familiar Latin of Virgil onto Chaucer's Middle English. Although Douglas's translation is largely faithful to Virgil's Latin (if not quite up to Junius's standards), in passages where Douglas deviates significantly from his original, Junius sometimes copied out several lines of Virgil's Latin for comparison. Where there is difference in form or orthography between Douglas and Chaucer, Junius sometimes noted this as well. For example, opposite Douglas's line "weill may I schaw, my bureil bustious thocht," Junius added "vide quid Chaucero sit Borell" and "vide quid Chaucero sit Boistous," directing his readers to the use of these same words in Chaucer.[84] Comparing Virgil with Douglas offered Junius a central core of corroborated definitions with which to begin his work on Chaucer. In effect, Douglas acts as a ready-made Latin–to–Middle English dictionary.

Though his Chaucer project was never fully completed, the glossaries give a sense of both the scope of Junius's plans and his method of executing them.

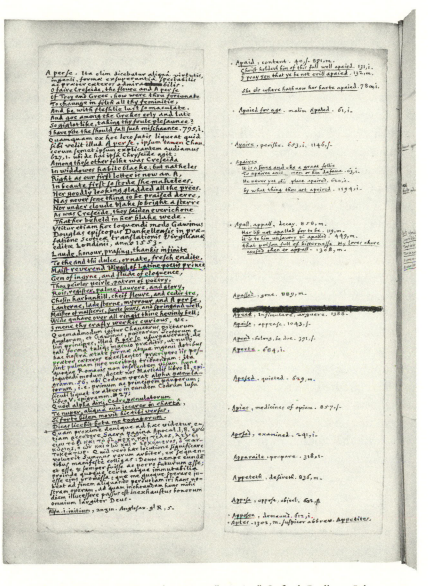

Figure 12. Franciscus Junius's note on "a per se," Oxford, Bodleian Library MS Junius 6, fol. 5v. By permission of the Bodleian Libraries.

In the Chaucer glossary, there are a representative number of entries for each letter *A–Y* (there is no grouping for *Z*), suggesting that Junius worked through the corpus rather than focusing on a single letter at a time. Junius appears to have at least entered all the terms he planned to gloss, leaving space to fill in definitions at a later date. As Johan Kerling notes, "this is obviously a sensible procedure, especially if you realize (as Junius did) that you might not live long enough to finish the work you have started, because in this way the possibility remains open for someone else to finish the work."[85]

Junius's glossary is groundbreaking in the detailed scholarly attention it affords Chaucer's words, but it is remarkable in other ways as well. As Johan Kerling notes, this is the first truly alphabetical Chaucer glossary, one that reveals a solid understanding of Middle English and wide-ranging but not uncritical use of other lexicographical sources such as Gerardus Vossius's *Etymologicon Linguae Latinae*.[86] In part because of its use of Latin, it seems that Junius compiled the glossary with a scholarly audience in mind, and he later drew on the material found here in his own *Etymologicon Anglicanum* (published posthumously in 1743).

Although the glossaries are the result of serious and sustained study, there is no evidence that Junius took further steps to prepare an edition of Chaucer for print.[87] This does not mean Junius's efforts were not useful to future scholars. Four hundred and sixty-eight examples drawn from the Chaucer glossary make their way into *Etymologium Anglicanum*.[88] Junius's materials were also known to later Chaucer editors, although they may have been disappointed with what they found. In his preface to the 1721 Urry edition of Chaucer, Timothy Thomas wrote: "There is a Copy of the Edition 1597 [*sic*] with MS. Notes of *Junius* in the *Bodleyan* Library amongst his MSS [No. 5121.9] but neither did those Notes nor his other Papers there of that nature (which I likewise consulted) afford that assistance which might be expected from so great a Name; most of them being very imperfect, or drawn up rather for his own use than for the information of others."[89] Thomas's dissatisfaction with their unfinished state notwithstanding, Junius's glossaries represent a sustained engagement with Chaucer on the part of one of the foremost European linguists of the seventeenth century. More than a simple record of reading, they reflect an increasingly rigorous and scholarly approach to Chaucer's language and text. The practice of reading Chaucer and studying Chaucer were becoming more and more closely aligned. Junius sought to understand Chaucer's language and to remedy corruption in his printed text. Both goals required deep linguistic knowledge and a career's worth of textual expertise.

Junius makes a fitting end to the sequence of readers I consider here not only because he participated in an ongoing tradition of learned responses to Chaucer, but because he was also a transitional figure in the history of Chaucer studies. With its lexicographical rigor and grounding in philological methods, his work looks forward to the future of Middle English linguistics. At the same time, it reflects concerns with source material and historical context similar to those that motivated earlier scholarly engagement with Chaucer. The fact that Junius pursued his work on Chaucer as ardently and in as focused a manner as he did still rests on his special appreciation for Chaucer as a writer. In a letter to William Dugdale he refers to Chaucer as "your archpoet," and, like Holland, he clearly approved of Sidney's comments on Chaucer in the *Defence of Poesie*, which emphasize both Chaucer's literary merit and his antiquity.[90] As Bremmer writes, for Junius, "Chaucer was a poet who, more than any other *deserved* to be studied. To Junius—and here we have an appreciative evaluation of Chaucer the author—he was an 'inventive poet,' a term used with significance in Junius's writings on art."[91] In this, Junius is still very much a part of a tradition of Chaucerian admiration that stretches back through antiquarians like Speght to the fifteenth-century tributes of poets Gower, Lydgate, Hoccleve, and their contemporaries.

A Shared Source?

Junius was clearly a reader of Chaucer as well as a student of his words, and his copy of the *Works* reflects this. In addition to his lexicographical notes, Junius also corrected individual line readings (usually to emend an obvious error in the text) and added a number of notes that identify sources or analogues for Chaucer's text.[92] These sources are most often classical, but he also added multiple references to the French text of the *Roman de la Rose* and to Boethius's *Consolation of Philosophy*. In addition, there are approximately fifty notes that direct the reader to some kind of additional material via a marginal directive to "vide annotat," or "vide annot" ("see annotations"). Although Bremmer asserts that Junius never refers to Speght's glossaries, which are missing from his copy of the 1598 edition, a large portion of the *vide annotationes* notes correspond to printed annotations found in the 1602 Speght edition.

Junius's copy of that edition is now Leiden, Universiteitsbibliotheek 364, with the full paratext intact.[93]

Junius's correspondence supports the idea that he made use of additional Chaucer commentary apart from Speght's notes. In a 1667 letter to his friend and former student Thomas Marshall, living in Oxford, Junius thanked him for a "comment upon Chaucer" that Marshall had apparently sent to his old teacher: "My kinsman Vossius [Isaac Vossius, Junius's nephew] thanketh you for Dr Windets dissertation, and I for the comment upon Chaucer, which I finde not otherwise then I exspected. Seeing I knew not how to looke for a Commentator that should give anie light to Chaucers old language, and so putt us in a way for to understand better the meaning of that inventive poët."[94] In a letter written after Junius's death to Vossius, Thomas Marshall refers to a "copy of the Index of this Chaucer" in Vossius's possession.[95] This might be a fair copy of the glossary to Chaucer that is now Bodleian Library MS Junius 6, but it might also be an additional notebook or set of papers.

If Junius did make use of some outside commentary, then it is worth considering the possibility that Ashmole may have had access to a similar set of notes, since both annotators single out many of the same words and passages for explication. Both Junius and Ashmole make several hundred notes in their copies of Chaucer's *Works*. Of Ashmole's notes, sixty-eight, or about one third, correspond to places also marked in Junius's copy, usually with the Latin notation *vide annotat*. The majority of these shared notes, about fifty, can also be found in Speght's printed commentary. In theory, as seventeenth-century readers, both Ashmole and Junius could have encountered difficulty because of historical or linguistic difference at the same points and turned to Speght's notes to help resolve their difficulties. The chances that two readers, separated by several decades, the North Sea, and two Anglo-Dutch wars, would spontaneously choose to excerpt so many of the same notes are, however, minimal.

Moreover, the similarities between the Junius and Ashmole copies do not end with material that can be traced to Speght. At several points, Ashmole and Junius made annotations or corrections that correspond to one another but that cannot be found in Speght. Of the annotations and emendations shared by Junius and Ashmole, thirteen fall into this category. While many of Junius's notes consist of nothing more than his usual *vide annotat*, comparing them with Ashmole's more extensive comments on these same points can illuminate the set of concerns shared between the two antiquarians. For

example, Ashmole and Junius both alight on lines in the *Knight's Tale*, where
Arcite wonders

> who shal give a lover any lawe?
> Love is a gretter law by my pan
> Than may be yeven to any erthly man.[96]

Each identifies it as coming from book 3 of Boethius's *Consolation of Philosophy*, a reasonable thing for Junius to recognize, but a more surprising note coming from the less philosophically oriented Ashmole. In the *Wife of Bath's
Tale*—a piece that garnered much less careful attention from early modern
readers than it does from present-day critics—both Ashmole and Junius connect the line "glad poverte is an honest thing" with Seneca.[97] This ongoing
interest in classical sources used in Chaucer speaks to a desire to demonstrate
that, as Speght wrote in 1602, Chaucer was a man of "great reading, & deep
judgement."[98]

In a different vein, both annotators also mark the moment in the *Reeve's
Tale* where the wife cries out and invokes the Holy Cross of Bromholm, a relic
also mentioned in *Piers Plowman*. Ashmole explains that Bromholm is "a Priory in Norfolke where was kept a piece of the Crosse of Christ," while Junius
adds a citation to Matthew of Paris, who describes in detail the arrival of the
relic in 1223.[99] Although this particular point is not found in Speght, it is
local medieval history of the sort that frequently makes its way into his annotations and that also predominates in Francis Thynne's commentary. Why did
it matter to Junius and Ashmole that, at this moment, Chaucer invokes an
actual relic? One possibility could be that, in 1598, Speght assumed the story
of the Bromholm cross was common knowledge but that—like the infamous
and now inscrutable reference to Wade's boat in Speght's glossary—by the
middle of the seventeenth century, it had become an increasingly obscure
detail.[100]

Junius and Ashmole are also both concerned with textual correctness. At
the beginning of the *Parson's Prologue*, both emend "tenne at clocke" to "two
at clocke" and change the zodiac sign in ascent from Libra to Taurus.[101] Ashmole adds an additional note, explaining "This must needes be 2: a'Clock, for
that at 10: the Son is in his Ascension."[102] (These changes are in fact made to
the *Parson's Prologue* in the 1687 reprint of the *Works*.)[103] They also both make
a note on Emily's crown of oak leaves in the *Knight's Tale*. In the 1532 and 1598
editions, the text has her wearing "a crowne of a grene oke unseryall." In their

notes, Ashmole and Junius both amend this to "serialle," a reference to the Turkey oak, or *Quercus cerrus*, and cite Pliny as a source.[104] (This same passage is discussed at length in Thynne's *Animadversions*, although he does not mention Pliny.)[105] Here, again, is a reference to a classical authority, used not only to explicate the text but to emend it. Another shared change, this time without the support of classical authority, occurs in the opening lines of the *Squire's Tale*. Both the 1532 and 1598 editions of the *Works* describe the setting of the tale as "Surrie." Ashmole and Junius make an identical change, crossing out "Surrie" and adding "Russie" in the margin.[106] This is the reading found in the better manuscripts, and one that is consistent with the mention of "Cambyuskan" (Genghis Khan) later in the passage. (Thynne discusses this passage as well.)

The correspondences between Ashmole's and Junius's annotations point toward the possibility of a shared body of notes on Chaucer—perhaps something like Francis Thynne's *Animadversions*—circulating in antiquarian communities in the middle decades of the seventeenth century. Although Ashmole and Junius read Chaucer in different countries and more than two decades apart, their professional networks overlapped. Junius was aware of Ashmole and his reputation as an antiquarian: he referred to him in a list of English antiquarians in a letter to Dugdale written in 1661 and asked for copies of his edition of the Gothic Gospels to be delivered to him in another 1667 letter to Thomas Marshall.[107] Ashmole and Junius's commentary is shaped and informed by the concerns of English antiquarianism more generally, but— given that there is no printed edition of Chaucer between 1602 and 1687—it is remarkable that it extends into a period that is otherwise notable for its *lack* of printed editions and commentary on Chaucer. Whatever their origins, the notes left by both Ashmole and Junius reveal the persistence of a certain kind of Chaucerian reading, motivated by a consistent subset of interests, shaped by the annotations offered by Speght, and taking place not just individually, but within a diffuse community of scholars, separated by time and location, but linked by an appreciation for and interest in the Middle English poet.

*   *   *

The work of Joseph Holland, Elias Ashmole, and Franciscus Junius shows how the Chaucerian reading experience was transformed in the seventeenth century, from something putatively accessible to all Englishmen (as the 1532 preface suggests) to the province of the scholar, the expert, and the antiquarian. In different ways, Holland, Ashmole, and Junius all make use of the explanatory materials offered by Speght to pursue their various ends. Their reliance on Speght (and, potentially, an additional body of antiquarian commentary) shows not only the growing practical necessity of glosses and other contextual guides for Chaucer, but also underscores the significant role that the 1598 and 1602 editions played in completing the process of specialization. Chaucer's status as "archpoet" (to borrow a term from Junius) was as secure as ever, but that status was now signaled not by deluxe manuscripts or robust praise of his singular eloquence, but by the evidence of scholarly and antiquarian study that would accompany his work moving forward.

Coda

Chaucer in the House of Fame

Early modern readers were relatively quiet about Chaucer's noisy dream vision the *House of Fame* and its extended meditation on the often fleeting and sometimes perplexing qualities of reputation and renown. Caxton first printed it in 1483, calling it "craftyly made" and "dygne to be wreton and knowen," despite its unfinished state.[1] The poem was printed again by Pynson in 1526, and included without much fanfare in the 1532 Thynne *Works* and those that follow from it.[2] Thomas Speght's headnote in the 1602 edition of the *Works* is relatively laconic: "In this booke is shewed how the deedes of all men and women, be they good or bad, are carried by report to posteritie."[3]

While Chaucer imagines his own reception at several points in his canon—perhaps most notably the Prologue to the *Legend of Good Women* and the ending of *Troilus and Criseyde*—in this enigmatic poem he offers a broader meditation on the fame itself. Although reputation appears primarily as an aural phenomenon in the House of Fame, the poet-narrator's first encounter with the capricious and fleeting nature of fame is a textual one. At the beginning of the poem's third book, Geoffrey finds himself at the foot of a large mountain of ice, contemplating the partially effaced names of "famous folkes" etched into its side:

> But wel unnethes koude I knowe
> Any lettres for to rede
> Hir names by; for, out of drede,
> They were almost ofthowed so
> That of the lettres oon or two
> Was molte away of every name
> So unfamous was woxe hir fame.
> But men seyn, "What may ever laste?"[4]

To borrow from the H.B poem for the 1598 *Works* that I discussed in the introduction, on this eroded slope, Chaucer finds the remains of "what Time and Writers had defaced." By contrast, on the other side of the mountain, shielded from the heat of the sun, he discovers,

> How hit was writen ful of names
> Of folkes that hadden grete fames
> Of olde tyme, and yet they were
> As fressh as men had writen hem here
> The selve day ryght, or that houre
> That I upon hem gan to poure.[5]

These names, preserved and protected, escape the depredations of time and are as legible as if they had been written an hour ago, even though the figures they name had fame "of olde tyme." They appear, as H.B. says of Chaucer's words after Speght's intervention, "so plain, that now they may be known of any."

What I mean to suggest by this comparison, of course, is that Chaucer's fate in the Renaissance was much more like that of the names etched on the shady side of the mountain of ice than those left to melt away on the sunny slope. His fame endured, so much so that in many contexts writers felt no need to articulate *why* Chaucer was famous, simply a need to remind their readers that he was (the open-endedness of this claim, like the capacious terms in which Chaucer's eloquence was described in the fifteenth-century, helped to make him available for appropriation in such a wide array of contexts). And yet, if we return to H.B.'s poem, a more complex perspective on long-term fame emerges, in which Chaucer is in "exile" and in need of the "grace" of Speght's editorial efforts. In response to the Reader's query "Where hast thou dwelt?" Chaucer responds,

> In haulks and herns, God wot, and in Exile,
> Where none vouchsaft to yeeld me words or lookes;
> Till one which saw me there, and knew my Friends,
> Did bring me forth: such grace sometime God sends.[6]

What the H.B. poem imagines is not a simple act of preservation, but an ongoing process of recovery and explication. It is as though the names etched into the mountain of ice that Chaucer reads as easily as if they had been written "that houre / That I upon hem gan to poure" must, in fact, be continually reinscribed.

Chaucer's fame—as well as the particular set of relations to Englishness past and present that made him such an ideologically flexible figure—was continually reiterated and rewritten in the sixteenth and seventeenth centuries, both through publication of his works and commentary on his life and writings. And it is through this process of inscription and reinscription that the vagaries of fame that Chaucer explores later in the *House of Fame* come into play. Fame, in Chaucer's account, is not a simple statement of fact that endures forever, but a mixture of "both sothe sawes [truths] and lesinges [falsehoods, fictions]," told and retold over time.[7]

"Sothe sawes and lesinges" are exactly what the narrator's eagle guide promises him he will find inside the House of Fame. A trip inside this capacious dwelling, which sits atop the icy mountain, reveals just how complex and capricious the process of making and maintaining fame can be. According to the eagle, this house stands in the center of the world, such that every sound in the world must pass through it, and when it does, that sound is transformed into the shape of the person who made it. Within its ruby walls, the narrator will discover musicians, historians, heralds, and poets, all doing the bidding of the mercurial goddess Fame. The sound they make is tremendous, so much so that it startles Geoffrey as he and the eagle approach from the air. It is the sound, the eagle tells him, of "bothe of feir speche and chidynges / And of fals and soth compouned" (1028–1029).

The sonically and epistemologically chaotic interior of the House of Fame mirrors the circumstances of Chaucer's reception in early modern England: there was no one narrative surrounding Chaucer, at least no narrative that definitively fixed to him a single realm of cultural significance. Instead, a diversity of input created a series of intersecting and overlapping discourses, each offering its own explanation of who Chaucer was and why his work mattered in the England of the sixteenth century. Chaucer was unquestionably canonical and widely recognized as "our most ancient and learned English poet"; the question was what to do with that. As Helen Cooper writes, "far from the processes of canon formation setting the seal of approval on him and offering him entry, there was a scramble to enlist his fame for each particular cause."[8] The project of etching Chaucer's fame into the proverbial mountain of literary history was the work of poets and dramatists, but as this book has shown, it also vitally involved the efforts of historians, heralds, lexicographers, and polemicists, all of whom found in Chaucer's renown a way of invoking authority or antiquity for their own particular causes.

One essential difference between Chaucer's fame in early modern England and the vision set forth in the House of Fame, however, is that while Chaucer does not describe any books inside the House of Fame, in the centuries after his death, books—and not just any books, but specifically printed books— would become a crucial instrument in maintaining his reputation and the circulation of his works. Such books not only reflected Chaucer's preexisting fame and made his texts available to a widening readership; they also inevitably made new claims for the importance of the poet and his works. It is tempting to speculate that, had Chaucer known the printing press, he would have placed it in the House of Fame or the nearby House of Rumor, where gossip and hearsay circulate at an even more frenetic pace.

*   *   *

While Chaucer's major works had been printed at regular intervals since the 1470s, the arrival of the edition of collected works in 1532 marked an evolution in Chaucer's posthumous fame, monumentalizing Chaucer the man and his ever-expanding canon and connecting them in newly explicit ways to court, crown, and nation. In the period this book considers, from roughly 1532 to the middle of the seventeenth century, these folio editions of Chaucer's collected works both drove and reflected a transformation in the transmission and reception of the poet and his works. Through these folios it is possible to trace how, while Chaucer never lost his special significance as a literary figure, extraliterary ideas about "Chaucer" came to shape how the medieval poet was discussed in literary and antiquarian circles and, even more importantly, how he was presented in print. A growing historical narrative around Chaucer gave him a lasting place in the antiquarian imagination and helped to bring about a number of paratextual features that remain standard in modern editions of Middle English texts. These include historical commentary, authorial biography, and linguistic glosses. While these features make it easier to read Chaucer, they also insist upon Chaucer's otherness and the linguistic and historical difference between the medieval poet and his latter-day readers.

Chaucer's story, of course, did not begin or end with these folio editions. For many readers, the primary encounter with Chaucer's name and reputation must have come not from copies of his works, but through the references and allusions to the poet found in best sellers like *Actes and Monuments* and literary trailblazers like the *Shepheardes Calender*, both of which leveraged (albeit to different ends) Chaucer's special status as a widely known and recognizably "antique" English poet. Dozens of other references from the sixteenth century mention Chaucer's alleged alchemical acumen, educational background, skills as an astrologer, and religious views, alongside or sometimes in place of the familiar praise for his distinctively English eloquence. The collected *Works* synthesize many of these views in their presentation of Chaucer and his writings, but these ideas continued to proliferate on their own as well.

New methods of engaging with Chaucer continued to proliferate in the seventeenth century, including Latin translations like Francis Kynaston's *Amorum Troili et Creseidae* (published in 1635), which renders *Troilus and Criseyde* into Latin hexameters, and modernizations like John Dryden's *Fables Ancient and Modern* (1700), which translates selections from the *Canterbury Tales* (as well as the apocryphal *Floure and the Leafe*) into heroic couplets. These are attempts to circumvent the difficulties of Middle English, but in their commitment to metrical regularity and classical poetic models, they also represent a continued effort to make Chaucer conform to contemporary (and thus continually changing) notions of what an ideal English poet and poetry should look like. For Kynaston, who compiled a fully annotated version of his Latin poem, and for Dryden, who discusses Chaucer at length in his preface to the *Fables*, Chaucer is both a figure of historical interest and a site of intense poetic admiration. In this, both Kynaston and Dryden represent the continuation of a literary-historical approach to Chaucer that began in the early decades of the sixteenth century and continued to develop throughout the sixteenth century and into the seventeenth, just as much as annotators like Junius, Ashmole, and Holland do.

*   *   *

"Chaucer" was many things in the Renaissance: a historical figure, a body of texts, a physical book, shorthand for both English literary tradition and earlier forms of the language itself. It has been the goal of this book to demonstrate that none of these versions of Chaucer can be fully disentangled from the others. Chaucer's presence in a diverse array of early modern historical and scholarly commentary shows that his significance far outstripped the comparatively narrow bounds of English literature, even if this commentary was predicated on an often-unspoken sense of his poetic importance. Conversely, literary representations of Chaucer and his works increasingly attended to their historical and linguistic context, borrowing ideas and methods from antiquarian commentary. If we look to the biographical writings of John Leland and Thomas Speght, we find not just narratives about Chaucer's life, but attempts to conceptualize the role of the vernacular in shaping national identity. If we trace the ongoing development of Chaucer's canon, we find it to be shaped by major efforts to construct a version of the English past suited to a Protestant present. And when we begin to track the sources and analogues of Speght's hard word lists, it becomes clear that this early lexicographical effort is spurred as much by the need to grapple with multiple forms of literary inheritance as it is about the need to define Chaucer's words. Much of this can be limned from the folio editions themselves, but when we step back and consider a wider archive, the story becomes still richer and more complex. The connection between scholarly and literary interest in Chaucer is always a two-way street.

Chaucer's presentation in print is especially important because, after 1532, poets, lay readers, historians, and antiquarians all relied primarily on the same set of collected editions. It was in these editions that Chaucer definitively emerged as the first literary historical figure in England, valued for his poetic achievements but approached from a significant temporal remove. These folios negotiate between a received idea of Chaucer's poetry as edifying and entertaining for all English readers and a growing need to provide those same readers with historical and linguistic resources for accessing the Chaucerian text. The tradition of Chaucerian praise grounded in fifteenth-century poetry was not equipped to provide those resources. Antiquarians, however, were. The ensuing mix of literary and antiquarian interest gave rise to a new way of reading Chaucer and provided a model for studying (rather than simply reading) vernacular English literature. The textual and linguistic concerns that typified medieval studies in the nineteenth and twentieth centuries, as well as the emphasis on historical context that continues to guide most readings of Middle English texts, all have their roots in early modern editions of and commentary on Chaucer.

Chaucer's ability to contribute meaningfully to wider conversations on English identity made him a singularly useful figure to early modern efforts to conceptualize the Middle Ages (and, as the scope and focus of this book suggest, makes him an exceptionally useful topic for modern scholars wishing to study those efforts today). In the sixteenth and seventeenth centuries, antiquarian readers and commentators focused closely on Chaucer. Their narrow focus contributed to a lasting perception of Chaucer as a poet with few (if any) immediate peers, a gap reflected not just in the amount of commentary generated but in the very availability of their texts. The eighty-five years between the printing of the 1602 Speght edition and the 1687 reprint mark the longest gap to date in Chaucer's print history (and, as my final chapter demonstrates, this does not necessarily indicate that Chaucer was not read). By contrast, after a 1590 edition of the *Serpent of Division*, no other work of John Lydgate's would be printed on its own until the nineteenth century, although *Fall of Princes* forms the core of the popular *Mirror for Magistrates* and the *Siege of Thebes* appears in the Speght editions of Chaucer. Langland and Gower fare equally poorly.

This Chaucerian exceptionalism, perhaps the most enduring legacy of Chaucer's early modern reception, is reflected today in diverse ways, including in the number of university classes taught on Chaucer and the existence of a separate Chaucer Division within the Modern Language Association. That this book has been conceived of, written, and published is yet another indicator of the special status of Chaucer in medieval studies today. More worrisome is the corollary to this exceptionalism, the comparative lack of scholarly attention given to other Middle English poets and the persistence of a myopic view of the late Middle Ages that implicitly or explicitly casts Chaucer as the only author from the period worth studying. In focusing on Chaucer, the goal of this book has not been to affirm this exceptionalism but to begin to explain it, with the hopes that in doing so we might not only understand Chaucer better, but consider anew the way the reception and transmission of his works have shaped, and continue to shape, the field of English literary history writ large.

NOTES

INTRODUCTION

1. *The Workes of our Antient and Learned English poet, Geffrey Chaucer, newly Printed* (London: Adam Islip for Thomas Wright, 1598), sig. a5v; *A Short-Title Catalogue of Books Printed in England, Scotland, and Ireland and English Books Printed Abroad, 1475-1604* (hereafter STC) 5079.

2. Stephanie Trigg, *Congenial Souls: Reading Chaucer from Medieval to Postmodern* (Minneapolis: University of Minnesota Press, 2002), 133.

3. A. C. Spearing, "Renaissance Chaucer and Father Chaucer," *English: The Journal of the English Association* 34, no. 148 (1985): 8. Helen Cooper notes Chaucer's selectivity in aligning himself with classical models rather than explicitly naming his vernacular contemporaries; see Cooper, "Choosing Poetic Fathers: The English Problem," in *Medieval and Early Modern Authorship*, ed. Guillemette Bolens and Lukas Erne (Tübingen: Narr Verlag, 2011), 29–49, esp. 37–14.

4. On this flexibility and its pervasiveness in Chaucer's canon, see especially Helen Cooper, "Chaucer's Self-Fashioning," *Poetica* 55 (2001): 55–74.

5. As this book does not consider Chaucer's reception in Ireland, Scotland, or Wales, I use the term "English" rather than "British" throughout. On the language politics of early modern England, initially framed as a contest between Latin and the English vernacular but increasingly a competition between a standardized "King's English" and a variety of competing nonstandard forms, see Paula Blank, *Broken English: Dialects and the Politics of Language in Renaissance Writings*, (London: Routledge, 1996).

6. Although only Chaucer's works were collected and presented together, his writings were not the only major pieces of Middle English literature printed in folio during this period. Thomas Berthelette printed folio editions of Gower's *Confessio Amantis* twice, in 1532 (STC 12143) and 1554 (STC 12144). Also in 1554, Richard Tottel and John Wayland printed folio editions of Lydgate's *Fall of Princes* (Tottel's, which also includes Lydgate's Middle English translation of the *Danse Macabre*, is STC 3177; Wayland's edition is STC 3177.5 and 3178). The following year, 1555, Thomas Marshe printed Lydgate's *Troy Book* (STC 5580), also in folio. Langland's *Piers Plowman* was printed three times by Robert Crowley in 1550 (STC 19906, 19907, and 19907a) and again by Owen Rogers in 1561 (STC 19908). All of these editions are in quarto. Numerous editions of minor works by Lydgate printed during this period also appear in smaller format; see Alexandra Gillespie, *Print Culture and the Medieval Author: Chaucer, Lydgate, and Their Books, 1473–1557* (Oxford: Oxford University Press, 2006).

7. As Helen Cooper notes, the way in which Chaucer's fame *precedes* his canonization on ideological grounds troubles the narrative of canonization advanced by John Guillory in his book *Cultural Capital: The Problem of Literary Canon Formation* (Chicago: University of Chicago Press, 1993). Rather, "Guillory's criteria of canon formation, in Chaucer's case, operate

largely retrospectively, to harness the fact that he was already so widely read." See Cooper, "Poetic Fame," in *Cultural Reformations: Medieval and Renaissance in Literary History*, ed. James Simpson and Brian Cummings (Oxford: Oxford University Press, 2011), 362.

8. Camden actually attributes these words to the Dutch geographer Ortelius. Philemon Holland's 1610 English translation renders the passage as follows: "Abraham Ortelius the worthy restorer of Ancient Geographie arriving heere in England, above thirty foure yeares past, dealt earnestly with me that I would illustrate this Ile of Britaine, or (as he said) that I would restore antiquity to Britaine, and Britain to his antiquity; which was as I understood, that I would renew ancientrie, enlighten obscuritie, cleare doubts, and recall home Veritie by way of recovery, which the negligence of writers and credulitie of the common sort had in a maner proscribed and utterly banished from amongst us" (William Camden, *Britain, or A chorographicall description of the most flourishing kingdomes, England, Scotland, and Ireland, and the ilands adjoyning*, trans. Philemon Holland [London: George Bishop and John Norton, 1610], sig. ¶4 [STC 4509]). On Camden's literary style and its relationship to antiquarian practice, see Angus Vine, "Copiousness, Conjecture and Collaboration in William Camden's *Britannia*," *Renaissance Studies* 28, no. 2 (2014): 225–41.

9. On the large body of work attributed to Chaucer in fifteenth-century manuscripts and early printed books, see Kathleen Forni, *The Chaucerian Apocrypha: A Counterfeit Canon* (Gainesville: University Press of Florida, 2001).

10. John Aubrey, *"Brief Lives," Chiefly of Contemporaries, Set Down by John Aubrey, Between the Years 1669 & 1696*, ed. Andrew Clark (Oxford: Clarendon Press, 1898), 1:193.

11. On the humanistic origins of antiquarianism, see Angus Vine, *In Defiance of Time: Antiquarian Writing in Early Modern England* (Oxford: Oxford University Press, 2010), 3–5. For the broader influence of humanism on early modern historiography in England, see Joseph Levine, *Humanism and History: Origins of Modern English Historiography* (Ithaca, NY: Cornell University Press, 1987) and F. J. Levy, *Tudor Historical Thought* (Toronto: University of Toronto Press, 1967), 33–78. For an important account of antiquarian scholarship in seventeenth-century England, see Graham Parry, *The Trophies of Time: English Antiquarians of the Seventeenth Century* (Oxford: Oxford University Press, 1995).

12. Lisa Jardine and Anthony Grafton, "'Studied for Action': How Gabriel Harvey Read His Livy," *Past and Present* 129 (1990): 30.

13. On Leland's life and work, see James P. Carley, "Leland, John (c. 1503–1552), Poet and Antiquary," in *Oxford Dictionary of National Biography* (Oxford: Oxford University Press, 2004), http://www.oxforddnb.com (hereafter *Oxford DNB*). For a discussion of the scope and motivation of Leland's travels, see John Scattergood, "John Leland's *Itinerary* and the Identity of England," in *Sixteenth-Century Identities*, ed. A. J. Piesse (Manchester: Manchester University Press, 2000), 58–74; and Jennifer Summit, "Leland's *Itinerary* and the Remains of the Medieval Past," in *Reading the Medieval in Early Modern England*, ed. Gordon McMullan and David Matthews (Cambridge: Cambridge University Press, 2007), 159–176.

14. The most comprehensive treatment of the period's scholarly engagement with medieval history remains May McKisack's *Medieval History in the Tudor Age* (Oxford: Clarendon Press, 1971).

15. See Timothy Graham, "Matthew Parker's Manuscripts: An Elizabethan Library and Its Use," in *The Cambridge History of Libraries in Britain and Ireland*, vol. 1, ed. Elisabeth Leedham-Green and Teresa Webber (Cambridge: Cambridge University Press, 2006), 322–324.

16. On the composition and publication of *Britannia*, see Wyman H. Herendeen, *William Camden: A Life in Context* (Woodbridge, Suffolk: Boydell and Brewer, 2007), 180–242.

17. On Cotton's relationship to antiquarianism and historical studies, see Kevin Sharpe, *Sir Robert Cotton, 1586–1631: History and Politics in Early Modern England* (Oxford: Oxford University Press, 1979), especially 17–32 on his role in the Society of Antiquaries. On the founding and development of the Society of Antiquaries, see Herendeen, *William Camden*, 309–333.

18. The fullest and most comprehensive study of the Elizabethan Society of Antiquaries remains Linda Van Norden, "The Elizabethan College of Antiquaries" (PhD diss., University of California, Los Angeles, 1946).

19. Herendeen, *William Camden*, 320–328.

20. A. S. G. Edwards offers an account of Stow's use of Middle English literary manuscripts in "John Stow and Middle English Literature," in *John Stow (1525–1605) and the Making of the English Past: Studies in Early Modern Culture and the History of the Book*, ed. Ian Gadd and Alexandra Gillespie (London: British Library, 2004), 109–118.

21. Cambridge, Trinity College MS R.3.19 and MS R.3.20. MS R.3.20 is in the hand of the noted fifteenth-century scribe and bibliophile John Shirley.

22. Thomas Hoccleve, in the *Regiment of Princes* (ca. 1412) was the first to call Chaucer "fadir." For John Lydgate, Chaucer's most prolific fifteenth-century admirer, the older poet was always "mayster." For an inclusive treatment of Chaucer's reception through the nineteenth century, see Caroline Spurgeon, *Five Hundred Years of Chaucer Criticism and Allusion*, 3 vols. (Cambridge: Cambridge University Press, 1925).

23. On Crowley's editions of *Piers Plowman*, see Lawrence Warner, *The Myth of Piers Plowman: Constructing a Medieval Literary Archive* (Cambridge: Cambridge University Press, 2014), 72–86. On Chaucer and alchemy, see Robert M. Schuler, "The Renaissance Chaucer as Alchemist," *Viator* 15 (1984): 305–333. On Lydgate and alchemy, and one fifteenth-century reader's determination to view *The Churl and the Bird* as an alchemic text, see Joel Fredell, "Alchemical Lydgate," *Studies in Philology* 107, no. 4 (2010): 429–464. Book 4 of Gower's *Confessio Amantis* discusses alchemy, and British Library Sloane MS 3847, a compendium of alchemical and magical texts, includes a seventeenth-century excerpt of Gower's discussion of the properties of stones and herbs.

24. The literature in this field is significant and wide-ranging, but see, for example, Catherine Sanok, "Good King Henry and the Genealogy of Shakespeare's First History Plays," *Journal of Medieval and Early Modern Studies* 40, no. 1 (2010): 37–63; Lucy Munro, "Speaking History: Linguistic Memory and the Usable Past in the Early Modern History Play," *Huntington Library Quarterly* 76, no. 4 (2013): 519–540; and Kurt A. Schreyer, *Shakespeare's Medieval Craft: Remnants of the Mysteries on the London Stage* (Ithaca, NY: Cornell University Press, 2014).

25. Alexandra Gillespie offers a comparative account of the fate of Lydgate and Chaucer in *Print Culture and the Medieval Author*. For discussion of texts less firmly marked with an authorial name, see Sarah A. Kelen, *Langland's Early Modern Identities* (New York: Palgrave Macmillan, 2007).

26. On Usk's text, see Anne Middleton, "Thomas Usk's 'Perdurable Letters': The 'Testament of Love' from Script to Print," *Studies in Bibliography* 51 (1998): 70–79. On the *Floure and the Leaf*, see D. A. Pearsall, ed. *The Floure and the Leafe; and The Assembly of Ladies* (Manchester: Manchester University Press, 1980), 2–4.

27. On the characteristic features of literary archaism, see Lucy Munro, *Archaic Style in English Literature, 1590–1674* (Cambridge: Cambridge University Press, 2013), 12–30.

28. See David Matthews, *The Making of Middle English, 1765–1910* (Minneapolis: University of Minnesota Press, 1999), 162–186.

29. Margreta de Grazia, "The Modern Divide: From Either Side," *Journal of Medieval and Early Modern Studies* 37, no. 7 (2007): 453.

30. The phrase is Christopher Cannon's; see "The Myth of Origin and the Making of Chaucer's English," *Speculum* 71, no. 3 (1996): 656.

31. Alice S. Miskimin's *The Renaissance Chaucer* (New Haven, CT: Yale University Press, 1975) remains a foundational study, although many of her conclusions have been supplanted or expanded on by more recent work by Gordon McMullan, David Matthews, Brian Cummings, Helen Cooper, and other scholars working across the medieval/early modern divide.

32. See Bart van Es, "Discourses of Conquest: *The Faerie Queene*, the Society of Antiquaries, and *A View of the Present State of Ireland*," *English Literary Renaissance* 32, no. 1 (2002): 118–151; and Vine, *In Defiance of Time*.

33. Vine, *In Defiance of Time*, 4.

CHAPTER I

1. See https://www.folger.edu/first-folio-tour.

2. Nor was the first First Folio Ben Jonson's 1616 *Workes*, which served as a model for the Shakespeare folio.

3. On the implications of this shift, which resulted in a stable bibliographic format but an increasingly corrupt text, see A. S. G. Edwards, "Chaucer from Manuscript to Print: The Social Text and the Critical Text," *Mosaic* 28, no. 4 (1995): 1–12.

4. For a reading that places Caxton's work with Chaucer in the context of early print capitalism, see William Kuskin, *Symbolic Caxton: Literary Culture and Print Capitalism* (Notre Dame, IN: University of Notre Dame Press, 2007), 118–154.

5. On the relationship between these early editions and their manuscript sources, see Alexandra Gillespie, "Caxton's Chaucer and Lydgate Quartos: Miscellanies from Manuscript to Print," *Transactions of the Cambridge Bibliographical Society* 12, no. 1 (2000): 1–25; and Seth Lerer, "Medieval Literature and Early Modern Readers: Cambridge University Library Sel. 5.51–5.63," *Papers of the Bibliographical Society of America* 97 (2003): 311–332.

6. On Pynson's editions, see Alexandra Gillespie's *Print Culture and the Medieval Author*, 126–134, as well as her "Poets, Printers, and Early English *Sammelbände*," *Huntington Library Quarterly* 67 (2004): 189–214.

7. Early supplements to Spurgeon's collection are noted in William L. Alderson, "A Check-List of Supplements to Spurgeon's Chaucer Allusions," *Philological Quarterly* 32 (1953): 418–427. See also updates by Jackson Campbell Boswell: "Chaucer and Spenser Allusions Not in Spurgeon and Wells," *Analytical and Enumerative Bibliography* 1 (1977): 30–32; and "Chaucer Allusions: Addenda to Spurgeon," *Notes and Queries* 222 (1977): 493–495. A comprehensive bibliography of printed references and allusions to Chaucer during the STC period can be found in Jackson Campbell Boswell and Sylvia Wallace Holton, *Chaucer's Fame in England: STC Chauceriana, 1475–1640* (New York: Modern Language Association of America, 2004).

8. The 1532 *Works* (STC 5068) were printed by Thomas Godfray. Richard Grafton printed the 1542 edition for booksellers William Bonham (STC 5069) and John Reynes (STC 5070). The *Works* were reprinted again in about 1550 by Nicholas Hill, for a consortium of booksellers including William Bonham (STC 5071), Richard Kele (STC 5072), Thomas Petit (STC 5073), and Robert Toye (STC 5074). The 1561 *Works* were printed by John Kynson for John Wight (STC 5075 and 5076), although a variant edition lists a Henry Bradsha as the printer (STC

5076.3). Adam Islip printed the *Works* in both 1598 and 1602. In 1598, Islip produced copies for sale by George Bishop (STC 5077), Bonham Norton (STC 5078), and Thomas Wight (STC 5079). In 1602, some copies are described as printed for Bishop (STC 5081), while others list only Islip as the printer (STC 5080).

9. While most texts were printed in black letter in the 1530s, by the end of the century, the typeface was largely reserved for works on the high end (legal and religious works) and low end (pamphlets and other "cheap print") of the publishing spectrum. See Zachary Lesser, "Typographic Nostalgia: Play-Reading, Popularity, and the Meanings of Black Letter," in *The Book of the Play: Playwrights, Stationers, and Readers in Early Modern England*, ed. Marta Straznicky (Amherst: University of Massachusetts, 2006), 99–126.

10. See Greg Walker, *Writing Under Tyranny: English Literature and the Henrician Reformation* (New York: Oxford University Press, 2005), 56–99, esp. 73–99, which situates the material added before Chaucer's poems within the broader context of humanistic "literature of counsel." On Stow's multifaceted antiquarian career, see the essays in Ian Gadd and Alexandra Gillespie, eds., *John Stow (1525–1605) and the Making of the English Past: Studies in Early Modern Culture and the History of the Book* (London: British Library, 2004). For Speght, see Derek Pearsall, "Thomas Speght (ca. 1550–?)," in *Editing Chaucer: The Great Tradition*, ed. Paul Ruggiers (Norman, OK: Pilgrim Books, 1984), 71–92; as well Pearsall's essay "John Stow and Thomas Speght as Editors of Chaucer: A Question of Class," in Gadd and Gillespie, *John Stow*, 119–125.

11. The most comprehensive overview of Chaucer editing remains Ruggiers, *Editing Chaucer*.

12. Jeffrey Todd Knight, drawing on work by Lerer and Gillespie, discusses the "open-ended" relationship between Thynne's edition and its predecessors in *Bound to Read: Compilations, Collections, and the Making of Renaissance Literature* (Philadelphia: University of Pennsylvania Press, 2013), esp. 159–165.

13. Godfray was probably a member of the Stationers' Company and was active between the end of 1530 and early 1537. On Godfray's career, with a discussion of the *Plowman's Tale*, see Peter W. M. Blayney, *The Stationers' Company and the Printers of London, 1501–1557* (Cambridge: Cambridge University Press, 2013), 1:277–282.

14. As Knight rightly observes, "the bibliographical composition of the early *Workes* volume is only surprising (or appalling) when the point of reference is the modern collection instead of the multiplying forms of vernacular compilation in the late medieval and early print period" (*Bound to Read*, 160). On Chaucer's apocrypha in both print and manuscript, see Forni, *The Chaucerian Apocrypha: A Counterfeit Canon*.

15. See Andrew W. Wawn, "The Genesis of *The Plowman's Tale*," *Yearbook of English Studies* 2 (1972): 21–40, as well as his "Chaucer, *The Plowman's Tale* and Reformation Propaganda: The Testimony of Thomas Godfray and *I Playne Piers*," *Bulletin of the John Rylands Library* 56 (1973–1974): 174–192. See also Gillespie, *Print Culture and the Medieval Author*, 189–195, on the addition of new printed marginalia in the 1542 reprint of Thynne by draper Richard Grafton.

16. Godfray's edition survives in one acephalous copy at the Huntington Library; while, like the *Works*, it is in folio format, it is printed on smaller paper stock than the *Works*. See Gillespie, *Print Culture and the Medieval Author*, 198.

17. The text does appear in manuscript, however, bound into a copy of the 1532 *Works* now held at the Harry Ransom Center at the University of Texas, described in Annie S. Irvine, "A Manuscript Copy of *The Plowman's Tale*," *University of Texas Studies in English* 12 (1932): 27–56. Irvine argues that the differences between this manuscript and sixteenth-century editions reflect the use of an exemplar predating any of the surviving print witnesses, suggesting that the poem was already circulating under Chaucer's name by the time it was printed in the

1530s. More recently, Joseph A. Dane has challenged Irvine's conclusions, arguing that the distinctive readings in the Ransom Center manuscript could also result from poor copying from a printed edition. See Dane, "Bibliographical History Versus Bibliographical Evidence: The Plowman's Tale and Early Chaucer Editions," *Bulletin of the John Rylands University Library of Manchester* 78, no. 1 (1996): 47–61.

18. See Anne Hudson, "John Stow," in Ruggiers, *Editing Chaucer*, 53–70.

19. Both are described fully by M. R. James in *The Western Manuscripts in the Library of Trinity College, Cambridge: A Descriptive Catalogue* (Cambridge: Cambridge University Press, 1900). Cambridge, Trinity College MS R.3.19 is a particularly important source for attribution of Chaucer's shorter poems. See Linne R. Mooney, "Scribes and Booklets of Trinity College, Cambridge, Manuscripts R.3.19 and R.3.21," in *Middle English Poetry: Texts and Traditions*, ed. A. J. Minnis (York, England: York Medieval, 2001), 241–66; A. S. G. Edwards and J. Hedley, "John Stowe, *The Craft of Lovers* and T.C.C. R.3.19," *Studies in Bibliography* 28 (1975): 265–268; and W. W. Greg, "Chaucer Attributions in MS R.3.19, in the Library of Trinity College, Cambridge," *Modern Language Review* 8, no. 4 (1913): 539–540.

20. On Shirley's life and manuscripts, see Margaret Connolly, *John Shirley: Book Production and the Noble Household in Fifteenth-Century England* (Aldershot: Ashgate, 1998).

21. See Pearsall, "John Stow and Thomas Speght as Editors of Chaucer," 122–123.

22. Both versions of Speght's dedication and letter to the reader, as well as Francis Beaumont's letter to Speght and the dedication to Henry VIII taken from the 1532 edition, are reprinted in Spurgeon, *Five Hundred Years of Chaucer Criticism and Allusion* (1:78–80, 145–148, 168–170).

23. Paul Greaves's *Vocabula Chauceriana* was appended to his *Grammatica Anglicana* (STC 12208) when it was published in 1594, but it contains only about 120 words, most with definitions derived from E.K.'s glosses to Spenser's language in the *Shepheardes Calender*.

24. On the marketing of early books, see Zachary Lesser, *Renaissance Drama and the Politics of Publication: Readings in the English Book Trade* (Cambridge: Cambridge University Press, 2004); and Adam G. Hooks, *Selling Shakespeare: Biography, Bibliography, and the Book Trade* (Cambridge: Cambridge University Press, 2016).

25. John Stow appears to have taken a special interest in Lydgate's canon and was responsible for compiling the list of Lydgate's works (including many spurious titles) that appears in Chaucer's *Works* in 1561. On Stow's interest in Lydgate, see Edwards, "John Stow and Middle English Literature," esp. 114–118.

26. Skelton's works were collected by John Stow and published in octavo in 1568 (STC 22608). The quarto edition of Heywood's collected writings was first published in 1562 by Thomas Powell (STC 13285) and reprinted in 1566 (STC 13286), 1577 (STC 13287), 1587 (STC 13288), and 1598 (STC 13289).

27. *The workes of Sir Thomas More Knyght, sometyme Lorde Chauncellour of England, wrytten by him in the Englysh tonge* (London: John Cawood, John Waly, and Richard Tottel, 1557); STC 18076.

28. Thomas Godfray's edition (STC 5099.5) is missing its title page, but William Hill's edition (1548?) clearly attributes the word to Chaucer in its title, *The plowmans tale compylled by syr Geffrey Chaucher knyght* (STC 5100). George Eld's 1606 quarto edition (STC 5101) added a number of printed marginal glosses drawn from the annotations printed with Speght's 1602 edition of the *Works*. In about 1536, John Gough published an octavo edition of *Jack up Lande Compyled by the famous Geoffrey Chaucer* (STC 5098), which also stresses the attribution to Chaucer on its title page.

29. On Thynne's copy-text, see James Blodgett, "William Thynne," in Ruggiers, *Editing Chaucer*, 35–53; Joseph A. Dane, "On 'Correctness': A Note on Some Press Variants in Thynne's 1532 Edition of Chaucer," *The Library* 17, no. 2 (1995): 156–167; and especially James Blodgett, "Some Printer's Copy for William Thynne's 1532 Edition of Chaucer," *The Library* 1, no. 2 (1979): 97–113. Blodgett identifies five extant Chaucer manuscripts owned by Thynne, of which two (Glasgow, University of Glasgow Library Hunterian V.3.7; and Longleat House MS 258) can be connected with the 1532 *Works* (the Longleat House copy of Caxton's edition of Chaucer's *Boece* also contains printer's marks consistent with that edition). He also hypothesizes an additional four manuscripts, related to surviving copies, used in his edition ("William Thynne," 39–41). In addition, as Robert Costomiris has shown, William Thynne made recourse to several earlier printed editions when preparing his *Works* (his sense of the scope and order of the *Canterbury Tales*, for example, can be traced to Caxton's first edition of 1477). See Costomiris, "The Influence of Printed Editions and Manuscripts on the Canon of William Thynne's *Canterbury Tales*," in *Rewriting Chaucer: Culture, Authority, and the Idea of the Authentic Text, 1400–1602*, ed. Thomas A. Prendergast and Barbara Kline (Columbus: Ohio State University Press, 1999), 237–257; as well as Costomiris, "Some New Light on the Early Career of William Thynne, Chief Clerk of the Kitchen of Henry VIII and Editor of Chaucer," *The Library* 4, no. 1 (2003): 3–15. As several twentieth- and twenty-first-century scholars have noted, there is little reason, on the basis of the text of the 1532 *Works*, to believe the claims made by Thynne's son Francis that his father undertook an extensive search of monasteries looking for Chaucer manuscripts; see Francis Thynne, *Animadversions upon the Annotacions and Corrections of some imperfections of impressiones of Chaucers workes (sett downe before tyme, and nowe) reprinted in the yere of oure lorde 1598*, ed. G. H. Kingsley, Early English Text Society, o.s. 9 (1865), rev. ed., ed. F. J. Furnivall (London: Trübner, 1875), 10. All subsequent page citations of the *Animadversions* refer to Furnivall's edition.

30. Urry heavily emends his text of the *Tales* with manuscript reading, but his base text is the 1602 Speght. His interleaved notes to the *Canterbury Tales* are preserved in Oxford, Bodleian Library MS Rawlinson Poet.40a.

31. John Stow made extensive use of two fifteenth-century miscellanies, now Cambridge, Trinity College MSS R.3.19 and R.3.20. Bradford Y. Fletcher has identified the manuscripts used by Stow (which also may have included Bodleian Fairfax 16, British Library Cotton Cleopatra D. VII and Harley 78) and finds him to be an accurate copyist of his fifteenth-century sources. See Fletcher, "Printer's Copy for Stow's *Chaucer*," *Studies in Bibliography* 31 (1978): 184–201.

32. On these additions, see Forni, *The Chaucerian Apocrypha: A Counterfeit Canon*, 21–88.

33. Stow's choice of texts is discussed in Hudson, "John Stow," 62–65.

34. In the 1561 *Works*, these added materials are introduced with the heading "Here foloweth certaine woorkes of Geffray Chauser, whiche hath not heretofore been printed, and are gathered and added to this booke by Ihon Stowe" (sig. 3P2).

35. Greg Walker argues that the preface and, potentially, the *Works* as a whole were the collaborative enterprise of William Thynne and Brian Tuke. Tuke's claim—written on the title page of a copy of the 1532 *Works* now at Clare College, Cambridge—that "this preface, I sir Bryan Tuke, knight, wrote at the request of the m[aste]r clerk of the kitchen, then being, tarrying for the tide and Greenwich" is supported by comments by John Leland and Francis Thynne concerning Tuke's involvement in the project (see *Writing Under Tyranny*, 59–72). R. F Yeager posits that Tuke's involvement was an unplanned response to the need to produce a suitable copy-text for the printer while Thynne was absent (see "Literary Theory at the Close of the Middle Ages: William Caxton and William Thynne," *Studies in the Age of Chaucer* 6 [1984]: 158); Walker argues for a more deliberate and sustained collaboration between the two.

Since the exact degree of Tuke's involvement is uncertain, and since the *Works* present themselves as the work of William Thynne, I follow Walker's practice and "leave [Thynne's] name unsullied by special punctuation, but on the understanding that . . . I am referring to a pseudo-fictional 'Thynne the Editor' who was, as I shall argue, a literary construct created by the combined authorship of Tuke and Thynne" (*Writing Under Tyranny*, 441).

36. On the role of these poems in the *Works*, see Walker, *Writing Under Tyranny*, 74–76; and Forni, *The Chaucerian Apocrypha: A Counterfeit Canon*, 45–54. On the print and manuscript circulation of the Chaucer/Merlin prophecy and its influence on Shakespeare, see Misha Teramura, "Prophecy and Emendation: Merlin, Chaucer, Lear's Fool," in *Postmedieval* 10.1 (forthcoming).

37. The connections between Thynne's preface and the tumultuous events of the early 1530s are discussed by Greg Walker in *Writing Under Tyranny*, 29–35, 56–99.

38. *Works* (1532), sig. a2.

39. On early sixteenth-century debates over how best to improve English as a language, see Alvin Vos, "Humanistic Standards of Diction in the Inkhorn Controversy," *Studies in Philology* 73 (1976): 376–396.

40. *Works* (1532), sig. a2–a2v.

41. *Works* (1532), sig. a2.

42. *Works* (1532), sig. a2.

43. *Works* (1532), sig. a2v.

44. *Works* (1532), sig. a2v.

45. *Works* (1532), sig. a2v.

46. Thomas Wilson, *The Arte of Rhetorique* (London: Richard Grafton, 1553), sig. Y2v; STC 25799.

47. The coat of arms title page appears only in STC 5076. *Hall's Chronicle* was printed by Richard Grafton, who was also responsible for the 1542 reprint of Thynne's edition of the *Works* (which does not contain the woodcut). There are two issues of Stow's 1561 Chaucer. STC 5075 does not include the Chaucer coat of arms on the title page, but does have portraits of the pilgrims in the *General Prologue*; STC 5076 includes the coat of arms on the title page but does not have the pilgrim portraits. From signature B on, the two issues are the same. (STC 5076.3 is a variant of 5076.) See Joseph Dane, "In Search of Stow's Chaucer," in Gadd and Gillespie, *John Stow*, 145–155.

48. Joseph Dane and Seth Lerer, "Press Variants in John Stow's Chaucer (1561) and the Text of 'Adam Scriveyn,'" *Transactions of the Cambridge Bibliographical Society* 11, no. 4 (1999): 468–479.

49. The large number of books and manuscripts that passed through Stow's hands are, as of 2019, being traced by the "John Stow's Books" project at the Old Books New Science Lab at the University of Toronto.

50. For a robust discussion of this image and Speed's work, see Martha W. Driver, "Mapping Chaucer: John Speed and the Later Portraits," *Chaucer Review* 36, no. 3 (2002): 228–249. Speed was a member of the circle of scholars centered on the Society of Antiquaries, and he contributed information on coins to William Camden's *Britannia*. See Sarah Bendall, "Speed, John (1551/2–1629)," in *Oxford DNB*.

51. M. H. Spielmann provides a broad, if incomplete, overview of the portrait tradition in *The Portraits of Geoffrey Chaucer: An Essay Written on the Occasion of the Quincentenary of the Poet's Death* (London: Kegan Paul, Trench, Trübner for the Chaucer Society, 1900). See also Driver, "Mapping Chaucer"; A. S. G. Edwards, "The Chaucer Portraits in the Harley and

Rosenbach Manuscripts," in *English Manuscript Studies, 1100–1700*, vol. 4, ed. Peter Beal and Jeremy Griffiths (Toronto: University of Toronto Press, 1993). 268–271; Sylvia Wright, "The Author Portraits in the Bedford Psalter-Hours: Gower, Chaucer, and Hoccleve," *British Library Journal* 18, no. 2 (1992): 190–201; and David R. Carlson, "Thomas Hoccleve and the Chaucer Portrait," *Huntington Library Quarterly* 54, no. 4 (1991): 283–300. Carlson argues that, were the *Regiment of Princes* portrait a fabricated likeness, Hoccleve would have lost face with potential patrons like Henry IV, who would have known Chaucer by sight; thus, Carlson concludes, the portrait probably really does resemble Chaucer in appearance.

52. Driver suggests the model for this portrait may have come from a manuscript in the possession of Speed's friend Robert Cotton, but also points to British Library Additional MS 5141, in which the poet holds his penner in the same unusual manner as he does in the Speed portrait ("Mapping Chaucer" 238, 247).

53. Chaucer's tomb, which was relocated in the middle of the sixteenth century, establishing what is now Poets' Corner, has been the subject of considerable scholarly attention. See Joseph Dane and Alexandra Gillespie, "Back at Chaucer's Tomb: Inscriptions in Two Early Copies of Chaucer's *Workes*," *Studies in Bibliography* 52 (1999): 89–96. On Chaucer's epitaph, see also Gillespie, *Print Culture and the Medieval Author*, 70–72; Seth Lerer, *Chaucer and His Readers: Imagining the Author in Late-Medieval England* (Princeton, NJ: Princeton University Press, 1993), 147–175; Thomas Prendergast, *Chaucer's Dead Body: From Corpse to Corpus* (New York: Routledge, 2004), 39–43; Derek Pearsall, "Chaucer's Tomb: The Politics of Reburial," *Medium Aevum* 64 (1995): 51–73; Dane, "Who Is Buried in Chaucer's Tomb?—Prolegomena," *Huntington Library Quarterly* 57 (1994): 99–123; Dane, *Who Is Buried in Chaucer's Tomb?* (East Lansing: Michigan State University Press, 1998), 11–32.

54. These shields are identified and described in E. A. Greening Lamborn, "The Arms on the Chaucer Tomb at Ewelme," *Oxoniensia* 5 (1940): 78–93.

55. David Griffith offers an instructive account of the route such rolls might take through antiquarian communities from the sixteenth century onward in "Owners and Copyists of John Rous's Armorial Rolls," in *Essays in Manuscript Geography: Vernacular Manuscripts of the English West Midlands from the Conquest to the Sixteenth Century*, ed. Wendy Scase (Turnhout, Belgium: Brepols, 2007), 203–228.

56. The nineteenth-century essayist and critic Walter Pater is said to have remarked that "this portrait, dight with heraldry, has as much within it as a vast number of the so-called commentaries of the Bible." See Thomas Wright, *The Life of Walter Pater* (New York: G. P. Putnam's Sons; London: Everett, 1907), 2:267–268.

57. See Trigg, *Congenial Souls*; Lerer, *Chaucer and His Readers*; and Prendergast, *Chaucer's Dead Body*.

58. Trigg, *Congenial Souls*, 134.

59. On the role of borders and frames in early modern art, see Victor I. Stoichita, *The Self-Aware Image: An Insight into Early Modern Meta-Painting*, trans. Anne-Marie Glasheen (Cambridge: Cambridge University Press, 1997), 30–63.

60. Driver, "Mapping Chaucer," 241.

61. For additional background on Paon de Roet, see Lindsay L. Brook, "The Ancestry of Sir Paon de Ruet, Father-in-Law of Geoffrey Chaucer and John 'of Gaunt,'" *Foundations* 1, no. 1 (2003): 54–56.

62. Helen Cooper, "Poetic Fame," in *Cultural Reformations: Medieval and Renaissance in Literary History*, ed. Brian Cummings and James Simpson (Cambridge: Cambridge University Press, 2010), 377.

63. Cooper, "Poetic Fame," 377.

64. *Confessio Amantis* (1532), sig. AA2v.

65. On the influence of Berthelette's presentation of Gower on the poet's later reception, see Helen Cooper, "'This Worthy Olde Writer': Pericles and Other Gowers, 1592–1640," in *A Companion to Gower*, ed. Siân Echard (Cambridge: D. S. Brewer, 2004), 99–113.

66. *Troy Book* (1555), sig. A2.

67. *Piers Plowman* (1550), sig. *2V (STC 19906).

68. Neither of Speght's editions comes close to providing the kind of detailed, dense marginal commentary found in sixteenth-century Italian editions of Petrarch, Boccaccio, and Dante. Indeed, the margins of all the Tudor Chaucers are strikingly bare, with the exception of manicules in the margins of some sections of the 1602 edition of Speght's Chaucer (see Clare Kinney, "Thomas Speght's Renaissance Chaucer and the Solaas of Sentence in *Troilus and Criseyde*," in *Refiguring Chaucer in the Renaissance*, ed. Theresa M. Krier [Gainesville: University Press of Florida, 1998], 66–84) and misinterpreted printers' marks in the 1550 edition (on this, see Joseph A. Dane, "Fists and Filiations in Early Chaucer Folios, 1532–1602," *Studies in Bibliography* 51 [1998]: 48–62). Moreover, unlike the Italian trecento poets, once collected into a single volume, Chaucer's works are always published in their entirety and in large, monumental folios.

69. On these conversations, see Catherine Nicholson, *Uncommon Tongues: Eloquence and Eccentricity in the English Renaissance* (Philadelphia: University of Pennsylvania Press, 2014).

70. See Munro, *Archaic Style in English Literature*.

71. This is true even though, as Cathy Shrank observes, Spenser's archaizing tendencies evoke mid-Tudor writing more than his own historical moment. See Cathy Shrank, *Writing the Nation in Reformation England, 1530–1580* (Oxford: Oxford University Press, 2004), 222–232. On Spenser's work in the context of archaism in early modern England, see Munro, *Archaic Style in English Literature*, 78–91.

72. See George Puttenham, *The Art of English Poesy*, ed. Frank Whigham and Wayne A. Rebhorn (Ithaca, NY: Cornell University Press, 2007), 229.

73. The rate of change within English outpaces that of other vernaculars, notably French and Italian, against which English poetry measures itself. See Terttu Nevalainen, "Early Modern English Lexis and Semantics," in *The Cambridge History of the English Language*, vol. 3, *1476–1776*, ed. John Algeo (Cambridge: Cambridge University Press, 1999), 332–458.

74. For one account of this change rooted in the Chancery courts of the late fourteenth and fifteenth centuries, see John H. Fisher, *The Emergence of Standard English* (Lexington: University Press of Kentucky, 1996). The particulars of the Great Vowel Shift have been the subject of much critical debate; for an overview, see Richard J. Watts, "Was the Great Vowel Shift Really 'Great'? A Reappraisal of Research Work on an Elusive Linguistic Phenomenon," in *English Core Linguistics*, ed. Cornelia Tschichold (Bern: Peter Lang, 2003), 13–30. On the implications for the study of Middle English poetry and meter, see Thomas Cable, "Fifteenth-Century Rhythmical Changes," in *"And Gladly Wolde He Lerne and Gladly Teache": Essays on Medieval English Presented to Professor Matsui Tahima on His Sixtieth Birthday*, ed. Yoko Iyeiri and Margaret Connolly (Tokyo: Kaibunsha, 2002), 109–125.

75. James Simpson, "Ageism: Leland, Bale, and the Laborious Start of English Literary History, 1350–1550," *New Medieval Literatures* 1 (1997): 217. Simpson writes elsewhere in his essay, under this still-present "'ageist' conception of cultural periodization . . . the 'medieval'

continues to figure all that is other to modernity, and . . . the function of scholarship is to define and reaffirm the 'medieval'" ("Ageism," 213).

76. On this, see Munro, *Archaic Style in English Literature*, 32–68; Chris Jones, "Anglo-Saxonism in Nineteenth-Century Poetry," *Literature Compass* 7, no. 5 (2010): 358–369, as well as his "New Old English: The Place of Old English in Twentieth- and Twenty-First-Century Poetry," *Literature Compass* 7, no. 11 (2010): 1009–1019. Despite the linguistic differences, the approach to Old English in these texts parallels early modern engagement with Chaucer. As Jones writes, in the nineteenth century, the thinking was "that Anglo-Saxon culture was primitive, or even uncivilised; and that Anglo-Saxon culture contained, in embryonic form, the expression of subsequent English (or British, or Anglo-Saxon American) national traits, therefore seen as somehow essential or even timeless" ("Anglo-Saxonism in Nineteenth-Century Poetry," 359).

77. For an overview of Anglo-Saxon scholarship in early modern England, see Rebecca Brackmann, *The Elizabethan Invention of Anglo-Saxon England: Laurence Nowell, William Lambarde, and the Study of Old English* (Cambridge: D. S. Brewer, 2012), 1–28; on etymological methods and their important place in Anglo-Saxon scholarship, see Hannah Crawforth, *Etymology and the Invention of English in Early Modern Literature* (Cambridge: Cambridge University Press, 2014), 7–18.

78. On the activities of Parker and his circle, see McKisack, *Medieval History in the Tudor Age*, 26–49. Jennifer Summit's account emphasizes the degree to which the collecting activities of Parker and his circle were selective, and informed by Protestantism. See Summit, *Memory's Library: Medieval Books in Early Modern England* (Chicago: University of Chicago Press, 2008), 106–121.

79. On the status of Old English in early modern England, see Carl T. Berkhout and Milton McCormick Gatch, eds., *Anglo-Saxon Scholarship: The First Three Centuries* (Boston: G. K. Hall, 1982); and Timothy Graham, ed., *The Recovery of Old English: Anglo-Saxon Studies in the Sixteenth and Seventeenth Centuries* (Kalamazoo: Western Michigan University Press, 2000). On its impact on literary practice, see Vine, *In Defiance of Time*; Munro, *Archaic Style in English Literature, 1590–1675*; and Hannah Crawforth, "Strangers to the Mother Tongue: Spenser's *Shepheardes Calender* and Early Anglo-Saxon Studies," *Journal of Medieval and Early Modern Studies* 41, no. 2 (2011): 293–316.

80. Lévi-Strauss writes, "We understand, too, that natural species are chosen [as totems] not because they are 'good to eat' but because they are 'good to think'" (*Totemism*, trans. Rodney Needham [London: Merlin Press, 1964], 89).

CHAPTER 2

1. On Thynne's edition, see Blodgett, "William Thynne"; Robert Costomiris, "Sharing Chaucer's Authority in Prefaces to Chaucer's Works from William Caxton to William Thynne," *Journal of the Early Book Society for the Study of Manuscripts and Printing History* 5 (2002): 1–13; and Walker, *Writing Under Tyranny*, 29–72.

2. On Chaucer's death, see Derek Pearsall, *The Life of Geoffrey Chaucer: A Critical Biography* (Oxford: Blackwell, 1992), 273–276. Shirley's note can be found in Cambridge, Trinity College MS R.3.20, p. 144. Two other manuscripts of "Truth" describe it as composed on Chaucer's deathbed (London, British Library Cotton MS Otho A.xviii and Oxford, Bodleian

Library MS Hatton 73), as does Thomas Speght's *Life of Chaucer*, which appears in the 1598, 1602, and 1687 editions of the *Works*.

3. Olive Sayce argues that Gascoigne's account is "undoubtedly" derived from the *Retraction*, but Míceál Vaughan disagrees. See Sayce, "Chaucer's 'Retractions': The Conclusion of the *Canterbury Tales* and Its Place in Literary Tradition," *Medium Aevum* 40, no. 3 (1971): 230–248; and Vaughan, "Personal Politics and Thomas Gascoigne's Account of Chaucer's Death," *Medium Aevum* 75, no. 1 (2006): 115. Vaughan also provides a full transcription and translation of Gascoigne's text.

4. In 1710–1712, the Oxford antiquary Thomas Hearne published eight volumes of material largely drawn from later transcripts of Leland's manuscripts, under the title *The Itinerary of John Leland the Antiquary*. All citations here are from John Leland, *De Viris Illustribus: On Famous Men*, ed. and trans. James P. Carley with the assistance of Caroline Brett (Toronto: Pontifical Institute of Medieval Studies, 2010), cited hereafter as *De Viris Illustribus*.

5. James Simpson offers an influential discussion of the relation between Leland and Bale in his "Ageism." While I share Simpson's conclusion that the work of Bale is in many ways more formative to narratives of literary periodization than is Leland's, Leland's writings nonetheless set the terms in which Chaucer's biography, in particular, was discussed in the early modern period.

6. On the rise of authorial biography during the sixteenth century, see Kevin Pask, *The Emergence of the English Author: Scripting the Life of the Poet in Early Modern England* (Cambridge: Cambridge University Press, 1996).

7. See Michel Foucault, "What Is an Author?" in *Aesthetics, Method, and Epistemology*, ed. James D. Faubion, trans. Josué V. Harari (New York: New Press, 1998), 205–222; and Gillespie, *Print Culture and the Medieval Author*, 17–19.

8. For an overview of Leland's life and work, see Carley, "Leland, John (c. 1503–1552)"; as well as *De Viris Illustribus*, xxi–xxv.

9. *The laboryouse Journey and serche of Johan Leylande . . .* (London: Printed by S. Mierdman for John Bale, 1549), sig. B8v; STC 15445. No documentary evidence of this charter, if it existed, survives. All subsequent references to Leland's *Laboryouse Journey* are to this edition.

10. For a discussion of the scope and motivation of Leland's travels, see Scattergood, "John Leland's Itinerary and the Identity of England"; and Summit, "Leland's Itinerary and the Remains of the Medieval Past."

11. Simpson, "Ageism," 221.

12. For further studies on Leland and Bale, see Simpson, "Ageism"; Ernst Gerhardt, "'No Quyckar Marchaundyce than Lybrary Bokes': John Bale's Commodification of Manuscript Culture," *Renaissance Quarterly* 60 (2007): 408–433; and Anne Hudson, "*Visio Baleii*: An Early Literary Historian," in *The Long Fifteenth Century: Essays for Douglas Gray*, ed. Helen Cooper and Sally Mapstone (Oxford: Clarendon Press, 1997), 314–329. James P. Carley's introduction in his edition and translation of *De Viris Illustribus* offers a detailed account of these journeys.

13. See James P. Carley, "John Leland's *Cygnea Cantio*: A Neglected Tudor River Poem," *Humanistica Lovaniensia* 32 (1983): 225–241; and Carley, "Polydore Vergil and John Leland on King Arthur: The Battle of the Books," *Interpretations* 15, no. 2 (1984): 86–100.

14. On this, see especially James Simpson, "The Melancholy of John Leland and the Beginnings of English Literary History," in *The Oxford English Literary History*, vol. 2, *1350–1547: Reform and Cultural Revolution* (Oxford: Oxford University Press, 2002), 7–33.

15. Simpson, "The Melancholy of John Leland," 17.

16. *Laboryouse Journey*, sig. C6v–C7.

17. *Laboryouse Journey*, sig. C7.

18. See Carley's introduction in *De Viris Illustribus*, xxiv.

19. Leland's holograph manuscript of the text is now Oxford, Bodleian Library MS Top. Gen. c. 4. Simpson emphasizes the degree to which Britishness itself was a "highly charged" category in the sixteenth century; see "The Melancholy of John Leland," 24.

20. James P. Carley, "The Manuscript Remains of John Leland, 'The King's Antiquary,'" *Text: Transactions for the Society for Textual Scholarship* 2 (1985): 114.

21. See *De Viris Illustribus*, 568–569.

22. Although the text was near completion when Leland died, the materials for it, along with Leland's other papers, were left in a notoriously disorganized state (see Carley, "The Manuscript Remains of John Leland," 111–120).

23. In his biographical study of Trithemius, Noel L. Brann emphasizes Trithemius's "monastic humanism" and the way in which his work synthesizes new ideas with monastic tradition. See Brann, *The Abbot Trithemius (1462–1516): The Renaissance of Monastic Humanism* (Leiden: E. J. Brill, 1981), xvi.

24. See Carley's introduction, in *De Viris Illustribus*, cv.

25. Benedict Anderson connects both the increasing fixity of language and the nationalism that endows linguistic community with such importance to the rise of print capitalism. See *Imagined Communities: Reflections on the Origin and Spread of Nationalism* (London: Verso, 1991), 37–46, esp. 44–45. The especially long period of reliance on imported texts in England affects development of the vernacular as well. As Lucien Febrve and Henri-Jean Martin note in *The Coming of the Book: The Impact of Printing, 1540–1800* (London: Verso, 1976), 324:

> At this time [the sixteenth century] there was a busy book trade in England, but much of it, especially up to 1540, was based on the import of books from the continent, from France and Spain in particular. Many of these were translated and soon in addition to the Latin and Greek classics were also translated into English. It was often thanks to this process of translation and publication that the English language, at the same time as it took on its final form, became enriched with numerous Spanish, French, and Latin expressions. These foreign additions to the language were so numerous that at the end of the century there was a violent reaction against their use—a sign of a real crisis in the development of the national language.

26. Chaucer's role in the inkhorn controversy is discussed in Vos, "Humanistic Standards of Diction in the Inkhorn Controversy."

27. Porcia, Jacopo di. *The Preceptes of Warre, set forth by James the erle of Purlilia, and translated into englysh by Peter Betham* (London: Edward Whitchurch, 1544 for William Tilotson, 1544), sig. A7 (STC 20116).

28. Leland's author-centricity automatically elides anonymous literature, no matter what the language, but the names of well-known English poets like Langland, Hoccleve, and Lydgate are also absent from his work (a contrast to Bale's drive to match every known text with an author). Leland also passes over prose works in the vernacular, even those he likely encountered in the course of his investigations into monastic libraries. *De Viris Illustribus* contains no information on the devotional writer Walter Hilton, for example, or the great Middle English

translator John Trevisa. When dealing with writers who left works in both Latin and the vernacular, Leland often omits mention of the second category. His bibliography for Richard Rolle (entry no. 372) silently passes over the hermit's Middle English work, and he makes no mention of the English language writings of the East Anglian hagiographer John Capgrave (no. 555).

29. Bourdieu describes the intersecting social and cultural factors that determine cultural position in "The Field of Cultural Production, or the Economic World Reversed," *Poetics* (Amsterdam) 12 (1983): 331–356.

30. See Siân Echard, "Gower in Print," in *A Companion to Gower*, ed. Siân Echard (Cambridge: D. S. Brewer, 2004), 115–135. See also Lucy Munro's discussion of Gower in *Archaic Style in English Literature*, 91–99. The *Confessio* had previously been printed by Caxton in 1483 (STC 12142).

31. One important exception is "Eneidos Bucolis," a sixteen-line Latin poem comparing Gower to Virgil that appears at the end of some manuscripts of the *Confessio Amantis* and the *Vox Clamantis* and which may have been written by Gower himself. See Michael P. Kuczynski, "Gower's Virgil," in *On John Gower: Essays at the Millennium*, ed. R. F. Yeager (Kalamazoo, MI: Medieval Institute Publications, 2007), 163–187.

32. On Gower's early print history, see Echard, "Gower in Print," 115–117.

33. *Confessio Amantis* (1532), sig. A2–A2v

34. *Confessio Amantis* (1532), sig. A2v.

35. *De Viris Illustribus*, 695.

36. *De Viris Illustribus*, 695.

37. "Scogan's Moral Balade," line 126, in *The Chaucerian Apocrypha: A Selection*, ed. Kathleen Forni (Kalamazoo, MI: Medieval Institute Publications, 2005), 151.

38. Cannon identifies two key themes in praise of Chaucer's language: "virtually boundless" originality and improvement or elevation of that language from "rude" to "faire." Cannon writes that "both claims license their esteem for Chaucer by gathering all the objective license of historical fact to that esteem, but, inasmuch as these claims specify *by means* of praise, they finally leave obscure just what Chaucer did." See Cannon, *The Making of Chaucer's English: A Study of Words* (Cambridge: Cambridge University Press, 1998), 10–11.

39. Cannon, *The Making of Chaucer's English*, 9.

40. *De Viris Illustribus*, 694–695. Alexandra Gillespie's work on the early print history of Chaucer and Lydgate, whose reputation comes closest to rivaling Chaucer's own in the pre-Reformation period, provides an illustrative contrast, as do the essays contained in *Caxton's Trace: Studies in the History of English Printing*, ed. William Kuskin (Notre Dame, IN: University of Notre Dame Press, 2003). See also Jennifer Summit's discussion of the suppression of anonymous religious writing in "*The Fifteen Oes* and the Reformation of Devotion," in *Lost Property: The Woman Writer and English Literary History, 1380–1589* (Chicago: University of Chicago Press, 2000), 111–126.

41. See Gillespie, *Print Culture and the Medieval Author*, 207–210.

42. See David Lawton, "Dullness and the Fifteenth Century," *English Literary History* 54 (1987): 761–799.

43. *De Viris Illustribus*, 711. Leland writes in Latin, "Nam, quemadmodum Richardo Burdegalensi, Anglorum regi, cognitus, et virtutum nomine charus fuit, ita etiam Henrico quarto, et eius filio, qui de Gallis triumphavit, eisdem titulis commendatissimus erat" (710).

44. *De Viris Illustribus*, 703.

45. Both men also receive their own entries in Leland (nos. 307 and 516), though only Nicholas's mentions the connection to Chaucer.

46. Thomas Hoccleve, *The Regiment of Princes*, ed. Charles R. Blyth, TEAMS Middle English Texts (Kalamazoo, MI: Medieval Institute Publications, 1999), line 1964; Thynne's edition of *The Workes of Geffray Chaucer newly printed* (London: Thomas Godfray, 1532), sig. A2v.

47. The need to construct an authorial figure equipped with the educational and cultural background perceived as necessary for his work has parallels in the ongoing controversies over Shakespearean authorship. See, for example, James Shapiro, *Contested Will: Who Wrote Shakespeare?* (London: Faber and Faber, 2010), esp. 312–313.

48. As Simpson notes in "Ageism," "however much the past is consistently rejected as obscure, it remains true that great figures need to be rescued from that obscurity" (218). See also Simpson, "Diachronic History and the Shortcomings of Medieval Studies," in *Reading the Medieval in Early Modern England*, ed. Gordon McMullan and David Matthews (Cambridge: Cambridge University Press, 2007), 17–30, esp. 27.

49. Carley, "John Leland's *Cygnea Cantio*," 232.

50. *De Viris Illustribus*, 694. Leland never specifically mentions Gower's vernacular writing in either English or French, although his reference to Ovid here implies familiarity with the *Confessio Amantis*, which had been printed as recently as 1532.

51. *De Viris Illustribus*, 47.

52. *De Viris Illustribus*, 39.

53. *Troilus and Criseyde* 5.1791–1792 (unless otherwise noted, quotations of Chaucer's poems are from the *Riverside Chaucer*, ed. Larry D. Benson [Boston: Houghton Mifflin, 1987]).

54. *De Viris Illustribus*, 705; emphasis added.

55. Bale prints his own list in his *Catalogus*, altering and adding to Leland's titles and providing both the number of books and Latin incipits for Chaucer's poems. Thus, the *General Prologue* becomes the *Praefationes earundem*, which begins, "Dum imbribus suavibus Aprilis" (*Scriptorum Illustrium majoris Brytanniae quam nunc Angliam & Scotium vocant: Catalogus* [Basel: Johannes Oporinus, (1557)], 1:525). Bale also increases the number of works attributed to Chaucer by providing Latin titles for individual poems within the *Legend of Good Women* (e.g., "De Phyllide Thracensi") and adding entries for works whose existence is extrapolated from Chaucer's account of his poems in the *Retraction* and the *Legend of Good Women* or derived from Lydgate's description of the Chaucerian canon in *Fall of Princes*.

56. See Warner, *The Myth of Piers Plowman*, 129–132. In *De Viris Illustribus*, Leland writes, "sed Petri Aratoris fabula, quae communi doctorum consensu Chaucero, tanquam vero parenti, attribuitur, in utraque editione, quia malos sacerdotum mores vehementer increpavit, suppressa est" (708–709; But the Tale of Piers Plowman, which is attributed by the common consent of scholars to Chaucer's authorship, has been suppressed in both editions because it vigorously attacked the bad morals of the clergy). This coincides with the account given in Francis Thynne's *Animadversions* (6–11) and also found, with attribution to Thynne, in the 1602 version of the *Life*, but there is little supporting evidence for Leland's claim that the poem was suppressed. The 1532 edition does not include the *Plowman's Tale*.

57. Gillespie, *Print Culture and the Medieval Author*, 74–75.

58. See *Greenes Vision: Written at the instant of his death* (London: E. Allde, 1592). Harvey's marginalia in his copy of the 1598 edition of Chaucer's *Works* (now London, British Library Additional MS 42518) are reproduced in *Gabriel Harvey's Marginalia*, ed. G. C. Moore Smith (Stratford-upon-Avon: Shakespeare Head Press, 1913). See also Francis Kynaston, trans.,

Amorum Troili et Creseidae Libri Duo Priores Anglico-Latini (Oxford: John Lichfield, 1635). The full text of Kynaston's translation, edited by Dana Sutton, is available at the Philological Museum website, http://www.philological.bham.ac.uk/troilus/.

59. *De Viris Illustribus* 709.

60. *De Viris Illustribus*, 705.

61. *De Viris Illustribus*, 705.

62. All three poems are included in a posthumously published quarto volume of Leland's Latin poetry, *Principum, ac illustrium aliquot & eruditorum in Anglia virorum, encomia, trophaea, genethliaca, & epithalamia* (London: Thomas Orwin, 1589; STC 15447). The collection includes poems on general and classical subjects, as well as short pieces addressed to sixteenth-century notables such as Dean John Colet, William Camden, and Brian Tuke, Thynne's collaborator on the 1532 *Works*.

63. *De Viris Illustribus*, 709.

64. *De Viris Illustribus*, 707. The reference is to Eclogue 5, lines 76–78:

Dum iuga montis aper, fluvios dum piscis amabit,
dumque thymo pascentur apes,
dum rore cicadae, semper honos nomenque tuom laudesque manebunt.

See *The Works of Virgil*, ed. John Conington and Henry Nettleship (Hildesheim: Georg Olms, 1963), 1:72.

65. According to Leland, this poem, twenty-one lines in hendecasyllables, was written at the request of Thomas Berthelette, Henry VIII's royal printer (see *De Viris Illustribus*, 706–709).

66. *De Viris Illustribus*, 707.

Linguam qui patriam redegit illam
In formam, ut venere et lepore multo,
Ut multo sale gratiaque multa
Luceret, velut Hesperus minora
Inter sydera; nec tamen superbe
Linguae barbariem exprobravit ulli.
(706)

67. I have been unable to discover a specific figure associated with the name Atticus who fits the usage here; the word can refer to any native of the region around Athens.

68. The *Life of Chaucer* was lightly revised for the 1602 edition. The changes are summarized by Eleanor Prescott Hammond in *Chaucer: A Bibliographical Manual* (New York: Macmillan, 1908), 35–36.

69. *The Workes of Our Antient and Lerned English Poet, Geffrey Chaucer* (London: Adam Islip, 1598), sig. b6v. Stow states in his *Annales* of 1600 that he contributed information on Chaucer's "life, preferment, issue and death, collected out of records in the towre and else where," which were then given "to *Thomas Spight* to be published and performed." Quoted in Pearsall, "Thomas Speght," 74.

70. See Simpson, "Ageism"; and Cathy Shrank, "John Bale and Reconfiguring the 'Medieval' in Reformation England," in *Reading the Medieval in Early Modern England*, ed. Gordon McMullan and David Matthews (Cambridge: Cambridge University Press, 2007), 179–192.

71. Bale's accounts of Chaucer's life are reproduced in Hammond, *Chaucer*, 8–13.

72. Trigg, *Congenial Souls*, 127.

73. *Works* (1598), sigs. b2–b2v.

74. See Martin M. Crow and Clair C. Olson, eds., *Chaucer Life-Records* (Oxford: Clarendon Press, 1966).

75. *Works* (1598), sig. b2, emphasis added. Speght and, later, Francis Thynne both recognize the etymology of "Chaucer" (see *Animadversions*, 13–14). In a passage that follows the one quoted above, Speght writes, "This Name was at the first a Name of Office or Occupation, which afterward came to be the Name of a Family, as *Smith, Baker, Skinner*, and others have done."

76. *Works* (1598), sig. c1.

77. *Works* (1598), sigs. b4, c1.

78. See, for example, Donald R. Howard, *Chaucer: His Life, His Works, His World* (New York: Dutton, 1987); Pearsall, *The Life of Geoffrey Chaucer*; and Paul Strohm, *Chaucer's Tale: 1386 and the Road to Canterbury* (New York: Viking, 2014).

79. *Works* (1598), sig. b3.

80. On this, see Edith Rickert, "Was Chaucer a Student at the Inner Temple?" in *The Manly Anniversary Studies in Language and Literature* (Chicago: University of Chicago Press, 1923), 20–31; and Joseph A. Hornsby, "Was Chaucer Educated at the Inns of Court?" *Chaucer Review* 22 (1988): 255–268.

81. Speed (1551–1629) is best remembered for his *Genealogies Recorded in the Sacred Scriptures* (included in editions of the Authorized Version of the Bible) and his *Theatre of the Empire of Great Britaine* (1611). The relationship between his career as mapmaker and genealogist and his engraving for the *Works* is examined by Martha W. Driver in "Mapping Chaucer." Driver offers a reading of the image within the context of Speed's biblical genealogies, arguing that "through genealogy and heraldic imagery, Chaucer is given a history and a stature both human and nearly divine" (243).

CHAPTER 3

1. John Foxe, *The first Volume of the Ecclesiasticall history contaynyng the Actes and Monumentes of thynges passed in every kynges tyme in this Realme, especially in the Church of England principally to be noted* (London: John Day, 1570), sig. 3D4; STC 11223. All subsequent references to *Acts and Monuments* are to this edition unless otherwise noted.

2. On Chaucer's often ambiguous engagement with issues related to Lollardy, see Frances M. McCormack, "Chaucer and Lollardy," in *Chaucer and Religion*, ed. Helen Phillips (Cambridge: D. S. Brewer, 2010), 35–40. See also Pearsall, *The Life of Geoffrey Chaucer*, 182–83.

3. Following on the work of Chaucer scholars Caroline Spurgeon and Thomas Lounsbury, Kathleen Forni identifies Foxe as a major conduit through which the idea that Chaucer was a proto-Protestant reached early modern audiences. See Forni, *The Chaucerian Apocrypha: A Counterfeit Canon*, 94–98.

4. *Works* (1598), sig. B3.

5. Thomas J. Heffernan, "Aspects of the Chaucerian Apocrypha: Animadversions on William Thynne's Edition of the Plowman's Tale," in *Chaucer Traditions: Studies in Honour of Derek Brewer*, ed. Ruth Morse and Barry Windeatt (Cambridge: Cambridge University Press, 1990), 156.

6. *Actes and Monuments of these latter and perillous dayes . . .* (London: John Day, 1563); STC 11222.

7. Linda Georgianna, "The Protestant Chaucer," in *Chaucer's Religious Tales*, ed. C. David Benson and Elizabeth Robertson (Cambridge: D. S. Brewer, 1990), 57.

8. The wide availability of Foxe's book does not necessarily imply an equally wide familiarity with its contents. As David Scott Kastan writes, "though these volumes of *Acts and Monuments*, when in fact they were set out in public, were certainly available for reading, unquestionably their function was as much iconic as discursive, their substantial presence in places of authority testifying to the triumph of the faithful every bit as compellingly as what was promised by the narratives within." Kastan, "Size Matters," *Shakespeare Studies* 28 (2000): 150.

9. On the circulation of Foxe, see John N. King, *Foxe's "Book of Martyrs" and Early Modern Print Culture* (Cambridge: Cambridge University Press, 2006), 267–84; King notes, "revered by many Protestants as a 'holy' book, it was frequently chained alongside the Bible for reading by ordinary people at many public places including cathedrals, churches, schools, libraries, guildhalls, and at least one inn" (1).

10. Elizabeth Evenden and Thomas S. Freeman, *Religion and the Book in Early Modern England: The Making of Foxe's "Book of Martyrs"* (Cambridge: Cambridge University Press, 2011), 135. On the idea that *Actes and Monuments* was mandated to be placed in every parish church, see King, *Foxe's "Book of Martyrs,"* 112–113, which notes that in 1570, "the rate of production was insufficient to keep up with demand from the more than 8,000 parish churches in England" (113).

11. Evenden and Freeman, *Religion and the Book*, 139.

12. King, *Foxe's "Book of Martyrs,"* 23.

13. Evenden and Freeman, *Religion and the Book*, 147.

14. On Foxe's contact with antiquarian networks, see Evenden and Freeman, *Religion and the Book*, 149–157.

15. For example, the July 29, 1681, issue of the *Weekly Pacquet of Advice from Rome; or, The History of Popery* includes Chaucer in a list of "famous men that have asserted the Pope to be Antichrist," noting that "our English Homer, the witty Sir Geofry Chaucer insinuates no less in his Plow-mans tale," a claim derived from Foxe. I thank Aaron Pratt for bringing this reference to my attention.

16. Holly A. Crocker, "John Foxe's Chaucer: Affecting Form in Post-Historicist Criticism," *New Medieval Literatures* 15 (2013): 149–182.

17. In more schematic terms, Chaucer might be said to signify both within Bourdieu's concept of the field of literary production and within the culture more generally. In both cases, this significance depends in part on the relation perceived between Chaucer and other figures—fellow poets like Gower and Lydgate in the case of the literary field, and the kind of figures like Colet and Erasmus to whom Foxe compares Chaucer and Gower more generally. See Bourdieu, "The Field of Cultural Production," 331–333.

18. *Actes and Monuments* (1570), sig. G3.

19. *Actes and Monuments* (1570), sig. G3.

20. E.K.'s commentary, which accompanies the twelve eclogues that make up the *Calender*, is discussed in detail in Chapter 4.

21. *Actes and Monumentes* (1570), sig. G3v.

22. Margreta de Grazia, "Shakespeare in Quotation Marks," in *The Appropriation of Shakespeare: Post-Renaissance Reconstructions of the Works and the Myth*, ed. Jean Marsden (New York: Harvester Wheatsheaf, 1991), 58.

23. P. L. Heyworth, ed., *Jack Upland, Friar Daw's Reply and Upland's Rejoinder* (Oxford: Oxford University Press, 1968), 9.

24. A related work, *Friar Daw's Reply*, appears in Bodleian MS Digby 41. The manuscript allows the antifraternal plowman the last word in the form of a third text called *Upland's Rejoinder*, with the result that while the debate is extended, the conclusion is very much the same. See Heyworth, *Jack Upland, Friar Daw's Reply and Upland's Rejoinder*.

25. "Jack Upland," in *Six Ecclesiastical Satires*, ed. James M. Dean (Kalamazoo, MI: Medieval Institute Publications, 1991), lines 82–90.

26. Heyworth, *Jack Upland, Friar Daw's Reply and Upland's Rejoinder*, 7.

27. As Katherine Little notes, "because of this vital tradition, in the sixteenth century plowmen were recognizable literary figures who carried with them a very specific set of associations. That is, they appear most commonly in texts that are concerned with a reform understood in both social and religious terms" (*Transforming Work: Early Modern Pastoral and Late Medieval Poetry* [Notre Dame, IN: Notre Dame University Press, 2013], 7).

28. Walter W. Skeat includes the poem in *Chaucerian and Other Pieces* (Oxford: Clarendon Press, 1897), 147–190. The text is also included in *The Plowman's Tale: The c. 1532 and 1606 Editions of a Spurious Canterbury Tale*, ed. Mary Rhinelander McCarl (New York: Garland, 1997); and in Dean, *Six Ecclesiastical Satires*.

29. This prologue creates a link to the *Tales* that is imperfect, at best. Dean, *Six Ecclesiastical Satires*, 51, writes:

> If the author or editor tried to adapt the *PlT* to the *CT* framework, he did not everywhere succeed. The evidence suggests rather that he wanted to write a tale in the debate tradition and that a sixteenth-century editor adapted the debate poem loosely to the *CT* mold through the Prologue (lines 1–52). The poem begins during the "midsummer moon," closer to the summer solstice than to April; and the Plowman is at home, plowing, rather than on pilgrimage, as with Chaucer's storytellers. Moreover, the ending of the *PlT* offers its own retraction. So it seems that the author or the interpolator meant the *PlT* to stand apart from the *CT* rather than to be included within the latter's fictional boundaries.

30. "The Plowman's Tale," lines 40, 46, 48, 62–64, 69, 71, 73, in Dean, *Six Ecclesiastical Satires*.

31. *The Man of Law's Epilogue*, line 1173 in *The Riverside Chaucer*.

32. Wawn, "The Genesis of *The Plowman's Tale*," 24–29. For an overview of bibliographic criticism of the *Plowman's Tale* through the twentieth century, see Dane, "Bibliographical History Versus Bibliographical Evidence," 47–61. Greg Walker argues in favor of a more complex pattern of revision and interpolation, spanning from the 1390s to the 1530s, in "The Archaeology of *The Plowman's Tale*," in *Studies in Late Medieval and Early Renaissance Texts in Honour of John Scattergood*, ed. Anne Marie D'Arcy and Alan Fletcher (Dublin: Four Courts Press, 2005), 375–401.

33. On *Gamelyn* and its place in manuscripts, A. S. G. Edwards, "The *Canterbury Tales* and *Gamelyn*," in *Medieval Latin and Middle English Literature: Essays in Honour of Jill Mann*, ed. Christopher Cannon and Maura Nolan (Cambridge: D. S. Brewer, 2011), 76–90.

34. See Heyworth, *Jack Upland, Friar Daw's Reply and Upland's Rejoinder*, 1–2.

35. Since the attribution in the Cambridge manuscript cannot be dated precisely, it remains possible that Chaucer's name was added to the text in manuscript by someone with knowledge of Gough's printed edition.

36. Gough's edition is STC 5098. On the John Day edition, see Bale, *Index Britanniae Scriptorum*, ed. R. L. Poole and M. Bateson (Oxford: Clarendon Press, 1902), 274. Heyworth notes that, although *Actes and Monuments* was printed by Day, the publication of the second edition (1570) postdates Bale's death in 1563 (*Jack Upland, Friar Daw's Reply, and Upland's Rejoinder*, 5).

37. Bale, *Index Britanniae Scriptorum*, 274.

38. For a full bibliographic description and analysis, see P. L. Heyworth, "The Earliest Black-Letter Editions of *Jack Upland*," *Huntington Library Quarterly* 30 (1967): 307–314.

39. *Jack up Lande* (1536), sig. A1v.

40. See *Actes and Monuments* (1570), sig. G3; and *Works* (1602), sig. 3O2.

41. *Actes and Monuments* (1570), sig. ☞4.

42. *Actes and Monuments* (1570), sig. 3D4.

43. On Chaucer's tomb, see Prendergast, *Chaucer's Dead Body*, 52–55. Foxe's description of Gower's tomb includes details that are not found in Bale or in the main *De Viris Illustribus* manuscript. This is unlikely to be a firsthand recollection and suggests, instead, that Foxe had access to some material on the poet beyond what is included in the principal surviving *De Viris Illustribus* manuscript. This may be information that was interpolated, for example, in a manuscript copy of Leland's materials that passed through Foxe's hands. (Although it is not in the Gower portion of *De Viris Illustribus*, this sort of material is common in Leland's work.)

44. See Bale, *Catalogus*, I:525–526; and Leland, *De Viris Illustribus*, 708–711.

45. *Actes and Monuments* (1570), sig. 3D4.

46. *Actes and Monuments* (1570), sig. 3D4.

47. Foxe would have encountered the *Testament* in the disordered form originally printed by Thynne. Anne Middleton hypothesizes the manuscript behind Thynne's edition in "Thomas Usk's 'Perdurable Letters.'"

48. *Actes and Monuments* (1570), sig. 3D4.

49. *Actes and Monuments* (1570), sig. 3D4–3D4v.

50. The term is also used in Spenser's *Shepheardes Calender* in a note to describe the tale of the Oak and the Briar in the Februarie eclogue, which Thenot, who narrates the tale, says he learned from Chaucer.

51. William Alley, *Ptochomuseion: The poore mans Librarie* (London: John Day, 1565), fol. 204v.

52. Robert Crowley's address to the reader in his 1550 editions of *Piers Plowman* discusses what he perceives to be the poem's prophetic content.

53. *Actes and Monuments* (1570), sig. 3D4.

54. Alexandra Gillespie notes that the language of the edict distinguishes "Canterbury Tales" and "Chaucer's Books." As authorial figures, Gower and Chaucer mark "licit" literature; a "Canterbury Tale," meanwhile, can be dismissed as a trifle. See Gillespie, *Print Culture and the Medieval Author*, 193–195.

55. *Actes and Monuments* (1570), sig. 3D4.

56. *Actes and Monuments* (1570), sig. 3D4v.

57. Foxe's notion that the *Plowman's Tale* has been removed from the canon shares some resonances with Francis Thynne's claims, made in 1599, that a pre-1532 edition of the *Works* had been suppressed by Cardinal Wolsey (see *Animadversions*, 6–10).

58. Attempts to understand the place of the *Plowman's Tale* in the early modern Chaucer corpus are complicated by comments made by Foxe, John Leland, and Francis Thynne, several of which contradict the available bibliographic evidence. In *De Viris Illustribus* (708–709), Leland names Thomas Berthelette, not Godfray, as the printer of William Thynne's edition of the *Works* and includes a "petri aratoris fabula" in his list of Chaucer's writings (the *Plowman's Tale* is not included in the 1532 edition). This entry, which James Carley dates to the 1530s, may refer to *Piers Plowman* or, alternatively, to the *Plowman's Tale*, which would mean that Leland knew the tale before its publication in the 1542 *Works*. Leland's comments are repeated by John Bale in his *Catalogus*, although Bale also includes an entry on Langland, to whom he assigns *Piers Plowman*. In *Actes and Monuments*, Foxe describes the *Plowman's Tale* as "restored agayne" to the *Works*, implying that it had been present, removed, and replaced again (sig. 3D4v). In 1599, Francis Thynne, son of William Thynne, claimed that a single-column edition of Chaucer's *Works*, predating the 1532 edition, was suppressed by Cardinal Wolsey because it contained the *Pilgrim's Tale*, another anticlerical work, and that the work was eventually printed again through the intervention of Henry VIII, with the *Plowman's Tale* "with muche ado permitted to passe with the reste" (*Animadversions*, 10). In the nineteenth century, Henry Bradshaw disproved the existence of such an edition (see Bradshaw's note *Animadversions*, 75–76). These issues are discussed at greater length by Dane in "Bibliographical History Versus Bibliographical Evidence."

59. Robert Costomiris argues that Thynne was not involved in the decision to add the *Plowman's Tale* in 1542. See "The Influence of Printed Editions and Manuscripts on the Canon of William Thynne's Canterbury Tales." On the *Retraction*'s absence, see Megan L. Cook, "'Here Taketh the Makere of This Book His Leve': The *Retraction* and Chaucer's Works in Tudor England," *Studies in Philology* 113, no. 1 (2016): 32–54; and Kathleen Forni, "The Chaucerian Apocrypha: Did Usk's 'Testament of Love' and the 'Plowman's Tale' Ruin Chaucer's Early Reputation?" *Neuphilologische Mitteilungen* 98, no. 3 (1997): 261–272.

60. See Georgianna, "The Protestant Chaucer," 56 n. 2. For more on Spenser's Protestant view of Chaucer and use of the spurious tales, see Miskimin, *Renaissance Chaucer*, esp. 93, 289–290.

61. A manuscript copy of the poem, potentially dating to the sixteenth century or later, is bound with a copy of the 1532 *Works* now at the Harry Ransom Center at the University of Texas at Austin.

62. Dane, "Bibliographical History Versus Bibliographical Evidence," 57.

63. Dane, "Bibliographical History Versus Bibliographical Evidence," 57.

64. Gillespie, *Print Culture and the Medieval Author*, 198.

65. See John N. King, *English Reformation Literature: The Tudor Origins of the Protestant Tradition* (Princeton, NJ: Princeton University Press, 1982), 51–52.

66. See Kathy Cawsey, "'I Playne Piers' and the Protestant Plowman Prints: The Transformation of a Medieval Figure," in *Transmission and Transformation in the Middle Ages: Texts and Contexts*, ed. Kathy Cawsey and Jason Harris (Dublin: Four Courts Press, 2007), 198; and McCarl, *The Plowman's Tale*, 39.

67. See Wawn, "Chaucer, *The Plowman's Tale* and Reformation Propaganda"; and Forni, *The Chaucerian Apocrypha: A Counterfeit Canon*, 53.

68. Heffernan, "Aspects of the Chaucerian Apocrypha," 162–163.

69. See Wawn, "Chaucer, *The Plowman's Tale* and Reformation Propaganda"; and Dane, "Bibliographical History Versus Bibliographical Evidence," 55. For a rebuttal, see Blayney, *The Stationers' Company*, 279–282, which argues that the materials shared between Godfray and

Berthelette reflect a commonplace sharing of resources (with ornamental borders in particular being quite scarce at this stage in English printing) and not a special collaborative relationship.

70. McCarl, *The Plowman's Tale*, 16.

71. Kathy Cawsey notes that, while the plowman prints (including other works without association with Chaucer) vary in format, "the overtly polemical Protestant works tend to be of lower quality and cheaper format than the expensive *Plowman's Tale* editions [in the *Works*], which may indicate a difference in purpose or readership" ("'I Playne Piers,'" 190).

72. Cawsey, "'I Playne Piers,'" 200.

73. On these marginal notes, which bring together the reform-minded Chaucer of Foxe and the apocryphal pamphlets with the laureate figure celebrated in the *Works*, see Paul J. Patterson, "Reforming Chaucer: Margins and Religion in an Apocryphal Canterbury Tale," *Book History* 8 (2005): 17–27. Patterson also discusses the possibility that Anthony Wotton, a Puritan divine, was responsible for these annotations.

74. Greg Walker and others have observed how Thynne's edition, with its dedication to Henry VIII, participates in Tudor policies of centralization and standardization. The *Troy Book's* large size reflects its involvement in these same discourses, as does its title page's use of a woodcut illustrating the houses of Lancaster and York. See Walker, *Writing Under Tyranny*, 29–72.

75. In the 1602 revision of the *Life of Chaucer*, Thomas Speght repeats Francis Thynne's account of the lost edition of the *Works* almost verbatim, including Thynne's claim that it was suppressed on account of the *Pilgrim's Tale* (*Works* [1602], sig. c1).

76. *Works* (1598), sig. b3.

77. Lerer, *Chaucer and His Readers*, 121.

78. *Works* (1598), sig. c1.

79. The last four items in the *Works* are the apocryphal *The Floure and the Leafe*, the *A.B.C.*, *Jack Upland*, and *Adam Scriveyn*. In 1598, the *Adam Scriveyn* follows *The Floure and the Leafe*. In both editions, *Adam Scriveyn* is followed by John Lydgate's *Siege of Thebes*, after an interior title page in 1598 and with a large title in 1602. In both cases, the work is clearly identified as Lydgate's.

80. *Works* (1598), sig. c5.

81. Pearsall, "Thomas Speght," 74.

82. *Works* (1598), sig. c1.

83. *Works* (1602), sig. c1.

84. *Works* (1602), sig. 3O2. The headnote is printed in roman type, while the quotation from the *Plowman's Tale* is printed in black letter.

85. The poem was printed by Reynold Wolfe in 1553 (STC 19904) and, as an addendum to *Piers Plowman*, by Owen Rogers in 1561 (STC 19908).

86. See Forni, *The Chaucerian Apocrypha: A Counterfeit Canon*, 209–210 n. 3. On Urry's edition, see William L. Alderson, "John Urry," in *Editing Chaucer: The Great Tradition*, ed. Paul G. Ruggiers (Norman, OK: Pilgrim Press, 1984): 93–117.

87. *The Works of Geoffrey Chaucer* (London: Bernard Lintot, 1721), sig. C1.

88. "The Former Age," "To Rosamund," and "Womanly Noblesse" were all first printed in the late nineteenth century.

89. On the relationship of Chaucer's text to its source, see Georgia Ronan Crampton, "Chaucer's Singular Prayer," *Medium Aevum* 59 (1990): 191–213.

90. A full list of the sixteen manuscripts of the *A.B.C.* is provided by the editors of *The Riverside Chaucer*, p. 1185.

91. Forni, *The Chaucerian Apocrypha: A Counterfeit Canon*, 25.

92. John Thompson, "Chaucer's *An ABC* in and out of Context," *Poetica* 37 (1993): 45.

93. Lines 19755–19762 in John Lydgate, *The Pilgrimage of the Life of Man*, ed. F. J. Furnivall and Katharine B. Locock, EETS e.s. 77, 83, 92 (London: Kegan Paul, Trench, Trübner, 1899–1904).

94. See George B. Pace, "Speght's Chaucer and MS. Gg.4.27," *Studies in Bibliography* 21 (1968): 225–235. Derek Pearsall writes that "the existence of a known manuscript exemplar puts us in the fortunate position of seeing Speght at work on an *editio princeps*: the sight is reassuring, for, apart from some obvious corrections and the inevitable modernizations of language, Speght keeps close to his original" ("Thomas Speght," 88). Noting that Gg.4.27 is known for its idiosyncratic orthography and lack of punctuation (Speght supplies it), Pace concludes that "Speght's copy is no better than what one might expect of a competent medieval scribe" but, significantly, no worse ("Speght's Chaucer," 231). Pace's comparison of the two texts shows that Speght could and did comprehend Chaucer's Middle English, even with the manuscript's unconventional spelling, and the version of the text he prints in 1602 is minimally and sensibly emended. In one case, for example, Speght substitutes the "pseudo-archaism" *bostaunce* for the unfamiliar *bobaunce* (boast) at line 84, having determined meaning based on context. There are occasional difficulties with transcription: Pace points to *y^e* for *þt* at line 77, and *sore* for the correct *yore* at line 150; the manuscript there reads *ʒore* (231–232). Both Pearsall and Pace believe Gg.4.27 to be the only manuscript used by Speght. Overall, he hews closely to his exemplar and does not seek to alter its content in any way. Gg.4.27 also includes the *Canterbury Tales*, the *Envoy to Scogan*, *Truth*, *Troilus and Criseyde*, the *Legend of Good Women*, *The Parliament of Fowles*, and Lydgate's Chaucerian homage, *Temple of Glas*, none of which Speght appears to have referred to in the course of his editorial work.

95. Speght may have received additional input on this title from John Stow, who knew the *A.B.C.* in a variety of manuscript contexts: Stow's marginalia are found in two other manuscripts of the *A.B.C.*, MS Fairfax 16 and MS Harley 2251, and he was familiar with both CUL MS Gg.4.27 and Pepys 2006. See Thompson, "Chaucer's *An ABC*," 44–48.

96. On this decision, see Thynne, *Animadversions*, 28. On the history of these titles and the two poems they designate, see Kathleen Forni, "'Chaucer's Dreame': A Bibliographer's Nightmare," *Huntington Library Quarterly* 64, nos. 1–2 (2001): 139–150.

97. Gg.4.27.1 is now missing its first four pages, which presumably would have included a title for the poem. A sister manuscript to Gg.4.27.1, Magdalene College Cambridge MS Pepys 2006, however, uses a similar French heading. George Pace notes that the CUL manuscript and the Pepys manuscript share a common exemplar and that a French title would be also be consistent with the headings used elsewhere in Gg.4.27.1, leading him to surmise that Gg may have also contained the French title prior to the loss of the initial folios.

98. See Lerer, *Chaucer and His Readers*, esp. 85–116.

99. *Works* (1602), sig. 3O1.

100. Pearsall, "Thomas Speght," 88. On this possibility, see Thompson, "Chaucer's *An ABC*," 47. Kay Gilliland Stevenson points out that, in addition to Chaucer's connection to Blanche in the *Book of the Duchess*, "the possibility that Blanche might have requested the translation is lent some plausibility by what is known about feminine patronage and ownership of manuscripts [of *La Pèlerinage*], on both sides of the Channel." See Stevenson, "Medieval Rereading and Rewriting: The Context of Chaucer's 'ABC,'" in *"Divers Toyes Mengled": Essays on Medieval and Renaissance Culture in Honour of André Lascombes*, ed. Michel Bitot with Roberta Mullini and Peter Happé (Tours: Université François Rabelais, 1996), 32.

101. Speght makes this connection in his headnote to the *Book of the Duchess* (which Thynne had titled "The dreame of Chaucer"). See *Works* (1598), sig. C5v.

102. See Marjorie Anderson, "Blanche, Duchess of Lancaster," *Modern Philology* 45, no. 3 (1948): 152–159.

103. See Walter Skeat, ed., *Romaunt of the Rose and Minor Poems*, vol. 1 of *The Complete Works of Geoffrey Chaucer* (1894; repr., Oxford: Clarendon Press, 1963), 59.

104. Skeat, *Romaunt of the Rose and Minor Poems*, 59. Skeat takes a rather dour view of the poem while, as John Thompson notes in his 1993 essay, in recent years "criticism has found much to praise in Chaucer's distinctive treatment of his Deguileville sourse, with the English version often considered an imaginative and skilled adaptation of the French rather than merely an early exercise in translation" ("Chaucer's *An ABC*," 38). See, for example, Crampton, "Chaucer's Singular Prayer." Critics have also noted that Chaucer's use of a decasyllabic line is more characteristic of his later work: see, e.g., Stevenson, "Medieval Rereading and Rewriting," esp. 36.

105. William A. Quinn, "Chaucer's Problematic *Priere: An ABC* as Artifact and Critical Issue," *Studies in the Age of Chaucer* 23 (2001): 109–110.

106. Stevenson, "Medieval Rereading and Rewriting," 37

CHAPTER 4

1. For an overview of the debates surrounding the identity of E.K., see Patsy Schere Cornelius, *E.K.'s Commentary on the Shepheardes Calender* (Salzburg: Institut für Englische Sprache und Literatur, 1974), 1–13, and Frances M. Malpezzi, "E.K., a Spenserian Lesson in Reading," *Connotations* 4, no. 3 (1994–1995): 181–191. See also Peter C. Herman, "Poets, Pastors, and Antipoetics: A Response to Frances M. Malpezzi, 'E.K., A Spenserian Lesson in Reading'," *Connotations* 6, no. 3 (1997): 316–325.

2. Studies of Chaucer's influence on Spenser are numerous and multifaceted, attending to Spenser's use of Chaucerian plot, language, and authorial persona. While Spenser draws on Chaucerian material in the *Calender* (see Clare Kinney, "Marginal Presence, Lyric Resonance, Epic Absence: *Troilus and Criseyde* and/in *The Shepheardes Calender*," *Spenser Studies* 18 [2003]: 25–39), it is the last of these two categories that are most salient here. On Spenser's use of Chaucerian authorial persona, see especially Glenn A. Steinberg, "Spenser's *Shepheardes Calender* and the Elizabethan Reception of Chaucer," *English Literary Renaissance* 35, no. 1 (2005): 31–51, which argues that Spenser follows Chaucer in adopting an ironically humble authorial persona. See also Anthony M. Esolen, "The Disingenuous Poet Laureate: Spenser's Adoption of Chaucer," *Studies in Philology* 87, no. 3 (1990): 285–311; David Lee Miller, "Authorship, Anonymity, and the *Shepheardes Calender*," *Modern Language Quarterly* 40 (1979): 219–236; and Alice E. Lasater, "The Chaucerian Narrator in Spenser's *Shepheardes Calender*," *Southern Quarterly* 12 (1974): 189–201. Though, as John A. Burrow observes in his entry on Chaucer in *The Spenser Encyclopedia*, ed. A. C. Hamilton (Toronto: University of Toronto Press, 1990), "the task of proving that this or that word or form could only have come directly from [Chaucer] seems less easy the more one knows about other late-medieval and Tudor poetry," Spenser's verse is shot through with Chaucerian resonances, and E.K. identifies a number of works in the *Calender* as having been taken from Chaucer. On Spenser's adaptation of Chaucerian language, see Edward Armstrong, *A Ciceronian Sunburn: A Tudor Dialogue on Humanistic Rhetoric and Civic Poetics* (Columbia: University of South Carolina Press, 2006); and Bruce Robert McElderry Jr., "Archaism and Innovation in Spenser's Poetic Diction," *PMLA* 47, no. 1 (1932):

144–170. For more on Chaucer's influence on Spenser, see especially the essays collected in Judith H. Anderson, *Reading the Allegorical Intertext: Chaucer, Spenser, Shakespeare, Milton* (New York: Fordham University Press, 2008); Clare Kinney, *Strategies of Poetic Narrative: Chaucer, Spenser, Milton, Eliot* (Cambridge: Cambridge University Press, 1992); and Kent Hieatt, *Chaucer, Spenser, Milton: Mythopoeic Continuities and Transformations* (Montreal: McGill-Queen's University Press, 1975). Chaucer was, of course, not the only medieval poet whose work inspired and influenced Spenser, and the *Faerie Queene*, especially, has strong parallels with William Langland's *Piers Plowman*. See Judith H. Anderson, *The Growth of a Personal Voice: "Piers Plowman" and "The Faerie Queene"* (New Haven, CT: Yale University Press, 1976); and Katherine Little, "The 'Other' Past of Pastoral: Langland's *Piers Plowman* and Spenser's *Shepheardes Calender*," *Exemplaria* 21 (2009): 160–178.

3. See Richard McCabe, "Annotating Anonymity, or Putting a Gloss on the *Shepheardes Calender*," in *Ma(r)king the Text: The Presentation of Meaning on the Literary Page*, ed. Joe Bray, Miriam Handley, and Anne C. Henry (Aldershot: Ashgate, 2000), 35–54. Ruth Luborsky notes that the placement of E.K. annotations after each eclogue is highly unusual, and, indeed, this interstitial model is not followed in Speght. See Luborsky, "The Allusive Presentation of *The Shepheardes Calender*," *Spenser Studies* 1 (1980): 44.

4. In "The Allusive Presentation of the *Shepheardes Calender*," Luborsky examines the self-authorizing design of the *Calender* in light of its complex interplay of textual and visual references, demonstrating that, in designing the *Calender*, Spenser drew on emblem books and illustrated editions of Latin and vernacular classics, as well as recent editions of Marot and Ronsard, to create a highly particularized mise-en-page. See also Ruth Luborsky, "The Illustrations to *The Shepheardes Calender*," *Spenser Studies* 2 (1981): 3–54. On the influence of Marot and Ronsard on Spenser, see Anne Lake Prescott, "The Laurel and the Myrtle: Spenser and Ronsard," in *Worldmaking Spenser*, ed. Patrick Cheney and Lauren Silberman (Lexington: University Press of Kentucky, 2000), 61–78; and Annabel Patterson, "Re-Opening the Green Cabinet: Clément Marot and Edmund Spenser," *English Literary Renaissance* 16 (1986): 44–70.

5. Johan Kerling suggests that, "the glosses, too, apart from actually helping the reader, also served to give greater weight to the poems by suggesting that the old words were authentic, and based on scholarly research, and thus helping to 'promote' the book in academic circles" ("English Old-Word Glossaries, 1553–1594," *Neophilologus* 63 [1979]: 140). Steven K. Galbraith argues that a similar impression of authentic Englishness and learned commentary is made through the use black-letter for the verse of the eclogues and roman type for the surrounding commentary; see Galbraith, "'English Black-Letter Type and Spenser's *Shepheardes Calender*," *Spenser Studies* 23 (2008): 13–40; as well as S. K. Heninger Jr., "The Typographical Layout of Spenser's *Shepheardes Calender* in *Word and Visual Imagination: Studies in the Interaction of English Literature and the Visual Arts*, ed. Karl Josef Höltgen, Peter M. Daly, and Wolfgang Lottes (Erlangen: Universitätsbund Erlangen-Nürnberg, 1988), 33–71.

6. Text and page and line numbers for the *Shepheardes Calender* are taken from *The Yale Edition of the Shorter Poems of Edmund Spenser*, ed. William A. Oram et al. (New Haven, CT: Yale University Press, 1989), 1–214; here, p. 14. Quotations from the eclogues are identified by month and line number; references to the prefatory epistles are by page.

7. "Februarie," line 4 and gloss.

8. "Maye," line 251 and gloss.

9. Ian Lancashire's Lexicons of Early Modern English project (http://leme.library.utoronto .ca/) has collected and cataloged many of these English word lists. On early French and English Latin lexicography, see especially chapters 2 and 3 of John Considine, *Dictionaries in Early*

Modern Europe: Lexicography and the Making of Heritage (New York: Cambridge University Press, 2008). On the particular importance of Estienne, see also Considine, "The Lexicographer as Hero: Samuel Johnson and Henri Esteinne," *Philological Quarterly* 79 (2000): 205–254; and Douglas A. Kibbee, "The Humanist Period in Renaissance Bilingual Lexicography," in *The History of Lexicography: Papers from the Dictionary Research Centre Seminar at Exeter*, ed. R. R. K. Hartmann (Amsterdam: Benjamins, 1986), 137–147.

10. R. F. Yeager, "Gower, John (1330–1408)," in Hamilton, *The Spenser Encyclopedia*, 337.

11. A. S. G. Edwards, "Lydgate, John (c. 1375–c. 1448)," in Hamilton, *The Spenser Encyclopedia*, 443.

12. Specifically, the *Troy Book* preface echoes the contrast between the "sleeping" state of literature in Chaucer's time and the flourishing "letters" of the present. Braham writes that in Chaucer's time "al good letters were almost aslepe, so farre was the grosenesse and barbarousnesse of that age from the understandinge of so devyne a wryter" (sig. A2v). Thynne writes of Chaucer's time that "doutlesse all good letters were layde aslepe throughout the world" (*Works* [1532], sig. A2v). Braham also writes that it without "the dylygence of one willyam Thime [*sic*] a gentilman who laudably studyouse to the polyshing of so great a Jewell, with ryghte good judgement travail, and great paynes causing the same to be perfected and stamped as it is nowe read, the sayde Chaucers workes had utterly peryshed, or at the lest bin so depraved by corrupcion of copies, that at the laste, there shoulde no parte of hys meaning have ben founde in any of them" (*Troy Book*, sig. A2–A2v).

13. *Troy Book*, sig. A2.

14. *Shepheardes Calender*, p. 14.

15. *Shepheardes Calender*, p. 15; citing Cicero, *De Oratore*, 3.153. James M. May and Jakob Wisse translate this passage as follows: "In the category of individual words, then, there are three types that an orator can employ to lend brilliance and distinction to speech: unusual words, new coinages, and metaphors. Unusual words are, for the most part, archaic ones, words that have long since been abandoned in everyday language because of their antiquity. Their use is more open to the license of the poets than to us, yet a poetic word is, by way of exception, dignified in speech as well. . . . When put in the right places, [unusual words] often tend to enhance the grandeur and antiquity of speech." See *Cicero: On the Ideal Orator*, trans. and ed. James M. May and Jakob Wisse (New York: Oxford University Press, 2001).

16. *Shepheardes Calender*, p. 16.

17. *Shepheardes Calender*, p. 19.

18. *Shepheardes Calender*, p. 16.

19. *Shepheardes Calender*, p. 13.

20. William Kuskin has attended to the oft-neglected role of Lydgate in both E.K.'s account and the prefatory materials to Speght's *Works* in "'The Loadstarre of the English Language': Spenser's *Shepheardes Calender* and the Construction of Modernity," *Textual Cultures* 2, no. 2 (2007): 9–33. Significantly, the phrase "uncouthe unkiste" is a misquotation from Chaucer. On the implications of this, see Alexandra Gillespie, "Unknowe, unkow, Vncovthe, uncouth: From Chaucer and Gower to Spenser and Milton," in *Medieval into Renaissance: Essays for Helen Cooper*, ed. Andrew King and Matthew Woodcock (Cambridge: D. S. Brewer, 2016), 15–33.

21. "Januarye," gloss on line 1. On Skelton's relationship to Spenser, see Kreg Segall, "Skeltonic Anxiety and Rumination in *The Shepheardes Calender*," *SEL* 47, no. 1 (2007): 29–56; and David Lee Miller, *The Poem's Two Bodies: The Poetics of the 1590 Faerie Queene* (Princeton, NJ: Princeton University Press, 1988), 44–49.

22. *Shepheardes Calender*, p. 13.

23. "Februarie," lines 92–93.

24. The influence of Virgil's career as a model for Spenser's has been well mapped by scholars, notably by M. L. Donnelly in "The Life of Vergil and the Aspirations of the 'New Poete,'" *Spenser Studies* 17 (2003): 1–35. On Virgil's specific influence in the *Calender*, see recent studies by Nancy Lindheim, "The Virgilian Design of the *Shepheardes Calender*," *Spenser Studies* 13 (1999): 1–22; Rebeca Helfer, "The Death of the 'New Poete': Virgilian Ruin and Ciceronian Recollection in Spenser's *The Shepheardes Calender*," *Renaissance Quarterly* 56, no. 3 (2003): 723–756; Patrick Cheney, *Spenser's Famous Flight: A Renaissance Idea of a Literary Career* (Toronto: University of Toronto Press, 1993); and Merritt T. Hughes, *Virgil and Spenser* (Berkeley: University of California Press, 1929). Virgil's *Eclogues* provide a generic model through which Spenser can align himself with a classical tradition, but, since Chaucer did not write pastoral, the link to a native tradition must be established through language and identification with the English poet. On this, see Patrick Cheney, "'Novells of His Devise': Chaucerian and Virgilian Career Paths in Spenser's *Februarie* Eclogue," in *European Literary Careers: The Author from Antiquity to the Renaissance*, ed. Patrick Cheney and Frederick A. de Armas (Toronto: University of Toronto Press, 2002), 231–267.

25. "Februarie," gloss for lines 92 and 102.

26. "June," gloss for line 81.

27. Colin Fairweather, "'I Suppose He Meane Chaucer': The Comedy of Errors in Spenser's *Shepheardes Calender*," *Notes and Queries* 46 (1999): 193–195.

28. *Calender*, p. 16.

29. Puttenham, *The Art of English Poesy*, ed. Frank Whigham and Wayne A. Rebhorn (Ithaca, NY: Cornell University Press, 2007), 229.

30. Miskimin, *Renaissance Chaucer*, 91.

31. Johan Kerling, *Chaucer in Early English Dictionaries: The Old-Word Tradition in English Lexicography Down to 1721 and Speght's Chaucer Glossaries* (Leiden: Leiden University Press, 1979), 15.

32. Writing of European and North American anthropologists working with oral cultures in sub-Saharan Africa, the anthropologist Jack Goody argues, "since the table is essentially a graphic (and frequently a literate device), its fixed two-dimensional character may well simplify the reality of oral communication beyond reasonable recognition, and hence decrease rather than increase understanding" (*The Domestication of the Savage Mind* [Cambridge: Cambridge University Press, 1977], 54). In the case of diachronic lexicography, something similar obtains, as the format of word lists like Speght's both reifies difference between old and new words and regularizes that difference for all pairs included in a given table.

33. *Works* (1602), sig. a2.

34. Similarly, in this same period, biographical claims for Chaucer's proto-Protestantism emerge alongside additions to the canon that seem to provide corroborating evidence of these views. This is discussed further in my second and third chapters.

35. See *Works* (1598) sig. 3B2–3B2v and *Works* (1602) sig. 3U6–3U6v.

36. See Cannon, "The Myth of Origin and the Making of Chaucer's English," 656.

37. *Works* (1602), sig. a2v; Richard Mulcaster, *The first part of the elementarie which entreateth chefelie of the right writing of our English tung* (London: Thomas Vautroullier, 1582), 142.

38. The 1613 edition of Robert Cawdrey's *A Table Alphabeticall* defines "Barbarisme" as "Rudness, a corrupt forme of writing or speaking" (sig. B3v).

39. *Works* (1602), sig. a2v.

40. For a discussion of the roots of this phenomenon and its long-term effects on nine-teenth- and twentieth-century lexicography in particular, see Cannon, *The Making of Chaucer's English*.

   41. *Works* (1602), sig. a3.

42. *Works* (1602), sig. a3. See *Troilus and Criseyde*, 5.1793–1796.

43. On the ways critical tradition presumes Chaucer's metrical innovation (and, implic-itly, metrical regularity), see Cannon, *The Making of Chaucer's English*, 45–47.

44. *Works* (1598), sig. a2v. It is important to note the highly rhetorical nature of some of these claims: although Speght purports to have "reformed" the "whole work" with manuscript witnesses, his interventions into the text are on a far more modest scale. See Derek Pearsall, "Thomas Speght," 79–80.

45. *Works* (1602), sig. a3v.

46. On the expansion of the Chaucerian canon, see Forni, *The Chaucerian Apocrypha: A Counterfeit Canon*.

47. Beaumont's epistle is significantly revised between the 1598 and 1602 printings. Speght himself was probably responsible for these revisions, since Beaumont died in 1598.

48. *Works* (1602), sig. a4. "Vinewed" (vinnied) is perhaps a telling choice of word here: the term, now archaic, was in use at the end of the sixteenth century and is identified by the *Oxford English Dictionary* as a regionalism from southwestern England. It ultimately derives, however, from the Old English *fen*, meaning mold or mildew, making Beaumont's use of it an example of the turn to ancient native words that he and other commentators on Middle En-glish advocate.

49. *Works* (1602), sig. a3v.

50. *Works* (1602), sig. a3v. Beaumont's Latin reads:

> Ut silvae foliis pronos mutantur in annos:
> Prima cadunt: ita verborum vetus interit aetas:
> Et juvenum ritu florent modo nata, vigentque.
> Debemur morti nos, nostraque, &c.

The quotation is taken from *Ars Poetica*, lines 60–63, which Leon Golden translates as "just as forests change their leaves year by year and the first drop to the ground, so the old generation of words perishes, and new ones, like the rising tide of the young, flourish and grow strong." See O. B. Hardison Jr. and Leon Golden, ed. and trans., *Horace for Students of Liter-ature: The "Ars Poetica" and Its Tradition* (Gainesville: University Press of Florida, 1995).

51. The *Riverside Chaucer* reads,

> *Ye* knowe ek that in forme of speche is chaunge
> Withinne a *thousand* yeer, and wordes tho
> That hadden pris, now wonder nyce and straunge
> Us thinketh hem, and yet thei spake hem so,
> And spedde as wel in love as men now do.
>   (2.22–26; emphasis added)

52. *Works* (1602), sig. a3v–a4.

53. *Works* (1602), sig. a4.

54. As William Kuskin has shown, Lydgate's proximity to Chaucer overshadows his own poetic achievements in the eyes of both Spenser and Beaumont; see "'The Loadstarre of the English Language,'" esp. 16–17 and 24–26. On the vicissitudes of Lydgate's reception earlier in the century, see also Gillespie, *Print Culture and the Medieval Author.*

55. *Works* (1602), sig. a4.

56. The lack of a more explicit reference to Spenser may be connected to Speght's awareness of the fraught relationship between Spenser and the William Cecil, Lord Burghley, the father of Robert Cecil, to whom the *Works* are dedicated. In his dedicatory epistle, Thomas Speght presents the *Works* as a remembrance of the financial support that Mildred Cecil, Robert's mother and the second wife of William, provided while he was a student at Cambridge. On the relationship between William Cecil and Spenser, see Bruce Danner, *Edmund Spenser's War on Lord Burghley* (New York: Palgrave Macmillan, 2011).

57. *Works* (1598), sig. a3v.

58. See Edmund Spenser, *The Faerie Queene*, ed. Hamilton et al. (London: Longman, 2001), IV.ii.32.

59. "Neither is *Plautus* nor *Terence* free in this behalfe: But these two last are excused above the rest, for their due observation of *Decorum,* in giving to their comicall persons such manner of speeches as did best fitt their dispositions. And may not the same be said for *Chaucer?*" (*Works* [1602], sig. a4).

60. *Works* (1602), sig. a4–a4v. The first passage here is *General Prologue*, lines 725–736. The second passage consists of four spurious lines, followed by lines 207–210 of the *Manciple's Tale.*

61. *Works* (1602), sig. a4v.

62. Reading for historical insight rather than literary merit is a major tendency in the later reception of Middle English texts. On the early study of Middle English, see Matthews, *The Making of Middle English.*

63. *Works* (1602), sig. a5.

64. As with the *Calender,* however, adding commentary disrupts notions of linguistic familiarity. On this dynamic in the *Calender,* see Nicholson, *Uncommon Tongues,* 105–106.

65. *Works* (1602), sig. a5. "Guillaume de Salust" is Guillaume de Salluste, Sieur du Bartas, a French Huguenot poet and author of biblical epics.

66. *Works* (1602), sig. c1. In this passage, "Alanus" is the French poet Alain Chartier (ca. 1392–ca. 1430), while "Johannes Mena" refers to the Spanish poet Juan de Mena (1411–1456). The Latin passage comes from a short poem printed in a 1598 collection of Leland's poems and included in Leland's entry on Chaucer in *De Viris Illustribus*. See Leland, *Principum, ac illustrium aliquot & eruditorum in Anglia virorum* (London, 1598), p. 80. Carley translates these Latin lines as, "Our England reveres the poet Chaucer, / To whom our native tongue owes its beauties." Speght was probably familiar with its quotation in Bale's *Illustrium Majoris Britanniae Scriptorum.*

67. For an overview of sixteenth-century debates on the incorporation of Latinate and Romance words into English, see Vos, "Humanistic Standards of Diction in the Inkhorn Controversy"; and Cannon, "The Myth of Origin and the Making of Chaucer's English."

68. *Works* (1602), sig. c3v.

69. This emphasis is charted in Matthews, *The Making of Middle English*; and Cannon, *The Making of Chaucer's English.*

70. That text is appended to Owen Rogers's 1561 reprint of Robert Crowley's edition of *Piers Plowman* (STC 19908).

71. Kerling, *Chaucer in Early English Dictionaries*, 33.

72. *Works* (1602), sig. 3T1. No terms are marked as Arabic outside of the "A" section, but the other etymologies appear consistently throughout the list. The dedication describes these etymological notes as "the significations of most of the old and obscure words, by the tongues and dialects, from whence they are derived," a formulation that simultaneously consigns Chaucer to the past and establishes another past behind Chaucer's past. For Camden's etymology of the word "Britain," see *Britain, or A chorographicall description of the most flourishing kingdomes*, 27.

73. In their layout, both volumes evoke the lexicographical work of Thomas Cooper and the Estiennes. E.K.'s commentary is especially reminiscent of the list of short definitions and more sustained explanations found in Cooper's *Thesaurus linguae Romanae & Britannicae* (1565). Both the *Calender* and the *Works* differ from these precedents, however, in that they are monolingual. In this way, E.K. and Speght synthesize these humanistic lexicographical works with an older tradition of lists of hard words and terms of art.

74. Jürgen Schäfer, "Chaucer in Shakespeare's Dictionaries: The Beginning," *Chaucer Review* 17, no. 2 (1982): 182–192. See also Kerling, *Chaucer in Early English Dictionaries*.

75. Pearsall, "Thomas Speght," 72.

76. The *Works* comes close to identifying an intended audience when Beaumont reminisces to Speght about those "ancient learned men of our time in Cambridge; whose diligence, in reading of his workes themselves, and commending them to others of the younger sort, did first bring you and me in love with him: and one of them at that time, and all his life after, was (as you know) one of the rarest men for learning, in the whole world" (*Works* [1602], sig. a5; see also *Works* [1598], sig. a4v). Stephanie Trigg writes that, in Beaumont's comments, "in conjunction with Speght's address to his readers and with H.B.'s poem, it is clear that the 'love' it is possible to feel for Chaucer is an important aspect of the bonds that link a company of gentlemen." She continues, "These gentlemen are not only the source of Speght's own love and knowledge of Chaucer, but also the main audience for the edition, a community of male readers" (Trigg, *Congenial Souls*, 134). Alison Wiggins's survey of written marginalia in fifty-four sixteenth-century copies of Chaucer suggests a less elite readership, at least in the long term, including women, members of the provincial gentry, and casual readers. See Wiggins, "What Did Renaissance Readers Write in the Copies of Chaucer?" *The Library* 9, no. 1 (2008): 3–36; see also Hope Johnston, "Readers' Memorials in Early Editions of Chaucer," *Studies in Bibliography* 59 (2015): 45–69. For an in-depth study of the readership of a single copy of the *Works*, see Antonia Harbus, "A Renaissance Reader's English Annotations to Thynne's 1532 Edition of Chaucer's *Works*," *Review of English Studies* 59 (2008): 342–355.

77. Similarly, the commonplace markers—promised in 1598, but only delivered in 1602—encourage the inclusion of Chaucer's *sententiae* alongside other authorities both ancient and modern and help to situate his proverbial comments in a matrix of received wisdom. For a discussion of the markers in Speght's edition of *Troilus and Criseyde*, see Kinney, "Thomas Speght's Renaissance Chaucer."

CHAPTER 5

1. Thomas Speght, "To the Reader," in *Works* (1602), sig. a2v.

2. As William Sherman notes, the "animadversion" emerged in the sixteenth century as a particular kind of critical commentary carrying with it new "intimations of an antagonistic relationship between the reader and the text, an awareness of the gap between the author's words on the page and the meaning particular readers want to derive from them." Sherman, *Used*

Books: Marking Readers in Renaissance England (Philadelphia: University of Pennsylvania Press, 2007), 22.

3. Thynne, *Animadversions*, 4.

4. See Leland, *Laboryouse journey* (STC 15445).

5. All quotations of the text are taken from Furnivall's edition. The *Animadversions* manuscript was purchased by Henry Huntington with the rest of the Bridgewater library in 1917 and is now San Marino, CA, Huntington Library MS EL.34.B.11.

6. Pearsall, "Thomas Speght," 84.

7. See Louis A. Knafla, "Thynne, Francis (1545?–1608)," in *Oxford DNB*.

8. These are Longleat House, Wiltshire, MS 178; and London, British Library, Additional MS 11388.

9. See Knafla, "Thynne, Francis."

10. On the relationship between alchemy and Thynne's financial straits, see David Carlson, "The Writings and Manuscript Collections of the Elizabethan Alchemist, Antiquary, and Herald Francis Thynne," *Huntington Library Quarterly* 52, no. 2 (1989): 205; and Knafla, "Thynne, Francis" in *ODNB*. British Library MS Lansdowne 27 contains two letters from Thynne to Burghley, dated March 1575, stating he has been imprisoned for a period of two years and two months, and begging him to secure his release. Their frantic tone is such that the Lansdowne cataloger describes them as the work of "F. Thynne, a madman." It is a testament to the unity and pervasiveness of Thynne's *outlook* that in the second of these letters he is able to reference and expand upon the mystical interpretation of the Burghley arms offered in his earlier *"Dyscourse upon the Creste of the Lorde Burghley.*

11. See *Animadversions*, 11–12. Whatever funds were raised proved insufficient for Thynne to avoid imprisonment over his £100 debt.

12. Francis Thynne, *The Perfect Ambassadour, Treating of the Antiquitie, Priveledges, and Behaviour of Men Belonging to That Function* (London: John Colbeck, 1652), sig. A.3.

13. Thynne's notes are preserved in three uniform manuscript volumes, now London, British Library MSS Cotton Faustina E.viii and E.ix, and San Marino, CA, Huntington Library MS EL.1137. The syndicate to publish this revision was organized by George Bishop, who was also involved in the publication of Speght's editions of Chaucer's *Works* in both 1598 and 1602.

14. See Carlson, "Francis Thynne," 208–209.

15. On the castration of the 1587 *Chronicles*, see Annabel Patterson, *Reading Holinshed's "Chronicles"* (Chicago: University of Chicago Press, 1994), 234–264. It is impossible to say what in Thynne's contribution caught the eye of the censors, though his long lists of officeholders could have provided ammunition for religious controversy. Here, as elsewhere in Thynne's work and in the writings of other antiquarians, it is possible to discern the ways in which seemingly objective work on offices and genealogy is recognized as politically relevant and responded to accordingly. For example, the historical role of offices like that of the Earl Marshall was of great interest to the Society of Antiquaries in the 1590s and early 1600s; they met to discuss "The Antiquity and Office of the Earl Marshal of England" on February 12, 1601/2, four days after the uprising undertaken by Robert Devereux, whom Elizabeth had appointed to the position of earl marshal in December 1597. See Herendeen, *William Camden*, 328–330.

16. Patterson, *Reading Holinshed's "Chronicles,"* 24.

17. Herendeen provides a useful overview of the operations of the society in *William Camden*, 309–328; see also F. Smith Fussner, *The Historical Revolution: English Historical Writing and Thought, 1580–1640* (London: Routledge and Kegan Paul, 1962), 92–99. Their principal source is Van Norden, "The Elizabethan College of Antiquaries."

18. See Thomas Hearne, ed., *A Collection of Curious Discourses Written by Eminent Antiquaries upon Several Heads in Our English Antiquities . . .* , 2 vols. (London: W. and J. Richardson, 1771). It is possible some of the additional papers that survive without authorial attribution were written by Thynne as well.

19. See Carlson, "Francis Thynne," 214.

20. Carlson, "Francis Thynne," 214.

21. British Library MS Lansdowne 75, art. 76, fol. 161. For Thynne's first attempt in 1588, see Thynne's letter to Burghley, quoted by Furnivall, in *Animadversions*, xci–xciii.

22. A contemporary account of Thynne's installation, written by Richard St. George, Norroy King of Arms, is preserved in Oxford, Bodleian Library, MS Rawlinson C.708, fol. 1r–1v.

23. On the probable date of Thynne's death, see Knafla, "Thynne, Francis."

24. Francis complains of gout in the opening lines of his 1606 *Discourse of the Dutye and Office of an Heraulde of Arms*, addressed to Henry Howard, Earl of Northampton; quoted here from Bodleian Library MS Ashmole 840, p. 79.

25. *Animadversions*, xlv.

26. *Britain, or A chorographicall description of the most flourishing kingdomes . . .* (1610), 160, 495.

27. See Carlson, "Francis Thynne," 203–272.

28. Carlson, "Francis Thynne," 203.

29. See, for example, folio 19r in London, British Library Additional MS 37666, Thynne's history of the Cobham family, which references the *Vox Clamantis*. This material was originally intended for inclusion in Holinshed's *Chronicles*, and Gower is in Thynne's list of historical writers on England. The *Vox Clamantis* was first printed for the Roxburghe Club in 1850.

30. Both appear in unique copies in Oxford, Bodleian Library, MS Ashmole 766.

31. Thynne's 1598 Chaucer is now Harvard University, Houghton Library, MS Eng 1221.

32. For example, Epigram 13, "A Puritane" (p. 59):

Dame *Lais* is a puritane by religion,
Impure in her deedes, though puer in her talke,
And therefore a purtane by condition,
or plurtane, which after manie doth walke;
For pruritie of wemenn, by lecherous direction,
Seekes pluritie of men to worke satisfaction.

Other titles include "Monument of a harlott" (p. 41); "Sundrie and strange effectes of wyne" (p. 54); "When a wife is badd, worse, and worst. When she is good, better, and best" (p. 59; the best wife is one who expires quickly and leaves her widower a substantial sum); "A tench and a wench" (p. 64); and "Drinkinge" (p. 65). All quotations here are taken from *Emblemes and Epigrames*, ed. Frederick Furnivall, EETS o.s. 64 (London: N. Trübner for the Early English Text Society, 1876).

33. *Emblemes and Epigrames*, 2.

34. See *Principum, ac illustrium aliquot & eruditorum in Anglia virorum* (STC 15447). For a discussion of Leland's short poems in their scholarly and social context, see Andrew Taylor, "John Leland's Communities of the Epigram," in *Neo-Latin Poetry in the British Isles*, ed. L. B. T. Houghton and Gesine Manuwald (London: Bloomsbury, 2012), 15–35.

35. See Trigg, *Congenial Souls*. On the provenance of the Ellesmere Chaucer, see C. W. Dutschke et al., *Guide to Medieval and Renaissance Manuscripts in the Huntington Library* (San Marino, CA: Huntington Library, 1989), 49–50.

36. *Emblemes and Epigrames*, 2–3.

37. Carlson, "Francis Thynne," 203.

38. *Emblemes and Epigrames*, 3.

39. In the *Life of Chaucer* in the 1598 *Works*, Thomas Speght and John Stow write of Chaucer's patrons that "Friends he had in the Court of the best sort: for besides that he alwaies held in with the Princes, in whose daies he lived, hee had of the best of the Nobility both lords & ladies, which favoured him greatly. But chiefly John of Gaunt Duke of Lancaster, at whose commandement he made the Treatise *Of the alliance betwixt Mars and Venus*: and also the booke of the Duchesse. Likewise the lady Isabel daughter to King Edward the third . . . also the lady Margaret daughter to the same King . . . did greatly love and favour Geffrey Chaucer" (sig. b6v).

40. *Emblemes and Epigrames*, 76–77.

41. I have not been able to identify a Waldronn (or Walden) associated with Thynne. Furnivall does not identify him in his edition of the poems.

42. In "Glasses" (p. 62), Thynne writes "besides, there is of glasse a temple faire and brighte, / which learned Chaucer builded hath with penn of heavenlie spright," a reference to the Temple of Glass in the *House of Fame*.

43. *Emblemes and Epigrames*, 71.

44. Joanna Bellis stresses the political importance of the connection this praise draws between Chaucer and Englishness. See *The Hundred Years War in Literature, 1337–1600* (Cambridge: D. S. Brewer, 2016), 127–130.

45. *Emblemes and Epigrames*, 71. Momus was the Greek god of satire and criticism, while Zoilus was a critic of Homer. See Henrietta V. Apfel, "Homeric Criticism in the Fourth Century B.C." *Transactions and Proceedings of the American Philological Association* 69 (1938): 250–252.

46. *De Viris Illustribus*, 706–707.

47. *Emblemes and Epigrames*, 93 (lines 7–12).

48. On the fundamental utility of this metaphor to the sixteenth-century construction of the past, see Simpson, "Ageism," 217–218.

49. Vergil was the frequent target of scorn on the part of English antiquarians. In annotated list of the names of authors at the back of the 1598 edition of Chaucer's *Works*, Lollius, the fictitious *auctor* cited by Chaucer in *Troilus and Criseyde*, is described as "an Italian Historiographer, borne in the citie of Urbine [Urbino]" (sig. 4B2v). There is nothing in Chaucer's text to support this identification, but the description does match Polydore Vergil, who was born outside of Urbino. The same note appears in the 1602 edition. On the conflict between Leland and Vergil, see Carley, "Polydore Vergil and John Leland on King Arthur."

50. *Emblemes and Epigrames*, 95 (lines 8–14).

51. *Emblemes and Epigrames*, 95 (lines 15–21).

52. *Works* (1602), sig. b1.

53. Both Deschamps's ballade to Chaucer and Stephanus Surigonus's epitaph for the poet compare him to Socrates, as well as other classical figures. Neither mentions Cicero.

54. Tasso's *La Gerusalemme liberata* had been translated in 1594 by the Cornish antiquary Richard Carew (STC 23697); Carew and Thynne would have known each other personally through their common involvement with the Society of Antiquaries.

55. The lines "What high renoune is purchas'd unto Spaine, / Which fresh *Dianaes* verses do distill" may be a reference to Jorge de Montemayor's *Diana*. An English translation by Bartholomew Young (STC 18044) was published in 1598 by George Bishop, who was also involved in the publication of the 1598 and 1602 *Works*. Thanks to David Carlson for bringing this to my attention.

56. While Thynne had a solid grammar school education and quotes extensively from Latin sources in his notes and in his writing, his only known Latin compositions are quite short. Similarly, although his knowledge of French literature appears substantial and in a dedicatory epistle to William Cecil, Lord Burghley he describes himself as one who "favorethe and savorethe the frenche tonge" (Bodleian MS Ashmole 766 fol. 3r), he did not write in French.

57. Notably, line 13 reads in print as "Or other motions by sweet Poets skill," but in Thynne's manuscript version as "Or other *natons* by swete poete skill" (the poems appear on the verso of the progeny leaf in Houghton MS Eng 1221).

58. Carlson writes that "attribution of these unsigned verses must seem tenuous," ("Francis Thynne," 242), but they are found, in Thynne's hand and with corrections, in his copy of the 1598 Chaucer at the Houghton Library (MS Eng 1221).

59. The title echoes that of the manuscript Thynne presented to Egerton in 1599, suggesting that Thynne, at least, regarded his own commentary on par with that provided by Speght.

60. *Works* (1602), sig. b1.

61. *Works* (1602), sig. a4.

62. *Animadversions*, 1.

63. This reference to Roman traditions in Britain might also have held special relevance during the decades in which successive editions of William Camden's *Britannia* were "restor[ing] antiquity to Britain, and Britain to its antiquity," and demonstrating how explorations of the local past might help situate Britain more comfortably in the company of its continental neighbors through a more explicit connection to the glories of Roman civilization. The bookseller George Bishop was involved with the 1590 edition of the *Britannia* and the two editions of Speght's Chaucer, as well as with the 1587 revised edition of Holinshed's *Chronicles*.

64. *Animadversions*, 4.

65. Trigg, *Congenial Souls*, 137.

66. *Animadversions*, 4.

67. *Animadversions*, 5. On Thynne's particular relation to his father's legacy, see Theresa M. Krier, "Introduction: Receiving Chaucer in Renaissance England," in *Refiguring Chaucer in the Renaissance*, ed. Theresa M. Krier (Gainesville: University Press of Florida, 1998), 5–9.

68. *Animadversions*, 6.

69. *Animadversions*, 7–8. For an overview of Francis Thynne's account of this event, and the problems with it, see Blodgett, "William Thynne," 38–39.

70. *Animadversions*, 10. According to Francis Thynne, his father had already aroused Wolsey's ire by sheltering John Skelton at his house in Kent while the poet composed his satire *Colin Clout*. Furnivall notes that, given Wolsey's supremely dramatic fall from power, this could have occurred no later than 1529. *Animadversions*, 10 n. 1.

71. In his introduction to the *Animadversions*, Furnivall suggests that the *Canterbury Tales* would have been suppressed in a nineteenth-century monastery (*Animadversions*, xiii). This comment reflects Furnivall's casual assurance in Chaucer's Protestant bona fides (even if he rejects claims for the Chaucerian authorship of the *Plowman's Tale* and similar works), but it also allows for a moment of identification between Furnivall and both Thynnes, as readers capable of recognizing and promoting Chaucer as a reformer *avant la lettre*.

72. That is, it is a reworking of the fifteenth-century reception of Chaucer, which, through a process of posthumous laureation, comes to view his works as interventions into a public sphere (see Anne Middleton, "The Idea of Public Poetry in the Reign of Richard II," *Speculum* 53, no. 1 [1978]: 94–114; and Lerer, *Chaucer and His Readers*, 14–19) and which idealizes the Chaucerian past as a time of both robust poetic production, and ample patronage and support for poets (see Lawton, "Dullness in the Fifteenth Century"). In 1606, Thynne dedicated a lavish copy of his *Dialogue between the Bath and Bachelor knights* to James I, now London, British Library Additional MS 12530.

73. Stephanie Trigg suggests that the connections between Francis Thynne, William Thynne, Thomas Speght, and Chaucer that are celebrated in the *Animadversions* may be in some sense "compensatory" for Thynne's lack of success in other endeavors and notes that "it is the Thynne family reputation that is at stake here" (*Congenial Souls*, 136). Theresa Krier draws on the psychoanalytical work of Jacques Lacan and Melanie Klein to argue that, in the *Animadversions*, Chaucer stands in for Francis Thynne's own absent father William, and that Chaucer's ability to fulfill this role for Francis is an expression of the "inexhaustibility" of Chaucer for Renaissance readers (*Refiguring Chaucer in the Renaissance*, 6–9).

74. See *Animadversions*, 9–10.

75. *Animadversions*, 5. In the 1605 edition of the *Annals* Stow refers to Thynne as his "good friend" (p. 1427). The two men may have reconciled, or, given Thynne's readiness to perceive slights, the enmity may have been one-sided to begin with. See Furnivall's hindwords in *Animadversions*, ciii.

76. Furnivall surmises that Thynne is the "one painefull antiquarie" referred to by Stow in Holinshed's *Chronicles* (1587) at vol. 2, p. 435, col. 2, line 56, as possessing a manuscript containing a prophecy of one Roger Wall. See *Animadversions*, ciii.

77. James E. Blodgett identifies five extant Chaucer manuscripts owned by Thynne, of which two (Glasgow, University of Glasgow Library Hunterian V.3.7 and Longleat House MS 258) can be connected with the 1532 *Works* (the Longleat House copy of Caxton's edition of Chaucer's *Boece* also contains printer's marks consistent with that edition). Blodgett also hypothesizes an additional four manuscripts, related to surviving copies, used in Thynne's edition. See Blodgett, "William Thynne," 39–41. As Robert Costomiris has shown, William Thynne made recourse to several earlier printed editions when preparing his *Works* (his sense of the scope and order of the *Canterbury Tales*, for example, can be traced to Caxton's first edition of 1477). See Costomiris, "The Influence of Printed Editions and Manuscripts on the Canon of William Thynne's *Canterbury Tales*"; Costomiris suggests that Thynne's reliance on Caxton's printed *Tales* lies behind his exclusion of the *Tale of Gamelyn* (237).

78. *Animadversions*, 6.

79. In a paper read at the 2010 meeting of the New Chaucer Society, Simon Horobin tentatively identified this manuscript as London, British Library MS Egerton 2726, a manuscript of the *Canterbury Tales*. Horobin suggests that Thynne may have overenthusiastically identified some corrector's marks as the endorsements of Chaucer himself. I am grateful to Professor Horobin for sharing his work with me. If this is indeed the manuscript that Thynne believed passed through Chaucer's hands, it is especially intriguing to note that it contains the apocryphal *Tale of Gamelyn*, which, though present in a large number of *Tales* manuscripts, is never printed with the *Tales*.

80. *Animadversions*, 11–12.

81. On Batman's activities as a book collector and agent for Matthew Parker, see Simon Horobin and Aditi Nafde, "Stephan Batman and the Making of the Parker Library," *Transactions*

of the Cambridge Bibliographical Society 15, no. 4 (2015): 561–581. See also Malcolm B. Parkes, "Stephen Batman's Manuscripts," in *Medieval Heritage: Essays in Honour of Tadahiro Ikegami*, ed. Masahiko Kanno et al. (Tokyo: Ushodo Press, 1997), 125–156; and Summit, *Memory's Library*, 108–123.

82. *Animadversions*, 12. This means that Thynne must have preserved at least a portion of the collection until after his imprisonment during 1574–1576.

83. *Animadversions*, 12. Thynne's anxieties about Speght's misuse of manuscript witnesses seem somewhat misplaced here, as the text of the 1598 *Works* is carried over from the 1561 edition with only minor alterations, which Derek Pearsall ascribes to compositional error rather than editorial intent (Pearsall, "Thomas Speght," 79).

84. *Animadversions*, 12.

85. *Animadversions*, 11.

86. *Animadversions*, 12–13. Both Speght and Thynne are incorrect in their identification of Chaucer's father: Speght names Richard Chaucer as Chaucer's father, when he was in fact the third husband of Chaucer's grandmother, Mary Chaucer. Thynne is correct that Chaucer's father was named John (he was the son of Mary Chaucer by her second husband, Robert Chaucer, possibly a relative of Richard), but John Chaucer appears to have been born in 1312 or 1313, so he cannot be the John Chaucer named in the materials cited here by Thynne. On Chaucer's ancestry, see Crow and Olson, *Chaucer Life-Records*, 2–8; and John M. Manly, "Mary Chaucer's First Husband," *Speculum* 9, no. 1 (1934): 86–88.

87. After citing several occurrences of the surname Chaucer in documentary record, Speght concludes "that the parents of Geffrey Chaucer were meere English, and he himselfe an Englishman borne. For els how could he have come to that perfection in our language, as to be called, The first illuminer of the English tongue; had not both he, and his parents before him, been borne & bred among us" (*Works* [1598], sig. b2v; the comment is made again in the 1602 edition).

88. See Crow and Olson, *Chaucer Life-Records*, 2–7.

89. See *Animadversions*, 14 n. 2.

90. See Oswald Barron, "A Fifteenth Century Book of Arms," *The Ancestor* 3 (1902): 185–213; and Cyril Ernest Wright, *Fontes Harleiani: A Study of the Sources of the Harleian Collection of Manuscripts in the British Museum* (London: British Museum, 1972), 79, 194–195.

91. *Animadversions*, 15.

92. Speght writes, "It may be that it were no absurditie to thinke (nay it seemeth likely, Chaucers skill in Geometry considered) that hee tooke the groundes and reasons of these armes out of Euclyde, the 27: and 28 Proposition of the first booke: and some perchaunce are of that opinion, whose skill therein is comparable to the best" (*Works* [1598], sig. b2v). This claim is removed in the 1602 edition.

93. *Animadversions*, 15; Thynne's rationale for the *Nun's Priest's Tale* correction is that it is "accordinge as Chaucer sett yt downe in myne and other written copies, which may stande with all mathematicall propertione, which Chaucer knewe and observed there" (*Animadversions*, 61).

94. *Animadversions*, 18.

95. *Animadversions*, 19–20.

96. Specifically, "the armes of this Sir Johne Gower, beinge argent, one a cheverone azure, three leopardes heddes or, do prove that he came of a contrarye howse to the Gowers of Styenhame in Yorke-shyre, who bare barrulye of argent & gules, a crosse patye florye sable" (*Animadversions*, 19).

97. It is important to note, however, that whereas Camden treats coins as a material record of pre-Roman Britain, Thynne turns to arms here as the quickest and easiest way to make his point, and the method that best supports his claim to the specialist knowledge required to properly interpret Chaucer and his works.

98. *Animadversions*, 15.

99. *Works* (1598), sig. b3–b3v. The claim is repeated in the 1602 edition.

100. *Animadversions*, 21. See Pearsall, "Thomas Speght," 78, for the broader scholarly response to this claim.

101. For a selection of papers on the topic, including Thynne's own, see Hearne, *Curious Discourses* (1771), 1:64–82. It is likely that other members presented additional papers that have not been preserved.

102. *Animadversions*, 23. In his treatise on the duties of a herald of arms, written a few years later, Thynne outlines twelve different kinds of bastards. See Hearne, *Curious Discourses*, 1:140.

103. Other significant bibliographical details, such as Chaucer's involvement in a suit brought by Cecily Chaumpaigne concerning charges of *raptus* against him, will likewise not be discovered by scholars until the nineteenth century.

104. See Carlson, "Francis Thynne," 234.

105. See *Animadversions*, 24–26.

106. *Animadversions*, 69.

107. *Animadversions*, 31. Joanna Bellis stresses the degree to which Chaucer's borrowing from French was figured originally as the spoils of the Hundred Years War, then elided in favor of his supposedly innate Englishness. See Bellis, *The Hundred Years War in Literature*, 182–187; as Bellis writes, "this reimagination of Chaucer's English was necessary because of the contradiction that he was simultaneously the figurehead of trenchant poetic nationalism, and famous for his borrowing" (185).

108. See Crawforth, *Etymology and the Invention of English*. For a comparative approach, see Considine, *Dictionaries in Early Modern Europe*.

109. *Animadversions*, 31.

110. *Animadversions*, 45. Thynne's claims about the exchequer, along with other claims concerning archival records, are an assertion of the privileged access gained by his association with members of the Society of Antiquaries.

111. *Animadversions*, 73.

112. *Animadversions*, 72.

113. *Works* (1602), sig. 3T5v. Thynne refers to Jean Molinet's prose moralization of the *Roman de la Rose*, published in at least three editions in Paris in the early sixteenth century, and Jean du Tillet's commentary on the French wars, first published in Frankfurt in 1579.

114. That copy of the *Works* is now Harvard University, Houghton Library MS Eng 1221.

115. *Animadversions*, 32 and 38. Speght corrects the definition accordingly in 1602.

116. See Schuler, "The Renaissance Chaucer as Alchemist."

117. *Animadversions*, 36.

118. *Animadversions*, 48.

119. *Animadversions*, 43.

120. *Animadversions*, 37–38.

121. These occur at lines 209, 6861–6864, and 7370.

122. A possible exception to this is John Stow, who was investigated for papistry in 1569. Derek Pearsall explores Stow's exceptionality further in "John Stow and Thomas Speght as Editors of Chaucer."

123. *Animadversions*, 43. There is also a note to this effect in Thynne's copy of the 1598 *Works*.

124. Elsewhere, Thynne writes to Speght, "but yf you saye, that in this and other thinges I am over-streyghte laced, and to obstinatlye bente to defende the former imperfecte editione,— in that I wolde rather allowe one imperfecte sence, and suche as must be understoode, when yt ys not fully expressed, then a playne style,—I will answere with a grounde of the lawe, 'quod frustra fit per plura, quod fieri potest per pauciora' [it is pointless to do with more what can be done with fewer] and 'quod subintelligitur non deest' [that which is understood is not lacking]" (*Animadversions*, 64).

125. *Animadversions*, 43.

126. *Animadversions*, 43-44; emphasis added.

127. *Animadversions*, 56.

128. *Animadversions*, 61.

129. *Animadversions*, 53.

130. *Animadversions*, 54.

131. *Animadversions*, 57.

132. See, for example, Paul Zumthor, *Toward a Medieval Poetics*, trans. Philip Bennett (Minneapolis: University of Minnesota Press, 1992), 45–49; and Bernard Cerquiglini, *In Praise of the Variant: A Critical History of Philology*, trans. Betsy Wing (Baltimore: Johns Hopkins University Press, 1999).

133. For a concise overview of the influence of continental legal scholarship on the English antiquarian movement, see Sharpe, *Sir Robert Cotton*, 5–13.

134. *Animadversions*, 75.

135. See "The Antiquity and Office of the Earl Marshall of England," *Curious Discourses*, 1:113; and "Of the Antiquity of Houses of Law," *Curious Discourses* 1:71.

CHAPTER 6

1. The 1687 edition resets the paratextual materials in Roman type but continues to use black letter for the text of Chaucer's writings. It adds, on a final page, two short passages that it describes as the endings to the *Cook's Tale* and the *Squire's Tale*. On these, see Hammond, *Chaucer: A Bibliographical Manual*, 276–277 and 312–313.

2. *Works* (1598), sig. a2v.

3. For an overview of Renaissance annotation practices, see Sherman, *Used Books*, 3–24. For a more specific survey of annotations in Chaucer folios, see Wiggins, "What Did Renaissance Readers Write in Their Printed Copies of Chaucer?"; and Hope Johnston, "Readers' Memorials in Early Editions of Chaucer."

4. On eighteenth- and nineteenth-century Middle English scholarship, see Matthews, *The Making of Middle English*.

5. A brief biography of Holland appears in Christina DeCoursey, "Society of Antiquaries (*act.* 1586–1607)," in *Oxford DNB*. See also Robert A. Caldwell, "Joseph Holand, Collector and Antiquary," *Modern Philology* 40, no. 4 (1943): 295–301.

6. Many of these papers are collected and published by Thomas Hearne in *A Collection of Curious Discourses . . .* , 2 vols. (1771). Holland spoke on topics including the "the Antiquity and Use of Heralds in England" (*Curious Discourses* [1771], 1:58–59), "the Antiquity, Use, and Privilege of Places for Students and Professors of the Common Law" (1:77–78), "the Antiq-

uity, Etymology, and Privileges" of both towns and parishes (1:192–195), and "the Variety and Antiquity of Tombs and Monuments" (1:258–260).

7. On William Camden and the Society of Antiquaries, see Herendeen, *William Camden*, 309–333. On Cotton's influence on the projects of the society, see Sharpe, *Sir Robert Cotton*, 17–37.

8. On Cotton's compilations, see Summit, *Memory's Library*, 136–196.

9. In addition to Gg.4.27, Holland at one time possessed what are now London, College of Arms MS Arundel 23 (containing the Middle English *Siege of Troye* and translation of Geoffrey of Monmouth's *Historia Regnum Britanniae*); and London, British Library Cotton MS Vespasian E.v (the cartulary of Reading Abbey); and his papers indicate familiarity with a range of historical and genealogical documents. See Caldwell, "Joseph Holand." (For a brief account of other manuscripts owned by London-based antiquarians, see McKisack, *Medieval History in the Tudor Age*, 67–68.)

10. The most recent comprehensive study of the manuscript is Matthew C. Wolfe, "Constructing the Chaucer Corpus: a Study of Cambridge, University Library, MS Gg.4.27" (PhD diss., West Virginia University, 1995). See also Jacob Thaisen, "Orthography, Codicology, and Textual Studies: The Cambridge University Library, Gg.4.27 'Canterbury Tales,'" *Boletín Millares Carlo* 24–25 (2005–2006): 379–394. CUL MS Gg.4.27 is "Gg" in *The Text of the Canterbury Tales*, ed. John M. Manly and Edith Rickert, 8 vols. (Chicago: University of Chicago Press, 1940).

11. For a full description of the manuscript and its contents, see M. B. Parkes and Richard Beadle, eds., *The Poetical Works of Geoffrey Chaucer: A Facsimile of Cambridge University Library MS GG.4.27*, 3 vols. (Cambridge: D. S. Brewer, 1979).

12. M. B. Parkes and Richard Beadle, "Commentary," in *Poetical Works*, 3:10.

13. Parkes and Beadle, *Poetical Works*, 3:63–64.

14. This scribe is also responsible for copying part 1 of Bodleian MS e Musaeo 116, as well as University of Missouri-Columbia MS Fragmenta Manuscripta 150 (a single leaf). On orthography in Gg and its relation to the spelling of exemplars used by Scribe A, see Parkes and Beadle, *Poetical Works*, 3:46–56; as well as Thaisen, "Orthography, Codicology, and Textual Studies"; and Robert A. Caldwell, "The Scribe of Chaucer MS Gg.4.27," *Modern Language Quarterly* 5 (1944): 33–46.

15. Parkes and Beadle, *Poetical Works*, 3:58–60.

16. Parkes and Beadle (*Poetical Works*, 3:10) suggest that whoever removed the illustrations was attempting to extricate them from a manuscript context that—because of its difficult orthography and increasingly archaic language—was no longer of interest.

17. For example, Holland could have worked along the lines of a sixteenth-century reader of MS Bodley 638, who updates the language of lines 1973–1988 of the *Legend of Good Women*.

18. See Pace, "Speght's Chaucer and MS Gg.4.27." The other text, the apocryphal *Jack Upland*, Speght took from John Foxe's *Actes and Monuments*, as discussed in Chapter 3.

19. Parkes and Beadle, *Poetical Works*, 3:67.

20. For further discussion of Gg.4.27.2, see Rosamund Allen, ed. *King Horn: An Edition Based on Cambridge University Library MS Gg.4.27.2* (New York: Garland, 1984), 2–6.

21. Parkes and Beadle, *Poetical Works*, 3:66.

22. Parkes and Beadle, *Poetical Works*, 3:10.

23. See Matthew C. Wolfe, "Placing Chaucer's *Retraction* for a Reception of Closure," *Chaucer Review* 33, no. 4 (1999): 427–431.

24. John Urry, for example, writing in the early eighteenth century, muses that "I fancy the Scriveners were prohibited from transcribing [the *Plowman's Tale*] and injoyn'd to subscribe

an Instrument at the end of the Canterbury Tales, call'd his Retraction" (*The Works of Geoffrey Chaucer* [1721], 178).

25. Gg.4.27.1, fol. 483v.

26. *Canterbury Tales* (Westminster: William Caxton, 1483), sig. L3v.

27. For a general overview, see Georgianna, "The Protestant Chaucer." While Holland's text aligns most closely with that found in Caxton's second edition, the possibility that an already-Protestantized text served as an exemplar for Holland's scribe cannot be excluded.

28. Shirley attributes the poem to Chaucer in Cambridge, Trinity College MS R.3.20, p. 9; the attribution is repeated in London, British Library MS Additional 29729, fol.132, a manuscript copied from a Shirley exemplar. The poem is printed for the first time in John Stow's 1561 edition of Chaucer's *Works*, where it appears alongside several other poems copied from the Trinity College manuscript.

29. In addition, sometime after the new pages were added, Holland copied Chaucer's short poem "Gentilesse" onto the very first folio of the manuscript. Holland's version of the poem contains a fourth stanza that is not attested in any other manuscript or printed version, suggesting that this text (unlike the pieces at the back of the book) was copied from a manuscript, now lost.

30. On this image, see Driver, "Mapping Chaucer."

31. Quoted in Spurgeon, *Five Hundred Years of Chaucer Criticism and Allusion*, 1:417–418.

32. For a detailed discussion and description of the tomb, see Greening-Lamborn, "The Arms on the Chaucer Tomb at Ewelme."

33. Gg.4.27.1, fol. 2v. The equivalent passage in the 1598 Speght *Works* appears on sigs. c1–c1v.

34. Gg.4.27.1, fol. 2v. The equivalent passage in the 1598 *Works* appears on sigs. c1v–c2r.

35. The passages quoted in Speght correspond to Hoccleve, *Regiment of Princes*, ed. Blyth (1999), lines 1958–1974 and 2077–2093, 2101–2107. Holland, however, quotes lines 2077–2079, followed by 1958–1966.

36. MS Gg.4.27.1, fol. 4v.

37. See *Works* (1598), sig. c2.

38. See Kuskin, "'The Loadstarre of the English Language.'"

39. Gg.4.27.1(b), fol. 5. See Dane and Gillespie, "Back at Chaucer's Tomb," 89–96.

40. Gg.4.27.1(b), fol. 7.

41. On Ashmole's life and career, see Michael Hunter, "Ashmole, Elias (1617–1692), Astrologer and Antiquary," in *Oxford DNB*.

42. These are Bodleian Library MSS Ashmole 766, 835, 856, and 840.

43. Bruce Janacek, "A Virtuoso's History: Antiquarianism and the Transmission of Knowledge in the Alchemical Studies of Elias Ashmole," *Journal of the History of Ideas* 69, no. 3 (2008): 396–397.

44. See C. H. Josten, ed., *Elias Ashmole (1617–1692): His Autobiographical and Historical Notes, His Correspondence, and Other Contemporary Sources Relating to His Life and Work* (Oxford: Clarendon Press, 1966), 1:18.

45. Gerarde is possibly the knight of that name mentioned in several legal records from Staffordshire circa 1600. See William Salt Archaeological Society, ed., *Collections for a History of Staffordshire*, vol. 13 (London: Harrison and Sons, 1892).

46. Skeat writes in his own edition of the tale that Urry's "spellings of the words are so fantastical, and the whole of his work so worthless and absurd, that it is hardly even possible to say what MS. he used" (*Chaucerian and Other Pieces*, xxxii).

47. The origins of *Gamelyn*'s association with the *Tales* are obscure. Skeat suggests that Chaucer may have intended to adapt the poem, and that a copy had been found among Chaucer's papers at the time of his death and posthumously put into circulation (Walter W. Skeat, ed., *The Tale of Gamelyn* [Oxford: Clarendon Press, 1884], xiv). Manly and Rickert rather noncommittally place the tale "in Chaucer's literary chest" (*The Text of the Canterbury Tales*, 2:172). On its place in the manuscripts, see Edwards, "The *Canterbury Tales* and *Gamelyn*." *Gamelyn*'s absence must be due at least in part to the fact that there is no ideological reason to add it, unlike *Jack Upland* (which fulfills a desire to read Chaucer as Protestant) or the short poems added by Stow (which meet a similar call for evidence of Chaucer as courtly poet). It is a reminder that we need to read decisions about Chaucer's canon as political ones, not just textual ones.

48. While Thynne, Stow, and Speght all made recourse to manuscripts in adding new pieces to their editions of the *Works*, the *Canterbury Tales* (with the important exceptions of the addition of the *Plowman's Tale* and the omission of the *Retraction*) always follows the pattern set by Caxton's first edition of 1477 (STC 5082).

49. Glanvill dedicates his work to Sir Francis Kynaston, who in the 1620s translated *Troilus and Criseyde* into Latin.

50. On this, see A. S. G. Edwards, "A New Text of *The Canterbury Tales*?" in *Studies in Late Medieval and Early Renaissance Texts in Honour of John Scattergood*, ed. Anne Marie d'Arcy and Alan J. Fletcher (Dublin: Four Courts Press, 2005), 121–128.

51. Later in the *Tales*, Ashmole also copies over a variant version of lines 803–826 of *The Tale of Sir Thopas*. These lines are absent from the 1532 text, but are printed in the "Annotations, with Some Corrections" in the 1598 Speght edition and incorporated into the main text in 1602.

52. MS Ashmole 1095, sig. V5.

53. Thynne does write that when the *Works* were reprinted a third time (he is counting the spurious one-column edition supposedly containing the *Pilgrim's Tale*, but means the 1542 edition), the *Plowman's Tale* was "with muche ado permitted to passe with the reste, in suche sorte that in one open parliamente (as I have herde Sir Johne Thynne reporte, being then a member of the howse,) when talke was had of Bookes to be forbidden, Chaucer had there for ever byn condempned, had yt not byn that his woorkes had byn counted but fables" (*Animadversions*, 10).

54. Oxford, Bodleian Library MS Ashmole 59, fol. 25.

55. MS Ashmole 1095, sig. 3V5v.

56. MS Ashmole 1095, sig. E6v.

57. *Works* (1602), 4B4. In his notes, Ashmole displays a characteristic antiquarian impulse to connect historical details with institutions familiar to postmedieval readers.

58. MS Ashmole 1095, sig. B6.

59. MS Ashmole 1095, sig. B6.

60. MS Ashmole 1095, sig. T6.

61. "Valerius in the 7: Chap: of his first Booke hath this History of Symonides the Poet, but here it is inlarged by Chaucer" (MS Ashmole 1095, sig. T6v).

62. MS Ashmole 1095, sig. N4.

63. *Britain*, trans. Holland, p. 194. Notably, Ashmole relies on Philemon Holland's translation rather than Camden's Latin original.

64. MS Ashmole 1095, sig. G5v.

65. See Kinney, "Thomas Speght's Renaissance Chaucer and the Solaas of Sentence in Troilus and Criseyde."

66. On this see Prendergast, *Chaucer's Dead Body*, 40.

67. See letter of June 3, 1667 (Bodleian Library MS Marshall 134) from Junius to Thomas Marshall.

68. On this manuscript, see J. A. Van Dorsten, "The Leyden 'Lydgate Manuscript,'" *Scriptorium* 14, no. 2 (1960): 315–25.

69. Junius's copy of the *Defence of Poesie* is now held at the University of Leiden. See Judith Dundas, "'A Mutuall Emulation': Sidney and *The Painting of the Ancients*," in *Franciscus Junius F.F. and His Circle*, ed. Rolf H. Bremmer Jr. (Amsterdam: Rodopi, 1998), 71–92. Junius's annotations to this book include references to the language of *Troilus and Criseyde* and to Spenser's *Shepheardes Calender* (Dundas, 74). Intriguingly, in *The Painting of the Ancients*, Junius also quotes, without attribution, from both E.K.'s prefatory epistle to the *Calender* and the prefatory epistle to the *Faerie Queen* (see Dundas, 84–87).

70. For a summary of Junius's biography, see Sophie van Romburgh, "Junius [Du Jon], Franciscus [Francis] (1591–1677)," in *Oxford DNB*.

71. Rolf H. Bremmer Jr., "Franciscus Junius Reads Chaucer: But Why? And How?" *Studies in Medievalism* 11 (2001): 38.

72. Bremmer, "Franciscus Junius Reads Chaucer," 39–40.

73. *A Restitution of Decayed Intelligence: In antiquities Concerning the most noble and renowmed English nation* (Antwerp: Robert Bruney), 203–204.

74. Bremmer, "Franciscus Junius Reads Chaucer," 41–42. For a discussion of Anglo-Dutch relations and their role in debates about language history, see Marjorie Rubright, *Doppelgänger Dilemmas: Anglo-Dutch Relations in Early Modern English Literature and Culture* (Philadelphia: University of Pennsylvania Press, 2014), 56–88.

75. For context, see Ph. H. Breuker, "On the Course of Franciscus Junius's Germanic Studies, with Special Reference to Frisian," in Bremmer, *Franciscus Junius F.F. and His Circle*, 154–155.

76. Bremmer, "Franciscus Junius Reads Chaucer," 43.

77. Bremmer, "Franciscus Junius Reads Chaucer," 46.

78. Gavin Douglas, trans., *The ·xiii. bukes of Eneados of the famose poete Virgill translatet out of Latyne verses into Scottish metir* (London: [William Copland], 1553) (STC 24797).

79. Quoted in Bremmer, "Franciscus Junius Reads Chaucer," 45.

80. Junius's "sparingly annotated" copy of the 1529 edition of *Le Rommant de la Rose* is now at Leiden. See Bremmer, "Franciscus Junius Reads Chaucer," 52.

81. "Ita olim dicatibus aliquam virtutis, ingenii, forma exsuperantiam spectabilis ac praeter caeteros admirabilis" (MS Junius 6, fol. 5v).

82. The passages correspond to line 78 of the *Testament of Cresseid* (printed following *Troilus and Criseyde* in all of the early modern *Works*) and *Troilus and Criseyde* 1.171–172. Spelling here is as recorded in Junius's note. For the text of the *Testament of Criseyde*, see *The Poems of Robert Henryson*, ed. Robert L. Kindrick (Rochester, NY: Medieval Institute Publications, 1997).

83. See MS Junius 54, sig. B1.

84. MS Junius 54, sig. B2. The use of both words is restricted to the *Canterbury Tales*. "Borell" and its variants ("burel," etc.) appear in the *Monk's Tale* (line 3145), the *Wife of Bath's Prologue* (line 356), the *Summoner's Tale* (lines 1872 and 1874), and the *Franklin's Tale* (line 716). "Boistous" appears in the *Manciple's Tale* (line 211).

85. Kerling, "Franciscus Junius, 17th-Century Lexicography and Middle English," in *LEXeter '83 Proceedings: Papers from the International Conference on Lexicography at Exeter, 2–12 September 1983*, ed. R. R. K. Hartmann (Tübingen: Niemeyer, 1984), 95.

86. See Kerling, "Franciscus Junius," 97. Gerardus Vossius was married to Junius's sister Elisabeth and the father of his nephew, the philologist Isaac Vossius.

87. On this, see Bremmer, "Franciscus Junius Reads Chaucer," 54. Johan Kerling suggests, to the contrary, that Junius had planned an edition of Chaucer. See Kerling, "Franciscus Junius," 16, 20.

88. On Chaucer's prominent role in seventeenth- and early eighteenth-century lexicography, see Kerling, *Chaucer in Early English Dictionaries*.

89. "The Preface," in *The Works of Geoffrey Chaucer* (1721), sig. L2v–M1.

90. See Sophie van Romburgh, ed. and trans., *"For My Worthy Freind Mr Franciscus Junius": An Edition of the Correspondence of Francis Junius F.F. (1591–1677)* (Leiden: Brill, 2004), 1030. On Sidney's influence on Junius's early art historical work, see Dundas, "'A Mutuall Emulation.'"

91. Bremmer, "Franciscus Junius Reads Chaucer," 44–45.

92. Bremmer offers a list of the sources cited by Junius in his notes on classical allusions and analogues. See "Franciscus Junius Reads Chaucer," 50.

93. Bremmer, "Franciscus Junius Reads Chaucer," 71 n. 67.

94. See Van Romburgh, *"For My Worthy Freind Mr Franciscus Junius,"* 1024.

95. Quoted in Bremmer, "Franciscus Junius Reads Chaucer," 54–55.

96. *Works* (1532), sig. C2v; *Works* (1598) sig. B2v. The passage is the *Knight's Tale*, 1164–1166, quoted here as it appears in the 1598 *Works*.

97. See MS Junius 6, fol. 38 and MS Ashmole 1095, sig. K3v.

98. "To the Readers," *Works* (1602), sig. A2.

99. See Bodleian MS Junius 9, fol. 16v; and MS Ashmole 1095, sig. F2. The reference appears at line 4286 of the *Reeve's Tale*.

100. On Speght's elliptical reference to the hero Wade and his mysterious boat, see Stephanie Trigg, "The Injuries of Time: Geoffrey Chaucer, Thomas Speght and Wade's Boat," *LaTrobe Journal* 81 (2008): 106–117.

101. See Bodleian MS Junius 9, fol. 85v; and MS Ashmole 1095, sig. V5. This passage corresponds to lines 5–12 of the *Parson's Prologue* in the *Riverside Chaucer*, which gives the time as "foure of the clokke" and sets events under the sign of Libra.

102. Ashmole 1095, sig. V5.

103. See the *Works* (1687), p. 168.

104. The reference is to *Historia Naturalis* 15.6.17. Junius writes "l. cerriall / for cerrus is a / kinde of tree / like an oke, / and bereth maste / vide Plinium." See Junius 9, fol. 7v. Ashmole writes "serialle serrus is a kinde of Tre / like an Oke, & beareth Mast vid. Plinius; see Ashmole 1095, sig. D3.

105. See *Animadversions*, 47–50.

106. See Bodleian MS Junius 9, fol. 23v; and MS Ashmole 1095, sig. G5.

107. See Van Romburgh, *"For My Worthy Freind Mr Franciscus Junius,"* 984 and 1026.

CODA

1. *The Book of Fame made by Gefferey Chaucer* ([Westminster]: William Caxton, [1483]).

2. Despite his claims to have sought out manuscripts, Thynne's edition appears to be based on Pynson's 1526 text. See A. S. G. Edwards, "Pynson's and Thynne's Editions of Chaucer's *House of Fame*," *Studies in Bibliography* 42 (1989): 185–186.

3. *Works* (1602), sig. 2Y6.

4. *House of Fame*, lines 1140–1147.

5. *House of Fame*, lines 1153–1158.

6. *Works* (1598), sig. A5v.

7. *House of Fame*, 646.

8. Cooper, "Poetic Fame," 365.

BIBLIOGRAPHY

MANUSCRIPTS

Cambridge, Cambridge University Library, MS Gg.4.27
Cambridge, Magdalene College, MS Pepys 2006
Cambridge, Trinity College, MS R.3.19
Cambridge, Trinity College, MS R.3.20
Cambridge, MA, Houghton Library, MS Eng 1221
London, British Library, Additional MS 11388
London, British Library, Additional MS 29729
London, British Library, Additional MS 37666
London, British Library, Additional MS 42518
London, British Library, Cotton MS Faustina E.viii
London, British Library, Cotton MS Faustina E.ix
London, British Library, Cotton MS Otho A.xviii
London, British Library, Cotton MS Vespasian E.v
London, British Library, MS Egerton 2726
London, British Library, MS Harley 2251
London, British Library, MS Lansdowne 27
London, British Library, MS Lansdowne 75
London, British Library, MS Lansdowne 76
London, British Library, Sloane MS 3847
London, College of Arms, MS Arundel 23
Oxford, Bodleian Library, MS 154
Oxford, Bodleian Library, MS Ashmole 59
Oxford, Bodleian Library, MS Ashmole 766
Oxford, Bodleian Library, MS Ashmole 835
Oxford, Bodleian Library, MS Ashmole 840
Oxford, Bodleian Library, MS Ashmole 856
Oxford, Bodleian Library, MS Ashmole 1095
Oxford, Bodleian Library, MS Bodley 638
Oxford, Bodleian Library, MS e Musaeo 116
Oxford, Bodleian Library, MS Fairfax 16
Oxford, Bodleian Library, MS Hatton 73
Oxford, Bodleian Library, MS Junius 6
Oxford, Bodleian Library, MS Junius 9

Oxford, Bodleian Library, MS Junius 54
Oxford, Bodleian Library, MS Junius 114
Oxford, Bodleian Library, MS Marshall 134
Oxford, Bodleian Library, MS Rawlinson C.708
Oxford, Bodleian Library, MS Rawlinson Poet.40a
Oxford, Bodleian Library, MS Top. Gen. c. 4
San Marino, CA, Huntington Library, MS EL.34.B.11
San Marino, CA, Huntington Library, MS EL.34.B.12
San Marino, CA, Huntington Library, MS EL.1137

PRIMARY TEXTS

STC numbers refer to A. W. Pollard and G. R. Redgrave, *A Short-Title Catalogue of Books Printed in England, Scotland, and Ireland and English Books Printed Abroad, 1475–1604,* 2nd ed., rev. and expanded by W. A. Jackson, F. S. Ferguson, and Katharine F. Pantzer (London: Bibliographical Society, 1976–1986).

Alley, William. *Ptochomuseion: The poore mans Librarie.* London: John Day, 1565; STC 374.

Bale, John. *Illustrium Majoris Britanniae Scriptorum.* Wesel: John Overton, 1548 and 1549; STC 1296.

———. *Scriptorum Illustrium majoris Brytanniae quam nunc Angliam & Scotiam vocant: Catalogus.* 2 vols. Basel: Johannes Oporinus, [1557–1559].

Brooke, Ralph. *A Discoverie of Certaine Errours Published in Print in the much commended Britannia 1594.* London: W. Wight and T. Judson, 1599; STC 3834.

Camden, William. *Britain, Or a Chorographicall Description of the Most flourishing Kingdomes, England, Scotland, and Ireland, and the Ilands adjoyning.* Translated by Philemon Holland. London: George Bishop and John Norton, 1610; STC 4509.

Carew, Richard. *Godfrey of Bulloigne, or The Recoverie of Hierusalem.* London: John Windet, 1594; STC 23697.

Cawdrey, Robert. *A Table Alphabeticall.* London: T. Snodham, 1613; STC 4885.

Chaucer, Geoffrey. *The Book of Fame made by Gefferey Chaucer.* [Westminster]: William Caxton, [1483]; STC 5087.

———. *[Canterbury Tales].* [Westminster: William Caxton, 1477]; STC 5082.

———. *[Canterbury Tales].* [Westminster: William Caxton, 1483]; STC 5083.

———. *[Works] The workes of Geffray Chaucer newly printed.* London: Thomas Godfray, 1532; STC 5068.

———. *[Works] The workes of Geffray Chaucer newly printed.* London: Richard Grafton for William Bonham, 1542; STC 5069.

———. *[Works] The workes of Geffray Chaucer newly printed.* London: Richard Grafton for John Reynes, 1542; STC 5070.

———. *[Works] The workes of Geffray Chaucer newly printed.* London: Nicholas Hill for William Bonham, [1550?]; STC 5071.

———. *[Works] The workes of Geffray Chaucer newly printed.* London: Nicholas Hill for Richard Kele, [1550?]; STC 5072.

————. [*Works*] *The workes of Geffray Chaucer newly printed.* London: Nicholas Hill for Thomas Petit, [1550?]; STC 5073.

————. [*Works*] *The workes of Geffray Chaucer newly printed, with dyvers workes whiche were never in print before.* London: John Kynson for John Wight, 1561; STC 5075.

————. [*Works*] *The woorkes of Geffrey Chaucer, newly printed with divers addicions, whiche were never in printe before.* London: John Kynson for John Wight, 1561; STC 5076.

————. [*Works*] *The woorkes of Geffrey Chaucer, newly printed, with divers addictions, whiche were never in printe before.* London: Henry Bradsha, 1561; STC 5076.3.

————. [*Works*] *The Workes of our Antient and lerned English poet, Geffrey Chaucer, newly Printed.* London: Adam Islip for George Bishop, 1598; STC 5077.

————. [*Works*] *The Workes of our Antient and Learned English poet, Geffrey Chaucer, newly Printed.* London: Adam Islip for Bonham Norton, 1598; STC 5078.

————. [*Works*] *The Workes of our Antient and Learned English poet, Geffrey Chaucer, newly Printed.* London: Adam Islip for Thomas Wight, 1598; STC 5079

————. [*Works*] *The Workes of our Ancient and learned English Poet, Geffrey Chaucer, newly Printed.* London: Adam Islip, 1602; STC 5080.

————. [*Works*] *The Workes of our Ancient and learned English Poet, Geffrey Chaucer, newly Printed.* London: Adam Islip for George Bishop, 1602; STC 5081.

————. [*Works*] *The Works of Our Ancient, Learned, and Excellent English Poet, Jeffrey Chaucer.* London, 1687.

————. [*Works*] *The Works of Geoffrey Chaucer, Compared with the Former Editions, and many valuable MSS.* London: Bernard Lintot, 1721.

Cooper, Thomas. *Thesaurus linguae Romanae & Britannicae.* London: Henry Wykes, 1565; STC 5686.

Douglas, Gavin, trans. *The ·xiii. Bukes of Eneados of the famose Poete Virgill Translatet out of Latyne verses into Scottish metir.* London: William Copland, 1553; STC 24797.

Foxe, John. *Actes and Monuments of these latter and perillous dayes.* . . . London: John Day, 1563; STC 11222.

————. *The first volume of the Ecclesiasticall history contaynyng the Actes and Monumentes of thynges passed in every kynges tyme in this Realme, especially in the Church of England principally to be noted.* London: John Day, 1570; STC 11223.

Gower, John. *De confessione Amantis.* London: Thomas Berthelette, 1532; STC 12143.

————. *De confessione Amantis.* London: Thomas Berthelette, 1554, STC 12144.

Greaves, Paul. *Grammatica Anglicana.* Cambridge: John Legatt, 1594; STC 12208.

Greene, Robert. *Greenes Vision: Written at the instant of his death.* London: E. Allde, 1592; STC 12261.

Hall, Edward. *The Union of the two noble and illustre famelies of Lancastre and Yorke.* London: Richard Grafton for Steven Mierdman, 1550; STC 12723.

Jack up Lande Compyled by the famous Geoffrey Chaucer. Southwark: J. Nicolson for John Gough, 1536; STC 5098.

Kynaston, Francis, trans. *Amorum Troili et Creseidae Libri duo priores Anglico-Latini.* Oxford: John Lichfield, 1635; STC 5097.

Langland, William. *The Vision of Pierce Plowman.* London: Robert Crowley, 1550; STC 19906.

————. *The vision of Pierce Plowman, newlye imprynted after the authours olde copy.* London: Owen Rogers, 1561; STC 19908.

Leland, John. *The laboryouse Journey and serche of Johan Leylande, for Englandes Antiquitees.* London: Printed by S. Mierdman for John Bale, 1549; STC 15445.

———. *Principum, ac illustrium aliquot & eruditorum in Anglia virorum, encomia, trophaea, genethliaca, & epithalamia.* London: Thomas Orwin, 1589; STC 15477.

Lydgate, John, trans. *A Treatise excellent and compendious, shewing and declaring, in the maner of Tragedye, the falles of sondry most notable Princes and Princesses with other Nobles, through the mutabilitie and change of unstedfast Fortune,* by Giovanni Boccaccio. London: Richard Tottel, [1554]; STC 3177.

———. *The tragedies, gathered by Jhon Bochas, of all such Princes as fell from theyr estates throughe the mutability of Fortune since the creacion of Adam, until his time.* London: John Wayland, [1554?]; STC 3178.

———. [*Troy Book*] *The Auncient Historie and onely trewe and syncere Cronicle of the warres betwixte the Grecians and the Troyans.* London: Thomas Marshe, [1555]; STC 5590.

Montemayor, Jorge de. *Diana of George of Montemayor: Translated out of Spanish into English by Bartholomew Yong of the Middle Temple Gentleman.* London: Edmund Bollifant for George Bishop, 1598; STC 18044.

More, Thomas. *The workes of Sir Thomas More Knyght, sometyme Lorde Chauncellour of England, wrytten by him in the Englysh tonge.* London: John Cawood, John Waly, and Richard Tottel, 1557; STC 18076.

Mulcaster, Richard. *The First Part of the Elementarie which Entreateth Chefelie of the right writing of our English tung.* London: Thomas Vautroullier, 1582; STC 18250.

Pierce the Ploughman's Crede. London: Reynold Wolfe, 1553; STC 19904.

[*The ploughman's tale*]. London: Thomas Godfray, 1535; STC 5099.5.

The Plough-mans tale: Shewing by the doctrine and lives of the Romish Clergie, that the Pope is Antichrist and they his Ministers. London: George Eld, 1606; STC 5101.

The plowmans tale compylled by syr Geffrey Chaucher knyght. London: William Hill, [1548]; STC 5100.

Porcia, Jacopo di. *The Preceptes of Warre, set forth by James the erle of Purlilia, and translated into englysh by Peter Betham.* London: Edward Whitchurch, 1544; STC 20116.

Skelton, John. *Pithy pleasaunt and profitable workes of maister Skelton, Poete Laureate.* London: Thomas Marshe, 1568; STC 22608.

Speed, John. *The Theatre of the Empire of Great Britaine: Presenting an Exact Geography of the Kingdomes of England, Scotland, Ireland, and the Iles adjoyning.* London: William Hall for John Sudbury and George Humble, 1611; STC 23041.

Spenser, Edmund. *The Shepheardes Calender.* London: Hugh Singleton, 1579; STC 23089.

Thynne, Francis. *The Perfect Ambassadour, Treating the Antiquitie, Priveledges, and Behaviour of Men Belonging to That Function.* London: John Colbeck, 1652.

Verstegan, Richard. *A Restitution of Decayed Intelligence: In antiquities Concerning, the most noble and renowmed English nation.* Antwerp: Robert Bruney, 1605; STC 21361.

Wilson, Thomas. *The Arte of Rhetorique, for the use of all suche as are studious of Eloquence, sette forth in English.* London: Richard Grafton, 1553; STC 25799.

SECONDARY SOURCES

Alderson, William L. "A Check-List of Supplements to Spurgeon's Chaucer Allusions." *Philological Quarterly* 32 (1953): 418–427.

————. "John Urry." In *Editing Chaucer: The Great Tradition*, edited by Paul G. Ruggiers, 93–117. Norman, OK: Pilgrim Books, 1984.

Allen, Rosamund, ed. *King Horn: An Edition Based on Cambridge University Library MS Gg.4.27.2*. New York: Garland, 1984.

Anderson, Benedict. *Imagined Communities: Reflections on the Origin and Spread of Nationalism*. London: Verso, 1991.

Anderson, Judith H. *The Growth of a Personal Voice: "Piers Plowman" and "The Faerie Queene."* New Haven, CT: Yale University Press, 1976.

————. *Reading the Allegorical Intertext: Chaucer, Spenser, Shakespeare, Milton*. New York: Fordham University Press, 2008.

Anderson, Marjorie. "Blanche, Duchess of Lancaster." *Modern Philology* 45, no. 3 (1948): 152–159.

Apfel, Henrietta V. "Homeric Criticism in the Fourth Century B.C." *Transactions and Proceedings of the American Philological Association* 69 (1938): 245–258.

Armstrong, Edward. *A Ciceronian Sunburn: A Tudor Dialogue on Humanistic Rhetoric and Civic Poetics*. Columbia: University of South Carolina Press, 2006.

Aubrey, John. *"Brief Lives," Chiefly of Contemporaries, Set Down by John Aubrey, Between the Years 1669 & 1696*. Edited by Andrew Clark. Oxford: Clarendon Press, 1898.

Bale, John. *Index Britanniae Scriptorum*. Edited by R. L. Poole and M. Bateson. Oxford: Clarendon Press, 1902.

Barron, Oswald. "A Fifteenth Century Book of Arms." *The Ancestor* 3 (1902): 185–213.

Bellis, Joanna. *The Hundred Years War in Literature, 1337–1600*. Cambridge: D. S. Brewer, 2016.

Bendall, Sarah. "Speed, John (1551/2–1629)." In *Oxford Dictionary of National Biography*. Oxford: Oxford University Press, 2004–. http://www.oxforddnb.com.

Berkhout, Carl T., and Milton McCormick Gatch, eds. *Anglo-Saxon Scholarship: The First Three Centuries*. Boston: G. K. Hall, 1982.

Blake, N. F. *Caxton's Own Prose*. London: Deutsch, 1973.

Blank, Paula. *Broken English: Dialects and the Politics of Language in Renaissance Writings*. London: Routledge, 1996.

Blayney, Peter W. M. *The Stationers' Company and the Printers of London, 1501–1557*. 2 vols. Cambridge: Cambridge University Press, 2013.

Blodgett, James E. "Some Printer's Copy for William Thynne's 1532 Edition of Chaucer." *The Library* 1, no. 2 (1979): 97–113.

————. "William Thynne." In *Editing Chaucer: The Great Tradition*, edited by Paul Ruggiers, 35–53. Norman, OK: Pilgrim Books, 1984.

Bonner, Francis W. "The Genesis of the Chaucer Apocrypha." *Studies in Philology* 48, no. 3 (1951): 461–481.

Boswell, Jackson C. "Chaucer Allusions: Addenda to Spurgeon." *Notes and Queries* 222 (1977): 493–495.

————. "Chaucer and Spenser Allusions Not in Spurgeon and Wells." *Analytical and Enumerative Bibliography* 1 (1977): 30–32.

Boswell, Jackson Campbell, and Sylvia Wallace Holton. *Chaucer's Fame in England: STC Chauceriana, 1475–1640*. New York: Modern Language Association of America, 2004.

Bourdieu, Pierre. "The Field of Cultural Production, or the Economic World Reversed." *Poetics* 12 (1983): 311–356.

Brackmann, Rebecca. *The Elizabethan Invention of Anglo-Saxon England: Laurence Nowell, William Lambarde, and the Study of Old English*. Cambridge: D. S. Brewer, 2012.

Brann, Noel L. *The Abbot Trithemius (1462–1516): The Renaissance of Monastic Humanism*. Leiden: E. J. Brill, 1981.

Bremmer, Rolf H., Jr. "Franciscus Junius Reads Chaucer: But Why? And How?" *Studies in Medievalism* 11 (2001): 37–72.

Breuker, Ph. H. "On the Course of Franciscus Junius's Germanic Studies, with Special Reference to Frisian." In *Franciscus Junius F.F. and His Circle*, edited by Rolf H. Bremmer Jr., 129–158. Amsterdam: Rodopi, 1998.

Brook, Lindsay L. "The Ancestry of Sir Paon de Ruet, Father-in-Law of Geoffrey Chaucer and John 'of Gaunt.'" *Foundations* 1, no. 1 (2003): 54–56.

Burrow, John A. "Chaucer, Geoffrey (c. 1343–1400)." In *The Spenser Encyclopedia*, edited by A. C. Hamilton, 144–148. Toronto: University of Toronto Press, 1990.

Cable, Thomas. "Fifteenth-Century Rhythmical Changes." In *"And Gladly Wolde He Lerne and Gladly Teache": Essays on Medieval English Presented to Professor Matsui Tahima on His Sixtieth Birthday*, edited by Yoko Iyeiri and Margaret Connolly, 109–125. Tokyo: Kaibunsha, 2002.

Caldwell, Robert A. "Joseph Holand, Collector and Antiquary." *Modern Philology* 40, no. 4 (1943): 295–301.

———. "The Scribe of Chaucer MS Gg.4.27." *Modern Language Quarterly* 5 (1944): 33–46.

Cannon, Christopher. *The Making of Chaucer's English: A Study of Words*. Cambridge: Cambridge University Press, 1998.

———. "The Myth of Origin and the Making of Chaucer's English." *Speculum* 71, no. 3 (1996): 656–675.

Carley, James P. "John Leland's *Cygnea Cantio*: A Neglected Tudor River Poem." *Humanistica Lovaniensia* 32 (1983): 225–241.

———. "Leland, John (c. 1503–1552), Poet and Antiquary." In *Oxford Dictionary of National Biography*. Oxford: Oxford University Press, 2004–. http://www.oxforddnb.com.

———. "The Manuscript Remains of John Leland, 'The King's Antiquary.'" *Text: Transactions for the Society for Textual Scholarship* 2 (1985): 111–120.

———. "Polydore Vergil and John Leland on King Arthur: The Battle of the Books," *Interpretations* 15, no. 2 (1984): 86–100.

Carlson, David R. "Thomas Hoccleve and the Chaucer Portrait." *Huntington Library Quarterly* 54, no. 4 (1991): 283–300.

———. "The Writings and Manuscript Collections of the Elizabethan Alchemist, Antiquary, and Herald Francis Thynne." *Huntington Library Quarterly* 52, no. 2 (1989): 203–272.

Cawsey, Kathy. "'I Playne Piers' and the Protestant Plowman Prints: The Transformation of a Medieval Figure." In *Transmission and Transformation in the Middle Ages: Texts and Contexts*, edited by Kathy Cawsey and Jason Harris, 189–206. Dublin: Four Courts Press, 2007.

Cerquiglini, Bernard. *In Praise of the Variant: A Critical History of Philology*. Translated by Betsy Wing. Baltimore: Johns Hopkins University Press, 1999.

Chaucer, Geoffrey. *The Text of the Canterbury Tales*. Edited by John M. Manly and Edith Rickert. 8 vols. Chicago: University of Chicago Press, 1940.

———. *The Riverside Chaucer*. Edited by Larry D. Benson. Boston: Houghton Mifflin, 1987.

Cheney, Patrick. "'Novells of His Devise': Chaucerian and Virgilian Career Paths in Spenser's *Februarie* Eclogue." In *European Literary Careers: The Author from Antiquity to the Renaissance*, edited by Patrick Cheney and Frederick A. de Armas, 231–267. Toronto: University of Toronto Press, 2002.

————. *Spenser's Famous Flight: A Renaissance Idea of a Literary Career*. Toronto: University of Toronto Press, 1993.

Cicero, Marcus Tullius. *On the Ideal Orator*. Translated and edited by James M. May and Jakob Wisse. New York: Oxford University Press, 2001.

Connolly, Margaret. *John Shirley: Book Production and the Noble Household in Fifteenth-Century England*. Aldershot: Ashgate, 1998.

Considine, John. *Dictionaries in Early Modern Europe: Lexicography and the Making of Heritage*. Cambridge: Cambridge University Press, 2008.

————. "The Lexicographer as Hero: Samuel Johnson and Henri Estienne." *Philological Quarterly* 79 (2000): 205–254.

Cook, Megan L. "'Here Taketh the Makere of This Book His Leve': The *Retraction* and Chaucer's Works in Tudor England." *Studies in Philology* 113, no. 1 (2016): 32–54.

Cooper, Helen. "Chaucer's Self-Fashioning." *Poetica* 55 (2001): 55–74.

————. "Choosing Poetic Fathers: The English Problem." In *Medieval and Early Modern Authorship*, edited by Guillemette Bolens and Lukas Erne, 29–49. Tübingen: Narr Verlag, 2011.

————. "Poetic Fame." In *Cultural Reformations: Medieval and Renaissance in Literary History*, edited by Brian Cummings and James Simpson, 361–378. Cambridge: Cambridge University Press, 2010.

————. "'This Worthy Olde Writer': Pericles and Other Gowers, 1592–1640." In *A Companion to Gower*, edited by Siân Echard, 99–113. Cambridge: D. S. Brewer, 2004.

Cormack, Bradin. *A Power to Do Justice: Jurisdiction, English Literature, and the Rise of Common Law, 1509–1625*. Chicago: University of Chicago Press, 2008.

Cornelius, Patsy Schere. *E.K.'s Commentary on the Shepheardes Calender*. Salzburg: Institut für Englische Sprache und Literatur, 1974.

Costomiris, Robert. "The Influence of Printed Editions and Manuscripts on the Canon of William Thynne's *Canterbury Tales*." In *Rewriting Chaucer: Culture, Authority, and the Idea of the Authentic Text, 1400–1602*, edited by Thomas A. Prendergast and Barbara Kline, 237–257. Columbus: Ohio State University Press, 1999.

————. "Sharing Chaucer's Authority in Prefaces to Chaucer's Works from William Caxton to William Thynne." *Journal of the Early Book Society for the Study of Manuscripts and Printing History* 5 (2002): 1–13.

————. "Some New Light on the Early Career of William Thynne, Chief Clerk of the Kitchen of Henry VIII and Editor of Chaucer." *The Library* 4, no. 1 (2003): 3–15.

Crampton, Georgia Ronan. "Chaucer's Singular Prayer." *Medium Aevum* 59 (1990): 191–213.

Crawforth, Hannah. *Etymology and the Invention of English in Early Modern Literature*. Cambridge: Cambridge University Press, 2014.

————. "Strangers to the Mother Tongue: Spenser's *Shepheardes Calender* and Early Anglo-Saxon Studies." *Journal of Medieval and Early Modern Studies* 41, no. 2 (2011): 293–316.

Crocker, Holly A. "John Foxe's Chaucer: Affecting Form in Post-Historicist Criticism." *New Medieval Literatures* 15 (2013): 149–182.

Crotch, W. J. B., ed. *The Prologues and Epilogues of William Caxton*. London: Early English Text Society, 1928.

Crow, Martin M., and Clair C. Olson, eds. *Chaucer Life-Records*. Oxford: Clarendon Press, 1966.

Dane, Joseph A. "Bibliographical History Versus Bibliographical Evidence: The Plowman's Tale and Early Chaucer Editions." *Bulletin of the John Rylands University Library of Manchester* 78, no. 1 (1996): 47–61.

————. "Fists and Filiations in Early Chaucer Folios, 1532–1602," *Studies in Bibliography* 51 (1998): 48–62.

————. "In Search of Stow's Chaucer." In *John Stow (1525–1605) and the Making of the English Past: Studies in Early Modern Culture and the History of the Book*, edited by Ian Gadd and Alexandra Gillespie, 145–155. London: British Library, 2004.

————. "On 'Correctness': A Note on Some Press Variants in Thynne's 1532 Edition of Chaucer." *The Library* 17, no. 2 (1995): 156–167.

————. *Who Is Buried in Chaucer's Tomb?* East Lansing: Michigan State University Press, 1998.

————. "Who Is Buried in Chaucer's Tomb?—Prolegomena." *Huntington Library Quarterly* 57, no. 2 (1994): 99–123.

Dane, Joseph A., and Alexandra Gillespie. "Back at Chaucer's Tomb: Inscriptions in Two Early Copies of Chaucer's *Workes*." *Studies in Bibliography* 52 (1999): 89–96.

Dane, Joseph A., and Seth Lerer. "Press Variants in John Stow's Chaucer (1561) and the Text of 'Adam Scriveyn.'" *Transactions of the Cambridge Bibliographical Society* 11, no. 4 (1999): 468–479.

Danner, Bruce. *Edmund Spenser's War on Lord Burghley*. New York: Palgrave Macmillan, 2011.

Dean, James M., ed. *Six Ecclesiastical Satires*. Kalamazoo, MI: Medieval Institute Publications, 1991.

DeCoursey, Christina. "Society of Antiquaries (*act.* 1586–1607)." In *Oxford Dictionary of National Biography*. Oxford: Oxford University Press, 2004–. http://www.oxforddnb.com.

de Grazia, Margreta. "The Modern Divide: From Either Side." *Journal of Medieval and Early Modern Studies* 37, no. 7 (2007): 453–467.

————. "Shakespeare in Quotation Marks." In *The Appropriation of Shakespeare: Post-Renaissance Reconstructions of the Works and the Myth*, edited by Jean Marsden, 57–71. New York: Harvester Wheatsheaf, 1991.

Donnelly, M. L. "The Life of Vergil and the Aspirations of the 'New Poete.'" *Spenser Studies* 17 (2003): 1–35.

Driver, Martha W. "Mapping Chaucer: John Speed and the Later Portraits." *Chaucer Review* 36, no. 3 (2002): 228–249.

Dundas, Judith. "'A Mutuall Emulation': Sidney and *The Painting of the Ancients*." In *Franciscus Junius F.F. and His Circle*, edited by Rolf H. Bremmer Jr., 71–92. Amsterdam: Rodopi, 1998.

Dutschke, C. W., et al. *Guide to the Medieval and Renaissance Manuscripts in the Huntington Library*. 2 vols. San Marino, CA: Huntington Library, 1989.

Echard, Siân. "Gower in Print." In *A Companion to Gower*, edited by Siân Echard, 115–135. Cambridge: D. S. Brewer, 2004.

Edwards, A. S. G. "The *Canterbury Tales* and *Gamelyn*." In *Medieval Latin and Middle English Literature: Essays in Honour of Jill Mann*, edited by Christopher Cannon and Maura Nolan, 76–90. Cambridge: D. S. Brewer, 2011.

————. "Chaucer from Manuscript to Print: The Social Text and the Critical Text." *Mosaic* 28, no. 4 (1995): 1–12.

————. "The Chaucer Portraits in the Harley and Rosenbach Manuscripts." In *English Manuscript Studies, 1100–1700*, vol. 4, edited by Peter Beal and Jeremy Griffiths, 268–271. Toronto: University of Toronto Press, 1993.

————. "John Stow and Middle English Literature." In *John Stow (1525–1605) and the Making of the English Past: Studies in Early Modern Culture and the History of the Book*, edited by Ian Gadd and Alexandra Gillespie, 109–118. London: British Library, 2004.

———. "Lydgate, John (c. 1375–c. 1448)." In *The Spenser Encyclopedia*, edited by A. C. Hamilton, 443. Toronto: University of Toronto Press, 1990.

———. "A New Text of *The Canterbury Tales*?" In *Studies in Late Medieval and Early Renaissance Texts in Honour of John Scattergood*, edited by Anne Marie d'Arcy and Alan J. Fletcher, 121–128. Dublin: Four Courts Press, 2005.

———. "Pynson's and Thynne's Editions of Chaucer's *House of Fame*." *Studies in Bibliography* 42 (1989): 185–186.

Edwards, A. S. G., and J. Hedley. "John Stowe, *The Craft of Lovers* and T.C.C. R.3.19." *Studies in Bibliography* 28 (1975): 265–268.

Esolen, Anthony M. "The Disingenuous Poet Laureate: Spenser's Adoption of Chaucer." *Studies in Philology* 87, no. 3 (1990): 285–311.

Evenden, Elizabeth, and Thomas S. Freeman. *Religion and the Book in Early Modern England: The Making of Foxe's "Book of Martyrs."* Cambridge: Cambridge University Press, 2011.

Fairweather, Colin. "'I Suppose He Meane Chaucer': The Comedy of Errors in Spenser's *Shepheardes Calender*." *Notes and Queries* 46 (1999): 193–195.

Febrve, Lucien, and Henri-Jean Martin. *The Coming of the Book: The Impact of Printing 1540–1800*. London: Verso, 1976.

Fisher, John H. *The Emergence of Standard English*. Lexington: University Press of Kentucky, 1996.

Fletcher, Bradford Y. "Printer's Copy for Stow's *Chaucer*." *Studies in Bibliography* 31 (1978): 184–201.

Forni, Kathleen. *The Chaucerian Apocrypha: A Counterfeit Canon*. Gainesville: University Press of Florida, 2001.

———, ed. *The Chaucerian Apocrypha: A Selection*. Kalamazoo, MI: Medieval Institute Publications, 2005.

———. "The Chaucerian Apocrypha: Did Usk's 'Testament of Love' and the 'Plowman's Tale' Ruin Chaucer's Early Reputation?" *Neuphilologische Mitteilungen* 98, no. 3 (1997): 261–272.

———. "'Chaucer's Dreame': A Bibliographer's Nightmare." *Huntington Library Quarterly* 64, nos. 1–2 (2001): 139–150.

Foucault, Michel. "What Is an Author?" In *Aesthetics, Method, and Epistemology*, edited by James D. Faubion, translated by Josué V. Harari, 205–222. New York: New Press, 1998.

Fredell, Joel. "Alchemical Lydgate." *Studies in Philology* 107, no. 4 (2010): 429–464.

Fussner, F. Smith. *The Historical Revolution: English Historical Writing and Thought, 1580–1640*. London: Routledge and Kegan Paul, 1962.

Gadd, Ian, and Alexandra Gillespie, eds. *John Stow (1525–1605) and the Making of the English Past: Studies in Early Modern Culture and the History of the Book*. London: British Library, 2004.

Galbraith, Steven K. "'English Black-Letter Type and Spenser's *Shepheardes Calender*." *Spenser Studies* 23 (2008): 13–40.

Georgianna, Linda. "The Protestant Chaucer." In *Chaucer's Religious Tales*, edited by C. David Benson and Elizabeth Robertson, 55–71. Cambridge: D. S. Brewer, 1990.

Gerhardt, Ernst. "'No Quyckar Marchaundyce than Lybrary Bokes': John Bale's Commodification of Manuscript Culture." *Renaissance Quarterly* 60 (2007): 408–433.

Gillespie, Alexandra. "Caxton's Chaucer and Lydgate Quartos: Miscellanies from Manuscript to Print." *Transactions of the Cambridge Bibliographical Society* 12, no.1 (2000): 1–25.

————. "Poets, Printers, and Early English *Sammelbände*." *Huntington Library Quarterly* 67 (2004): 189–214.

————. *Print Culture and the Medieval Author: Chaucer, Lydgate, and Their Books, 1473–1557*. Oxford: Oxford University Press, 2006.

————. "Unknowe, Unkow, Vncovthe, Uncouth: From Chaucer and Gower to Spenser and Milton." In *Medieval into Renaissance: Essays for Helen Cooper*, edited by Andrew King and Matthew Woodcock, 15–33. Cambridge: D. S. Brewer, 2016.

Goody, Jack. *The Domestication of the Savage Mind*. Cambridge: Cambridge University Press, 1977.

Graham, Timothy. "Matthew Parker's Manuscripts: An Elizabethan Library and Its Use." In *The Cambridge History of Libraries in Britain and Ireland*, vol. 1, edited by Elisabeth Leedham-Green and Teresa Webber, 322–324. Cambridge: Cambridge University Press, 2006.

————, ed. *The Recovery of Old English: Anglo-Saxon Studies in the Sixteenth and Seventeenth Centuries*. Kalamazoo: Western Michigan University Press, 2000.

Green, Richard Firth. *Poets and Princepleasers: Literature and the English Court in the Late Middle Ages*. Toronto: University of Toronto Press, 1980

Greg, W. W. "Chaucer Attributions in MS R.3.19, in the Library of Trinity College, Cambridge." *Modern Language Review* 8, no. 4 (1913): 539–540.

Griffith, David. "Owners and Copyists of John Rous's Armorial Rolls." In *Essays in Manuscript Geography: Vernacular Manuscripts of the English West Midlands from the Conquest to the Sixteenth Century*, edited by Wendy Scase, 203–228. Turnhout, Belgium: Brepols, 2007.

Guillory, John. *Cultural Capital: The Problem of Literary Canon Formation*. Chicago: University of Chicago Press, 1993.

Hamilton, A. C., gen. ed. *The Spenser Encyclopedia*. Toronto: University of Toronto Press, 1990.

Hammond, Eleanor Prescott. *Chaucer: A Bibliographical Manual*. New York: Macmillan, 1908.

Harbus, Antonia. "A Renaissance Reader's English Annotations to Thynne's 1532 Edition of Chaucer's *Works*." *Review of English Studies* 59 (2008): 342–355.

Hardison, O. B., Jr., and Leon Golden, ed. and trans. *Horace for Students of Literature: The "Ars Poetica" and Its Tradition*. Gainesville: University Press of Florida, 1995.

Harvey, Gabriel. *Gabriel Harvey's Marginalia*. Edited by G. C. Moore Smith. Stratford-upon-Avon: Shakespeare Head Press, 1913.

Hearne, Thomas, ed. *A Collection of Curious Discourses Written by Eminent Antiquaries upon Several Heads in Our English Antiquities*. 2 vols. London: W. And J. Richardson, 1771.

Heffernan, Thomas J. "Aspects of the Chaucerian Apocrypha: Animadversions on William Thynne's Edition of the Plowman's Tale." In *Chaucer Traditions: Studies in Honour of Derek Brewer*, edited by Ruth Morse and Barry Windeatt, 155–167. Cambridge: Cambridge University Press, 1990.

Helfer, Rebeca. "The Death of the 'New Poete': Virgilian Ruin and Ciceronian Recollection in Spenser's *The Shepheardes Calender*." *Renaissance Quarterly* 56, no. 3 (2003): 723–756.

Heninger, S. K., Jr. "The Typographical Layout of Spenser's *Shepheardes Calender*." In *Word and Visual Imagination: Studies in the Interaction of English Literature and the Visual Arts*, edited by Karl Josef Höltgen, Peter M. Daly, and Wolfgang Lottes, 33–71. Erlangen: Universitätsbund Erlangen-Nürnberg, 1988.

Henryson, Robert. *The Poems of Robert Henryson*. Edited by Robert L. Kindrick. Rochester, NY: Medieval Institute Publications, 1997.

Herendeen, Wyman H. *William Camden: A Life in Context.* Woodbridge, Suffolk: Boydell and Brewer, 2007.

Herman, Peter C. "Poets, Pastors, and Antipoetics: A Response to Frances M. Malpezzi, 'E.K., a Spenserian Lesson in Reading.'" *Connotations* 6, no. 3 (1997): 316–325.

Heyworth, P. L. "The Earliest Black-Letter Editions of *Jack Upland.*" *Huntington Library Quarterly* 30 (1967): 307–314.

———, ed. *Jack Upland, Friar Daw's Reply and Upland's Rejoinder.* Oxford: Oxford University Press, 1968.

Hieatt, A. Kent. *Chaucer, Spenser, Milton: Mythopoeic Continuities and Transformations.* Montreal: McGill-Queen's University Press, 1975.

Hoccleve, Thomas. *The Regiment of Princes.* Edited by Charles R. Blyth. TEAMS Middle English Texts Series. Kalamazoo, MI: Medieval Institute Publications, 1999.

Hooks, Adam G. *Selling Shakespeare: Biography, Bibliography, and the Book Trade.* Cambridge: Cambridge University Press, 2016.

Hornsby, Joseph A. "Was Chaucer Educated at the Inns of Court?" *Chaucer Review* 22 (1988): 255–268.

Horobin, Simon, and Aditi Nafde. "Stephan Batman and the Making of the Parker Library." *Transactions of the Cambridge Bibliographical Society* 15, no. 4 (2015): 561–581.

Howard, Donald R. *Chaucer: His Life, His Works, His World.* New York: Dutton, 1987.

Hudson, Anne. "John Stow." In *Editing Chaucer: The Great Tradition*, edited by Paul Ruggiers, 53–70. Norman, OK: Pilgrim Books, 1984.

———. "*Visio Baleii*: An Early Literary Historian." In *The Long Fifteenth Century: Essays for Douglas Gray*, edited by Helen Cooper and Sally Mapstone, 314–329. Oxford: Clarendon Press, 1997.

Hughes, Merritt T. *Virgil and Spenser.* Berkeley: University of California Press, 1929.

Hunter, Michael. "Ashmole, Elias (1617–1692), Astrologer and Antiquary." In *Oxford Dictionary of National Biography.* Oxford: Oxford University Press, 2004–. http://www.oxforddnb .com.

Irvine, Annie S. "A Manuscript Copy of *The Plowman's Tale.*" *University of Texas Studies in English* 12 (1932): 27–56.

James, M. R. *The Western Manuscripts in the Library of Trinity College, Cambridge: A Descriptive Catalogue.* Cambridge: Cambridge University Press, 1900.

Janacek, Bruce. "A Virtuoso's History: Antiquarianism and the Transmission of Knowledge in the Alchemical Studies of Elias Ashmole." *Journal of the History of Ideas* 69, no. 3 (2008): 395–417.

Jardine, Lisa, and Anthony Grafton. "'Studied for Action': How Gabriel Harvey Read His Livy." *Past and Present* 129 (1990): 30–78.

Johnston, Hope. "Readers' Memorials in Early Editions of Chaucer." *Studies in Bibliography* 59 (2015): 45–69.

Jones, Chris. "Anglo-Saxonism in Nineteenth-Century Poetry." *Literature Compass* 7, no. 5 (2010): 358–369.

———. "New Old English: The Place of Old English in Twentieth- and Twenty-First-Century Poetry." *Literature Compass* 7, no. 11 (2010): 1009–1019.

Josten, C. H., ed. *Elias Ashmole (1617–1692): His Autobiographical and Historical Notes, His Correspondence, and Other Contemporary Sources Relating to His Life and Work.* 5 vols. Oxford: Clarendon Press, 1966.

Kastan, Scott. "Size Matters." *Shakespeare Studies* 28 (2000): 149–153.

Kelen, Sarah A. *Langland's Early Modern Identities.* New York: Palgrave Macmillan, 2007.

Kerling, Johan. *Chaucer in Early English Dictionaries: The Old-Word Tradition in English Lexicography Down to 1721 and Speght's Chaucer Glossaries.* Leiden: Leiden University Press, 1979.

———. "English Old-Word Glossaries, 1553–1594." *Neophilologus* 63 (1979): 136–147.

———. "Franciscus Junius, 17th-Century Lexicography and Middle English." In *LEXeter '83 Proceedings: Papers from the International Conference on Lexicography at Exeter, 9–12 September 1983,* edited by R. R. K. Hartmann, 92–100. Tübingen: Niemeyer, 1984.

Kibbee, Douglas A. "The Humanist Period in Renaissance Bilingual Lexicography." In *The History of Lexicography: Papers from the Dictionary Research Centre Seminar at Exeter,* edited by R. R. K. Hartmann, 137–147. Amsterdam: Benjamins, 1986.

King, John N. *English Reformation Literature: The Tudor Origins of the Protestant Tradition* Princeton, NJ: Princeton University Press, 1982.

———. *Foxe's "Book of Martyrs" and Early Modern Print Culture.* Cambridge: Cambridge University Press, 2006.

Kinney, Clare. "Marginal Presence, Lyric Resonance, Epic Absence: *Troilus and Criseyde* and/in *The Shepheardes Calender.*" *Spenser Studies* 18 (2003): 25–39.

———. *Strategies of Poetic Narrative: Chaucer, Spenser, Milton, Eliot.* Cambridge: Cambridge University Press, 1992.

———. "Thomas Speght's Renaissance Chaucer and the Solaas of Sentence in *Troilus and Criseyde.*" In *Refiguring Chaucer in the Renaissance,* edited by Theresa M. Krier, 66–84. Gainesville: University Press of Florida, 1998.

Knafla, Louis A. "Thynne, Francis (1545?–1608)." In *Oxford Dictionary of National Biography.* Oxford: Oxford University Press, 2004–. http://www.oxforddnb.com.

Knight, Jeffrey Todd. *Bound to Read: Compilations, Collections, and the Making of Renaissance Literature.* Philadelphia: University of Pennsylvania Press, 2013.

Krier, Theresa M. "Introduction: Receiving Chaucer in Renaissance England." In *Refiguring Chaucer in the Renaissance,* ed. Theresa M. Krier, 1–18. Gainesville: University Press of Florida, 1998.

———, ed. *Refiguring Chaucer in the Renaissance.* Gainesville: University Press of Florida, 1998.

Kuczynski, Michael P. "Gower's Virgil." In *On John Gower: Essays at the Millennium,* edited by R. F. Yeager, 163–187. Kalamazoo, MI: Medieval Institute Publications, 2007.

Kuskin, William, ed. *Caxton's Trace: Studies in the History of English Printing.* Notre Dame, IN: University of Notre Dame Press, 2003.

———. "'The Loadstarre of the English Language': Spenser's *Shepheardes Calender* and the Construction of Modernity." *Textual Cultures* 2, no. 2 (2007): 9–33.

———. *Symbolic Caxton: Literary Culture and Print Capitalism.* Notre Dame, IN: University of Notre Dame Press, 2007.

Lamborn, E. A. Greening. "The Arms on the Chaucer Tomb at Ewelme." *Oxoniensia* 5 (1940): 78–93.

Lasater, Alice E. "The Chaucerian Narrator in Spenser's *Shepheardes Calender.*" *Southern Quarterly* 12 (1974): 189–201.

Lawton, David. "Dullness and the Fifteenth Century." *English Literary History* 54, no. 4 (1987): 761–799.

Leland, John. *De Viris Illustribus: On Famous Men*. Edited and translated by James P. Carley with the assistance of Caroline Brett. Toronto: Pontifical Institute of Medieval Studies, 2010.

Lerer, Seth. *Chaucer and His Readers: Imagining the Author in Late-Medieval England*. Princeton, NJ: Princeton University Press, 1993.

———. "Medieval Literature and Early Modern Readers: Cambridge University Library Sel. 5.51–5.63." *Papers of the Bibliographical Society of America* 97 (2003): 311–332.

Lesser, Zachary. *Renaissance Drama and the Politics of Publication: Readings in the English Book Trade*. Cambridge: Cambridge University Press, 2004.

———. "Typographic Nostalgia: Play-Reading, Popularity, and the Meanings of Black Letter." In *The Book of the Play: Playwrights, Stationers, and Readers in Early Modern England*, edited by Marta Straznicky, 99–126. Amherst: University of Massachusetts Press, 2006.

Levine, Joseph. *Humanism and History: Origins of Modern English Historiography*. Ithaca, NY: Cornell University Press, 1987.

Lévi-Strauss, Claude. *Totemism*. Translated by Rodney Needham. London: Merlin Press, 1964.

Levy, F. J. *Tudor Historical Thought*. Toronto: University of Toronto Press, 1967.

Lindheim, Nancy. "The Virgilian Design of the *Shepheardes Calender*." *Spenser Studies* 13 (1999): 1–22.

Little, Katherine C. "The 'Other' Past of Pastoral: Langland's *Piers Plowman* and Spenser's *Shepheardes Calender*." *Exemplaria* 21 (2009): 160–178.

———. *Transforming Work: Early Modern Pastoral and Late Medieval Poetry*. Notre Dame, IN: Notre Dame University Press, 2013.

Luborsky, Ruth. "The Allusive Presentation of *The Shepheardes Calender*." *Spenser Studies* 1 (1980): 29–67.

———. "The Illustrations to *The Shepheardes Calender*." *Spenser Studies* 2 (1981): 3–53.

Lydgate, John. *The Pilgrimage of the Life of Man*. Edited by F. J. Furnivall and Katharine B. Locock. 3 vols. Early English Text Society, e.s. 77, 83, 92. London: Kegan Paul, Trench, Trübner, 1899–1904.

Malpezzi, Frances M. "E.K., a Spenserian Lesson in Reading." *Connotations* 4, no. 3 (1994–1995): 181–191.

Manly, John M. "Mary Chaucer's First Husband." *Speculum* 9, no. 1 (1934): 86–88.

Matthews, David. *The Making of Middle English, 1765–1910*. Minneapolis: University of Minnesota Press, 1999.

McCabe, Richard. "Annotating Anonymity, or Putting a Gloss on the *Shepheardes Calender*." In *Ma(r)king the Text: The Presentation of Meaning on the Literary Page*, edited by Joe Bray, Miriam Handley, and Anne C. Henry, 35–54. Aldershot: Ashgate, 2000.

McCarl, Mary Rhinelander, ed. *The Plowman's Tale: The c. 1532 and 1606 Editions of a Spurious Canterbury Tale*. New York: Garland, 1997.

McCormack, Frances M. "Chaucer and Lollardy." In *Chaucer and Religion*, edited by Helen Phillips, 35–40. Cambridge: D. S. Brewer, 2010.

McElderry, Bruce Robert, Jr. "Archaism and Innovation in Spenser's Poetic Diction." *PMLA* 47, no. 1 (1932): 144–170.

McKisack, May. *Medieval History in the Tudor Age*. Oxford: Clarendon Press, 1971.

Middleton, Anne. "The Idea of Public Poetry in the Reign of Richard II." *Speculum* 53, no. 1 (1978): 94–114.

———. "Thomas Usk's 'Perdurable Letters': The 'Testament of Love' from Script to Print." *Studies in Bibliography* 51 (1998): 70–79.

Miller, David Lee. "Authorship, Anonymity, and the *Shepheardes Calender*." *Modern Language Quarterly* 40 (1979): 219–236.

———. *The Poem's Two Bodies: The Poetics of the 1590 "Faerie Queene."* Princeton, NJ: Princeton University Press, 1988.

Miskimin, Alice S. *The Renaissance Chaucer*. New Haven, CT: Yale University Press, 1975.

Mooney, Linne R. "Scribes and Booklets of Trinity College, Cambridge, Manuscripts R.3.19 and R.3.21." In *Middle English Poetry: Texts and Traditions*, edited by A. J. Minnis, 241–266. York, England: York Medieval, 2001.

Munro, Lucy. *Archaic Style in English Literature, 1590–1674*. Cambridge: Cambridge University Press, 2013.

———. "Speaking History: Linguistic Memory and the Usable Past in the Early Modern History Play." *Huntington Library Quarterly* 76, no. 4 (2013): 519–540.

Nevalainen, Terttu. "Early Modern English Lexis and Semantics." In *The Cambridge History of the English Language*, vol. 3, *1476–1776*, edited by John Algeo, 332–458. Cambridge: Cambridge University Press, 1999.

Nicholson, Catherine. *Uncommon Tongues: Eloquence and Eccentricity in the English Renaissance*. Philadelphia: University of Pennsylvania Press, 2014.

Pace, George B. "Speght's Chaucer and MS Gg.4.27." *Studies in Bibliography* 21 (1968): 225–235.

Parkes, Malcolm B. "Stephen Batman's Manuscripts." In *Medieval Heritage: Essays in Honour of Tadahiro Ikegami*, edited by Masahiko Kanno et al., 125–156. Tokyo: Ushodo Press, 1997.

Parkes, M. B., and Richard Beadle, eds. *The Poetical Works of Geoffrey Chaucer: A Facsimile of Cambridge University Library MS GG.4.27*. 3 vols. Cambridge: D. S. Brewer, 1979.

Parry, Graham. *The Trophies of Time: English Antiquarians of the Seventeenth Century*. Oxford: Oxford University Press, 1995.

Pask, Kevin. *The Emergence of the English Author: Scripting the Life of the Poet in Early Modern England*. Cambridge: Cambridge University Press, 1996.

Patterson, Annabel. *Reading Holinshed's "Chronicles."* Chicago: University of Chicago Press, 1994.

———. "Re-Opening the Green Cabinet: Clément Marot and Edmund Spenser." *English Literary Renaissance* 16 (1986): 44–70.

Patterson, Paul J. "Reforming Chaucer: Margins and Religion in an Apocryphal Canterbury Tale." *Book History* 8 (2005): 17–27.

Pearsall, D. A., ed. *The Floure and the Leafe; and The Assembly of Ladies*. Manchester: Manchester University Press, 1980.

Pearsall, Derek. "Chaucer's Tomb: The Politics of Reburial." *Medium Aevum* 64 (1995): 51–73.

———. *The Life of Geoffrey Chaucer: A Critical Biography*. Oxford: Blackwell, 1992.

———. "John Stow and Thomas Speght as Editors of Chaucer: A Question of Class." In *John Stow (1525–1605) and the Making of the English Past: Studies in Early Modern Culture and the History of the Book*, edited by Ian Gadd and Alexandra Gillespie, 119–125. London: British Library, 2004.

———. "Thomas Speght (ca. 1550–?)." In *Editing Chaucer: The Great Tradition*, edited by Paul Ruggiers, 71–92. Norman, OK: Pilgrim Books, 1984. Prendergast, Thomas. *Chaucer's Dead Body: From Corpse to Corpus*. New York: Routledge, 2004.

Prescott, Anne Lake. "The Laurel and the Myrtle: Spenser and Ronsard." In *Worldmaking Spenser*, edited by Patrick Cheney and Lauren Silberman, 61–78. Lexington: University Press of Kentucky, 2000.

Puttenham, George. *The Art of English Poesy*. Edited by Frank Whigham and Wayne A. Rebhorn. Ithaca, NY: Cornell University Press, 2007.

Quinn, William A. "Chaucer's Problematic *Priere: An ABC* as Artifact and Critical Issue." *Studies in the Age of Chaucer* 23 (2001): 109–141.

Rickert, Edith. "Was Chaucer a Student at the Inner Temple?" In *The Manly Anniversary Studies in Language and Literature,* 20–31. Chicago: University of Chicago Press, 1923.

Rubright, Marjorie. *Doppelgänger Dilemmas: Anglo-Dutch Relations in Early Modern English Literature and Culture*. Philadelphia: University of Pennsylvania Press, 2014.

Ruggiers, Paul, ed. *Editing Chaucer: The Great Tradition*. Norman, OK: Pilgrim Books, 1984.

Sanok, Catherine. "Good King Henry and the Genealogy of Shakespeare's First History Plays." *Journal of Medieval and Early Modern Studies* 40, no. 1 (2010): 37–63.

Sayce, Olive. "Chaucer's 'Retractions': The Conclusion of the *Canterbury Tales* and Its Place in Literary Tradition." *Medium Aevum* 40, no. 3 (1971): 230–248.

Scattergood, John. "John Leland's *Itinerary* and the Identity of England." In *Sixteenth-Century Identities*, edited by A. J. Piesse, 58–74. Manchester: Manchester University Press, 2000.

Schäfer, Jürgen. "Chaucer in Shakespeare's Dictionaries: The Beginning." *Chaucer Review* 17, no. 2 (1982): 182–192.

Schreyer, Kurt A. *Shakespeare's Medieval Craft: Remnants of the Mysteries on the London Stage*. Ithaca, NY: Cornell University Press, 2014.

Schuler, Robert M. "The Renaissance Chaucer as Alchemist." *Viator: Medieval and Renaissance Studies* 15 (1984): 305–334.

Segall, Kreg. "Skeltonic Anxiety and Rumination in *The Shepheardes Calender*." *SEL* 47, no. 1 (2007): 29–56.

Shapiro, James. *Contested Will: Who Wrote Shakespeare?* London: Faber and Faber, 2010.

Sharpe, Kevin. *Sir Robert Cotton, 1586–1631: History and Politics in Early Modern England*. Oxford: Oxford University Press, 1979.

Sherman, William. *Used Books: Marking Readers in Renaissance England*. Philadelphia: University of Pennsylvania Press, 2008.

Shrank, Cathy. "John Bale and Reconfiguring the 'Medieval' in Reformation England." In *Reading the Medieval in Early Modern England*, edited by Gordon McMullan and David Matthews, 179–192. Cambridge: Cambridge University Press, 2007.

———. *Writing the Nation in Reformation England, 1530–1580*. Oxford: Oxford University Press, 2004.

Simpson, James. "Ageism: Leland, Bale, and the Laborious Start of English Literary History, 1350–1550." *New Medieval Literatures* 1 (1997): 213–236.

———. "Chaucer's Presence and Absence, 1400–1550." In *The Cambridge Companion to Chaucer*, edited by Piero Boitani and Jill Mann, 251–269. Cambridge: Cambridge University Press, 2003.

———. "Diachronic History and the Shortcomings of Medieval Studies." In *Reading the Medieval in Early Modern England*, edited by Gordon McMullan and David Matthews, 17–30. Cambridge: Cambridge University Press, 2007.

———. "The Melancholy of John Leland and the Beginnings of English Literary History." In *The Oxford English Literary History*, vol. 2, *1350–1547: Reform and Cultural Revolution*, 7–33.

Oxford: Oxford University Press, 2002. Skeat, Walter W., ed. *Chaucerian and Other Pieces.* Vol. 7 of *The Complete Works of Geoffrey Chaucer.* Oxford: Clarendon Press, 1897.

———, ed. *Romaunt of the Rose and Minor Poems.* Vol. 1 of *The Complete Works of Geoffrey Chaucer.* 1894. Reprint, Oxford: Clarendon Press, 1963.

———, ed. *The Tale of Gamelyn.* Oxford: Clarendon Press, 1884.

Spearing, A. C. "Renaissance Chaucer and Father Chaucer." *English: The Journal of the English Association* 34, no. 148 (1985): 1–38.

Spenser, Edmund. *The Yale Edition of the Shorter Poems of Edmund Spenser.* Edited by William A. Oram, Einar Bjorvand, Ronald Bond, Thomas H. Cain, Alexander Dunlop, and Richard Schell. New Haven, CT: Yale University Press, 1989.

———. *The Faerie Queene.* Edited by A. C. Hamilton, with Hiroshi Yamashita, Toshiyuki Suzuki, and Shohachi Fukuda. London: Longman, 2001.

Spielmann, M. H. *The Portraits of Geoffrey Chaucer: An Essay Written on the Occasion of the Quincentenary of the Poet's Death.* London: Kegan Paul, Trench, Trübner for the Chaucer Society, 1900.

Spurgeon, Caroline. *Five Hundred Years of Chaucer Criticism and Allusion.* 3 vols. Cambridge: Cambridge University Press, 1925.

Steinberg, Glenn A. "Spenser's *Shepheardes Calender* and the Elizabethan Reception of Chaucer." *English Literary Renaissance* 35, no. 1 (2005): 31–51.

Stevenson, Kay Gilliland. "Medieval Rereading and Rewriting: The Context of Chaucer's 'ABC.'" In *"Divers Toyes Mengled": Essays on Medieval and Renaissance Culture in Honour of André Lascombes,* edited by Michel Bitot with Roberta Mullini and Peter Happé, 27–42. Tours: Université François Rabelais, 1996.

Stoichita, Victor I. *The Self-Aware Image: An Insight into Early Modern Meta-Painting.* Translated by Anne-Marie Glasheen. Cambridge: Cambridge University Press, 1997.

Strohm, Paul. *Chaucer's Tale: 1386 and the Road to Canterbury.* New York: Viking, 2014.

Summit, Jennifer. "Leland's *Itinerary* and the Remains of the Medieval Past." In *Reading the Medieval in Early Modern England,* edited by Gordon McMullan and David Matthews, 159–176. Cambridge: Cambridge University Press, 2007.

———. *Lost Property: The Woman Writer and English Literary History, 1380–1589.* Chicago: University of Chicago Press, 2000.

———. *Memory's Library: Medieval Books in Early Modern England.* Chicago: University of Chicago Press, 2008.

Taylor, Andrew. "John Leland's Communities of the Epigram." In *Neo-Latin Poetry in the British Isles,* edited by L. B. T. Houghton and Gesine Manuwald. London: Bloomsbury, 2012.

Thaisen, Jacob. "Orthography, Codicology, and Textual Studies: The Cambridge University Library, Gg.4.27 'Canterbury Tales.'" *Boletín Millares Carlo* 24–25 (2005–2006): 379–394.

Thompson, John. "Chaucer's *An ABC* in and out of Context." *Poetica* 37 (1993): 38–48.

Thynne, Francis. *Animadversions uppon the Annotacions and Corrections of some imperfections of impressiones of Chaucers workes (sett downe before tyme, and nowe) reprinted in the yere of oure lorde 1598.* Edited by G. H. Kingsley. Early English Text Society, original series, no. 9, 1865. Revised edition, edited by F. J. Furnivall. London: Trübner, 1875.

———. *Emblemes and Epigrames.* Edited by Francis J. Furnivall. Early English Text Society o.s. 64. London: N. Trübner for the Early English Text Society, 1876.

Trigg, Stephanie. *Congenial Souls: Reading Chaucer from Medieval to Postmodern.* Minneapolis: University of Minnesota Press, 2002.

————. "The Injuries of Time: Geoffrey Chaucer, Thomas Speght and Wade's Boat." *LaTrobe Journal* 81 (2008): 106–117.

Usk, Thomas. *The Testament of Love.* Edited by R. A. Shoaf. Kalamazoo, MI: Medieval Institute Publications, 1998.

Van Dorsten, J. A. "The Leyden 'Lydgate Manuscript.'" *Scriptorium* 14, no. 2 (1960): 315–325.

van Es, Bart. "Discourses of Conquest: *The Faerie Queene*, the Society of Antiquaries, and *A View of the Present State of Ireland*." *English Literary Renaissance* 32, no. 1 (2002): 118–151.

Van Norden, Linda. "The Elizabethan College of Antiquaries." PhD diss., University of California, Los Angeles, 1946.

van Romburgh, Sophie, ed. and trans. *"For My Worthy Freind Mr Franciscus Junius": An Edition of the Correspondence of Francis Junius F.F. (1591–1677).* Leiden: Brill, 2004.

————. "Junius [Du Jon], Franciscus [Francis] (1591–1677)." In *Oxford Dictionary of National Biography.* Oxford: Oxford University Press, 2004–. http://www.oxforddnb.com.

Vaughan, Mícéál F. "Personal Politics and Thomas Gascoigne's Account of Chaucer's Death." *Medium Aevum* 75, no. 1 (2006): 103–122.

Vine, Angus. "Copiousness, Conjecture and Collaboration in William Camden's *Britannia*," *Renaissance Studies* 28, no. 2 (2014): 225–241.

————. *In Defiance of Time: Antiquarian Writing in Early Modern England.* Oxford: Oxford University Press, 2010.

Virgil. *The Works of Virgil.* Edited by John Conington and Henry Nettleship. 3 vols. Hildesheim: Georg Olms, 1963.

Vos, Alvin. "Humanistic Standards of Diction in the Inkhorn Controversy." *Studies in Philology* 73 (1976): 376–396.

Walker, Greg. "The Archaeology of *The Plowman's Tale*." In *Studies in Late Medieval and Early Renaissance Texts in Honour of John Scattergood,* edited by Anne Marie D'Arcy and Alan Fletcher, 375–401. Dublin: Four Courts Press, 2005.

————. *Writing Under Tyranny: English Literature and the Henrician Reformation.* New York: Oxford University Press, 2005.

Warner, Lawrence. *The Myth of Piers Plowman: Constructing a Medieval Literary Archive.* Cambridge: Cambridge University Press, 2014.

Watts, Richard J. "Was the Great Vowel Shift Really 'Great'? A Reappraisal of Research Work on an Elusive Linguistic Phenomenon." In *English Core Linguistics,* edited by Cornelia Tschichold, 13–30. Bern: Peter Lang, 2003.

Wawn, Andrew N. "Chaucer, *The Plowman's Tale* and Reformation Propaganda: The Testimony of Thomas Godfray and *I Playne Piers*." *Bulletin of the John Rylands Library* 56 (1973–1974): 174–192.

————. "The Genesis of *The Plowman's Tale*." *Yearbook of English Studies* 2 (1972): 21–40.

Wiggins, Alison. "What Did Renaissance Readers Write in Their Printed Copies of Chaucer?" *The Library* 9, no. 1 (2008): 3–36.

William Salt Archaeological Society, ed. *Collections for a History of Staffordshire,* vol. 13. London: Harrison and Sons, 1892.

Wolfe, Matthew C. "Constructing the Chaucer Corpus: A Study of Cambridge, University Library, MS Gg.4.27." PhD diss., West Virginia University, 1995.

————. "Placing Chaucer's *Retraction* for a Reception of Closure." *Chaucer Review* 33, no. 4 (1999): 427–431.

Wright, Cyril Ernst. *Fontes Harleiani: A Study of the Sources of the Harleian Collection of Manuscripts in the British Museum.* London: British Museum, 1972.

Wright, Sylvia. "The Author Portraits in the Bedford Psalter-Hours: Gower, Chaucer, and Hoccleve." *British Library Journal* 18, no. 2 (1992): 190–201.

Wright, Thomas. *The Life of Walter Pater.* 2 vols. New York: G. P. Putnam's Sons; London: Everett, 1907.

Yeager, R. F. "Gower, John (1330–1408)." In *The Spenser Encyclopedia*, edited by A. C. Hamilton, 337–338. Toronto: University of Toronto Press, 1990.

———. "Literary Theory at the Close of the Middle Ages: William Caxton and William Thynne." *Studies in the Age of Chaucer* 6 (1984): 135–164.

Zumthor, Paul. *Toward a Medieval Poetics.* Translated by Philip Bennett. Minneapolis: University of Minnesota Press, 1992.

ACKNOWLEDGMENTS
_____

John Dryden wrote that, upon reading Chaucer, he found he had "a soul congenial to his." I make no such lofty claims about my affinity to Chaucer, but it is a deep pleasure to say that I have had the good fortune to work on this book in the company of many congenial souls.

An account of the intellectual and personal generosity from which I have benefited while writing this monograph could fill a book on its own. I am grateful to all my teachers, whose mentorship continues to shape my teaching and my scholarship on a daily basis. David Wallace is a tireless advocate; his faith in this project never wavered, even when my own did, and it has gained tremendously from his boundless Chaucerian wisdom. Margreta de Grazia helped me to see that there was still much more to be said about Middle English poetry, print culture, and the Renaissance and challenged me to say it. Emily Steiner, Rita Copeland, Zachary Lesser, and Peter Stallybrass all offered me support and scholarly acumen at timely moments, and through their work I have learned firsthand what ambitious and engaged premodern scholarship looks like.

This book could not have been written without access to libraries and the knowledgeable assistance of those who staff them. In particular, I would like to thank the librarians and staff of Van Pelt Library, University of Pennsylvania; the Houghton Library, Harvard University; the Folger Shakespeare Library; the Harry Ransom Center, University of Texas at Austin; the Henry E. Huntington Library; the British Library; the Bodleian Library; Gonville and Caius College, Cambridge; Trinity College, Cambridge; the Pepys Library at Magdalene College, Cambridge; the University of Cambridge Library; and the College of Arms. I would also like to acknowledge the meticulous and often anonymous labor of catalogers and bibliographers, whose work has been a necessary precondition for my own.

Throughout the process of research and writing, my work and my life have been deeply enriched by a community of friends and fellow scholars who have sharpened my thinking, expanded my knowledge, and listened patiently as I attempted to explain yet again why early modern heralds are the key to understanding Middle English literature. David Carlson, Helen Cushman, Megan Heffernan, Jennifer Jahner, Courtney Rydel, Elizaveta Strakhov, and Thomas Ward all read portions of this manuscript in draft; my thinking and my writing have been much improved by their insights and suggestions. I would also like to thank the faculty and graduate students at Boston College, Harvard University, the University of California, Berkeley, the University of Pennsylvania, and the University of Texas at Austin who invited me to share portions of this project with them as a work in progress.

I am someone who does her best thinking in conversation with others; as a result, many of the ideas in this book got their first airing in bars, over long phone conversations, or on social media. Any list of those who helped along the way will inevitably be incomplete, but for their encouragement and camaraderie I would especially like to thank (in addition to those already mentioned) Alexis Becker, Marina Bilbija, Cal Biruk, Heather Blatt, Claire M. L. Bourne, Piers Brown, Brantley Bryant, Tekla Bude, Taylor Cowdery, Daniel Davies, Alexander Devine, Sonja Drimmer, Tony Edwards, Stephanie Elsky, Devin Fitzgerald, Andrew Fleck, Damian Flemming, Ari Friedlander, Jack Giesking, Alexandra Gillespie, Rick Godden, David Hadbawnik, Aaron Hanlon, Zachary Hines, Adam Hooks, Simon Horobin, Jonathan Hsy, Boyda Johnstone, Jamison Kantor, Michelle Karnes, Michael King, András Kiséry, Jeffrey Todd Knight, Greta LaFleur, Elon Lang, Laura Massey, Sarah Montross, Marissa Nicosia, Catherine Nicholson, Rosemary O'Neill, Laurie Osborne, Brooke Palmieri, Steve Perkinson, Ryan D. Perry, Noelle Phillips, Aaron Pratt, Thomas Prendergast, Elizabeth Sagaser, Adriana Salerno, Brien Saputo, Anita Savo, Elizabeth Scala, Kurt Schreyer, Josh Smith, Juliet Sperling, Karl Steel, Zach Stone, Spenser Strub, Chris Taylor, Simran Thadani, Sara Torres, Lawrence Warner, Eric Weiskott, Emily Weissbourd, and Sarah Werner. I would also like to recognize the hard work of the baristas and bartenders of Philadelphia, London, and Portland, Maine, without whose assistance writing this book would have been a much more arduous task.

Short-term fellowships from the Henry E. Huntington Library, the Harry Ransom Center at the University of Texas, and the Folger Shakespeare Library enabled much of my research with early printed books. A 2012 NEH seminar, "Tudor Books and Readers," allowed me to lay the groundwork for further research with primary sources in the United Kingdom. I am extremely grateful for the financial support from Colby College that has allowed me to complete that research and for the junior leave during which much of this book was written. I thank Sean Gilsdorf and the Standing Committee on Medieval Studies at Harvard University for their hospitality during the fall semester of that leave. The Mellon Fellowship in Critical Bibliography at Rare Book School has introduced me to an intellectually diverse and highly sociable cohort of fellow travelers in book history, and both this book and the process of writing it have been greatly enriched by their company.

I would like to thank Jerry Singerman and the staff of the University of Pennsylvania Press, as well as Siân Echard and Lucy Munro, whose comments have made it a much stronger piece of scholarship. Anne Bramley and Audra Woolf offered indispensable pragmatic advice and guidance as I prepared the manuscript for initial submission, while my research assistants at Colby, Eva Neczypor and Alison Zak, provided essential assistance in compiling the bibliography and checking references, averting numerous mistakes and infelicities. Those errors that remain are, of course, entirely my own.

A version of Chapter 4 originally appeared as "Managing the Past: Lexical Commentary in Spenser's *Shepheardes Calender* (1579) and Chaucer's *Works* (1598/1602)," *Spenser Studies* 25 (2011): 179–222; a version of the material on Joseph Holland in Chapter 6 appeared as "Joseph Holland and the Idea of the Chaucerian Book," *Manuscript Studies: A Journal of the Schoenberg Institute for Manuscript Studies* 1, no. 2 (2016): 165–188. I am grateful to the University of Chicago Press and to the University of Pennsylvania Press for permission to reprint this material here.

My final and greatest thanks are due to my family, especially my parents, David and Chris Cook, for their unstinting support for any and all intellectual ambitions and for making sure I grew up surrounded by books. I owe an unquantifiable debt to Ben Mason, who has lived with this project for as long as I have. This book is dedicated to my grandmothers, Ruthann VanZanten and Linda Cook-Toren, whose lives as teachers and readers continue to be a model for my own.